The Political Representation of Kurds in Turkey

Kurdish Studies Series

Series Editors

Zeynep Kaya, Middle East Centre, London School of Economics and Political Science, UK & Department of Development Studies, School of Oriental and African Studies, UK
Robert Lowe, Middle East Centre, London School of Economics and Political Science, UK

Advisory Board

Sabri Ateş, Dedman College of Humanities & Sciences, USA
Mehmet Gurses, Florida Atlantic University, USA
Janet Klein, University of Akron, USA
David Romano, Missouri State University, USA
Clemence Scalbert- Yücel, University of Exeter, UK
Güneş Murat Tezcür, University of Central Florida, USA
Nicole Watts, San Francisco State University, USA

Titles

The Kurds in a Changing Middle East: History, Politics and Representation,
edited by Faleh A. Jabar & Renad Mansour
Kurdish Nationalism on Stage: Performance, Politics and Resistance in Iraq,
Mari R. Rostami
The Kurds of Northern Syria: Governance, Diversity and Conflicts,
Harriet Allsopp & Wladimir van Wilgenburg
The Kurds and the Politics of Turkey: Agency, Territory and Religion, Deníz Çifçi

The Political Representation of Kurds in Turkey

New Actors and Modes of Participation in a Changing Society

Cengiz Gunes

With a Foreword and Comment by
Thomas Jeffrey Miley and Luqman Guldivê

I.B. TAURIS
LONDON • NEW YORK • OXFORD • NEW DELHI • SYDNEY

I.B. TAURIS
Bloomsbury Publishing Plc
50 Bedford Square, London, WC1B 3DP, UK
1385 Broadway, New York, NY 10018, USA
29 Earlsfort Terrace, Dublin 2, Ireland

BLOOMSBURY, I.B. TAURIS and the I.B. Tauris logo are trademarks of
Bloomsbury Publishing Plc

First published in Great Britain 2021
This paperback edition published in 2022

Copyright © Cengiz Gunes, 2021

Cengiz Gunes has asserted his right under the Copyright, Designs and Patents Act, 1988, to be identified as Author of this work.

For legal purposes the Acknowledgements on p. xvi constitute an extension of this copyright page.

Series design by Adriana Brioso
Cover image © ILYAS AKENGIN/AFP/Getty Images

All rights reserved. No part of this publication may be reproduced or transmitted in any form or by any means, electronic or mechanical, including photocopying, recording, or any information storage or retrieval system, without prior permission in writing from the publishers.

Bloomsbury Publishing Plc does not have any control over, or responsibility for, any third-party websites referred to or in this book. All internet addresses given in this book were correct at the time of going to press. The author and publisher regret any inconvenience caused if addresses have changed or sites have ceased to exist, but can accept no responsibility for any such changes.

A catalogue record for this book is available from the British Library.

A catalog record for this book is available from the Library of Congress.

ISBN:	HB:	978-0-7556-0189-9
	PB:	978-0-7556-4117-8
	ePDF:	978-0-7556-0634-4
	eBook:	978-0-7556-0633-7

Series: Kurdish Studies

Typeset by Integra Software Services Pvt. Ltd.

To find out more about our authors and books visit www.bloomsbury.com and sign up for our newsletters.

Contents

List of figures and tables	vi
List of contributors	viii
Preface	ix
Foreword *Thomas Jeffrey Miley with Luqman Guldivê*	xii
Acknowledgements	xvi
List of abbreviations	xvii
Introduction: Political representation of Kurds in Turkey	1
1 Kurdish political parties in Turkey	13
2 Electoral politics and the Kurds in Turkey	35
3 Tribes and political representation	57
4 Religious groups and political representation	73
5 The modern classes and political representation	91
6 Women and youth and political representation	113
7 Representative democracy and the democratic confederal project *Thomas Jeffrey Miley with Luqman Guldivê*	131
Conclusions: Re-thinking Kurdish political representation in Turkey	161
Notes	177
Bibliography	212
Index	231

List of figures and tables

Figures

2.1	Percentage of votes the AKP obtained in the 2002 and 2007 general elections in the Kurdish majority provinces	38
2.2	Percentage of votes the AKP obtained in the June 2011 and June 2015 general elections in the Kurdish majority provinces	41
2.3	Percentage of votes the AKP obtained in the November 2015 and June 2018 general elections in the Kurdish majority provinces	42
2.4	Percentage of votes the DEHAP obtained in the 2002 general election and the pro-Kurdish independent candidates obtained in the 2007 general election in the Kurdish majority provinces	44
2.5	Percentage of votes the pro-Kurdish parties obtained in the 2009 and 2014 local elections in the Kurdish majority provinces	44
2.6	Percentage of votes the pro-Kurdish independent candidates obtained in the June 2011 election and the HDP obtained in the June 2015 elections in the Kurdish majority provinces	46
2.7	Percentage of votes the pro-Kurdish candidates and political parties obtained since 2011 in the western and southern provinces of Turkey	47
2.8	Percentage of votes the HDP obtained in the November 2015 and June 2018 general elections in the Kurdish majority provinces	49
2.9	Percentage of votes Recep Tayyip Erdoğan and Selahattin Demirtaş obtained in the 2014 and 2018 presidential elections in the Kurdish majority provinces	50
3.1	Members of Kurdish tribes' political attitudes	66
3.2	Members of Kurdish tribes' desired political representatives	66
3.3	Action Kurdish tribe members take to achieve desired representation	70
3.4	Action Kurdish tribe members take when no one is representing them	70
4.1	Religious Kurds' political representatives	85
4.2	Religious Kurds' desired political representatives	87
4.3	Action religious Kurds take to achieve desired representation	89
4.4	Action religious Kurds take when no one is representing them	89
5.1	Political representatives (upper business)	102

5.2	Political representatives (medium business)	105
5.3	Action taken to achieve desired representation (upper business)	106
5.4	Action taken to achieve desired representation (medium business)	106
5.5	Action taken to achieve desired representation (professional strata)	107
5.6	Action taken to achieve desired representation (working class)	108
5.7	Action taken when no one is representing them (upper business)	109
5.8	Action taken when no one is representing them (medium business)	110
5.9	Action taken when no one is representing them (professional strata)	110
5.10	Action taken when no one is representing them (working class)	110
6.1	Women's political representatives	123
6.2	Women's desired political representatives	124
6.3	Action women take to achieve desired representation	125
6.4	Action women take when no one is representing them	126
6.5	Youth's and students' political representatives	127
6.6	Youth's and students' desired political representatives	129
6.7	Action youth and students take to achieve desired representation	129
6.8	Action youth and students take when no one is representing them	130

Table

5.1	Types of business enterprise in 2015 in Diyarbakır and Van	95

List of contributors

Dr Cengiz Gunes is an Associate Lecturer in Politics and International Relations at The Open University. He received his PhD from the University of Essex (2010). His main research interests are in the areas of autonomy and the accommodation of minorities, peace and conflict studies, the Kurds in the Middle East, the international relations of the Middle East and Turkish politics. He is the author of *The Kurdish National Movement in Turkey: From Protest to Resistance* (London: Routledge, 2012) and *The Kurds in a New Middle East: The Changing Geopolitics of a Regional Conflict* (London: Palgrave MacMillan, 2018) and co-editor of *The Kurdish Question in Turkey: New Perspectives on Violence, Representation, and Reconciliation* (London: Routledge, 2014).

Dr Thomas Jeffrey Miley is a Lecturer of Political Sociology at the University of Cambridge. He is a member of the executive board of the European Union Turkey Civic Commission (EUTCC) and is a patron of Peace in Kurdistan. His scholarship focuses on comparative nationalisms, religion and politics, and empirical democratic theory. He has published broadly on the dynamics of nationalist conflict and accommodation in Spain and, increasingly, in Turkey. He is co-editor, with Federico Venturini, of *Your Freedom and Mine: Abdullah Öcalan and the Kurdish Question in Erdoğan's Turkey* (Montreal: Black Rose Books, 2018). He is currently working on a project on struggles for self-determination in the twenty-first century.

Dr Luqman Guldivê is an editor and columnist at the bilingual Kurdish-Turkish daily newspaper Yeni Ozgur Politika. He lectured at University of Erfurt Kurdish History and Politics, and gave Kurdish Literature and Language classes at the University of Goettingen. He has a PhD in Iranian Studies with a focus on Kurdish oral culture and literature from the University of Goettingen in 2009. He obtained his MA degree from INALCO in Paris in 2002. He is a member of the Scientific Advisory Board of Kurd-AKAD (Network of Kurdish Professionals). He has a special scientific and political interest in Kurdish Politics in Turkey, Syria, Iraq, Iran and Europe.

Preface

This is the first book-length study to analyse Kurdish political representation in Turkey. Its primary focus is the form Kurdish political representation took in the first two decades of the twenty-first century, but the discussion is contextualized within the post-1950 period to highlight the dominant trends of Kurdish political representation since Turkey's transition to electoral democracy. The guiding question is 'how the Kurds in Turkey represent themselves' and this question is answered via an in-depth examination of the forms of representation carried out by different political actors and social groups within the Kurdish society in Turkey. To accurately portray the complexity of Kurdish political representation and shed new light on it, the analysis presented here pays special attention to the types of political activities the different segments of Kurdish society engage in, and the avenues, organizations and networks Kurds use in their efforts to represent themselves.

The book provides an account of the emergence of the main Kurdish political parties that are active in Turkey and involved in the representation of the Kurds. The activities and initiatives of Kurdish political leaders within political parties at national and local levels as well as the activities of Kurds who are members of Turkish political parties are also examined. Before the re-emergence of the Kurdish national movement in Turkey during the 1970s, the tribal and religious elite were the main political actors that represented the Kurds. Their role has significantly changed over the years and their influence and power have declined, but their relevance to the political representation of the Kurds remains. The spread of education and migration of Kurds to cities in Turkey's west has brought about a significant transformation in the Kurdish society including the rise of Kurdish business and professional classes. One of the key objectives of this book is to set out the activities and actions that Kurds from different social backgrounds in Turkey, as individuals or as a group, engage in as they attempt to represent themselves and their interests. Other significant developments discussed here include the impact of the participation of women and youth in large numbers in politics.

Turkey's institutional set-up and political culture, both of which have been strongly influenced by Turkish state nationalism formulated by modern Turkey's founder, Mustafa Kemal Atatürk, have placed multiple barriers on the representation of the Kurds as a group. As Kurdish political representation continues to be severely restricted, consequently, this book also discusses the difficulties and challenges the Kurds face when representing themselves and their interests, and the actions they take to overcome these challenges and difficulties.

The analysis offered here is mainly based on primary research that was conducted in Turkey during the second half of 2015 and autumn of 2016. In total, survey data from 373 respondents from different segments of Kurdish society was collected, and I analyse this data to inquire deeper into the political attitudes and activities of Kurds from different tribal, religious, social and political backgrounds. In addition, I have used a number of other primary sources to supplement the survey data, including political discourse, publications by the Kurdish political parties, interviews with the leading members of the Kurdish political parties and those who are active in the Turkish political parties, newspaper reports of events and developments, data from recent elections and also the existing secondary literature in the Turkish and English languages. A brief review of the theoretical literature on political representation is also presented to unpack the meaning attached to the concept and highlight the main debate in the literature on the political representation of national minorities.

This book was written at a time when Kurdish political representatives were experiencing severe repression, which resulted in the arrest and detention of many Members of Parliament (MPs) from the pro-Kurdish Peoples' Democratic Party (*Halkların Demokratik Partisi*, HDP) and the removal from their position of almost all city and district mayors belonging to the pro-Kurdish Democratic Regions Party (*Demokratik Bölgeler Partisi*, DBP) and the HDP, and the appointment of 'trustees' as their replacements. The exceptional results of the pro-Kurdish political parties in national and local elections since 2014, together with the concurrent electoral decline of the governing Justice and Development Party (*Adalet Ve Kalkınma Partisi*, AKP) precipitated this ongoing crisis. The escalation of the violence in the conflict between the Kurdistan Workers' Party (*Partiya Karkerên Kurdistanê*, PKK) guerrillas and the state security forces from autumn 2015 onwards created the ideal context for the government to start the process of elimination of Kurdish political representation in Turkey. This instance of repression came after the HDP has firmly established itself as the main representative of the Kurds in Turkey. This is not the first time Turkey has taken repressive measures to eliminate Kurdish political representation, but the sheer numbers involved mark this occasion of political repression as unique in Turkey's recent history.

In Chapter 1, I provide an account of the dominant Kurdish political actors and the main political parties and movements that are involved in the representation of Kurds in Turkey at national and local levels. In Chapter 2, I discuss the electoral competition between the pro-Kurdish parties and the AKP since 2002 at local as well as national levels. In Chapters 3 and 4, an account of the activities of Kurdish traditional elites and leaders such as those who occupy a high position in tribal hierarchies and religious orders are provided. The analysis examines the role they play in representing the Kurds in Turkey, the functions they fulfil in society, the types of activities that they are engaged in and their political attitudes. Chapter 5 examines the representation of Kurdish modern classes and their political attitudes, the activities they engage in and the differences that exist across the classes but also in terms of geographic locations. In particular, there is also an exploration of the business class and how they represent themselves, what types of activities they engage in and the extent to which they represent Kurdish group interests and demands. In Chapter 6, the focus turns to the role of women and I explore their political attitudes, what types of political activities they engage in and what kind of organizational networks they use when representing their interests. Chapter 6 also examines how Kurdish youth represent themselves, the types of activities in which they engage and their political attitudes. In Chapter 7, written by Thomas Jeffrey Miley with Luqman Guldivê, a theoretical reflection on the current issues affecting the political representation of Kurds in Turkey is offered. The discussion unpacks the issues affecting the political representation of the Kurds in Turkey highlighting the challenges Kurdish actors face in their attempt to represent Kurdish constituencies and obtain Kurdish group rights.

Foreword

Thomas Jeffrey Miley with Luqman Guldivê

The book that you have in your hands, by Cengiz Gunes, constitutes the culmination of the late Dr Faleh Abdul Jabar's last major comparative research project, a collaborative endeavour, organized and supported by the Iraq Institute for Strategic Studies in Beirut. The project was conceived in the spring of 2014, under the title of 'Governing Diversity: Representing the Kurds in the New Middle East'. It grew out of a conference that was held in Beirut at the end of 2013, dedicated to the changing political and social conditions faced by Kurds in Turkey, Iraq, Syria and Iran. At the conference, one of the main themes that surfaced, again and again, was that 'gaps in knowledge and literature on the Kurds continue to problematize any genuine analysis of the region'. A consensus thus emerged around 'the need for a renewed and rigorous empirical and theoretical research effort', focused on the concept of and problems associated with political representation.

In the research proposal that gave birth to the project, Dr Jabar and his associates at the Iraq Institute were adamant about the importance of combining theoretical sophistication with empirical rigour in order to adequately address this important subject. To this end, they included in the proposal a brief sketch of their theoretical point of departure, in which they emphasized and explained:

> Political Representation, as a concept, requires further scrutiny. Stemming from the Latin 'repraesentare', meaning literally 'to make present', representation is a dynamic and multi-faceted association between the principal, i.e. the representative, and the agent, i.e. the represented. This relationship and the power distribution between the two players, or the legitimacy that the agent holds or the principal affords to the agent, varies with different modes of representation. Legitimacy is essential in this relationship, as the representative must maintain an effective claim to speak on behalf of the agent(s).

In designing their research agenda, Dr Jabar and his colleagues were especially sensitive to the intimate connection between representation and legitimacy, in its many manifestations. To this end, they noted that, in the Kurdish context, there have been multiple, sometimes contradictory, 'channels' for making claims 'to legitimately speak' on behalf of the Kurdish populations. These include:

> (1) dynastic legacies, such as the Barzinji or Barzani family name in the southern Kurdistan context; (2) coercive control, quite common for most of the twentieth century, which allowed tribal leaders and warlords to effectively control a population and thus speak on behalf of the people; (3) relations with international actors, which were (and still are) perceived as legitimizers, insofar as the leader

who is backed by an external power, be it the UK previously or the US today, was given both material and symbolic support to further his claim; in addition to (4) local legitimacy that granted a representative with a democratic mandate to represent a population.

Dr Jabar and his associates were at the same time careful to stress that '[r]epresentation is not a static concept, but a dynamic institution that entails a plethora of "principals", both official and unofficial, that have various legitimate claims'. Accordingly, they set out to examine empirically the following set of questions: (1) 'how Kurdish societies are coping with problems of representation and how, in this course, they are developing, or, in certain cases, mutating beyond recognition'; (2) 'how these changes are or would be transforming the ways of seeing the Kurdish ethnic-self or the strategies for representation adopted by their active socio-political groups'; and (3) 'how and to what extent the hosting nation-states are reforming their course vis-à-vis ethno-linguistic and cultural groups in their realm'.

To answer these questions, Dr Jabar and his colleagues assembled a research team to 'investigate the modes of political representations that the Kurdish leadership uses' in each of the four different parts of Kurdistan – in Iraq, Turkey, Syria and Iran. The project thus aimed to provide 'an unprecedented scholarly focus on the issue of Kurdish representation', and it sought not only to identify 'local regional problems/solutions', but also to 'assist policy and decision-makers interested in stability, peaceable resolution of conflicts, and the promotion of genuine structures for "governing diversity"', in accordance with 'a broad concept of legitimate pluralistic representation'.

The project was therefore conceived as a contribution to empirical democratic theory, very much with the same ethos, in the same spirit, as the work of two of my mentors, Juan Linz and Al Stepan, who emphasized, in their influential 1996 book, *Problems of Democratic Transition and Consolidation*, the profound tensions – indeed contradiction – between 'nationalizing state policies' and the logic of democracy. Like Linz and Stepan, too, Dr Jabar and his colleagues were very much concerned to 'dispel misinformed myths', to counter the misleading claims of those to whom Burckhardt famously referred as '*terribles simplificateurs*'. For, as they would insist in their project proposal:

> The Kurds have become an essential component to the future structure of governance in the Middle East. In Turkey, Iraq, Syria and Iran, Kurds are consolidating, negotiating, actively seeking, or clandestinely pursuing some form of self-rule, which by necessity entails an institutional and constitutional recognition of pluralism, anchored in the broad concept of 'governing diversity' and embedded in a formal system (or systems) of representation. The problem of pluralistic representation is dual by definition: the inclusion of the Kurds into the system of federal or unitary states and the facilitation of representing diversity within the Kurdish community itself. Nationalism, as a discourse, may lend claims of representation a holistic aura but ultimately fails to bury the socio-economic and cultural diversity within. Kurdish society at large still lingers in a semi-modern, semi-traditional state. A lack of the levelling and modernizing power of a modern economy renders this society 'prismatic' in nature. Modern strata,

such as the middle and business classes, women, youth, among others, yearn for ways and means of representation to defend their sectoral-generational interests. This extends also to cultural-linguistic groups (three major dialects or languages exist), religious sects (Alawis, Yezedis, Kakais, among others), and traditional groups like clerics, Sufi orders (Naqshbandiya, Qadiriya, among others), tribal Aghas and village peasant (Miskin) communities. Political parties, organized along modern lines, be it nationalist, Islamist or leftist, show tendencies to co-opt a multitude of diverging interests, but fail to have a universal mandate, and reveal inadequate channels of representation. Hence the countless forms and modalities of representation tend to defy any simplistic and holistic approach.

To combat still-prevalent misconceptions and oversimplifications, Dr Jabar and his associates decided to embark on an ambitious research agenda, organized around multiple research 'clusters', beginning with (1) an 'examination of government structures and leading parties'; followed by (2) '[a] theoretical and empirical examination of the very concept of representation as a conflictual space, its scope and meaning in a semi-modernized society, where modern and traditional structures overlap, or act independently, producing both theoretical and empirical complexities'; as well as (3) 'empirical research to examine the problems of representations for modern groups, which include the middle and business strata, the underclasses, women, youth, and a focus on their civil organizations (trade and professional unions, NGOs, etc.)'; (4) 'an assessment of the case of religious sects, namely the Yezidis, Kakais, and Alawites'; (5) 'an examination of the traditional clerics and Sufi orders'; and finally, (6) 'a look at tribal chiefs (Aghas) and their webs of client villages'.

In so doing, Dr Jabar and his colleagues hoped 'to locate fundamental problems of political representation', and in the process to provide empirically robust evidence about the diversity of the Kurdish regions, as well as empirically grounded answers to a host of pressing questions, ranging from 'the impact of the so-called "Arab-Spring" on the political culture', to 'the level of appetite for guerrilla-type (or any type) of armed struggle', to 'the problems with pan-Kurdish nationalism, the linguistic, religious and cultural differences that divide Kurds', to the nature of the 'newly emerging socioeconomic formations', and even 'the effect of a patriarchal structure on gender relations'. All of this within the overarching rubric of 'the problem of political representation'.

An ambitious research agenda, indeed. And one which was forced to overcome many obstacles, perhaps especially in Turkey, where the onset of field research coincided with and was significantly hindered by, a rapid escalation of hostilities, political persecution and human rights atrocities in the Kurdish region in the aftermath of the definitive breakdown of peace negotiations in July 2015. Yet, where there is a will, there is a way. With considerable bravery and resilience, Luqman Guldivê and other researchers managed to carry out interviews in Turkey over the course of the summer and autumn of 2015 and autumn 2016, and thus provide a substantial, original empirical basis for this text, so skilfully elaborated by Cengiz Gunes.

Unfortunately, Dr Jabar did not live to see the project to its completion. He did, however, get to complete the introductory volume to this series, with Renad Mansour, titled *The Kurds in a Changing Middle East: History, Politics and Representation*;

and he also got to see the important companion volume by Harriet Allsopp, titled *Representing the Kurds in Syria*. We can only hope that this volume would have met with his approval as well.

In his life, Dr Jabar made many crucial contributions to the political sociology of the Middle East, including several path-breaking books such as *Post-Marxism and the Middle East* (1997), *Ayatollahs, Sufis and Ideologues: State, Religion and Social Movements in Iraq* (2002), *The Shiite Movement in Iraq* (2003), *Tribes and Power: Nationalism and Ethnicity in the Middle East* (co-edited with Hosham Dawod, 2003) and *The Kurds: Nationalism and Politics* (2007). This was in addition to his many invaluable reports for *International Crisis Group*, not to mention his dedication and efforts as the Director of the Iraq Institute for Strategic Studies in Beirut.

We consider ourselves fortunate to have met Dr Jabar and to have played a role in the production and completion of this important volume by Cengiz Gunes, which adds considerably to our understanding of the problems and dynamics of representation of the Kurds in Turkey.

Moshi, Tanzania
September 2018

Acknowledgements

This book could not have come into being had it not been for the collective effort of several persons. I would like to express my sincere gratitude to my friends and colleagues Yasin Duman, Luqman Guldivê, Çetin Gürer, Zeki Gürür and Güllistan Yarkın for their hard work and diligence in assisting me with the research that forms this book. Luqman Guldivê also provided an initial analysis of the survey data used in Chapters 1 and 2. I would like to thank Thomas Jeffrey Miley for providing feedback on the entire manuscript that helped me to reorient the book's focus. I would like to thank Heval Çakmakçı for helping me find several primary sources I used in this book, and Ruhat Kemaloğlu for helping me identify and contact several research participants. Finally, I would like to thank the team at the Iraq Institute, the late Faleh Abdul Jabar, Renad Mansour and Abir Khaddaj, who were very helpful and supportive throughout this project. The project's inception and development owed much to the efforts of Faleh Abdul Jabar, whose untimely death in February 2018 prevented him from seeing the publication of this book.

List of abbreviations

AKP	Adalet Ve Kalkınma Partisi (the Justice and Development Party)
BDP	Barış ve Demokrasi Partisi (the Peace and Democracy Party)
CHP	Cumhuriyet Halk Partisi (the Republican People's Party)
DDKO	Devrimci Doğu Kültür Ocakları (The Revolutionary Cultural Hearths of the East)
DEHAP	Demokratik Halk Partisi (the Democratic People's Party)
DEP	Demokrasi Partisi (the Democracy Party)
Diyanet	Diyanet İşleri Başkanlığı (the Directorate of Religious Affairs)
DP	Demokrat Parti (the Democrat Party)
DTP	Demokratik Toplum Partisi (the Democratic Society Party)
ERNK	Eniya Rizgariya Netewa Kurdistan (The National Liberation Front of Kurdistan)
HADEP	Halkın Demokrasi Partisi (the People's Democracy Party)
HDP	Halkların Demokratik Partisi (the Peoples' Democratic Party)
HEP	Halkın Emek Partisi (the People's Labour Party)
HPG	Hêzên Parastina Gel (the People's Defence Forces)
Hüda-Par	Hür Dava Partisi (the Free Cause Party)
ISIS	Islamic State of Iraq and Syria
KADEK	Kongreya Azadî û Demokrasiya Kurdistanê (the Kurdistan Freedom and Democracy Congress)
KCK	Koma Civakan Kurdistan (The Council of Communities of Kurdistan)
KDP	Kurdistan Democrat Party – Iraq
KNK	Kongreya Netawa Kurdistan (the Kurdistan National Congress)
Kongra-Gel	Kongra Gelê Kurdistan (the People's Congress of Kurdistan)
MGK	Milli Güvenlik Kurulu (the National Security Council)
PJA	Partiya Jina Azad (the Party of Free Women)

PKK	Partiya Karkerên Kurdistanê (the Kurdistan Workers' Party)
SHP	Sosyaldemokrat Halkçı Parti (the Social Democratic Populist Party)
TİP	Türkiye İşci Partisi (the Workers' Party of Turkey)
TKDP	Türkiye Kürdistan Demokrat Partisi (the Kurdistan Democrat Party of Turkey)
TKSP	Türkiye Kürdistanı Sosyalist Partisi (the Socialist Party of Turkish Kurdistan)
YTP	Yeni Türkiye Partisi (the New Turkey Party)

Introduction:
Political representation of Kurds in Turkey

The political representation of the Kurds in Turkey's political structures has been a thorny issue ever since the foundation of the republic in 1923. Political activism by the Kurds or around Kurdish-related political demands continues to be viewed with deep suspicions by Turkey's political establishment. Despite the difficulties and dangers involved, whether through acts of dissent or active participation, Kurds from all walks of life have been taking part in politics and trying to represent their interests and demands. Kurds who did not publicly assert their identity were able to rise through the ranks. For those who did assert their identity, it was a completely different story. Turkey's unitary and highly centralized political system and the definition of national identity as exclusively Turkish have created major barriers for the Kurds to represent their interests and pursue their demands.

Since Turkey began holding regular competitive elections in 1950, many Kurdish individuals have been elected to political office at the national and local levels. These individuals tended to be selected by Turkish political parties from the top echelons of tribal and religious hierarchy and, as time went by, they became co-opted into Turkey's political elite. They established themselves as the dominant political actors within the Kurdish society in Turkey and acted as the link between the state and the masses of Kurdish peasants. They have been a voice to their constituents but, by and large, have steered well clear of demanding Kurdish group rights and the recognition of Kurdish identity. This trend continues in the present day but has been significantly weakened as a result of the rise of the Kurdish national movement in the second half of the twentieth century.

During the 1960s and 1970s, the combined effects of the development of capitalism, the mechanization of agriculture, the spread of education and increasing levels of urbanization in Turkey created the conditions for the emergence and rise of a Kurdish national movement and brought about significant changes to the way Kurds participate in the politics of the country. However, the Turkish state's repression of Kurdish dissent convinced many Kurdish political activists in the second half of the 1970s that a forceful challenge of the state authority was necessary to bring about political change. This led to the radicalization of an increasing number of Kurds and the mass mobilization of a significant section of the Kurdish population by the PKK from the late 1980s onwards. The PKK's insurgency against Turkey from 1984 onwards resulted in a conflict that continues to date. Hence, in the past four decades, the contest over Kurdish political representation has been taking place in the context of an ongoing violent conflict, which has been used by the state to justify its repression of peaceful Kurdish attempts to represent themselves in the political structures and campaigns for constitutional reform to broaden Kurdish political rights in Turkey.

With the establishment of the People's Labour Party (Halkın Emek Partisi, HEP) on 7 June 1990, we have witnessed the emergence of the pro-Kurdish democratic movement. Its rise in Turkey has faced many challenges as the state's repression targeted the pro-Kurdish political parties in particular. Several pro-Kurdish political parties were closed down during the 1990s and 2000s, hundreds of their members and activists were murdered and thousands of them were imprisoned and tortured. In fact, such repressive practices became routine during the 1990s and included the removal of legal immunity from Kurdish MPs and their imprisonment in 1994. However, despite the repression and state violence directed at the pro-Kurdish political parties, they have remained committed to achieving Kurdish rights within the framework of a democratic Turkey and continued their efforts to participate in elections for Turkey's political institutions. As this brief overview highlights, Kurdish political representation in Turkey has a complex history and, before we attempt to answer the question of 'Who represents the Kurds' or whether Kurdish political representation in Turkey is possible, we first need a discussion of what political representation refers to.

Political representation

Suzanna Dovi defines political representation as 'the activity of making citizens' voices, opinions, and perspectives "present" in public policy-making processes. Political representation occurs when political actors speak, advocate, symbolize, and act on the behalf of others in the political arena.'[1] 'Political actors' here refer to persons holding elected office, such as members of parliament and district and provincial mayors, and are formally involved in the representation of their constituency. This definition is based on Hanna Pitkin's seminal study, *The Concept of Representation*, which, being the first major study on political representation, has had a major impact on the subsequent discussion on the topic. Pitkin's account discusses four views of representation: formalistic, descriptive, symbolic and substantive.[2] A formalistic view of representation centres around the concept of authorization and accountability. Accordingly, a representative is either someone who 'is authorized to act in place of others' or 'someone who is to be held to account, who will have to answer to another for what he does', with elections seen as the occasions when the represented hold their representatives to account.[3]

The descriptive representation that Pitkin discusses relates to the notion of 'standing for'. On this account, representatives 'stand for' the represented 'by virtue of correspondence and connection between them, a resemblance or reflection'.[4] The representatives have to be similar to or share a descriptive likeness with the represented, and in the debate on the representation of minorities, this often refers to similarities in terms of ethnic, religious or cultural background. The third view of representation also relates to the notion of 'standing for' and is known as 'symbolic representation'. A similar link between the representatives and the represented is highlighted on the basis of symbols: 'a political representative is to be understood on the model of a flag representing a nation, or an emblem representing a cult'.[5] Pitkin's fourth view is based on the notion of representation as 'substantive acting for' others, which is known as substantive representation.[6] Here representation is seen as an activity and the importance of representatives advocating the 'best interest' of the represented is emphasized.

Although these different views of representation are distinct, they should not be seen as mutually exclusive or in opposition to each other. In many ways, they are connected and impact on each other; for example, an increase in descriptive representation can and often does lead to an increase in substantive representation. This argument has been developed more fully by Manbridge who argues that descriptive representation enhances the substantive representation of a group's interests 'by improving the quality of deliberation'.[7] Especially in contexts where a minority is severely marginalized or subordinated, descriptive representation empowers that minority and increases their feeling of attachment to the country's political institutions.[8] The importance of descriptive representation for the empowerment of a minority is also confirmed by the comparative study of the US and New Zealand by Banducci et al.[9]

Pitkin's account of representation has been critiqued by Michael Saward on grounds that it does not sufficiently consider the non-electoral forms of representation as well as the issue of the contestability of political representation. On this interpretation, representation is something that is claimed by the actors involved and is framed as an 'ongoing, dynamic process in which a great variety of actors and organizations take part, electoral actors through elective process and other actors through other processes'.[10] Saward's approach reorients the focus from representatives to the represented and sees representation in politics as a two-way process: 'the represented play a role in choosing representatives, and representatives "choose" their constituents in the sense of portraying them or framing them in particular, contestable ways'.[11] Hence, non-elective and self-authorized forms of representation can enjoy strong legitimacy and support among a constituency and needs to be considered when thinking about political representation.

The changing context of Kurdish political representation in Turkey

The debate on political representation presented above is highly useful for highlighting the forms Kurdish political representation has taken and the representative claims that Kurdish political actors in Turkey make. If we derive a conception of representation based on descriptive representation, then we can identify a long list of Kurdish representatives in Turkey who have taken part in Turkey's national politics. Since 1950, party competition created suitable conditions for Kurds to engage in politics, leading to an increase in Kurdish descriptive representation. This process was initiated by the Democrat Party (Demokrat Parti, DP), which was keen to increase its support base in the Kurdish majority regions. Kurdish tribal chiefs and religious leaders who were exiled by Kemalists to western Turkey during the 1930s were allowed to return and the

DP utilized the Kurdish tribal and religious elite in its attempt to mobilize the Kurdish electorate during the 1950s. A common practice employed by the DP in the 1950s and other centre-right political parties subsequently was to choose locally influential Kurdish tribal leaders from populous tribes as their parliamentary candidates to win the support from the Kurdish voters. Almost all Kurdish political representatives during the 1950s and 1960s were drawn from the tribal and religious elite and, as a result, several leading tribal and religious families became active in centre-right politics. These included the Kartal family in the province of Van, a leading family in the Bruki tribe. Similarly, the Zeydan family in Hakkari, a leading family of the Pinyanişi tribe, have played an important role in the politics of the Hakkari province in the past fifty years. It was not only the tribal leaders who become political actors, but sheikhs also. These include Abdulmelik Fırat, who was the grandson of Sheikh Said – a Naqshibandiyya sheikh and leader of the Kurdish revolt of 1925 – and the Gaydalı-İnan family, who dominated the politics of Bitlis province during the past fifty years. There are many other tribal and religious figures who were active in politics and I discuss these in greater detail in Chapters 3 and 4.

Nevertheless, having Kurdish descriptive representation did not lead to the development of Kurdish substantive representation as most of these political actors remained loyal to their political parties and, in the main, refrained from articulating Kurdish political or group demands. An attempt to pursue a more independent line was made when the New Turkey Party (Yeni Türkiye Partisi, YTP) was established in 1961. Although the YTP was a centre-right political party aiming to attract the support of a cross-section of the Turkish population, its establishment was an important development for Kurdish representation in Turkey because the party included several high-profile Kurds among its founders, such as Yusuf Azizoğlu, who was active in the DP, served as the mayor of Silvan district of Diyarbakır between 1946 and 1950 and was an MP for the Diyarbakır province during the 1950s. The YTP managed to gain significant support from the Kurds in the 1961 general election and served as a junior coalition partner in the government between 1962 and 1965. Additionally, its leading figures campaigned to address the disproportionate inequality the Kurds were experiencing in Turkey.[12] However, Turkey's political system remained very much unresponsive to popular Kurdish political demands, which began to be expressed more vocally from the late 1960s onwards by several other political actors.

With the spread of education and increase of urbanization in Turkey and the Kurdish majority regions from the 1960s onwards, the strong connection between tribal leaders and political representatives started to weaken. The rise of Turkey's left-wing movement during the 1960s and later the Kurdish movement in Turkey from the late 1960s onwards further weakened the power of the Kurdish traditional elite and reduced their influence over Kurdish society. Hence, from the 1960s onwards, as more Kurds began to take part in political activities, a wider set of Kurdish political demands began to be voiced by different political actors and movements. The absence of a genuinely democratic political order and a functioning representative democratic system in Turkey during the 1960s and 1970s meant that the Kurds' attempts to establish their own organizations and represent their interests were repressed, which pushed them more towards dissent and resistance-orientated political practices.

Several meetings, collectively known as the 'Meetings of the East', took place in the Kurdish majority regions during the late 1960s and, as the high number of Kurds attending these meetings indicates, Kurdish political activism active within Turkey's left-wing movement was able to mobilize large numbers of Kurds in that period. From the late 1960s onward, Kurds' activism within the left in Turkey gradually led to the emergence of a Kurdish socialist movement, which began to draw the support of a wider section of the Kurdish society in Turkey. In fact, from the late 1960s onwards, with increasing vigour, Kurds began to organize collectively around their group rights and demands. In the mid-1970s, this took a radical turn and led to the formation of clandestine political groups and parties, which advocated a forceful challenge of the authority of the state.

The late 1970s also witnessed the pro-Kurdish candidates Mehdi Zana and Edip Solmaz winning the 1977 and 1979 local elections in Diyarbakır and Batman, respectively. However, soon after Kurds' representation at local government level faced repression from the state: Edip Solmaz was killed in 1979 and Mehdi Zana was arrested in 1980 and imprisoned at the Diyarbakır Prison until 1991.[13] From 1990, Kurdish political representation in Turkey took a new dimension with the establishment of the pro-Kurdish political movement. From then on, pro-Kurdish political parties have been part of Turkey's political system and have provided the Kurds with a channel to represent themselves and pursue their demands. However, the repression that they have been experiencing, particularly during the mid-1990s, bears testimony to the difficulties Kurds face as they try to represent themselves via legal political channels and in the institutions of the state. Despite the repression, the pro-Kurdish movement has been gaining more support in the past decade, and from 2007 onwards, it managed to get its independent candidates elected and form a political bloc in the Turkish parliament.

In line with the past trend of the popularity of centre-right conservative parties among the Kurdish electorate, the AKP has also managed to consistently draw strong support from the Kurds from 2002 onwards. However, its increasing authoritarianism and Turkish nationalist rhetoric have led to Kurds withdrawing their support from it over the years. The party lost much of its support base in the Kurdish majority regions in the June 2015 election but, in the re-run of the election on 1 November 2015, it has recovered some of the votes it lost to HDP, though not enough to challenge the HDP as the main representative of the Kurds in Turkey. Currently, many of the mainstream Turkish political parties have local branches in the majority Kurdish regions but none other than the AKP manage to gain a significant amount of support from the Kurdish electorate. As discussed in Chapter 1, there are smaller political parties, such as the leftist HAK-PAR and the Islamist Hüda-Par active in the Kurdish majority regions but these parties are yet to win a seat at the parliament or mayoralty of districts and provinces.

With the growth of Kurdish business, professional and working classes since the 1960s, there has been an increase in the number of civil society and non-governmental organizations that represent the Kurds in Turkey. These include trade unions, business associations, human rights groups, associations representing a region or province, women's rights groups and religious groups. The trade unions with a strong presence in Kurdish majority areas are the Confederation of Public Employees Trade Union (KESK) and the Education and Science Workers' Union (Eğitim ve Bilim Emekçileri

Sendikası, Eğitim-Sen). These trade unions have local branches in the Kurdish areas and those in western Turkey have many Kurdish members among its ranks. With the increase in the rate of urbanization and education, Kurds have become much more integrated into Turkish society and the avenues they use to represent themselves have also increased. New and more diverse representative organizations have been added to the already established traditional forms of representation.

The legal and political order and Kurdish political representation in Turkey

An account of the constitutional and legal framework in Turkey and how it conceives of the non-dominant minorities, of which the Kurds are the most significant, is needed when discussing the legal impediments that Kurdish representatives continue to face. Such an account will also provide useful context to the Kurds' political representation at local and national levels in Turkey. Following the proclamation of the republic in 1923, the Turkish state nationalism or Kemalism became the official state ideology and the guiding principle behind the widespread socio-political reforms.[14] The transformation of the multinational Ottoman Empire to a nation-state required wide-ranging social and political reforms that the new nationalist elite that came to power in Turkey felt was necessary to build their westernized and secular Turkish nation. The Treaty of Lausanne signed between Turkey and the Allied Powers on 24 July 1923 is the main document that contains some protection for minorities in Turkey. Although the treaty does not mention any specific minority group by name, the state officials have long claimed that its provisions apply only to the non-Muslim Armenian, Greek and Jewish minorities, and in practice, these communities have only benefited from the protection afforded by it.[15] The remaining minorities in Turkey were integrated through a policy of assimilation and the policy adopted by the newly established state in Turkey did not extend any public recognition to the Kurds as a distinct group:

> The traditional assimilationist perspective perceived the Kurds as an assimilable community or as prospective 'Turks' and did not recognise or exclude them systematically on a racial or ethnic basis. The conventional policy of the Turkish state and official Turkish nationalism was rather based on [the] denial of the presence of the Kurdish identity in Turkey.[16]

The Kurds resisted the new regime that came into being in a series of revolts during the 1920s and 1930s but their attempts to counter the hegemony of Turkish nationalism ultimately failed. The new nationalist elite constructed the political system in Turkey as a unitary and highly centralized republic and Turkishness as both a national and ethnic identity was placed firmly at the centre of citizenship. In all of Turkey's constitutions, the category of 'Turk' has been used to describe the citizens of Turkey and both an ethnic/cultural and national connotation is attached to the definition of a Turk.[17] Grigoriadis describes this ambiguity in the following terms: 'Every Muslim citizen of the republic regardless of his ethnic origins was invited – and obliged – to adopt the republican

Turkish national identity. There was no room for separate ethnic or religious groups. Kurdish, Alevi or any other group identities were persistently denied by the state.[18] This ambiguity proved useful for the promotion of Turkishness and the Turkification of other non-Turkish groups. The exclusivist way Turkish citizenship was defined had significant consequences for the Kurds as the category of universal national rights were assigned only to the Turkish nation, and the Kurds' subsequent articulation of their group-specific demands was considered illegitimate.[19]

As Bayır argues, 'the Turkish legal system has persistently failed to accommodate ethno-religious diversity in the country, a failure attributable to the state's founding philosophy – Turkish nationalism – and its influence upon legislation in judicial bodies'.[20] In fact, the judiciary has played a key role in the criminalization of any form of Kurdish political activism (described as Kurdism in court judgements) and it justified its decisions on the ground that articulating Kurdish political demands 'conflicted with Turkish nationalism, which has been defined by the judiciary as the founding principle of the Turkish state and legal system'.[21] Turkish judiciary has been described as 'one of the guardians of the foundational values of the Turkish state' and they used their position to negate and suppress Kurdish national demands and punish anyone who advocated the recognition of Kurdish identity and group rights, which was described as 'Kurdism' (*Kürtçülük*).[22] Based on her extensive examination of the judgements Turkish courts produced on the cases of Kurdish political activists since the 1970s, Bayır argues:

> ... the judiciary's representation of the Kurds has been based on three overlapping yet distinguishable positions: (1) denying the Kurds' separate existence and claiming their Turkishness; (2) acknowledging the Kurds while denying Kurdism; and (3) portraying the Kurds' traditional law, culture and social structure as deficient.[23]

The Turkish judiciary's representation of the Kurds relied on all three of these positions. In some of their judgements, the Kurds' separate existence as a nation was rejected and the claim that they were Turks was put forward. In other cases, the judges' decisions did not completely reject the Kurds' different identity but rejected what they termed 'Kurdism', and any claim that the Kurds were entitled to group rights and articulated their cultural, linguistic and cultural demands were seen as Kurdism and prosecuted. The third position that Turkish judiciary took portrayed the Kurds as inter alia 'backward' and 'primitive'.[24]

The failure to recognize the Kurds as a separate national group and Kurdish identity and group rights in Turkey has been functioning as a barrier to Kurdish representation in Turkey. Claims that advocate or articulate the separate existence of a Kurdish nation in Turkey are interpreted as a threat to Turkey's national security and the indivisible unity of its territory and nation. This meant that articulations of Kurdish political demands or rights were criminalized and individuals and political parties that demanded group rights for the Kurds were prosecuted.

In 1991, the veteran politician and the leader of the True Path Party (Doğru Yol Partisi, DYP) Süleyman Demirel announced, 'we recognize the Kurdish reality', and, in 1995, the leader of the Motherland Party (Anavatan Partisi, ANAP) Mesut Yılmaz linked Turkey's EU prospects to solving the Kurdish question.[25] In reality, however, these overtures to the Kurds led neither to the recognition of Kurdish group rights nor to a policy change to accommodate Kurdish political demands and group rights. Hence, the way Kemalism framed the Kurdish identity and demands continues to remain the dominant view by the political establishment in Turkey and Kemalism's anti-pluralist logic continues to create barriers for the Kurds' political representation. For example, a political party that advocates the rights of Kurdish people is seen as committing an act of separatism, which is a ground for closing down a political party. The restrictions placed on the formation of political parties create significant barriers for Kurdish political representation and these restrictions have been used extensively to prevent the pro-Kurdish political parties' attempts to represent the Kurds. On 3 July 1992, the Supreme Court's Attorney General filed a case at the Constitutional Court to close down the HEP. The indictment accused the HEP of engaging in activities to weaken Turkey's territorial and national unity by proposing to change the 'unchangeable' principles of the constitution and for expressing that ethnic, linguistic and cultural groups exist in Turkey. The HEP was closed down by the Constitutional Court on 14 July 1993.[26] On 7 May 1993, the Kurdish political leaders in Turkey established the Democracy Party (Demokrasi Partisi, DEP) as a replacement in the case of the HEP's closure but it too was closed down on 16 June 1994. On 17 March 1994, six DEP MPs were arrested, with two more being arrested on 1 July 1994. The trial ended on 8 August 1994 with Hatip Dicle, Orhan Doğan, Leyla Zana, Ahmet Türk and Selim Sadak each receiving fifteen-year sentences and Sedat Yurtdaş receiving a sentence of seven-and-a-half years. Ahmet Türk's and Selim Sadak's sentences were revoked on appeal. As a result, the Kurdish political representation in the Turkish Assembly was eliminated in 1994, and, subsequently, Kurdish political demands were equated with separatism and terrorism, thereby limiting the channels through which they could be raised.[27] The Constitutional Court closed down the pro-Kurdish People's Democracy Party (Halkın Demokrasi Partisi, HADEP) in 2003 and the Democratic Society Party (Demokratik Toplum Partisi, DTP) in 2009. The reasons cited by the Constitutional Court for the closure of the pro-Kurdish parties is summarized neatly by Derya Bayır:

> Thus, to speak about the existence of the Kurds as a national entity ... to aim to create facilities for ethnic and religious minorities to enhance their culture in a free environment or claim the use of the mother language in the legal system and in education, to speak about the existence of a Kurdish nation which has been persecuted and has been under pressure of assimilation, to differentiate the Kurds from Turks and to anticipate a Kurdish nation outside of the Turkish nation, and to establish a new state order to this end were all considered as justifiable reasons for closure of political parties.[28]

Over the years, parliament passed legislation to make party closures more difficult but other features of the system that have created significant barriers for the Kurds to represent their interests and demands remain very much intact.

A second formal barrier to Kurdish political representation in Turkey has been the 10 per cent election threshold introduced in 1983 (Law no. 2839). On several occasions during the 1990s and 2000s, the pro-Kurdish political parties took part in the elections as a party and were prevented from entering the parliament because they could not gain 10 per cent of the national vote. In 1991, the HEP worked closely with the Social Democratic Populist Party (Sosyaldemokrat Halkçı Parti, SHP) and managed to get twenty-two MPs elected to parliament. However, after the elimination of the pro-Kurdish representation in 1994 until 2007, pro-Kurdish political parties were not represented in the parliament. At the 2007 general elections, twenty-two of the independent pro-Kurdish candidates supported by the DTP were elected to the parliament. In the 2011 election, again a similar strategy of supporting independent candidates was adapted and a total of thirty-five MPs were elected. The HDP decided to take part in the June 2015 election as a party and managed to win 13.1 per cent of the national vote and eighty seats in the parliament. The coalition negotiations between the AKP and the Republican People's Party (Cumhuriyet Halk Partisi, CHP) did not produce a result and, consequently, new elections were held on 1 November 2015, during which the HDP won 10.76 per cent of the vote and fifty-nine seats. The HDP managed to obtain 11.7 per cent in the June 2018 election, and through electoral alliances and incorporating diverse political actors into its structures, the pro-Kurdish democratic movement has overcome the barrier to representation placed by the electoral threshold.

The articulation of Kurdish political rights and demands in Turkey is also restricted by the existing laws that promote the use of the Turkish language in public life. In fact, the Turkish state has devised a complex legal mechanism for banning the use of Kurdish language in many areas of life, which has a significant political implication as it prevents and penalizes Kurdish attempts to raise their political demands connected to linguistic rights. Although there are not any legal prohibitions on the public use of the Kurdish language, a *de facto* ban exists through the imposition of the use of Turkish language, which is the state's official language, in public affairs.[29] A number of legal reforms carried out in the 2000s as part of attempts to meet Turkey's obligations under the EU accession process have broadened Kurdish language rights and led to the increasing use of Kurdish language in areas of education and broadcasting. These reforms have broadened the rights of Kurds as well as other minorities in Turkey but, by and large, the system has retained its essential features. The constitutional amendment of 2001 (Law no. 4709) paved the way to broadcasting in the Kurdish language and the legal reforms carried out in 2002 enabled the teaching of the Kurdish language in private courses.[30] In 2009, the Institute of Living Languages was established at the Mardin Artuklu University to teach the Kurdish language and, in 2012, an elective Kurdish language course began to be offered as part of the secondary school curriculum in Kurdish majority regions. The state's broadcasting network, Turkish Radio and Television Corporation (TRT) began forty-five-minute-long Kurdish language news broadcasts in 2004, and in 2006 this was extended to private broadcasters. On 1 January 2009, a twenty-four-hour Kurdish language TV station (initially known as *TRT-6* but since January 2015 known as *TRT-Kurdî*) was established as part of the TRT network.[31] The establishment of the Kurdish-language TV station and provision of Kurdish language courses in state schools are often offered as proof of the governing AKP's tolerance of ethnocultural diversity in Turkey. However, doubts remain over the extent of the AKP's tolerance because of its consistent refusal to commit to the full recognition of the Kurds' linguistic rights, such as the provision of education in the Kurdish language. Also, there remain many practical problems and prohibitions that restrict the use of these limited language rights. The legal reforms and the associated regulations are vague and do not clearly provide guarantees for the protection and development of the Kurdish language in Turkey. Another significant reform that had a compelling impact on the representation of the Kurds is the changes made to the Associations Law (Law no. 5253) in November 2004, which made it possible for regional and local associations to have the status of non-profit associations working for the good of the public. The changes made it easier to establish and manage associations and in the subsequent decades led to a significant increase in the number of associations that were active in the Kurdish majority region of Turkey.

Turkey is administratively divided into eighty-one provinces (*il/vilayet*) but it has a unitary and centralized state structure. The provinces are further divided into districts (*ilçe*) and into towns (*belde*), villages (*köy*) or neighbourhoods (*mahalle*), depending on whether the settlement is in an urban or rural area. All these administrative units have elected officials: the head of a village or neighbourhood is known as a *muhtar* and the elected leader of a province and a district is a mayor (*il* or *ilçe Belediye Başkanı*). The highest state official at the provincial level is a governor (*vali*), who is appointed by and responsible to the central government. Services such as maintaining water supply and gas networks, rubbish collection, public works, licensing, fire services and the city police (*zabıta*) at a provincial level are provided by the municipal councils, and provinces that have a large population are classified as a metropolitan municipality (*Büyükşehir Belediyesi*). The budget of the municipal councils is allocated by the central government based on the needs of the province. Even though Turkey is a signatory to the European Charter of Local Self-Government, so far there has been little progress towards empowering the local governments and granting them more political and administrative freedom. Given the strong attachment in Turkey to the principle of the unitary state, any attempts to empower the local administrations are seen as a threat to Turkey's unitary structure and rejected.[32]

Kurdish population in Turkey

Because of the lack of current census data on the Kurdish population in Turkey, accurate information about the exact number of Kurds or their socio-economic conditions is hard to find.[33] Initially, the languages people spoke at home was included in the census questionnaire but the last time that was asked was in the 1965 census. Also, given the Kurds in Turkey have been facing widespread discrimination in Turkey, it is highly likely that some Kurds will be unwilling to identify themselves as Kurds when asked, which makes any attempts to estimate the Kurdish population in Turkey more difficult. In 2013, columnist Taha Erdem estimated the Kurdish population in Turkey to be 13.4 million constituting 17.7 per cent of the country's population.[34] This figure was based on the surveys carried out with the Kurds in Turkey and other available statistics but it has been challenged by others for significantly underestimating the number of Kurds in Turkey.[35] Other estimates of the Kurdish population range between 15 million and 20 million, constituting roughly between 18 and 25 per cent of Turkey's population. Despite the ongoing out-migration from the Kurdish heartlands, between 65 per cent and 80 per cent of the total population of the following provinces is Kurdish: Adıyaman, Ağrı, Batman, Bingöl, Bitlis, Diyarbakır, Elazığ, Hakkari, Mardin, Muş, Şanlıurfa, Siirt, Şırnak, Tunceli and Van. A significant number of Kurds populate the adjacent area of the above provinces such as Erzurum, Gaziantep, Kahramanmaraş, Kayseri, Malatya and Sivas.[36]

Because of the adverse economic conditions in eastern and south-eastern regions, many Kurds have been migrating to western Turkey in search of work since the 1950s.[37] Also, many Kurds, while being permanently based in the Kurdish regions, move to western Turkey on a temporary basis to work in agricultural jobs during harvesting seasons and in construction, restaurant or hospitality sectors during part of the year. From the late 1980s until the early 2000s, with the intensification of conflict, many rural Kurds who were forced out of their settlements by the army and security services moved to cities in western Turkey. It is estimated that between 3 million and 4 million Kurds were forcibly displaced during the late 1980s and 1990s.[38] Consequently, large Kurdish populations reside in western Turkey, particularly in Adana, Ankara, Antalya, Bursa, Istanbul, Izmir, Kocaeli and Mersin. Kurds make up as much as 20 per cent of Istanbul's population of fourteen million and almost 35 per cent of Kurds that reside outside of the majoritively Kurdish regions live in Istanbul.[39] The Kurdish population in Ankara is also significant and estimates suggest that it constitutes nearly 10 per cent of the province's population.[40] In addition, there are Kurds in districts of Bala, Haymana and Polatlı and it is thought they settled there as early as the seventeenth century. Hence, given the lack of available population statistics and the fact that the Kurds have dispersed around Turkey, it is difficult to provide accurate population data for the Kurds.

Diyarbakır is often seen as the unofficial capital of the Kurdish region and in 2015, the province had a total population of 1,654,196 people.[41] In 1990, the population of Diyarbakır stood at 1,094,996 of which 381,114 resided in Diyarbakır city. The remaining 494,356 people resided in the rural areas and 219,496 resided in the surrounding towns.[42] The same figures for 2000 for Diyarbakır province, Diyarbakır city and the population residing in the surrounding towns and villages were 1,362,708, 812,962 and 545,016, respectively.[43] Being an important regional centre, Diyarbakır received a significant number of forcibly displaced people. In 2007, 58.6 per cent of the population resided in the urban settlements (the city centre and the surrounding towns) and this rate increased to 72.6 per cent in 2012.[44] In 2012, the rate of urbanization in Turkey was at 77.3 per cent and in comparison with western parts of Turkey, the Kurdish south-east and east are lower.[45] The mean age of the population is 22.2 compared to Turkey's average of 30.7.[46] This is in line with the other Kurdish regions which indicate that the Kurdish population in Turkey is much younger than Turkey's population. In 1990, the population of Van stood at 637,433, which twenty-five years later in 2015 reached 1,096,397, and it is ranked fifteenth in terms of the most populous provinces of Turkey.[47] In 2007, 511,678 or 51.04 per cent of the province's total population of 979,671 resided in urban areas, with this figure reaching 548,717 or 52.11 per cent in 2012.[48] According to the 2015 statistics, the population of other Kurdish majority provinces were as follows: Adıyaman, 602,774; Ağrı, 547,210; Bingöl, 267,184; Bitlis, 340,449; Hakkari, 278,775; Kars, 292,660; Mardin 796,591; Muş, 408,728; Şanlıurfa, 1,892,320; Siirt, 320,351; Şırnak, 490,184; and Batman, 566,633.[49]

1

Kurdish political parties in Turkey

This chapter provides an account of the emergence and development of the main political movements and parties that represent the Kurds in Turkey and highlights their ideological inclinations and approach to the accommodation of Kurdish rights. It also assesses how these parties relate to each other and the institutions of the state. It uses a wide range of primary sources and secondary literature to chart the development of political parties that have a Kurdish constituency or advocate Kurdish rights. It also provides brief profiles of the leading figures in these political parties and the extent to which different sections of the Kurdish community are represented within them.

The study of political parties has been a key topic for political scientists since the beginning of the twentieth century and, consequently, the academic literature on the subject is vast and ever-growing. The interest in political parties is unsurprising due to the fact that they fulfil an essential function in a representative democracy. Political parties play a key role in the public deliberation of political issues and policies and the representation and aggregation of citizens' interests and political demands.[1] Consequently, political parties are generally seen as the most significant political actors in representative democracy and as 'vehicles of representation' they are essential for the functioning of democracy and formation of governments.[2]

Turkey held its first multi-party parliamentary election in July 1946, but the subsequent election held on 14 May 1950 is generally considered to be the country's first free and fair election. This liberalization of the political system was initiated and orchestrated by the political elite and mainly as a response to the changing domestic and global developments. The existing literature on Turkey's transition to multi-party democracy highlights the importance of intra-elite competition and the growing influence of the US in Europe and its promotion of democracy as the key factors.[3] However, despite nearly seventy years of holding elections, Turkey is yet to consolidate its democracy and become a fully functional democratic state. The military's dominance in politics throughout the twentieth century has historically prevented the development of a democratic system. The AKP government's growing authoritarianism since 2015 has reversed much of the progress Turkey made in instituting a more open and liberal political system during the first decade of the twenty-first century. The limits and shortcomings of Turkish democracy become more visible when we look at the experiences of political parties that tried to represent the demands and interests of the Kurds in Turkey. As discussed in the introductory section, Turkey's dominant political norms and restrictive legal order created a situation where political parties representing the interests of Kurds were repressed, with some facing closure in the past three decades on grounds that they threatened the country's national unity and territorial integrity.

While Turkey's political system remained firmly against the collective representation of Kurdish political demands, as Chapters 3 and 4 discuss in more detail, from 1950 onwards, many Kurdish individuals have been elected to the positions of political office mainly via the centre-right political parties. The same period also witnessed the emergence of a new generation of political activists who began to challenge, through their writings and dissent-orientated political practices, the repression the Kurds faced in Turkey. During the 1960s, Kurds also increased their involvement in Turkish left-wing organizations and in the 1965 parliamentary elections: a Kurd from Diyarbakır – Tarık Ziya Ekinci – was elected as an MP for the Workers Party of Turkey (Türkiye İşçi Partisi, TİP).[4] The demands for political and economic equality the nascent Kurdish movement voiced resonated with the Kurdish masses, especially during the 'Meetings of the East' held in Kurdish majority regions in 1967.[5] This led to the emergence in 1969 of a Kurdish left-wing political group, the Revolutionary Cultural Centres of the East (Devrimci Doğu Kültür Ocakları, DDKO) in Ankara and Istanbul, but they were closed down and their leaders and activists prosecuted during the military rule between 1971 and 1973.

The repression Kurdish political activists experienced during the military regime pushed many of them to take part in dissent and resistance-orientated political activities, particularly from the mid-1970s onwards.[6] Their efforts resulted in the establishment of new political groups or parties and during the late 1970s; the following Kurdish groups or parties were active: the Socialist Party of Turkish Kurdistan (Türkiye Kürdistanı Sosyalist Partisi, TKSP) in 1974; Rizgarî (Liberation, 1976); the Kurdistan Workers' Party (PKK, 1978); the Kurdistan National Liberationists (KUK, 1978); Kawa (1978); Ala Rizgarî (the Flag of Liberation, 1979); and Tekoşin (Struggle, 1979). Due to the violent political environment of the 1970s and the repression unleashed by the military coup of 12 September 1980, few of them managed to survive.[7] Since the early 1980s, the PKK managed to establish itself as the dominant Kurdish political force in Turkey. The PKK members, including its leader Abdullah Öcalan, moved to Syria in 1979 and subsequently established a military base in Lebanon's Beqaa Valley, where preparations for its guerrilla campaign against Turkey were made, which it embarked upon on 15 August 1984. During the 2000s and 2010s, the PKK ceased its military activities for long periods of time to facilitate the development of a political solution of the conflict but has not totally ended its armed campaign.

Since 1990, numerous pro-Kurdish political parties have also been active in Turkey raising Kurdish demands, challenging the established order in Turkey to recognize Kurdish identity and cultural rights, and putting forward proposals to end the conflict peacefully. In addition, during the past decade, Islamist political actors have increased their visibility in Kurdish politics in Turkey and have organized themselves within the Free Cause Party (Hür Dava Partisi).

The Kurdistan Workers' Party (PKK)

The PKK was formally established on 27 November 1978 in the Lice district of Diyarbakır province as a clandestine political party advocating the unification of Kurdistan under a united socialist republic. Its emergence as a political/ideological group dates back to 1973 and to the political activism of the left-wing university circles.[8] By the end of 1975, the group moved most of its cadres to the Kurdish regions in the south-east of Turkey and expanded its efforts to build its support base there. This was initiated during a series of meetings held secretly in Kars, Bingöl, Diyarbakır, Elazığ and Gaziantep during April and May 1977, when the group's ideas and political programme were shared with a larger group of sympathizers by its leading figure in the movement, Abdullah Öcalan. The PKK interpreted the Kurdish-state relations as a form of colonialism and proposed that Kurdistan's colonial exploitation and national oppression could only be achieved through armed resistance and by a revolutionary movement.[9] The PKK's rhetoric also targeted the Kurdish feudal elite who were described as partly responsible for Kurdistan's national fragmentation because of their cooperation with the state.

A significant number of the PKK members, prior to the military coup in 1979 and 1980, relocated to Syria and Lebanon, and during the early 1980s, the PKK formed close links with the Palestinian organizations there and established its guerrilla training camps, where it provided ideological and military training to its cadres.[10] Also, starting in the early 1980s, the PKK began to build a strong presence in Europe, mainly in Germany, through a network of community organizations. The PKK's activities in Europe, Lebanon and Syria provided it with the necessary organizational and financial resources to begin its guerrilla campaign against Turkey in August 1984.[11] As the scope and depth of its guerrilla war increased significantly, the PKK managed to mobilize many Kurds in Turkey during the late 1980s and early 1990s. In this period, the PKK guerrillas were able to connect with local populations and establish a local network of supporters who provided important logistic support.[12] Also, the mountainous terrain alongside the Turkey–Iraq border provided a highly suitable environment to conduct a guerrilla campaign.

In March 1985, the National Liberation Front of Kurdistan (Eniya Rizgariya Netewa Kurdistan, ERNK) was established to carry out the political development and mobilization of the masses.[13] Within the ERNK organization in Europe, there were numerous sub-organizations established during the late 1980s and early 1990s to represent different segments of the Kurdish society, such as women, youth and different religious groups.[14] In 1993, more organizations representative of the religious groups were established, including the Islamic Movement of Kurdistan (Herekata Îslamiya Kurdistanê), the Union of Alevis of Kurdistan (Kürdistan Aleviler Birliği) and the Union of Yezidis of Kurdistan (Yekîtiya Êzîdiyan Kurdistan) to mobilize the Muslim, Alevi and Yezidi religious communities.

As I discuss in more detail in Chapter 6, from the late 1980s onwards, with the gradual increase in the activities of the Kurdish national movement, more and more Kurdish women started to engage in politics. In particular, women participated in large numbers in the numerous *serhildan* (popular uprisings) and one of the most significant developments that the PKK initiated, especially in the early 1990s, was the mobilization of women, which had a significant impact on the PKK's overall mobilization. Not only did the mobilization of women significantly increase the PKK's overall support base and fighting force, the presence of a significant number of female guerrillas within the ARGK ranks lessened the appeal and force of traditional values. As a result, the increasing levels of participation in the past thirty years has meant Kurdish women have become a significant political actor in Turkey.

From 1990 onwards, the popular expression of Kurdish identity demands and open support for the PKK became much more commonplace in Turkey as Kurdish political activism evolved into a vocal social movement. This was demonstrated in several instances of *serhildan* between 1990 and 1993, to which large numbers of ordinary Kurds across Kurdish towns participated and who often fought with the police and the gendarmeries. Furthermore, numerous mass rallies and other forms of protest such as shop closures and school boycotts were organized in Diyarbakır, Batman, Şırnak and Siirt. Additionally, many people attended the funerals of the PKK guerrillas, which became a political act in itself and a sign of support for the PKK's struggle. In the early 1990s, Kurds in Turkey became much more visible and actively voiced their demands for the recognition of their identity. The PKK-led Kurdish rebellion has been the most radical and has lasted the longest in the history of the Kurds in Turkey. The conflict cost the lives of more than 45,000 people (mainly soldiers, guerrillas, village guards and Kurdish civilians), and resulted in the forced evacuation of 3,500 villages and hamlets.[15]

As I have argued in greater detail in my previous work, in order to represent its struggle as the 'embodiment of Kurdish national struggle' to its target groups, the PKK re-activated the myth of Newroz and the Legend of Kawa in its discourse.[16] This enabled the PKK to construct a contemporary myth of resistance in its discourse that it used to narrate this struggle. It adopted a sensitive approach to religion and sought to connect with religious Kurds. Consequently, the PKK was able to articulate the demands of the various sections of Kurdish society and address the problems that they faced within its national liberation discourse. It established various cultural and political organizations in Europe and through these was able to reach out to a large section of Kurdish diaspora and mobilize them in support of its struggle.[17] The Kurdish diaspora was an important source of human and financial resources for the PKK.

However, due to the stalemate that the PKK experienced in its guerrilla war, from the early 1990s onwards, it started to concede that the revolutionary overthrow of the Turkish rule through a popular uprising and the construction of a 'united', 'socialist' and 'independent' Kurdistan were no longer achievable and realistic. In subsequent years throughout the 1990s, as part of its attempts to formulate a political solution to the conflict, the PKK began appropriating the democratic discourse. After the PKK's leader, Abdullah Öcalan, was captured by the state of Turkey in February 1999, it began to change its political objectives and construct a more coherent and condensed democratic discourse. The discursive transformation and ideological repositioning were guided by the ideas that Abdullah Öcalan put forward in his trial in 1999.[18]

During his trial, Öcalan called for a new relationship between the Kurds as a political community and the state in Turkey based on the principles of equality and freedom and he rejected the separatist approach his movement had previously taken.¹⁹ He called for measures to address the Kurdish demands within a democratic Turkey and expanded on his democratic solution proposals through the defences he submitted to the European Court of Human Rights (ECHR) in 2001 that considered his appeal. His defence was published as a two-volume book at the end of 2001, where he proposed a 'nation of Turkey' as an inclusive identity for all citizens and argued that such a framework would be a major step in the direction of the democratic solution: 'All that is necessary is loyalty to the democratic system, to renounce the chauvinist fascist claims and for each group [in Turkey] to experience its cultural identity and education without denying the formal system.'²⁰ In 2004, Öcalan submitted another defence text to the ECHR that expanded on his democratic solution and was published as a book in the same year titled *Bir Halkı Savunmak* (Defending a Nation).²¹ In this new text, the issue of the formal legal status of the Kurds and Kurdistan within the existing states gained more emphasis. Here, Öcalan proposed a framework whereby the 'people's own democratic administration in Kurdistan' will co-exist with the 'state as the general public authority'.²²

Öcalan's new theorization has been used by the PKK to re-orient its political objectives and demands for the Kurds and has generated a lively debate on the resolution of the Kurdish question and the possible steps that can be taken to accommodate Kurdish demands within the borders of the existing states in the Middle East.²³ Parallel to its discursive transformation, the PKK also established new representative organizations during the early 2000s. The first one of these was the Kurdistan Freedom and Democracy Congress (Kongreya Azadî û Demokrasiya Kurdistanê, KADEK) in 2002. In 2003, KADEK was abolished and a new organization People's Congress of Kurdistan (Kongra Gelê Kurdistan, Kongra-Gel) was established. However, this has not resulted in any change in the proposed solution to the Kurdish question in Turkey.²⁴

In the new party programme the PKK accepted in 2005, its proposal for the solution of the Kurdish question was described as the 'democratic solution'; the central tenet of which was described as the 'democratic transformation' of the current state system in the Middle East into federal and confederal entities. It put forward the proposals to reconstitute the Kurds as a nation without constructing a Kurdish nation-state, and the confederal Kurdish entity it proposed would neither challenge the established and internationally recognized boundaries nor resort to nationalism or establishing a nation-state.²⁵ While the construction of a Kurdish nation-state is seen as unnecessary, the central focus would be on developing an administrative framework for Kurdish self-government.

The mid-2000s noticed the establishment of a new entity, the Union of Kurdistan Communities (Koma Civakan Kurdistan, KCK), which was established with the specific objective of putting into practice the 'democratic confederalism' proposals. The KCK is described as 'the people's non-state based democratic system' and has, as its basic principle, 'the democratic solution of the Kurdish question, the recognition of Kurdish identity on all levels and the development of Kurdish language and culture'.²⁶ It is the umbrella organization bringing together the decentralized autonomous Kurdish administrations and is designed as an alternative 'hybrid' institutional framework to provide political representation to the Kurds and allow them to organize themselves as a nation within the existing state boundaries in the Middle East. It is a bottom-up organization where Kurds are organized at a local level, but these self-governing communities are connected to higher city, regional and national levels: 'Democratic confederalism is based on grassroots participation. Its decision-making processes lie with the communities. Higher levels only serve the coordination and implementation of the will of the communities that send their delegates to the general assemblies.'[27] Democratic confederalism is proposed as an alternative institutional framework for resolving the Kurdish question in the Middle East and is seen as a structure that will allow the Kurds to organize themselves as a nation and obtain their national rights within the existing states in the Middle East.

In addition to the 'democratic confederalism' proposal, since August 2010, the 'Democratic Autonomy' proposal has also been developed as a framework to organize the relations between the states and the various Kurdish communities.[28] More specifically in the Kurdish context in Turkey, it concerns the nature of the relationship between the Kurds and the Turkish state and seeks to accommodate Kurdish rights and demands within Turkey's territorial integrity: 'Democratic autonomy is about the Turkish state and the Kurds agreeing on a new contract for their unity. It is the establishment of a democratic political union instead of a union based on force and assimilation.'[29] It is seen as a way of limiting the power and authority of the central state and an important step in this direction involves the recognition of Kurdish identity and cultural rights:

> A fundamental characteristic of democratic autonomy is that the Turkish state accepts the constitutional recognition of the national identity of the Kurdish people. Together with the recognition of national identity, it is necessary to remove all obstacles in front of the Kurdish language and cultural development and to enable Kurdish to become a language of education.[30]

In addition, decentralization is demanded as part of a general democratization of state structures and the right of the Kurdish communities to organize themselves through a network of local and regional councils and thereby create their self-governments. These representative councils will have responsibility for solving societal problems in areas that do not directly concern the state.[31] The state's recognition of Kurdish rights should include the freedom of assembly to allow Kurds to express freely their collective identity and establish political parties.

As well as organizing Kurdish communities within decentralized administrative levels, the democratic autonomy proposals involves the establishment of Kurdish national representative bodies, which would have decision-making power on specific issues relevant to the Kurds but whose areas of influence are not confined to a particular region or territory: 'Within the territorial integrity framework, many identities can establish their administrative structures and exercise self-governance.'[32] It is described as a 'form of multiple administrations in a single territory. On such basis, different national groups can have education in their mother tongue in all levels.'[33] It is designed as a formula for the exercise of national cultural autonomy without resorting to the creation of a nation-state, which has similarities to the models of non-territorial autonomy (NTA) practised in Central and Eastern Europe. For example, under these proposals, Kurdish communities residing in western parts of Turkey can organize themselves in their own representative bodies and make the decisions relating to specific issues concerning their community, such as education in the Kurdish language.[34]

The PKK has managed to establish itself as the dominant actor in Kurdish politics in Turkey and it maintains a pan-Kurdist inclination. Since its formation, it has been led by Abdullah Öcalan, who has been serving his sentence of life imprisonment in İmralı Island since February 1999. Öcalan continues to be the dominant figure in the movement despite his imprisonment. The ideological and strategic transformations that the PKK experienced were initiated by Öcalan. In Öcalan's absence, the PKK has been led by a collective leadership comprising of Cemil Bayık, Duran Kalkan, Murat Karayılan, Rıza Altun, Mustafa Karasu and Ali Haydar Kaytan. In recent years, other senior figures have assumed leadership positions and these include Bese Hozat, who is the co-president of the KCK; Fehman Hussein, a Kurd from Syria who served as the military commander of the PKK's forces People's Defence Forces (Hêzên Parastina Gel, HPG) and remains active in the movement at a leadership capacity; Ronahi Serhat, who is a member of the KCK Executive Council; and Sozdar Avesta, who is part of the PKK's women's branch.

There are other representative political bodies that are linked to the PKK such as the Kongra-Gel, whose leadership is drawn from the wider Kurdish movement, including Remzi Kartal and Zübeyir Aydar, both of whom were MPs for the DEP during the early 1990s and escaped to Belgium in 1994 to avoid imprisonment. The PKK has a membership that reflects the general Kurdish population and is able to draw support from different religious and ethnic groups within the Kurdish nation. It has also Turkish members such as Duran Kalkan and one of its first members to be killed was Haki Karer, who was also a Turk from the Black Sea province of Ordu. Some of its early members, such as Mazlum Doğan and Sakine Cansız, were Alevi Kurds. In addition to Kurds in Turkey and Kurdish diaspora communities in Europe, it has also managed to recruit from Kurdish communities in Syria and Iran.

The pro-Kurdish democratic movement

The pro-Kurdish democratic movement in Turkey came into being with the establishment of the HEP on 7 June 1990.[35] The HEP was established by a group of Kurdish and Turkish socialist MPs who were expelled from the SHP.[36] The Kurds constituted the majority of its members, but several Turkish socialist politicians and activists also took part in its formation and activities. However, the predominantly Kurdish support created unease among Turkish socialists and led to them severing their ties from the HEP. The democratization of the state and society and bringing about a democratic and peaceful solution to the Kurdish conflict in Turkey were the HEP's key objectives and, rather than being a party for the Kurds, it was committed to representing the wider Turkish society and described itself as a party representing the whole of Turkey.[37] In the parliamentary elections held on 20 October 1991, the HEP candidates were selected on the SHP list with twenty-two winning a seat in the parliament. However, soon after the election, the HEP became the target of state repression. On 22 May 1992, the state Security Court prepared a case for stripping the HEP MP's parliamentary immunity and on 3 July 1992, the Supreme Court's Attorney General filed a case at the Constitutional Court to close down the HEP. On 14 July 1993, the Constitutional Court reached its verdict and closed down the HEP. From then on, the pro-Kurdish parliamentary opposition was organized within the DEP, which was established on 7 May 1993 and had an almost identical political programme to the HEP.[38] The DEP was closed on 16 June 1994.[39]

The next decade or so following the closure of the DEP and the elimination of the Kurdish parliamentary opposition was spent by attempts to rebuild the pro-Kurdish democratic movement. The HADEP, established on 11 May 1994, and its sister party the Democratic People's Party (Demokratik Halk Partisi, DEHAP), established on 24 October 1997, were the representatives of the pro-Kurdish movement in that period. Due to the 10 per cent national election threshold restricting the parliamentary representation, neither the HADEP nor the DEHAP was able to gain a seat in the parliament. However, as Chapter 2 discusses in more detail, they both enjoyed some level of success at a local level and more importantly managed to construct a grassroots organization and a wide-ranging organizational network covering many of the cities in Turkey.

In April 2004, the former DEP MPs were released from prison and they initiated the formation of the DTP in November 2005.[40] The DTP was established to represent broader sections of society and attract other political groups in Turkey that its predecessors were unable to connect with. After the 22 July 2007 general election, the pro-Kurdish parliamentary opposition returned with the election of twenty-two DTP MPs who stood as independent candidates to avoid the 10 per cent national election threshold. The DTP remained active until it was closed down by the Constitutional Court on 12 December 2009.

From then on, the Peace and Democracy Party (Barış ve Demokrasi Partisi, BDP), which was established on 3 May 2008, became the main pro-Kurdish party in Turkey. The efforts to unify the demands for economic, political and gender equality and represent different ethnic, religious and social groups in Turkey accelerated from the late 2000s onwards. The pro-Kurdish political parties began to appeal to a broader section of Turkey's population and started to construct a more condensed democratic discourse reflective of the demands and values of different sections of Turkish society that began to emerge. The BDP supported independent candidates in the June 2011 general elections and formed the pro-democracy 'Labour, Peace and Democracy' bloc. In addition to the leading members of the pro-Kurdish BDP, independent socialist and pro-democracy candidates were also included in the list, including the film director and columnist Sırrı Süreyya Önder for Istanbul, the leader of the Labour Party (Emeğin Partisi, EMEP) Abdullah Levent Tüzel for Istanbul and the socialist activist and journalist Ertuğrul Kürkçü for Mersin. In total, thirty-five pro-Kurdish MPs were elected as independent candidates. In the local elections held on 30 March 2014, the BDP consolidated its position as the leading party of the Kurdish regions when it won more than 50 per cent of the votes in many towns and cities.[41] In total, it won 102 councils including the Municipalities of Ağrı, Batman, Bitlis, Diyarbakır, Hakkari, Iğdır, Mardin, Siirt, Şırnak, Tunceli and Van.[42]

The current representative of the pro-Kurdish political movement at a national level is the HDP, which was established to bring together various political movements, parties and civil society organizations that represent different social and minority ethnic and religious groups in Turkey. As a precursor to the HDP foundation, the Peoples' Democratic Congress (Halkların Demokratik Kongresi, HDK) was established as a representative body for the diverse oppositional social and political groups and parties in Turkey. Each political group or party that is part of the HDK is described as a component and maintains its independent existence. The HDP is the national-level parliamentary representative of the HDK, and in the Kurdish majority regions at a local level, the DBP is active, which is the continuation of the BDP, having changed its name and party symbol at the third congress on 11 July 2014. The DBP is one of the main components of the HDK. In addition, the EMEP, the Socialist Party of the Oppressed (Ezilenlerin Sosyalist Partisi, ESP), the Green Left Party (Yeşil Sol Parti, YSP) and numerous organizations that represent women, the Alevi community, the Armenian community, the LGBT community and workers also participated in the establishment of the HDK.

The HDP's key political objective is to represent the demands of the sections of the society that have been historically marginalized by the state, such as the Kurds, Alevis and other minority ethnic and religious groups in Turkey. A new democratic constitution that strengthens the parliamentary system and guarantees the civil and political rights of citizens in Turkey is another of the HDP's key political demands. The new constitution should embody the ethos of pluralism and promote multiculturalism by recognizing and protecting Turkey's ethnic, linguistic and religious diversity. The new constitution should offer a platform to resolve Turkey's long-standing Kurdish question by addressing Kurdish demands and providing stronger safeguards for the rights of all minority groups in Turkey. The HDP proposes a decentralized political system for Turkey to break the domination of the centre over the regions and develop models of local self-governance to meet the needs of different minority groups to protect and develop their culture and identity.

This alternative administrative framework for Turkey that the HDP proposes is described as 'democratic autonomy' and its origins dates back to the second half of the 2000s. The democratic autonomy proposals were first discussed by the DTP during its second party congress in 2007 when it accepted the democratic autonomy as a framework to accommodate Kurdish rights in Turkey. It argued that extensive reform of Turkey's political structure was needed, and the DTP's democratic autonomy proposals envisage decentralization of power and the establishment of between twenty and twenty-five self-governing regions in Turkey. These regions would bring together two or three existing provinces that have dense social, cultural and economic relations and would have a regional parliament and administration, which would make decisions relating to matters of education, culture, social services, agriculture, environment etc. The decision on matters relating to policing and legal services would be jointly decided by the central government and regional assemblies and those that pertain to foreign affairs, finance and national security would be conducted by the central government.[43] It argued that such a decentralized framework would enable the participation and representation of citizens in the decision-making processes and greatly contribute to the advancement of democracy in Turkey. In order to enable the participation and representation of all of the ethnic and national groups in Turkey, a more inclusive definition of nationality in Turkey's constitution was needed. Such steps, it argued, would facilitate the development of the democratic solution of the Kurdish question in Turkey.[44]

As mentioned above, following the closure of the DTP, the BDP took the centre stage in pro-Kurdish politics. Similar to its predecessors, the BDP also advocated the need for a more inclusive and pluralist notion of national identity and citizenship and demanded that the collective rights of the Kurdish people, including education in the Kurdish language, needed to be recognized and protected by the constitution. Furthermore, the BDP's party programme argued that decentralization in Turkey's political system was needed to solve the Kurdish question and listed the implementation of the recommendations of the Council of Europe's European Charter of Local Self-Government in Turkey among its key political objectives. It argued that such a framework would empower the local communities and administrations and thereby would be a major step towards deepening democracy in Turkey.[45] In September 2011, at its second party congress, the BDP began to use 'Democratic Autonomy' to describe its proposals for reform of Turkey's political system and solution of the Kurdish question. It had significant similarities with the DTP's democratic autonomy proposal and proposed the decentralization of Turkey's centralist political and administrative structure and creation of between twenty to twenty-five self-governing regions that would exercise extensive autonomy. It argued that such a framework was needed to strengthen democracy and pluralism in Turkey.[46]

The Diyarbakır-based Democratic Society Congress (DTK) is another Kurdish representative organization that is associated with the development of democratic autonomy proposals and is an important political actor in the majority Kurdish populated areas that campaigns for realizing democratic autonomy. The DTK was formally established in October 2007 to politically organize Kurds and develop and implement the democratic autonomy proposals that Öcalan has been developing. The DTK is an umbrella organization that brings together civil society groups, trade unions, political parties and many local Kurdish political actors based in the Kurdish-majority regions. During 2010 and 2011, it held many meetings where Öcalan's ideas were discussed in detail and a more detailed democratic autonomy framework was developed.[47] The DTK's democratic autonomy framework embodies the principle of decentralization, grassroots democracy and people organizing themselves in local councils and actively taking part in debating issues and decision-making at a local level and electing delegates to represent the local council in higher representative bodies such as at district, province and regional levels. It 'aims to organize Kurdistan society in eight dimensions: Political, Legal, Self-Defense, Social, Economic, Cultural, Ecology and Diplomacy, and to build political autonomy and to build Democratic Autonomous Kurdistan'.[48]

The DTK sees itself as the representative body for the Kurds in Turkey and the main vehicle for the implementation of Kurdish democratic autonomy in Turkey.[49] It seeks to organize Kurdish society within a democratic and autonomous administrative body. The lowest level administrative body is the commune which is usually comprised of the residents of a village or a street in the urban context. The neighbourhood council is the higher-level representative body that offers representation to communes as well as people representing different ethnic and political groups, followed by the district council. It is also a representative body for the local, district and provincial councils and citizens' assemblies that were established in the Kurdish majority regions since 2005. In addition to aspiring to represent the Kurdish community, it has sought the inclusion of representatives of the different ethnic and religious groups, such as the Syriac community, that are historically based in the Kurdish majority regions.

The HDP's 'Democratic Autonomy' model for Turkey is built around the idea of decentralization of state power to autonomous and self-governing regional administrations.[50] Such decentralization of the state in Turkey is needed to ensure citizens' direct participation in the decision-making processes at local, regional and national levels and to develop socio-economic policies that address the needs of the whole of society.[51] Such a decentralized framework is seen as sufficient for addressing the demands of the Kurdish minority for autonomy and paves the way to a peaceful solution for the Kurdish conflict.[52]

Also, as I discuss in more detail in Chapter 6, similar to its predecessors, the HDP has been very successful in providing representation to Kurdish women. It aspires to achieve gender equality in representation and runs a system of co-presidency where each executive position of the party is shared between a man and a woman. This is part of the HDP's long-term objective of achieving gender equality and having at least 50 per cent women in all its representative bodies and parliamentary group. Twenty-three of the HDP's fifty-nine MPs elected in November 2015 were women and there has been a strong representation of women at a local level as city and district mayors and local and provincial party representatives. Twenty-five of the sixty-seven HDP MPs elected in the June 2018 general election were women and many women were elected as co-mayors at the March 2019 local elections.

One of the main figures in the HDP is its former co-president Selahattin Demirtaş who was first elected to the parliament as an independent candidate supported by the DTP in 2007 but has risen rapidly through the ranks to become the co-chair of BDP in 2010. He was born in Palu, Elazığ in 1973 to a working-class Zaza Kurdish family but spend most of his childhood in Diyarbakır after the family moved there. He graduated from the Law Faculty of Ankara University and, before entering the parliament, he practised law and was actively involved in the Diyarbakır branch of the Human Rights Association (İnsan Hakları Derneği, İHD), the main human rights group in the Kurdish majority regions of Turkey, and served as its chairman in 2004.

The HDP also incorporated candidates that would appeal to religious and tribal Kurds, such as Altan Tan for Diyarbakır and Mehmet Mir Dengir Fırat for Mersin, both of whom were active in Islamist-leaning political parties before. Nimettullah Erdoğmuş, who was the mufti of Diyarbakır and Abdullah Zeydan, is a member of the leading family of the Pinyanişi tribe and was selected as one of the candidates for the Diyarbakır and Hakkari provinces, respectively. Similarly, Mahmut Celadet Gaydalı who is from the Gaydalı-İnan family that dominated the politics of Bitlis since the 1950s was selected for the Bitlis province. Additionally, candidates that could appeal to specific ethnic and religious minorities, such as the Arabs in Şanlıurfa and Mardin provinces and Alevis in Turkey's western provinces were chosen as HDP parliamentary candidates. Consequently, by including diverse candidates, the HDP successfully mobilized a larger section of Turkey's population and managed to win votes from religious and tribal Kurds, ethnic Turks and Turkey's other ethnic or religious minorities. Several Turkish socialists have played a significant role in the formation of the current pro-Kurdish political party, the HDP. These include Ertuğrul Kürkçü, is the Honorary President of the HDP, and Figen Yüksekdağ and Sezai Temelli, the HDP's former and current co-presidents, respectively.

On 20 May 2016, the Turkish parliament passed legislation to lift the immunity of MPs, which can be understood as a measure designed to end or at least significantly weaken the HDP representation in Turkey's parliament. Legal proceedings began against a number of HDP MPs and on 4 November 2016, eleven HDP MPs were detained and currently nine are remanded in custody, including its former co-presidents Selahattin Demirtaş and Figen Yüksekdağ. Several other HDP MPs were detained on numerous occasions but released after questioning.[53] The MPs and co-presidents are charged with offences ranging from 'carrying out propaganda for a terror organization' and 'being a member of an armed terror organization' and prosecutors are demanding long sentences for all of them. On 6 October 2017, Burcu Çelik, the HDP MP for Muş province, received a six-year sentence for 'aiding and abetting a terror organization' and the HDP MP for Diyarbakır province, İdris Baluken, received a sentence of sixteen years and eight months on 4 January 2018 for 'membership of a terror organization' and 'carrying propaganda for a terror organization'.[54]

During 2017 and early 2018, the MP status of several HDP MPs was removed, including Figen Yüksekdağ, Nursel Aydoğan, Leyla Zana and Ferhat Encü. In addition, two HDP MPs, Faysal Sarıyıldız and Tuğba Hezer, have escaped Turkey to Europe in order to avoid arrest and, currently, around 6,000 HDP members remain under arrest.[55] The government has targeted the local level representation of the pro-Kurdish parties and on 15 August 2016 passed a delegated decree (Kanun Hükmünde Kararname, KHK) that enabled the removal of the elected mayors from office and their replacement with appointed trustees. This measure targeted the pro-Kurdish political representation in particular, and on 11 September 2016, the mayors of the following municipal councils – Ağrı, Batman, Bitlis, Diyarbakır, Hakkari, Mardin, Şırnak, Siirt, Tunceli and Van – were removed from their office and replaced by the provincial governor or their deputy and the district governor.[56] In total, ninety-four of the 102 councils have been taken over by the government-appointed trustees. Ninety-three of the DBP co-mayors have been detained since September 2016, and by the end of 2018, a total of fifty-three remained under arrest. Several co-mayors have been convicted and are serving jail sentences, including the former co-mayor of Diyarbakır municipal council, Gültan Kışanık.[57]

Despite the severe repression the HDP has been experiencing since 2015 and the arrest of its prominent politicians, the party managed to maintain its support base and obtain 11.7 per cent at the general election on 24 June 2018, winning sixty-seven seats in the parliament. Most of the MPs were elected for the first time and the change in personnel was partly enforced as many of the HDP's previous prominent MPs either chose not to stand again or were imprisoned. For example, İdris Baluken, Burcu Çelik,

Çağlar Demirel, Selahattin Demirtaş, Ferhat Encü, Selma Irmak, Figen Yüksekdağ and Abdullah Zeydan are currently held in prison either serving sentences or being remanded in custody.[58] Osman Baydemir has left Turkey to avoid serving his prison sentence. Altan Tan severed his ties with the party following the HDP's refusal to select him as a candidate in Diyarbakır and stood as a candidate for the Islamist Felicity Party (Saadet Partisi, SD) in Istanbul, but did not get elected.

Throughout its existence, the pro-Kurdish political parties have been seen as the political wing of the PKK by the state and the mainstream political parties in Turkey. The pro-Kurdish political parties have rejected that they are connected to the PKK and ascertaining whether there is a relationship between them is beyond the scope of this study. The pro-Kurdish political parties' refusal to describe the PKK as a terror group has been interpreted by the mainstream media and political parties in Turkey as evidence of sympathy towards the PKK's struggle. Several incidents such as removing the Turkish flag from the HADEP's second congress in June 1996 and protests by the party members against the capture of Abdullah Öcalan in February 1999 have strengthened the popular belief that the pro-Kurdish movement is the PKK's political wing.[59]

The pro-Kurdish parties often stress that they share the same social base with the PKK and it is possible that there are personal relations between their members and persons active within the PKK. However, they emphasize that their movement neither advocates violence nor condones the PKK's use of violence. In an interview with the German newspaper *Süddeutsche Zeitung* in September 2016, the HDP co-president Selahattin Demirtaş rejected the suggestion that his party has an organic link to the PKK or condones violence. Furthermore, he stated that the HDP does not define the PKK in the same way as the government or the state but saw it as a violent organization that emerged as a result of the state terror that the Kurdish people in Turkey have been suffering for a century.[60] Demirtaş's statements are reflective of the views that other members of the pro-Kurdish parties have been putting forward concerning the PKK. Abdullah Öcalan's niece Dilek Öcalan was elected an MP from the Şanlıurfa Province in June 2015 and served until 2018, and his nephew Ömer Öcalan, also from the Şanlıurfa Province, was elected at the June 2018 general election. In the past, occasionally the HDP officials called for the improvement of Abdullah Öcalan's prison conditions and the state to end his isolation on grounds that such actions will make a positive contribution to ending the conflict peacefully. Such statements have been used by the state to prosecute the HDP officials and as proof that it is the legal front for the PKK.

Although the pro-Kurdish MPs and mayors have been arrested and remanded in custody on terror-related charges, these offences relate to speeches that they delivered rather than inciting violence or being involved in it. In some cases, attending the funerals of PKK guerrillas has been interpreted by state authorities as 'carrying out propaganda for a terror organization'. The similarities between the demands both the PKK and the HDP raise for the Kurds can also be seen to contribute to the view that they are related. Both these parties describe their approach to the accommodation of Kurdish demands in Turkey as 'democratic autonomy' but there is a significant difference between the PKK's and HDP's actual proposals. For the HDP, democratic autonomy is a model for decentralization of Turkey's political system but for the PKK it is part of a larger project of establishing Kurdish self-governing communities in the Middle East and unifying them through higher-level representative institutions.

In addition to the HDP, there are several other smaller pro-Kurdish political parties in Turkey, including the Freedom and Rights Party (Hak ve Özgürlükler Partisi, HAK-PAR, 2002), the Participatory Democracy Party (Katılımcı Demokrasi Partisi, KADEP, 2006), Kurdistan Freedom Party (Partiya Azadiya Kurdistan, PAK, 2014), the Azadi Movement (Hereketa Azadi, 2012) and the Kurdistan Democratic Party-Turkey (Türkiye Kürdistan Demokrat Partisi, TKDP, 2014). HAK-PAR has established branches in a total of nineteen provinces in the Kurdish majority regions as well as in the main Turkish cities that have a significant Kurdish population.[61] The party was established under the leadership of Abdülmelik Fırat and for a long period the party was led by Bayram Bozyel, and other former party leaders include Fehmi Demir and Sertaç Bucak. In 2012, Kemal Burkay became its leader, and it is now currently led by Refik Karakoç. It is closely aligned with the Kurdistan Socialist Party (Partiya Sosyalîst a Kurdistan, PSK; known as Türkiye Kürdistan Sosyalist Partisi, TKSP, before 1992), which was led by Kemal Burkay from its establishment in 1974 until his return to Turkey from exile in Sweden in 2012. HAK-PAR advocates the recognition of Kurdish identity and all of its associated national rights and proposes a solution to the Kurdish question based on ethnic federalism to ensure the equality of the Kurdish and Turkish nations and enable the Kurds to exercise their right to national self-determination.[62] They demand the Kurdish language to be recognized as an official language in Turkey and publicly funded education to be provided in Kurdish.[63] HAK-PAR has been taking part in elections over the past decade and, while it has been making steady progress, it is far from establishing itself as a credible force in Kurdish politics in Turkey.

The KADEP was formed by Şerafettin Elçi and political activists close to the Kurdistan Democratic Party (KDP) in Iraq in 2006. Şerafettin Elçi was an MP in 1977 in Mardin Province from the Justice Party (Adalet Partisi, AP) but subsequently resigned and served as the Minister for Public Works in the minority government formed by the CHP between 5 January 1978 and 12 November 1979. The KADEP cooperated with the BDP in the 2011 election and Şerafettin Elçi was elected as an independent candidate from the Diyarbakır province and served until his death on 25 December 2012. In May 2016, the KADEP joined the TKDP and continues to be active and advocates autonomy as a solution to the Kurdish question in Turkey. The Azadi Movement was established as a representative of the Kurdistan Islamic Movement, which is made up of conservative and religious Kurds. It cooperated with the HDP in the June 2015 election and one of its members, Adem Geveri, was elected as an MP for the Van province. However, whether the Azadi Movement and the TKDP will be able to maintain their unity and expand their organizational network remains to be seen, but in the current context, it is difficult to see the above-discussed political parties challenging the dominance of the HDP in Kurdish politics. Several of the smaller pro-Kurdish parties cooperated with the HDP at the 2019 local elections and supported joint candidates, which shows the potential for the HDP to bring together pro-Kurdish parties under a single bloc.

Islamism among Kurds: Hizbullah and the Hüda-Par

Another movement that has had influence among the Kurds in Turkey is the group that was known as Hizbullah and that transformed itself to the Free Cause Party (Hür Dava Partisi, Hüda-Par) in 2012. However, rather than being associated with the advocacy of Kurdish rights in Turkey, Hizbullah is best known for its murderous campaign during the 1990s against the Kurdish rights activists and PKK sympathizers in the majority Kurdish region, in particular in Diyarbakır and Batman. In the past decade, it began to rebrand itself as a Kurdish Islamist movement and describe itself as an advocate of Kurdish rights in Turkey. Hizbullah's first-known publication was published in 2004 and is titled *Hizbullah in Its Own Words and Important Selections from the History of Its Struggle*.[64] It is thought to be written by its current leader, İsa Altsoy, and presents an account of the political developments from its perspective, particularly its conflict with the PKK during the 1990s.[65] Hizbullah maintains a website, Hüseyni Sevda, which hosts propaganda material on the group and shares regular statements about current political developments.[66] However, despite its online presence, it remains a close-knit underground group and there is much that is unknown about it.

Hizbullah was established by Hüseyin Velioğlu, who led it until his death in 2000. Its origin dates back to 1979 and it was initially active in Batman but the group's base moved to Diyarbakır in the early 1980s, where it began organizing around the İlim (knowledge) bookshop from 1983 onwards.[67] Diyarbakır subsequently became its recruiting ground and main base of operations until 1991 when Velioğlu moved to Mardin.[68] In addition to the İlim bookshop, the rival Menzil bookshop run by Fidan Güngör was also a hub of Islamist activities in the early 1980s Diyarbakır. Both groups were committed to jihad and the use of violence to bring about the establishment of an Islamic State in Turkey.[69]

As I discuss in more detail in Chapter 4, Islam has had a significant influence on Kurdish society and there are numerous Sufi orders that retain significant influence in Kurdish politics and society. However, in terms of ideology and practices, Hizbullah shares more with other jihadist groups than with traditional Kurdish Islam. Also, these groups were in receipt of support from the Iranian regime in their early days: 'During the 1980s, both groups were in regular contact with elements in the Iranian intelligence services and members travelled to Iran for training'.[70] The group members were recruited in high schools and mosques in the main urban centres of the Kurdish majority region, in particular Diyarbakır, Batman and Mardin, and their activities brought a significant number of high schools and mosques under Hizbullah's control during the early 1990s.[71] This allowed Hizbullah to build a significant organizational network in the Kurdish majority regions and significantly increase its membership.

Hizbullah's conflict with the PKK erupted in 1991, lasted throughout the 1990s and resulted in the death of around 1,000 people.[72] The conflict began when the PKK killed Şerif Karaaslan – a local Hizbullah leader in İdil, Şırnak Province – on 8 May 1991, and as an act of revenge Hizbullah killed a well-known PKK sympathizer, Mikail Bayru, on 3 December 1991, also in İdil.[73] The conflict continued throughout the 1990s and mainly involved Hizbullah killing people who were known to be supporters of the PKK in the urban centres of the Kurdish region, in particular Diyarbakır and

Batman. Hizbullah carried out many attacks against rival religious groups such as the Menzil group in the 1990s and it was involved in the abduction and murder of İzzettin Yıldırım in 2000, who was the president of the Zehra Foundation, a Kurdish Islamist organization.[74] In 1992, Hizbullah murdered Ubeydullah Dalar, a leading figure in the Menzil group and subsequently intensified its attacks against the group. Given that the Menzil group lacked Hizbullah's capacity for violence, it was defeated with ease and eliminated when its leader Fidan Güngör and his bodyguard were kidnapped in September 1994 in Istanbul. The body of his bodyguard was found subsequently but Güngör's body was never recovered. Hizbullah carried out many kidnapping and ransoms of businessmen and ordinary Kurds for money.[75] Other high-profile murders committed by Hizbullah include the Islamist Feminist writer Konca Kuriş in 1998.[76] The assassination of the head of security in Diyarbakır province Gaffar Okkan on 24 January 2001 is also attributed to the organization.[77]

It is generally believed that Hizbullah had close links with the Turkish security establishment. This is because its main activities involved attacks against the PKK mainly in urban centres in Diyarbakır and Batman and on many occasions the security forces tolerated Hizbullah's activities. Even if it is impossible to establish a clear link between the state and Hizbullah, it is generally assumed that Hizbullah was used in the counter-insurgency operations against the PKK.[78] Furthermore, the fact that during the 1990s Hizbullah did not carry out any attacks against the Turkish security forces seems to strengthen the presumed link. Both Hizbullah and the Turkish state deny these claims but there is ample evidence to suggest that 'in the early 1990s there was a measure of low-level collusion between Ilim [Hizbullah] militants and state officials, particularly members of the Turkish intelligence community'.[79] The state authorities usually turned a blind eye to the activities of Hizbullah and left it alone to operate with impunity. From 1995 onwards, the police increased its operations against Hizbullah, which seemed to suggest the end of the tolerance shown by the security forces. The crackdown on its activities and the death of its leader Hüseyin Velioğlu on 17 January 2000 weakened the organization significantly.[80]

The military defeat Hizbullah experienced during the early 2000s, particularly the death of its leader, the dismantling of its organizational network and the arrest and imprisonment of many of its members, did not result in its end. After Velioglu's death and the arrests of many of its leading members, it is thought that Isa Altsoy has been leading Hizbullah. Altsoy was on Hizbullah's Shura Council before becoming its leader, and currently his whereabouts are unknown. Turkish media reported that in 2007 he was arrested by German authorities, but the story subsequently proved to be false.[81] In January 2011, many of the senior members of Hizbullah were released from prison because of the legal changes made to the Criminal Procedure Code.[82] However, many did not comply with the conditions of their release and went underground soon after. Some of the Hizbullah members, such as Hacı İnan, were subsequently arrested again, but other senior figures, including Cemal Tutar and Edip Gümüş, have avoided arrest and remain at large.[83] Since the release of the leading members of Hizbullah, it is likely that a more collective leadership style has been adopted.

Hizbullah has not carried out an act of violence in recent years, but it is thought that it maintains its capacity to use violence and since the release of its members has increased its efforts to increase its organizational capacity. Although the details are not very well known, it is thought that Hizbullah is also part of larger Islamist jihadist networks. An important indication that confirms this link is the leader of Islamic State in Iraq and Syria (ISIS) in Turkey, Halis Bayuncuk (Abu Hanzala), who is the son of a jailed senior leader of Hizbullah, Hacı Bayuncuk.[84] It is also known that Hizbullah is active amongst the Kurdish diaspora community, especially in Germany, and is able to draw financial support for its activities in Turkey.

Hizbullah is often described as a Kurdish actor as it is made of Kurds but the extent to which it is genuinely committed to Kurdish rights is doubtful. Since 2004, Hizbullah has been attempting to present itself as a defender of Kurdish rights in Turkey as well as an Islamist movement.[85] This meant that its discourse increasingly makes references to Kurdish rights and frames itself as part of the Kurds' national struggle:

> Hizbullah is an Islamic movement, centered in Kurdistan, dedicated to defending the Muslim Kurds' Islamic and human rights and to finding solutions to historical, social, political, economic, and cultural problems through an Islamic approach. Hizbullah's duty is to struggle against oppression, tyranny, and injustice to make Kurds free.[86]

It has also begun to appropriate the religious Kurdish leaders that were involved in Kurdish revolts in the early twentieth century, such as Sheikh Said. Hizbullah also emphasizes the influence of the ideas of Kurdish religious scholar Said-i Nursi on its ideological development.[87] The link to previous Kurdish religious leaders and scholars is made to situate Hizbullah within the tradition of Kurdish Islam to increase its appeal among a greater number of the Kurds and move away from its image as an extremist jihadist organization. Hizbullah's embrace of Kurdish rights does not extend to becoming more tolerant towards the cultural pluralism prevalent in Kurdish society as it remains committed to establishing the dominance of Islam in Kurdish society.

The changing political context in Turkey during the 2000s, especially the rise of the AKP and democratization reforms carried out as part of the EU accession process, has created opportunities for Hizbullah to revitalize and establish itself as a vocal social movement with an extensive media and organizational network.[88] Hizbullah's evolution towards a social movement occurred during the 2000s and started with the establishment of the Association for Solidarity with the Oppressed (Muztazaflar ile Dayanışma Derneği, Muztazaf-Der) by circles close to Hizbullah in 2004.[89] Other branches of the Muztazaf-Der were opened in the Kurdish majority region and it remained active until 2010 when it was closed by state authorities on grounds that it was linked to Hizbullah.[90] In addition, circles close to Hizbullah have been involved in the provision of courses to study the *Qu'ran* and manage a number of bookstores in Kurdish majority regions that have become hubs of Hizbullah activity and meeting points for Hizbullah supporters and activists.[91]

In December 2012, Hizbullah followers established the Hüda-Par as a legal political party under the leadership of Zekeriya Yapıcıoğlu and the party remains active in the majority regions of Turkey.[92] The Hüda-Par's party programme identifies broad democratic demands, such as a civilian constitution to replace Turkey's current constitution, respect for basic human rights and freedoms, ensuring respect for the rule of law and freedom of religion and association. In addition, it articulates more specific demands for the Kurdish group rights, such as the constitutional recognition of Kurdish identity and the recognition of Kurdish language as an official language in Turkey. It calls for education in the Kurdish language to be provided and the village guards system to be abolished. The party advocates a form of decentralization whereby the municipal authorities are empowered and provided with more resources. Such a system is seen as more effective in decision-making and essential to increase the participation of citizens in the decision-making processes.[93]

Hüda-Par has managed to create a grassroots organization and has branches in many of the provinces across Turkey and in all majority Kurdish provinces and districts. It has so far managed very limited success at elections but established notable pockets of stronghold in Diyarbakır and Batman. In the past year, it has on a number of occasions cooperated with the AKP, such as during the referendum for the executive presidency in April 2017. This cooperation has continued and increased since then as the AKP government intensified its repression of the pro-Kurdish movement. The AKP hopes to strengthen its position in Kurdish majority regions by empowering political actors that are ideologically close to it and use them to mobilize religious Kurds to further weaken the pro-Kurdish movement.

To date, Hüda-Par has been involved in organizing political meetings and rallies that have attracted large crowds. Events organized as part of the 'Blessed Birth Week' (*Kutlu Doğum Haftası*) to celebrate the birth and life of Prophet Mohammed have been attracting significant crowds in Kurdish majority cities such as Diyarbakır. The events are held around 14–20 April every year and are organized by the 'Platform for Lovers of the Prophet' (Peygamber Sevdalıları Platformu), which is a nationwide organization affiliated with Hizbullah and has branches in the main cities of the Kurdish majority regions in Turkey. This is a religious/cultural event popularized by Turkey's Directorate of Religious Affairs (Diyanet İşleri Başkanlığı, Diyanet) and in Kurdish majority areas has become an event organized and associated with Hizbullah or its successor, the Hüda-Par. The event has been used as a show of strength for the Hüda-Par and as an alternative to the Newroz celebrations popularized by the pro-Kurdish movement in Turkey.

The ongoing repression of the pro-Kurdish political parties is creating more space and opportunities for the Hüda-Par to consolidate itself as an important political actor in the Kurdish majority regions of Turkey. However, the Hüda-Par's close association with Hizbullah and Hizbullah's widespread use of violence in the 1990s and its connection, in the minds of ordinary Kurds, to the state's counter-terrorism operations and 'dirty war' against the Kurdish movement are likely to be a barrier preventing it from attracting a larger section of the Kurds in Turkey. Many Kurds remain resentful and hostile to the Hüda-Par and its Islamist ideology makes it very difficult to genuinely accommodate the demands of Kurdish religious groups, such as the Alevi Kurds and Yazidis. Hence, its rise is unlikely to be able to challenge the HDP as the pre-eminent Kurdish political actor in Kurdish politics in Turkey.

Analysis of the survey data

The survey responses of the representatives of the above discussed political parties/ movements enable us to further elaborate on their political inclination and views concerning the representation of Kurds in Turkey. In total, twenty-two representatives (seventeen male; five female) of political parties completed the survey and a non-probability sampling technique was used for selecting the respondents. Persons with a high level of political involvement and who were in a representative position for their respective political parties completed the survey. While the use of the non-probability sampling technique means we are unable to generalize the findings of the sample to the whole of the population, our aim is to generate a deeper understanding of the attitudes of the political elites and activists closely involved in the representation of the Kurds in Turkey and the non-probability sampling technique is fit for this purpose. Moreover, it enables us to include the important political actors in the study and reflect on their experiences, attitudes and motivations.[94]

The respondents included representatives of the Azadi Movement, DBP, HDP, HAK-PAR, Hüda-Par, KADEP, Kurdistan National Congress (Kongreya Netawa Kurdistan, KNK), Kongra-Gel and PAK. All but one of the interviewees was Kurdish and some of the respondents stated a tribal affiliation. Most identified themselves as Sunni Muslims with a minority identifying themselves as atheists and one respondent identifying herself as an Alevi. Almost all representatives of political parties who completed the survey have stated their dissatisfaction with the current system of representation in Turkey and described it as being unable or incapable of representing the Kurdish people. Numerous respondents described Turkey's political system as 'colonialist' and serving only the interests of the Turkish nation. They argued that the Kurds were forcefully incorporated into Turkey and the fundamental principles underpinning the political system in Turkey needed to change before it can represent the Kurds and respond to their political demands. Turkey needed a political system that protected cultural pluralism and acknowledged the Kurds as a nation and recognized Kurdish national and group rights.

The view that nations had a right to national self-determination and form their own independent state was shared by many of the respondents who argued that an independent state for the Kurds would offer the best solution to the problem of the Kurds' political representation. However, many also shared the view that, given the multifarious barriers to the establishment of an independent Kurdish state, alternative frameworks that enable the participation and representation of Kurds should be developed and implemented. All respondents expressed the need for a new administrative framework in Turkey that enabled the Kurds to exercise their right to self-determination through the devolution of political power to a Kurdish administration. These ranged from the decentralization of political power and greater empowerment of the local authorities (Hüda-Par) to regional self-government (HDP) to regional autonomy or ethnic federation (HAK-PAR and KADEP).

Also, the accommodation of Kurdish rights within Turkey through alternatives institutional frameworks are seen as more realistic and achievable than an independent Kurdish state in Turkey. The co-chair of Kongra-Gel Remzi Kartal emphasized the need to build and develop Kurdish self-governments with decision-making power. Such self-governments would empower Kurds and could be united together under a higher entity operating according to the framework of democratic confederalism.

Regional autonomy is also seen as a suitable approach by the representatives of organizations that advocate the democratic autonomy and democratic confederalism model. In such a model, autonomy should be granted to self-governing regions as well as to cultural groups such as nations, ethnic groups and religious communities to build a genuinely plural society in Turkey. Widespread constitutional amendments are seen as necessary to democratize the state and create structures that enable the participation of different nations, ethnic groups and religious communities. The former co-president of the HDP Figen Yüksekdağ argued that decentralization offers the best option for the representation of Kurds because it will allow 'self-governance' for different Kurdish social and cultural identities and in doing so promote a more diverse and democratic Kurdish society.

The representative political organizations that are influenced by the PKK's ideology, such as the KNK, share a vision of a decentralized and democratic Turkey where local and district level assemblies offer citizens the chance to participate in decision-making processes. Political power should be decentralized as far as possible and most of the decisions that concern the lives of the local population should be taken by regional parliaments and self-governments. These local self-governing entities should be represented at the national parliament and take part in the national decision-making processes. Although the model involves features of direct democracy and the political participation of the citizens is at its heart, it also proposes that a fair and just electoral system should be used for the election of representative officials.

Several respondents have stated their preference for a federal solution and gave the example of the Kurdistan Region of Iraq (KRI) as a possible model for the Kurds in Turkey. The idea of a federal Kurdish region in Turkey dates to the TKDP and was initially discussed in the 1960s. Subsequently, in the 1970s, it was defended by Kemal Burkay and circles close to the TKSP and HAK-PAR. In the current period, politicians such as Kemal Burkay and Bayram Bozyel argue that a federal solution is not only capable of offering Kurds genuine representation but also desirable as it would empower the Kurdish nation and guarantee the realization of its national rights. According to Kemal Burkay, this would facilitate the transformation of Turkey into a 'Turkish–Kurdish republic'. Hüda-Par representatives proposed the 'empowerment of local governments' as a realistic and preferable solution to guaranteeing the representation of diverse cultural groups in Turkey.

A representative of the Azadi Movement argued that '[i]n the current system only people who see themselves as Turkish can be represented' and stressed that the Kurds should be given the space to decide for themselves what would be the ideal institutional approach for their representation. Some respondents have argued that Turkey's current political system was not able to accommodate and represent national diversity and it needs to be reformed so that it became more pluralistic. Pluralism was seen as the pre-condition for building a democratic system and such a system is only possible if the existing constitution is amended. The respondents highlighted that the current system placed many barriers in front of the Kurdish representation and that there was a need to build a consensus in Turkey about a new framework for the accommodation of Kurdish rights. All Kurdish representatives stressed that the electoral system used for parliamentary elections needed to change with a fairer system. The requirement that a party obtain at least 10 per cent of the national vote before it can be represented in the parliament needed to be removed. The electoral threshold is seen as an important barrier for the representation of the Kurds and its removal would be a significant step towards ensuring people representing different ethnic and cultural groups are able to take part in politics at the state level. The view that constitutional amendments to remove the barriers that prevent the representation of the Kurds should be undertaken by the government was put forward by some of the representatives from the HAK-PAR, KADEP and the Hüda-Par. These representatives also argued that the government should start a genuine dialogue and engagement with the Kurdish representatives and design a new institutional framework for Turkey that allows for genuine Kurdish representation. Some of the smaller parties such as the Azadi Movement proposed the establishment of a regional parliament in the Kurdish majority regions as the main institution for the representation of the Kurds in Turkey.

The Kurdish political parties rely on a number of methods and undertake different activities to build a base among the Kurds in Turkey. The Azadi Movement, KADEP, HAK-PAR representatives have stated that they use media and social media campaigns to increase the visibility and presence of their party. However, running a media campaign has been difficult for these parties due to the costs and financial burden associated with it. These political parties also use other more conventional methods such as protests, political mobilization, negotiations and lobbying activities. Given they are small parties and lack manpower and resources, they are often involved in building networks and alliances with other Kurdish political parties and use these to reach a large section of the Kurdish society. The representatives of the Azadi Movement emphasized that they believe in 'legal' methods and that in their view violence is 'not legitimate' and cannot solve the Kurdish Question in Turkey. Similar sentiments were echoed by the representative of the Hüda-Par, who also emphasized that his party uses 'legitimate' methods and means, such as lobbying and negotiation.

The representatives of the HDP also stated the importance of media and social media campaigns, mobilization and protest. In fact, protests and similar forms of collective action are widespread and effective forms of putting forward political demands. They also, where possible, use negotiations and lobbying activities, but these efforts were seen as not very effective in achieving its aims. In addition, the HDP puts greater efforts into building grassroots-level organizations that they use to recruit new members and sympathizers as well as organize and mobilize the wider society. Having a parliamentary group also allows the HDP to voice its demands and represent the interests of the Kurdish people through the parliament. The HDP and its constituent organizations advocate legal political practices and see forms of mass protests and political mobilization as necessary to overcome the state's frequent encroachments. The idea of the right to 'self-defence' has been used by the representatives of the KNK and Kongra-Gel, who emphasize the need for the Kurds to defend themselves against the violence used by the state. In the PKK's discourse, the concept of 'self-defence' is frequently used to offer justification for its use of violence against the state security forces. The PKK's use of violence is seen as necessary to preserve or protect its own existence and counter the threat of the state's forced assimilation and repression of the Kurdish nation in Turkey.

Many of the Kurdish political parties are active in only some of the Kurdish majority provinces and generally have a very small membership base drawn exclusively from the Kurds. The HDP, on the other hand, has a mass membership and presence across Turkey. It appeals to Kurds from different tribal and religious backgrounds. It seeks to build stronger relations with left-wing and socialist political parties in Europe and often organizes meetings and conferences in European countries. It has an office in Brussels and in Washington DC and regularly organizes events attended by the HDP MPs and the leading figures in the party and uses such events to inform the western public and media about political developments in Turkey. As discussed above, the HDP has been severely repressed by the state and the AKP government, with many of the elected representatives at local and national levels removed from their position. The other Kurdish political parties have been so far spared such repression and are able to continue their activities. Some of the Kurdish political parties have seen this as an opportunity and seek to fill in the space left by the HDP's repression. The Hüda-Par, for example, has struck closer relations with the AKP in recent years and campaigned for a yes vote in the referendum for the executive-style presidency held in April 2017. Due to the Hüda-Par's association with Hizbullah and the continued animosity between the PKK and Hizbullah supporters, the Hüda-Par political activities often are met with hostility. This takes place during the election campaigns and often results in fights but, so far, these have remained local and not escalated into larger clashes. Many of the smaller political parties have sought to cultivate friendly ties with the KDP in Iraqi Kurdistan and the KRI to establish themselves as stronger political actors in Turkey. They see such an association as beneficial to their credibility and as a token of their commitment to Kurdish rights in Turkey and elsewhere.

2

Electoral politics and the Kurds in Turkey

This chapter analyses the election results in the Kurdish majority regions since 2002 and seeks to unpack the factors at play in the mobilization of Kurdish voters in Turkey. The analysis highlights the views of Kurdish elected officials on the accommodation of Kurdish rights as well as their ideological inclinations and leanings. Although it is possible to find Kurds active in many of the political parties in Turkey, the main contest for the political representation of the Kurdish voters during the past two decades has been waged by the AKP and the pro-Kurdish democratic movement, which is currently represented by the HDP.

Turkey's restrictive political space during the 1990s prevented Kurdish voices to be heard, but it has not deterred large numbers of Kurds from attempting to engage with the political process and to raise their demands. During the 2000s, due to the significant transformation in the armed conflict between the PKK and the state security forces and the democratization reforms the AKP government carried out to meet the EU accession conditions, the domestic context in Turkey began to change, which in turn created more space for Kurdish political parties and actors. Consequently, some rights to the Kurds were granted, particularly around Kurdish language tuition and broadcasting. Also, to facilitate the development of civil society, the process of establishing charities and non-governmental organizations was simplified.

In 1999, the pro-Kurdish democratic movement managed to secure representation at a local level and, in 2004, the number of municipal councils the pro-Kurdish parties controlled increased. This institutional base enabled the movement to grow and increase its base in the Kurdish majority provinces in the south-east of Turkey. This process coincided with a transformation in the Kurdish conflict towards significantly less violence compared to the 1980s and 1990s. The PKK ceased armed activity during the early 2000s after the capture and trial of Abdullah Öcalan in 1999. The PKK returned to violence after 2004 and restarted its insurgency against the Turkish state but its use of violence was not as intense or extensive as that of the 1990s and was interrupted by frequent unilateral ceasefires. Also, the conflict between Hizbullah and the PKK subsided towards the end of the 1990s following the elimination of Hizbullah's leadership. Consequently, the decline in violence helped to generate a new debate on how to resolve the Kurdish conflict through political means.

While efforts to find a political settlement to end the conflict were not successful, the 2000s was a period of reflection and search for peace. Minor shifts and changes in Turkish state policy towards the Kurds can be interpreted as partial responses to Kurdish demands. With the rise of the pro-Kurdish movement in the past decade and the electoral successes it has had, the pressure for reform has been growing. Initially, the AKP seemed to respond to this pressure but, without a coherent policy framework for reform, its efforts did not bear much fruit. Reforming the political institutions, decentralizing power to enable the full representation of Kurds and improving the rights of its Kurdish minority never fully became a part of the reform initiatives or debate. The reform process came to an end in the summer of 2015 and since then the AKP government intensified its efforts to repress and eliminate the Kurdish political representation at both local and national levels.

Competition over Kurdish votes

During the 1980s, it was mainly the centre-right Motherland Party (Anavatan Partisi, ANAP) and the centre-left Populist Party (Halkçı Parti) and the Social Democratic Populist Party (Sosyaldemokrat Halkçı Parti, SHP) that dominated electoral politics in the Kurdish regions. Several centre-right political parties such as the True Path Party (Doğru Yol Partisi, DYP) drew significant support in the Kurdish majority provinces. Islamist political parties have been quite successful in winning the support of the Kurdish electorates. This started during the 1990s when the Islamist Welfare Party (Refah Partisi, RP) managed to win the support of the Kurdish voters to establish itself as a significant force in the Kurdish majority regions. At the 1995 general election, the RP managed to win more than thirty MPs from the Kurdish majority provinces. The strength of the support for the RP showed the force of the appeal of Islam and its potential to mobilize the Kurds.[1] During the 1990s, despite the severe state repression and failure to secure parliamentary representation, the pro-Kurdish democratic movement also managed to establish itself as a significant political actor in the region.

During the 2000s, the competition over the Kurdish votes was mainly waged between the pro-Kurdish political parties and the AKP. The AKP's nucleus is traced to the RP but it additionally represents the political space previously taken by the conservative and centrist political parties and it is also possible to describe the AKP as the contemporary representative of Turkey's right-wing populist political tradition, which was previously represented by the DP of Adnan Menderes during the 1950s and ANAP of Turgut Özal in the 1980s. It is important to note here that, since 1950, right-wing populist parties have been more willing to engage with the Kurds and have drawn strong support from the Kurdish majority regions.

Apart from the Tunceli province, where the CHP has tended to perform strongly, and Elazığ, which has a notable Nationalist Movement Party (Milliyetci Hareket Partisi, MHP) presence, Turkey's other opposition parties have received very little electoral support in the majority Kurdish regions. In the provinces with a Kurdish Alevi minority, such as Erzincan, Kahramanmaraş, Kayseri, Malatya and Sivas, a high percentage of Kurdish Alevi voters tend to support the CHP. Historically, Alevi Kurdish voters strongly associate with centre-left parties such as the CHP currently and the SHP during the 1980s and 1990s.

The AKP has been successful in winning the backing of conservative Kurds and it recruited many Kurds to its ranks from the beginning. It has been the main political party that represents the religious Kurds even though there are various other centre-right parties and Kurdish political parties with a religious leaning. At the general elections in 2007 and 2011, it won more votes in the Kurdish majority regions than any other political party. The religious orders and networks and other religious organizations that are active within the Kurdish community and in the Kurdish majority region participate in national-level politics through the AKP. Also, under the AKP rule since 2002, religion acquired a central role in the state's management of the Kurdish question and has been used to diminish the appeal of Kurdish nationalism.[2] Islamist critiques of Turkish nationalism and secularism have not been extended to counter the oppression the Kurds have been experiencing in Turkey.[3]

To counter the advances the AKP has made among the Kurdish voters and to challenge the state's propaganda that depicted the Kurdish movement as undermining the Kurds' Islamic heritage and attempting to enforce a secular way of life on the religious Kurdish society, Kurdish national movement began to incorporate elements from Islam into its discourse. In addition, several political actors previously associated with Islamist parties, Islamic civil society organizations or the religious establishment, such as Nimettullah Erdoğmuş, who was the former mufti of Diyarbakır, became members of the pro-Kurdish political parties and were elected as MPs.

The AKP's Kurdish vote between 2002 and 2019

As mentioned above, the AKP has been drawing strong support from the Kurds since its establishment and it can be argued that no mainstream Turkish political party has been as successful as the AKP in mobilizing the Kurdish voters. Its Islamist discourse, democratization reforms and promise of future reform to broaden the area of Kurdish rights in Turkey received strong support from the Kurdish voters throughout the 2000s. The Islamist parties that preceded the AKP also had a strong presence in the region and many religious Kurds shifted their support to the AKP when the party was established in 2001. The Kurds' association with the AKP has been strengthened through the inclusion of several prominent Kurds in its ranks and it has managed to utilize the existing religious networks to increase its support base. The AKP incorporated locally influential Kurdish tribal and religious leaders into its structures throughout the 2000s and 2010s. In the Kurdish majority provinces where tribal relations and religion remain strong, such as Şanlıurfa, Adıyaman and Bingöl, the AKP has been performing very strongly.

There were many Kurdish figures active within the AKP and some have risen to become ministers, such as Hüseyin Çelik who served as the Minister for National Education between 2003 and 2009, Mehmet Mehdi Eker who served as the Minister for Agriculture in successive AKP governments between 2003 and 2015 and Mehmet Şimşek who was the Minister of Finance between 2009 and 2015. Abdulrahman Kurt, who served as an MP for the Diyarbakır province between 2007 and 2011, was another Kurd active within the AKP. Other Kurds within the AKP included Mehmet Metiner who served as an MP for the Adıyaman and Istanbul provinces between 2011 and 2018 and Orhan Miroğlu who served as an MP for the Mardin Province between 2015 and

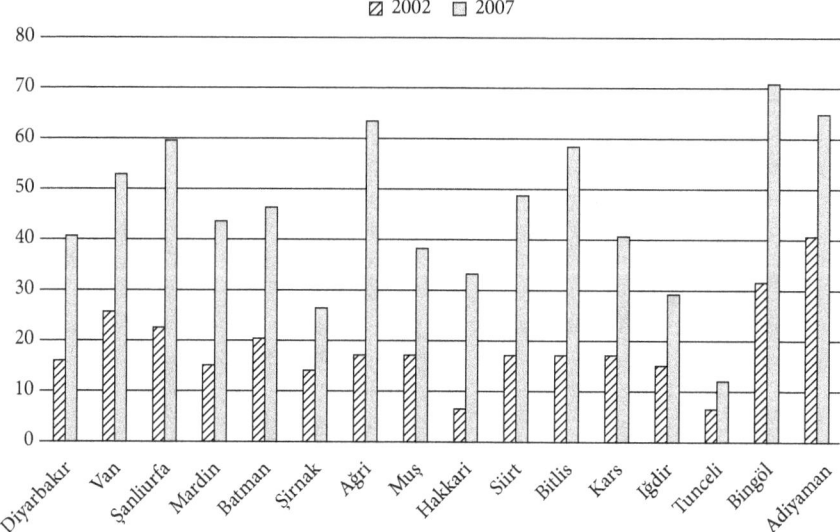

Figure 2.1 Percentage of votes the AKP obtained in the 2002 and 2007 general elections in the Kurdish majority provinces.

2018. Galip Ensarioğlu, who is a tribal leader from Diyarbakır, was elected as an AKP MP for the Diyarbakır province between June 2011 and June 2015 and again between November 2015 and June 2018.

Another approach taken by the AKP to increase its support base in the Kurdish majority region has centred on expanding welfare service provision. Throughout the 2000s, the social assistance payments to the Kurds increased and it has been argued that they are 'disproportionately directed to the Kurdish minority and to the Kurdish region on an ethnic basis'.[4] Additionally, Islamist civil society organizations were utilized in service provisions and there has been a rapid growth in the number and activities of such organizations in the past two decades.[5] Charitable activities have also been provided by the governor's office in many of the provinces in the Kurdish majority regions and such efforts are generally seen as part of the AKP's charity distribution. Ensar Vakfı (The Ensar Foundation) is one of the main pro-government associations that are active in many of the cities and towns of the majority Kurdish region, and as well as providing meals for the poor, it is also involved in managing student dormitories.

More recently, the Islamist and pro-government charities and other civil society associations have been brought together under the Platform for The National Will (Milli İrade Platformu). This serves the purpose of coordinating the activities of pro-government civil society organizations and actively mobilizes the population in support of the government's policies and has been especially effective in the aftermath of the popular mobilizations following the failed coup attempt in July 2016. In the past decade, activities by Islamist charities and the extensive network of civil society associations have been playing an important role at the local level to build the support base for the AKP and the other Islamist political actors.

The Islamist discourse has been a source of ideological challenge against the pro-Kurdish democratic movement in the past two decades and, in addition to the AKP and its affiliates, there are several Islamist actors, such as the Hüda-Par and the Gülen Movement, which were organized through a network of civil society organizations and charities. In addition, the Felicity Party (Saadet Partisi, SP), which is a minor Islamist party established in 2001 and sees itself as the current representative of Erbakan's Islamist Milli Görüş (National Outlook) movement is also active in Diyarbakır and has a similar organization network of charities and civil society associations.[6] There are charitable organizations that were established and managed by the Diyarbakır municipality council, such as Sarmaşık and Gün Işığı, which could be considered a part of the pro-Kurdish political movement. As part of the crackdown on the activities of the pro-Kurdish movement in 2016 and 2017, alongside other Kurdish civil society organizations and associations, the state has closed these charities down.

The support for Islamist political actors under the AKP rule enabled them to increase their power in the Kurdish majority regions and to challenge the pro-Kurdish movement: 'Religious politics has been the main component of the AKP strategy to cope with the Kurdish question in its territories as well as in neighbouring countries.'[7] The charity activities the AKP coordinated sought to also empower its Kurdish Islamist allies, who became more active because of the political space and opportunities the AKP governments created:

> After decades long Kemalist domination in the country, AKP rule has provided pro-Islamist Kurdish groups with considerable material and normative resources to reorganize themselves in the economic, social, cultural and political arenas against or alongside Kurdish national and secular groups in general, and the KM [Kurdish Movement] in particular.[8]

The AKP's association with the Kurdish religious and tribal actors is likely to draw Kurdish voters who are resident in Turkey's western cities and towns because of the stronger connection it creates. In fact, the AKP has been performing well in the working-class districts of Istanbul and other major cities where a sizeable Kurdish population resides. The role of religious and ideological affiliation is likely to be an important factor as the AKP draws support predominantly from the religious conservative Sunni Muslim Kurds. This affiliation is strengthened by the AKP's relatively more tolerant approach to accepting Turkey's ethnic pluralism. While ideology plays a faciliatory role, social assistance programmes also play an important role in the AKP's mobilization of the Kurds in cities and towns in western Turkey, many of whom are internally displaced and continue to suffer from economic hardship. Through its wide charitable networks and service provisions to the poor, the AKP could reach and persuade a significant number of Kurdish voters.[9] Also, being associated with the AKP's social network that offers other advantages such as finding jobs or promotion can also be a motivating factor in Kurds voting for the AKP. In fact, the AKP has successfully utilized service provision not only for its election campaigns but as a broader tool for managing the conflict via pacifying and controlling the Kurds.[10]

In comparison to other Turkish political parties and especially during the early years of its existence, the AKP displayed more tolerance towards Kurdish identity. During the 2000s, the AKP has been carrying numerous democratization reforms as part of which a limited recognition of the Kurdish identity has been granted. The establishment of the Kurdish language TV station, TRT Şeş, as part of the state broadcasting network in January 2009, is often given as proof of AKP's tolerance of ethnocultural diversity in Turkey. However, doubts remain over the extent of AKP's tolerance because of its consistent refusal to commit to the full recognition of the Kurds' linguistic rights, such as the provision of education in the Kurdish language. Additionally, by emphasizing commonalities such as the Islamic heritage, the aim of the AKP government's political reforms has been to also lessen the appeal of Kurdish nationalism and depoliticize Kurdish identity.[11] With the declaration of the 'Kurdish initiative' in August 2009, the search for a political solution started to take a more central position in the public debate in Turkey.

Although the AKP toyed with the idea of peace with the Kurds and Prime Minister Recep Tayyip Erdoğan often indicated that he was willing to carry reforms to broaden Kurdish rights in Turkey, in practice, very little effort was put into developing policies to address the rights of the Kurds or end the insurgency.[12] There was a dialogue between the state and the PKK in 2009 and during 2013 and 2014 and a framework on future negotiations was agreed upon and made public in February 2015, which came to be known as the Dolmabahçe Agreement. However, signs of tension appeared as early as 22 March 2015, when President Erdoğan declared that the so-called 'Dolmabahçe Agreement' did not exist and he did not approve of a negotiated end to the conflict with the PKK.[13]

In the past decade, the AKP government also developed good relations with the Kurdistan Regional Government (KRG) and several Iraqi Kurdish leaders have been hosted in Turkey. Visits to Kurdistan Region in Iraq by Turkish officials have also taken place, including by Foreign Minister Ahmet Davutoğlu in 2009 and Prime Minister Recep Tayyip Erdoğan in 2011. The AKP used its close relations with the KRG to argue that it was in favour of cultivating strong relations with the Kurds and was willing to carry out reforms to improve the conditions for them in Turkey. The visits by KRG representatives often turned into symbolic gestures and took place as part of activities designed to increase the AKP's appeal amongst the Kurds in Turkey. For example, in November 2013, the President of the Kurdistan Region of Iraq, Massoud Barzani, visited Diyarbakır and attended several events with Prime Minister Erdoğan. In his speech, Erdoğan uttered the word 'Kurdistan' and made several promises of improving Turkey's relations with the Kurds. In the same meeting, Erdoğan and Barzani were joined by the exiled Kurdish singer Sivan Perwer who sang in the Kurdish language.[14] In February 2017, Massoud Barzani again visited Turkey and the flag of Kurdistan Region was hoisted when he was received at the State Guest House in the Istanbul Airport.[15]

While the AKP has been relatively successful in the general elections in the Kurdish majority provinces, it has not been able to replicate its success at the local elections. It won the municipal councils in the provinces of Adıyaman, Ağrı, Bingöl, Bitlis, Kars, Mardin, Muş and Şanlıurfa in 2009 but lost Ağrı, Bitlis, Kars and Mardin at the 2014 local elections. The MHP won the control of the Kars municipal council to the MHP

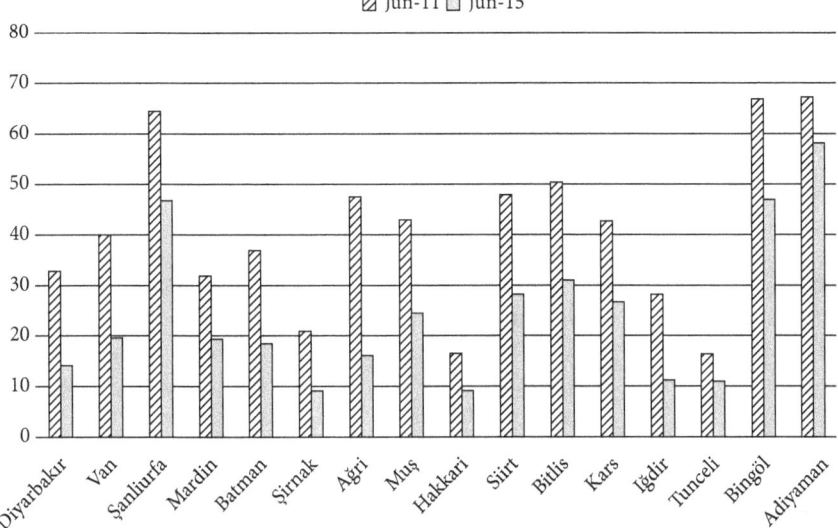

Figure 2.2 Percentage of votes the AKP obtained in the June 2011 and June 2015 general elections in the Kurdish majority provinces.

and the Ağrı, Bitlis and Mardin councils were won by the BDP. The AKP was not able to defeat the candidate of the pro-Kurdish party in the main cities in the east and south-east of Turkey in subsequent local elections. In March 2019, the AKP won the Ağrı, Bingöl, Bitlis, Elazig, Muş, Şanlıurfa and Şırnak municipal councils.

The Kurdish support for the AKP began to fall significantly from 2013 onwards and, as the above figure shows, this fall became apparent at the June 2015 election. In earlier elections, the AKP was keen to promote itself as a party that had a moderate and sympathetic approach to the accommodation of the Kurdish demands in Turkey and it credited itself with the democratization reforms and the peaceful approach to resolving the conflict. It depicted itself as the chief architect of the dialogue process with the PKK that began in January 2013 and received much support from the Kurds. However, from 2013 onwards, after the Gezi Park protests, the AKP began to lose its image as a force for democratization and increasingly turned towards authoritarianism and Turkish nationalism. The growing opposition to the AKP's social conservatism and free-market economic policies began to be met with a stronger challenge and its heavy-handed approach and repression of dissent and incidents of collective mobilization by opposition groups undid the image that it was a force for democratization in Turkey.

The trust between the AKP and the Kurds further disintegrated during the election campaign for the June 2015 election. The AKP made the HDP its main target and based its strategy on preventing it from winning any parliamentary representation. This would have been realized if the HDP had failed to pass the 10 per cent election threshold – the HDP's failure would have handed the AKP a big majority in parliament to change the constitution and introduce an executive form of the presidency that

President Erdoğan has been demanding. The AKP's desire to further centralize power was a major concern amongst the voters and pushed many people to side with the HDP with a significant number choosing to support it for tactical reasons to prevent the AKP winning an overwhelming majority. Strong opposition to an executive-style presidential system and popular discontent with the government allowed the HDP to position itself as the only party that could prevent the AKP from further eroding the power of Turkey's democratic institutions.

AKP's foreign policy choices in the Syrian conflict also had a bearing on the election result. An important rupture point occurred during the siege of the Kurdish town of Kobani by ISIS in autumn 2014. The government's refusal to aid the Kurdish fighters in Kobani was met with widespread protest by Kurds across Turkey between 6 and 8 October 2014 and the excessive use of police violence to suppress the protests that resulted in the death of forty-six people left many Kurds feeling deeply disappointed with the AKP attitude. President Erdoğan and other government representatives were keen to interpret the developments in Kobani as a fight between two terror organizations, which was not received well by the Kurdish public in Turkey as many strongly identified with and supported the struggle of the Kurds in Syria against ISIS.

Despite a significant fall in the Kurdish support for the AKP, a detailed analysis of the 7 June 2015 election results were provided by the Istanbul-based research consultancy company KONDA and the report states that 19 per cent of 18.8 million AKP voters are of Kurdish background and 1 per cent are identified as Zaza.[16] In the June 2015 election in Şanlıurfa, Adıyaman and Bingöl, the AKP obtained 356,537 (46.7 per cent), 178,282 (58.2 per cent) and 61,294 (46.9 per cent) votes, respectively.

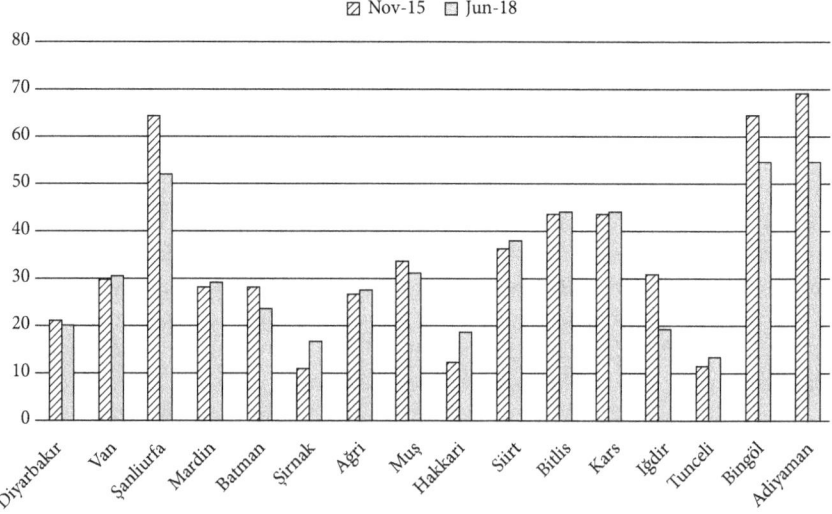

Figure 2.3 Percentage of votes the AKP obtained in the November 2015 and June 2018 general elections in the Kurdish majority provinces.

In the November 2015 election, the AKP increased its efforts to engage with the religious and tribal actors to increase its share of the Kurdish vote. Since then, the AKP has managed to maintain its electoral base in the Kurdish majority provinces. This is confirmed by the result of the referendum for the presidency held in April 2017 and the parliamentary and presidential elections held on 24 June 2018. The AKP improved its share of the vote in the provinces where it has a very low base, such as Şırnak and Hakkari, but overall it has not managed to significantly improve on its November 2015 results for the Kurdish majority provinces. This is despite the harsh conditions and severe repression its main rival for Kurdish votes, the HDP, faced.

The pro-Kurdish movement's electoral performances between 2002 and 2019

As discussed in Chapter 1, the pro-Kurdish movement's articulation of Kurdish rights has made it the target of state repression and one of the key barriers to the pro-Kurdish parties were that they were perceived by the mainstream Turkish political parties and society as a threat to Turkey's territorial integrity. Despite this, the pro-Kurdish political movement has managed to build an institutional base in the majority of Kurdish regions in Turkey and grassroots organizations. The pro-Kurdish parliamentary representation was eliminated in 1994 and subsequent attempts by HADEP to regain it during the mid-1990s were not successful. However, its performance at a local level was more encouraging and enabled it to build a stronger base for the movement. In the municipal elections held on 18 April 1999, the HADEP obtained 1.95 million votes and managed to win the control of thirty-seven towns and cities across the majority Kurdish regions, including the municipal councils of Ağrı, Batman, Bingöl, Diyarbakır, Hakkari, Siirt and Van.[17]

In the 2004 municipal elections, the DEHAP took part in the election in an electoral alliance with the SHP and increased the number of the councils it held to fifty-four, winning the municipal councils of Batman, Diyarbakır, Hakkari, Mardin and Şırnak. The pro-Kurdish political parties HADEP and DEHAP took part in the general elections held in 1999 and 2002 and obtained 4.75 per cent and 6.14 per cent of the national vote, respectively. Since the late 1990s, the pro-Kurdish parties have been the main political party with a mass membership and following in the Kurdish majority regions.

On 22 July 2007, Kurdish representation in parliament returned with the elections of the twenty-two DTP MPs as independent candidates. In western Turkey, the DTP supported Turkish pro-democratic socialist candidates mainly from the EMEP and the Freedom and Solidarity Party (Özgürlük ve Dayanışma Partisi, ÖDP). One DTP MP, Sebahat Tuncel, was elected in the city of Istanbul with another of its Istanbul candidates and its candidate in the province of Mersin losing narrowly.[18] The election success resulted in the return of the pro-Kurdish parliamentary opposition in Turkey at the July 2007 general elections. The election of the DTP into the parliament – after thirteen years of absence – restored the pro-Kurdish parliamentary opposition in Turkey and brought new momentum to Kurdish political activism in Turkey. It has also placed the DTP at the centre stage of Kurdish politics in Turkey. In the municipal elections held on 29 March 2009, the DTP consolidated its position as the leading party of the Kurdish regions when winning more than 50 per cent of the votes in many

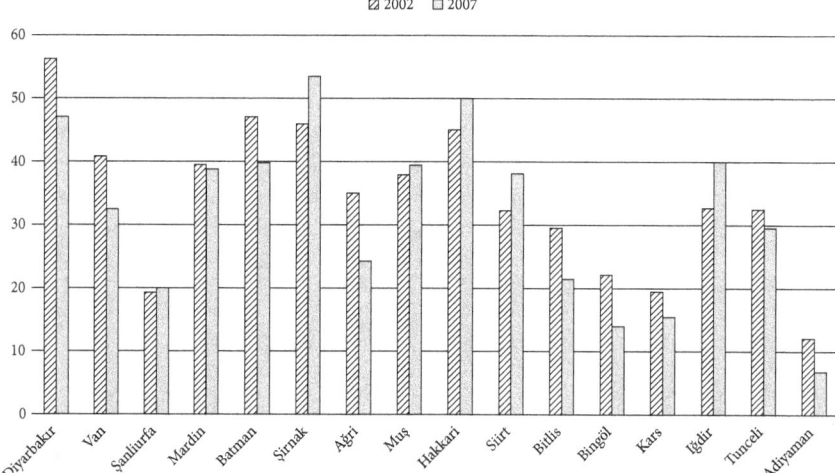

Figure 2.4 Percentage of votes the DEHAP obtained in the 2002 general election and the pro-Kurdish independent candidates obtained in the 2007 general election in the Kurdish majority provinces.

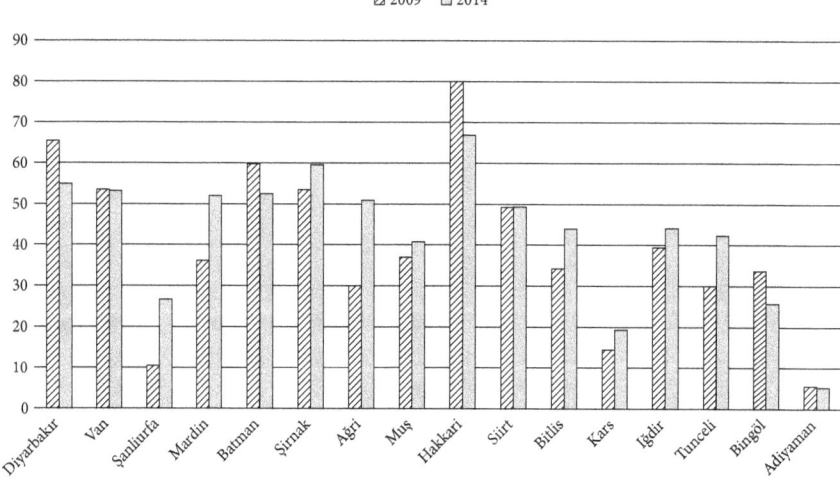

Figure 2.5 Percentage of votes the pro-Kurdish parties obtained in the 2009 and 2014 local elections in the Kurdish majority provinces.

towns and cities and a respectable 2,339,729 votes nationally. In total, it won ninety-nine councils including the Municipalities of Diyarbakır, Van, Batman, Tunceli, Iğdır, Şırnak, Siirt and Hakkari.[19]

The election of the DTP MPs and the success it achieved in the municipal election was viewed as a chance to build bridges between the different political groups to foster greater understanding. Crucially, having parliamentary representation provided the

DTP with a legal democratic platform where Kurdish rights and demands can be raised. Being represented in the national assembly and having the experience of running many of the local authorities in the Kurdish regions has enabled the DTP to establish a strong regional and national presence. This allowed for the establishment and sustenance of links and associations with various other social and political groups in Turkey, which fosters the exchange of views and better understanding. Having an institutional base also enabled the DTP to intensify its efforts to campaign for a democratic and peaceful solution to the Kurdish question in Turkey.

The DTP remained active until it was closed down by the Constitutional Court on 12 December 2009. From then onwards, the BDP, which was established on 3 May 2008, took the task of Kurdish representation in Turkey. In April 2011, the BDP in alliance with seventeen other political parties and non-governmental organizations formed the pro-democracy 'the Labour, Peace and Democracy Bloc' and supported independent candidates in the general elections scheduled for 12 June 2011. In addition to the leading members of the pro-Kurdish BDP, independent socialist and pro-democracy candidates were also included in the list, including the film director and columnist Sırrı Süreyya Önder for Istanbul, the leader of the EMEP Abdullah Levent Tüzel for Istanbul and the socialist activist and journalist Ertuğrul Kürkçü for Mersin. Broad democratic demands such as gender equality, better working conditions, comprehensive constitutional reform and political reconciliation are the key demands articulated in the election campaigns. In total, thirty-five pro-Kurdish MPs were elected as independent candidates. The BDP took part in the local elections held in 2014 and it consolidated its position by winning a total of 102 councils.

The difficulties that the pro-Kurdish democratic movement experienced throughout its existence continue to affect the current pro-Kurdish political party the HDP in Turkey. However, unlike its predecessors, the HDP managed to perform better in the general elections in which it took part. On 7 June 2015, it managed to win 13.1 per cent of the popular vote and secure eighty seats in the parliament in Ankara. Judged by the electoral performance of any of its predecessors, the HDP's success is unparalleled in the history of Turkish democracy. Its achievement represents the overcoming of barriers created by the marginalization of the pro-Kurdish movement. By choosing parliamentary candidates from a wider network and representatives of diverse political, social and cultural groups, the HDP managed to connect with a much larger portion of the electorate, win their support and establish itself as the voice of the left in Turkey. Given that the June 2015 election was the first parliamentary election that the HDP contested, it is difficult to make a direct comparison with any previous election results.

Overall, the HDP's support increased significantly in the traditional heartlands of the pro-Kurdish movement in the south-east of the country and it was the number one party in the following provinces: Ağrı, Batman, Bitlis, Diyarbakır, Hakkari, Kars, Mardin, Muş, Siirt, Şırnak, Tunceli and Van.[20] Although the pro-Kurdish political parties had performed well in these provinces for more than a decade, the HDP received significantly more votes in all of the provinces, and in the provinces of Hakkari and Şırnak it managed to gain 86.4 per cent and 85.36 per cent of the vote, respectively. In the most populous provinces in the Kurdish majority regions, such as Diyarbakır and Van, the HDP managed to get more than 70 per cent of the votes.

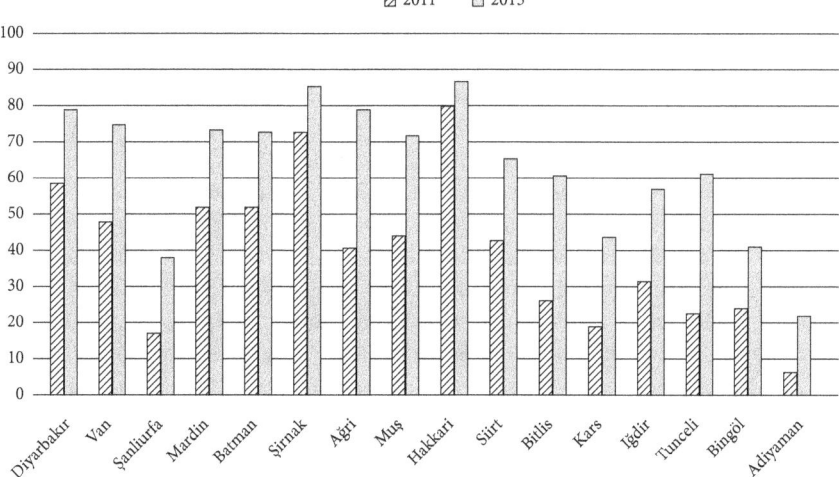

Figure 2.6 Percentage of votes the pro-Kurdish independent candidates obtained in the June 2011 election and the HDP obtained in the June 2015 elections in the Kurdish majority provinces.

The HDP also performed well and came second in the Kurdish majority provinces of Şanlıurfa, Adıyaman and Bingöl, where it obtained 293,841, 69,513 and 53,519 votes, respectively. Also, there was a surge in support for the HDP in Istanbul where it gained 1,030,761 votes to become the third party in the province and win eleven seats in the parliament. It performed well in Turkey's other provinces in the south and west of the country too. It gained 273,089 votes in Izmir, 183,934 votes in Mersin, 177,359 votes in Adana, 167,634 votes in Ankara, 138,678 votes in Gaziantep, 96,513 votes in Bursa and 90,644 votes in Antalya. In the previous election, the pro-Kurdish independent candidates were fielded only in provinces where they had a realistic chance of winning. In contrast, participating in the elections as a party meant that the HDP fielded candidates in all of the provinces and gave its supporters across Turkey a chance to vote for HDP candidates. Also, the HDP ran a successful campaign abroad especially in European countries that have a significant Kurdish and Turkish population and obtained 211,299 votes that were distributed among all the provinces.

According to the analysis of the 7 June 2015 election provided by research consultancy firm KONDA, the Kurds are the main supporters of the HDP and they make as much as 87 per cent of its voters (this figure includes the Zazas, who are generally considered to be another Kurdish ethnic group in Turkey but often counted separately).[21] Only 9 per cent of the HDP voters are defined as Turkish, 1 per cent are estimated to be of Arab origin and, in the case of 3 per cent of voters, ethnic background was not classified.

On a broader level, the transformation in Turkey's Kurdish conflict during the 2000s and the country's EU accession process since 2005 can be singled out as the two

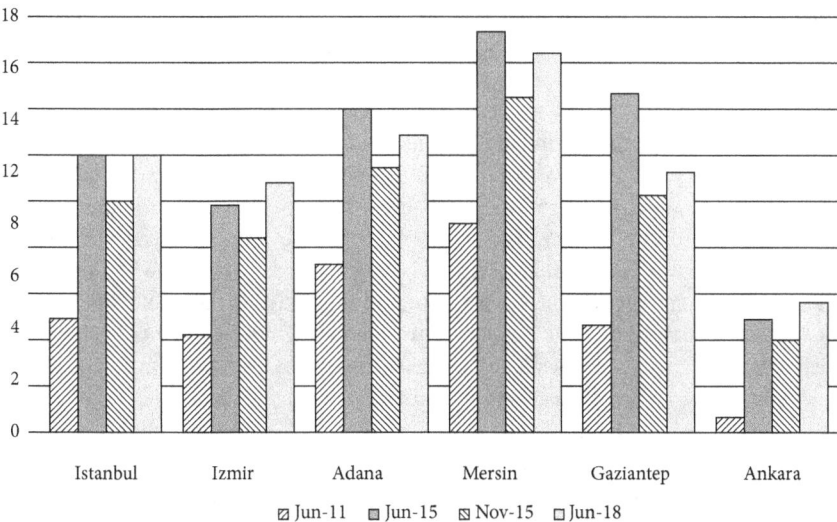

Figure 2.7 Percentage of votes the pro-Kurdish candidates and political parties obtained since 2011 in the western and southern provinces of Turkey.

most important developments that facilitated the HDP's rise in Turkish politics.[22] The legal reforms the government carried out to meet the EU accession conditions have increased the democratic space for the pro-Kurdish political movement to broaden its activities and become a more effective political actor. Reforms carried out in the subsequent years, such as in the area of Kurdish language broadcasting and tuition, enhanced the legitimacy of Kurdish demands in Turkey. The transformation of the conflict in the past two decades is also a significant factor in the rise of the HDP. The past two decades witnessed a significant reduction in the violent incidents between the PKK and the state security forces in Turkey, and, although the violence returned after 2004, its intensity was far less than the violence of the 1990s. This transformation in the conflict created space for the pro-Kurdish political parties to promote reconciliation and a democratic solution to the Kurdish question. Their efforts received a significant impetus with the return of Kurdish representation to parliament in 2007. Being represented in the national assembly and having the experience of running many of the local authorities in the majority Kurdish regions had enabled the pro-Kurdish movement to establish a strong regional and national presence. This allowed for the establishment and sustenance of links with various other social and political groups and foster better understanding and more cooperative relations between the different pro-democracy political groups in Turkey.

The HDP also played a key role in facilitating the communication between the state representatives and the PKK during the dialogue process that lasted from January 2013 to April 2015. The dialogue process involved regular meetings between government representatives, the HDP delegation, the jailed PKK leader Abdullah Öcalan and the PKK representatives, and they produced some milestones, such as the ceasefire from March 2013 to July 2015 and a ten-point route map for future negotiations that was made public on 28 February 2015 jointly by an HDP delegation and government representatives in Istanbul's Dolmabahçe Palace. Throughout the dialogue process, the HDP MPs involved in the dialogue process and its leaders had the opportunity to address the mainstream media, which gave more visibility to the HDP and provided it with an opportunity to disseminate its political discourse to a much larger audience. Being one of the central actors of the dialogue process allowed the HDP to be seen by a greater number of people as a legitimate actor working towards the good of the whole of Turkish society. The performance of the HDP's co-leader Selahattin Demirtaş is another factor that needs to be highlighted. Demirtaş was a candidate in the presidential elections in August 2014 and subsequently became the public face of the HDP. The presidential election campaign gave Demirtaş and the HDP more visibility in the media and enabled them to reach out to a larger section of society and disseminate the HDP's message across Turkey. Demirtaş proved to be a very strong media performer and his confident and calm approach has won much praise.

The election strategy that the HDP followed also significantly contributed to its success. In western Turkey, the HDP selected candidates that represent and appeal to different sections of society and political movements. It had several Alevi community leaders such as Turgut Öker and Ali Kenanoğlu in Istanbul and Müslüm Doğan in Izmir. Well-known socialist activists such as Ertuğrul Kürkçü and Sırrı Süreyya Önder have been part of the HDP from the beginning and stood as candidates for Izmir and Ankara, respectively. Feminist activist Filiz Kerestecioğlu, Armenian rights activist Garo Paylan and Islamic feminist writer and journalist Hüda Kaya stood as candidates in Istanbul. Another experienced politician changing his allegiance to the HDP in 2015 is Celal Doğan who was previously active in the SHP and CHP and was the mayor of the Gaziantep province between 1989 and 2004. As discussed in Chapter 1, the HDP incorporated several political actors in the Kurdish majority areas who would appeal to religious and tribal Kurds.

Soon after the election in June 2015, however, the HDP came under increasing pressure and state repression. The intensification of violence in the conflict between the PKK and the state security forces in Turkey's majority Kurdish regions from summer 2015 onwards has led to an increase in instances of violent attacks by Turkish nationalists against the HDP. The anti-HDP fervour reached its height on 8 September 2015 when large-scale mob attacks targeted and vandalized the HDP's offices in many cities in western Turkey, including its headquarters in Ankara and many of the district offices in Istanbul. In addition, ISIS terror attacks targeting Turkey's pro-Kurdish peace network in Suruç and Ankara on 20 July 2015 and 10 October 2015, respectively, made running a campaign for the November election very difficult for the HDP.[23] As a result, there was a reduction in the HDP's vote in the repeated election on 1 November 2015, but, despite that, it still managed to obtain 10.75 per cent of the popular vote and fifty-nine seats in the parliament.

Despite the ongoing repression and imprisonment of many of the leaders of the HDP, the party performed strongly in the Kurdish majority regions. Although its vote decreased slightly in the Kurdish majority provinces, the results confirm that it is maintaining its support base. In total, the HDP obtained 11.7 per cent of the national vote and won sixty-seven seats in the parliament.

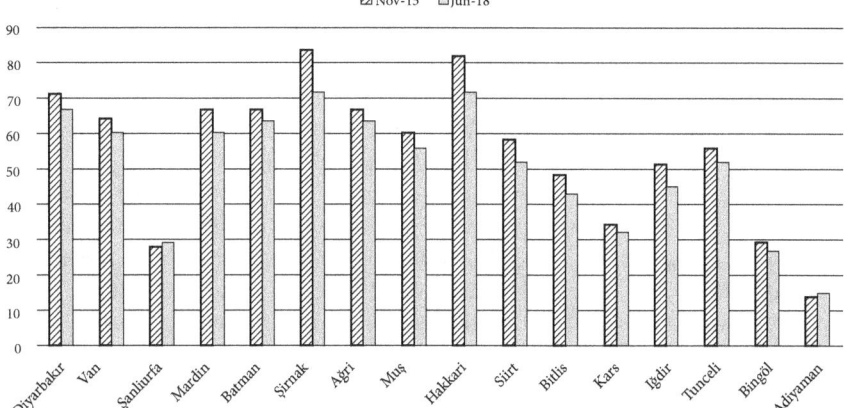

Figure 2.8 Percentage of votes the HDP obtained in the November 2015 and June 2018 general elections in the Kurdish majority provinces.

As noted above, almost all of the pro-Kurdish mayors elected in 2014 were replaced by trustees appointed by the government. At the local elections held on 31 March 2019, the HDP concentrated its efforts in the Kurdish majority provinces and its main objective was to take back control over the municipal and district councils won in 2014 but taken over by government-appointed 'trustees' in 2016. Despite the decline in its overall share of the vote, it managed to win a total of sixty-nine councils. The HDP candidates won the election in six other districts and towns, but they were not able to take their position on grounds that they were removed from their positions in the civil service by a delegated decree issued by the government in the aftermath of the failed coup attempt in 2016. The HDP won the municipal councils of Batman, Diyarbakır, Hakkari, Iğdır, Kars, Mardin, Siirt and Van. In addition, it won fifty district and eleven town councils.[24] However, prior to the elections, Erdoğan hinted that the government policy of removing the elected mayors and replacing them with district and provincial governors will continue. On 19 August 2019, the HDP co-mayors of Diyarbakır, Mardin and Van municipal councils were removed from their positions and replaced by the provincial governors who were appointed as 'trustees'. Since then, more of the HDP mayors in other municipal and districts councils have been removed by the central government and replaced by a trustee. By 16 November 2019, the co-mayors of twenty-four councils have been removed from their position and it is expected that more HDP-run councils will be taken over by the government-appointed 'trustees'.[25]

The HDP chose not to field candidates in most of western Turkey and encouraged its supporters to back the opposition candidates in an attempt to weaken the AKP's power base. This support proved crucial and enabled the opposition to take back the municipal councils of Istanbul, Ankara, Adana, Antalya and Mersin form the AKP and its nationalist ally MHP. On 7 May 2019, Turkey's Supreme Electoral Council (YSK) decided to repeat the Istanbul mayoral election and the HDP's Kurdish votes have proved decisive again in the outcome of the election held on 23 June 2019. In addition, the HDP supported the opposition candidates, Sabahattin Cevheri and Ahmet Faruk Ünsal of the Saadet Partisi (Felicity Party, SP) in Şanlıurfa and Adıyaman, respectively, and Celal Doğan of the Democratic Left Party (DSP) in Gaziantep, all of whom lost the election but increased the opposition's vote significantly.

Previously, the presidency was a ceremonial post elected by the parliament for a period of seven years. Since 2014, Turkey has been transitioning to a presidential system and held its first presidential election on 10 August 2014. In 2017, the AKP government with the support from the MHP amended the constitution to empower the position of the presidency and change Turkey's political parliamentary system into a presidential system. The constitutional amendment was put to a referendum on 16 April 2017, which narrowly won amidst widespread intimidation and irregularities.[26] Selahattin Demirtaş was the HDP's presidential candidate in both of the elections and the percentage of the vote he obtained in the Kurdish majority provinces broadly corresponds with the percentage the HDP has been obtaining at the parliamentary elections in 2015 and 2018.

The other Kurdish political parties also taking part in the election include the leftist HAK-PAR and the Islamist Hüda-Par, but they have not managed to win sufficient votes in either the parliamentary or the local elections. At the local elections in 2009, HAK-PAR obtained 26,431 votes nationally and this figure increased to 43,863 in the local elections held in 2014. It obtained 58,645 votes or 0.13 per cent of the total votes cast in the June 2015 general election. It increased its votes to 109,722 in the November 2015 general election, but did not participate in the 2018 general election and the 2019 local elections.[27]

The Hüda-Par has also been taking part in the recent elections and the first election it took part in was the 2014 local elections where it managed to get 89,655 votes nationally. At the local elections held in 2014, the Hüda-Par candidates received 12,733 votes in the province of Batman, 1,510 in Bingöl, 1,294 in Bitlis, 34,543 in

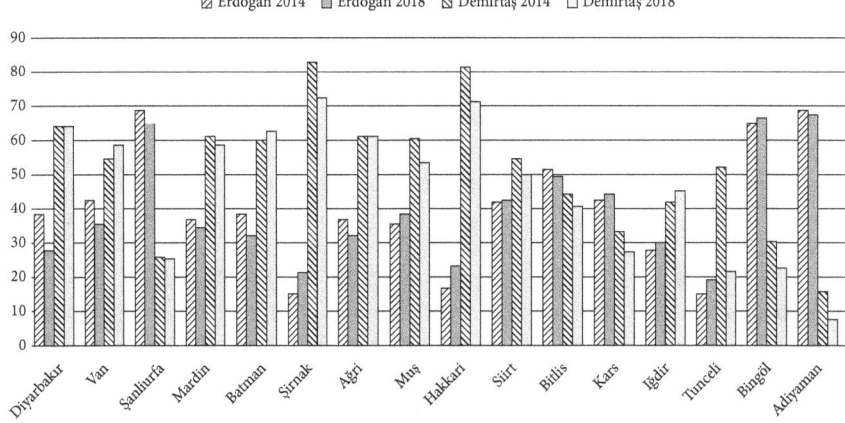

Figure 2.9 Percentage of votes Recep Tayyip Erdoğan and Selahattin Demirtaş obtained in the 2014 and 2018 presidential elections in the Kurdish majority provinces.

Diyarbakır, 6,456 in Mardin, 6,077 in Şanlıurfa and 2,879 in Van.[28] In the June 2015 general election, the party fielded independent candidates in nine provinces. Its leader, Zekeriya Yapıcıoğlu, stood as an independent candidate for the Diyarbakır province and received 22,923 votes but below the number of required votes to win a seat in the parliament. Its candidates for Batman and Bingöl received 14,000 votes and 4,488 votes, respectively. All the other candidates received less than 2 per cent of the votes cast in the provinces they stood.[29] In the November 2015 election, the Hüda-Par withdrew from participating in the elections in favour of the AKP. Hüda-Par continued its cooperation with the AKP and supported the AKP's constitutional amendment in the referendum and presidential candidate in the 2018 presidential election. However, rather than support the AKP in the 2018 general elections, it fielded its own candidates and won 157,324 votes, but it has not managed to win any seats at the parliament. It obtained 4.48 per cent of the vote in Bingöl province, 1.52 per cent in Elazığ province, 2.14 per cent in Mardin province, 1.52 per cent in Muş province, 1.6 per cent in Şanlıurfa province, 1,21 per cent in Siirt province and 2.14 per cent in Şırnak province. Its vote share in the rest of the provinces was less than 1 per cent. Hüda-Par leader, Zekeriya Yapıcıoğlu, was again unsuccessful in his attempt to get elected as an independent candidate for the Diyarbakır province as he received only 35,239 votes, which was nearly 20,000 votes shorter than the winning candidates.[30]

Views and political attitudes of Kurdish representatives

In an interview broadcasted on the state's television network TRT in 2010, the then Prime Minister and current president of Turkey Recep Tayyip Erdoğan claimed that as many as seventy MPs from his party and nearly 25 per cent of the MPs at the parliament were of Kurdish origin.[31] His objective in making such a claim was to emphasize the argument that there are no barriers preventing Kurds from participating in Turkey's social, economic and political life. This is a claim that Erdoğan frequently makes and one that he repeated in a speech he delivered to Kurdish students attending a summer educational camp organized by the Diyanet on 5 August 2017: 'I have Kurdish brothers and sisters in our cabinet, in my party, among our top managers. Mr Bekir [Bozdağ] who just addressed you is a Kurd. He is the government spokesperson at the same time.'[32]

During a panel discussion at the World Economic Forum in Davos and as a response to the rise of sectarianism in the Middle East, Mehmet Şimşek, Turkey's then Deputy Prime Minister, who is an ethnic Kurd from the Batman province, stated: 'Globally, usually Turkey is portrayed as if like we have a quarrel with the Kurds. I am a Kurd myself. Turkey does not have a quarrel with the Kurds, exactly the opposite: the largest Kurdish city in the world is not in the south-east part of Turkey, it is Istanbul. But you cannot divide Turkey according to ethnic lines'.[33] Similar sentiments have been echoed by other Kurdish politicians active within the AKP in the past citing the deep and strong connections between the Kurds and Turks in Turkey. The view has wide support amongst the AKP's electorate and entails some level of recognition of Kurdish identity in Turkey. However, this is limited to private affairs and does not extend to the constitutional recognition of the Kurds in Turkey as a distinct national group. As often uttered by President Erdoğan, the AKP's guiding principles are 'single nation, single flag, single homeland and single state'.[34]

Hence, the AKP's ability or willingness to represent the Kurds needs to be assessed within its overall Kurdish policy. The AKP has many Kurds active within its structures and it is important to note here that throughout the second half of the twentieth century, as discussed in Chapters 3 and 4, right-wing populist parties have been more willing to engage with the Kurds and have drawn strong support from the Kurdish majority provinces. The AKP is often credited with carrying out many of the reforms that have broadened Kurdish rights in Turkey in the past fifteen years. The AKP's policy throughout the 2000s has been one of toleration without formal recognition but it did not abandon its insistence on integrating Kurds through depoliticizing the Kurdish identity. The positive steps that the AKP governments took often combined and were followed by repressive measures. The AKP refused to commit to the full recognition of the Kurds' linguistic rights, such as the provision of education in the Kurdish language. Additionally, by emphasizing commonalities such as the Islamic heritage, the aim of the AKP government's political reforms has been to lessen the appeal of Kurdish nationalism and depoliticize Kurdish identity.[35] Therefore, it is not a coincidence that many Kurds have been employed by the Diyanet and, in fact, the former head of Diyanet, Mehmet Görmez, who was in charge between November 2010 and July 2017, is of Kurdish background. During one of his sermons in 2013 in the Silvan district of Diyarbakır province, he briefly spoke in the Kurdish language.[36] This was a symbolic gesture to prove that the religious authorities were tolerant of the Kurdish language and tacitly allowed its use in sermons in the rural areas where the congregation was entirely Kurdish.[37]

While the AKP government has indicated a willingness to go beyond the 'hegemonic' security discourse in its framing of the Kurdish question, its approach also embeds the security discourse with the elimination of the PKK being a stated objective of all the proposals it devised to end the conflict. It has been keen to express the existence of many ethnic groups in Turkey, but this is often expressed as part of the desire to keep the unitary nation-state model in Turkey. The actions AKP governments took included the detention and prosecution of Kurdish political activists on grounds that they were involved in subversive activities towards Turkey. The cases brought against Kurdish politicians have been described as 'politicide' and serve the eventual aim of eliminating Kurdish representation in Turkey.[38] The AKP's attitude towards the Kurdish political representatives also reveals the limits of its toleration of political pluralism in Turkey. The moderate approach to the management of the Kurdish question the AKP adopted during its early years has been replaced by an authoritarian approach reminiscent of the state policies during the 1990s. Since summer 2015 and in line with the state's long-established security discourse, the AKP government set out to implement a policy to destroy the PKK's presence in the region, leading to the escalation in the conflict with losses on both sides, which is ongoing at the time of writing.

Although there were Kurdish women MPs elected from the AKP in the past, most of the Kurdish elected officials from the AKP tend to be men. Furthermore, in contrast with the success the AKP had in winning seats at the parliament from the Kurdish majority regions, it has not been able to dominate the elections at the district and provincial level. In Diyarbakır, after the 2014 election, only the mayors of the districts of Çermik and Çüngüş were from the AKP and all the remaining fifteen district mayors were from the DBP. For example, there are no women elected from the AKP to the provincial assembly in Diyarbakır and Van provinces. The representatives of the AKP that were interviewed were mainly from an upper-middle-class background and usually involved in business and had a strong connection to a tribe. Similarly, the members of the Istanbul provincial assembly elected from the AKP that were interviewed were involved in business and had connections to a tribe. Most of the members of the provincial assembly from the AKP that were interviewed expressed their full satisfaction with the existing political system in Turkey and stated that they felt that no legal obstacles hindered the representation of Kurds in Turkey. A minority were partly satisfied but expressed the need for amendment of the constitution and empowerment of the local governments.

The CHP has been the main opposition party in Turkey since 2002 when the AKP came to power and had a rather hostile attitude towards the Kurds throughout the 2000s. However, its successive failure in several elections prompted a leadership change with the moderate Kemal Kılıçdaroğlu replacing Deniz Baykal in 2010. Under Kılıçdaroğlu's leadership, the CHP lessened its Turkish nationalist rhetoric and showed more willingness to acknowledge Turkey's ethnocultural diversity. Kurdish human rights activists Sezgin Tanrıkulu and Hüseyin Aygün were elected to the parliament, with the former currently the deputy leader of the party. The CHP has a notable Kurdish support base, particularly among the Alevi Kurds living in the urban centres in Turkey's west. According to the aforementioned KONDA report, an estimated 6 per cent of the CHP voters are either Kurdish or Zaza.[39] The CHP has been generally supportive of the attempts to resolve the conflict peacefully and stressed the need to construct a national consensus to generate policy proposals to resolve the Kurdish question. Other long-serving CHP MPs of Kurdish origin included Hikmet Çetin, who was active in the party from the late 1970s to the late 1990s and served as the Foreign Minister between 1991 and 1994 in the DYP-CHP coalition government. The CHP retains a strong appeal among the older Kurdish Alevi voters and has several other Kurdish MPs but, by and large, these do not openly associate themselves with the Kurds or describe themselves as Kurdish representatives.

The CHP's 2011 and 2015 election manifestos specify numerous democratization proposals such as political pluralism, respect for diversity and the promotion of fundamental rights and freedoms.[40] While concepts such as 'equality' and 'societal peace' find frequent mention in the party's discourse and the speeches its leading figures make, it is not possible to determine the extent of the CHP's willingness to respond to widespread popular demands for equality that Kurds and other groups have. Sezgin Tanrıkulu authored the CHP's Kurdish question report in 2013, which listed numerous democratization measures to resolve the conflict. In an interview with the Cumhuriyet newspaper, Tanrıkulu discussed the CHP's approach to the Kurdish question. He argued: 'Mother tongue is accepted by the CHP as a basic human right. In addition to learning the common language Turkish, it is CHP's priority to remove the obstacles to citizens learning and using their mother tongue.'[41] Tanrıkulu does not describe himself as a representative of the Kurds and when interviewed for this study he stated: 'People think that I would be representing a special ethnic group, but I do not want to push [representation] into a tied identity.' Tanrıkulu's response indicates the secondary character of identity in the question of representation, which is reflective of the ideology of the CHP and its views on the level of recognition that ethnic and cultural groups should enjoy.

When interviewed, a Kurdish representative in Istanbul, formerly a CHP member but an independent member of the provincial assembly, provided a similar reply to Tanrıkulu and did not see himself as a representative of the Kurds. Hence, even if there are people of Kurdish background active within the CHP, they are not very vocal about asserting their Kurdish identity and moreover do not see themselves as representing the Kurds.

Nevertheless, the CHP has maintained an interest in the human rights abuses committed against the Kurdish people, especially during the long curfews that the government declared during 2015–16 in the urban centres in the Kurdish majority regions. The CHP also uses a rights discourse when articulating the demands and concerns of the Kurds and often expresses Kurdish demands for representation as general demands for human rights. This is also reflected in the answers provided by several Kurds elected from the CHP to the provincial assembly in Istanbul who stressed the need for a new constitution that respects the people's rights to freely express themselves. However, they did not discuss their views on the suitability of the political system in Turkey for the representation of the Kurdish demands or whether a new institutional structure in Turkey was needed to enable Kurdish representation.

As discussed previously, the great majority of the HDP voters are Kurds and the majority of the Kurds in Turkey voted for the HDP in 2015. However, the party does not describe itself as an exclusively Kurdish political party and aspires to represent other sections of society in Turkey. Several of its MPs are ethnic Turks, including its former co-chair Figen Yüksekdağ and current co-chair Sezai Temelli. This approach is expressed in the party programme in the following way:

> We are a party for Turkey's working classes, labourers, peasants, tradespeople, pensioners, women, youth, intellectuals, artists, LGBT individuals, the disabled, the oppressed and the exploited of all nations, languages, cultures and faiths who joined forces to reach the goal of moving towards establishing people's democratic power and government.[42]

This diversity is also reflected in the background of the elected representatives of the HDP. Among the HDP representatives, working-class or professional people dominated and few of them were involved in business. Also, a higher number of women were involved in the local level party activities of the DBP. For example, the DBP had twenty-three women members of the Diyarbakır provincial assembly and fifteen women elected to the provincial assembly in Van. A high number of women are elected as mayors at provincial and district levels.

The majority of the HDP's Kurdish MPs were from a Sunni Muslim background. These include the former mufti of Diyarbakır Nimetullah Erdoğmuş who saw himself as a representative of Kurds but emphasized the importance of the Zaza language and saw himself as a representative of the Zazas too. Currently, the HDP has two MPs who are Yazidis, one of whom, the MP for Diyarbakır, Feleknas Uca, argued that in her role she represented the Yazidi community, many of whom had to migrate from Turkey and settle in Europe, mainly Germany. Alevi Kurds are also elected as MPs from the HDP. The majority of the HDP representatives explicitly stated that they represented Kurds in general and also saw themselves as representing Kurdistan as a region. For example, Erdal Ataş, who is the HDP MP for Istanbul, described himself as a Kurd who speaks Zaza and is of Alevi background. He stated he saw himself as a representative of Kurds, Alevis and the region of Kurdistan. Others have expressed that they do not exclusively represent the Kurds and claimed to be representing all other ethnic and religious groups in Turkey who collectively make up the HDP's electorate.

All the HDP and DBP representatives that we interviewed did not think Turkey's institutional framework was suitable for the representation of the Kurdish people. They argued that the problem of Kurdish representation had a constitutional dimension and the fact that the Kurds were not recognized as a distinct national group was a major barrier for Kurdish representation. This was expressed explicitly by the co-leader of the HDP Figen Yüksekdağ who argued that 'the system as a whole is not pluralistic. It doesn't recognize the right of existence for different identities. It leans towards the hegemony of the political elite in Turkey.' She described the existing legal framework as a handicap for democratic representation and pointed out the importance of decentralization of the state and the need of constitutional amendments to make it possible for different identities to be represented. She argued that a new constitution that paves the way to regional self-governance and the foundation of necessary institutions such as local parliaments was needed for the representation of the Kurds. Other MPs expressed similar views and argued that Turkey's existing legal and institutional framework hindered the representation of Kurds and that widespread democratization was needed to enable the representation of not only the Kurds but also people from different ethnic and religious backgrounds who are not represented. HDP MP for Van province Adem Geveri argued that the state needed to officially recognize the Kurds as a nation for their fair political representation.

3

Tribes and political representation

This chapter discusses the tribes' changing role in the political representation of the Kurds in Turkey. It first provides an overview of Kurdish tribes and the role they have been playing in Kurdish political representation in Turkey since 1950. The socio-political developments in the subsequent decades, which have significantly changed their role in Kurdish politics in Turkey, are also discussed. Then, it discusses the results of the survey conducted in the provinces of Diyarbakır, Mardin, Şanlıurfa and Van with tribe members to highlight their dominant political attitudes and behaviour.

It is generally accepted that a significant percentage of Kurds in Turkey belong to a tribe and that tribal bonds continue to play an important role in Kurds' lives. The transformation Kurdish society experienced from the 1960s onwards, as a result of the spread of education and socio-economic modernization, weakened tribes' influence in the region. Also, with the gradual migration from the rural to urban areas since the 1950s onwards and the forced displacement of nearly 4 million Kurds during the conflict in the 1980s and 1990s, has weakened tribes' territorial concentration to further undermine their influence and traditional way of life. Hence, at present, tribes' influence and the strength of tribal bonds show a significant degree of variation across Kurdish populated provinces in Turkey.

Kurdish tribes' influence did not merely exist in the social and economic realm; there was a strong political dimension to their power too. From 1950 onwards, the tribal elite established itself as the dominant Kurdish political actors in Turkey. The centre-right political parties were keen to draw the tribal elite to their ranks to win the Kurdish vote. This, in turn, has enabled the tribal elite to establish themselves as intermediaries between the state and Kurdish population. The patron-client relationship that came into being after 1950 has begun to be challenged by the Kurdish national movement from the mid-1970s onwards. Many of the newly established Kurdish political organizations felt it was necessary to dislodge the power and influence of the tribal elite to advance the Kurdish national cause. In the Kurdish national liberation discourse, which became the dominant discourse among the Kurdish political parties in the 1970s and 1980s, tribes were often depicted as socially backward, oppressive and exploitative groups and the influence of the tribal elite was seen as a major barrier to the Kurds' national liberation and unification. Tribal elite's involvement in Turkey's political system was interpreted by the Kurdish political groups as evidence of their complacency and involvement in the exploitation and oppression of the Kurds in Turkey.

Consequently, the rising power of the Kurdish national movement in Turkey from the 1980s onward led to a reduction in the power and influence of the tribal elite. With the emergence of the pro-Kurdish democratic political movement in Turkey in 1990 and its rise during the past three decades, the dominant role that tribal chiefs have been playing as the political representatives of the Kurds has weakened significantly. This is reflected in the decline of the number of tribal chiefs being elected as MPs or mayors of towns and cities in recent years. However, some tribes have chosen to form a closer alliance with the Kurdish movement while others allied themselves with the state against the Kurdish national movement. From 1985 onwards, some tribes began to take part in the village guard system that was assembled by the state as a pro-state paramilitary force and used in the state's counter-insurgency efforts against the PKK guerrillas. Tribes saw the PKK's rise as a threat to their existence, but it was not only their fear of the PKK that determined their decision to take arms: many tribes were involved in bloody feuds against their local rivals and participated in the village guard system to increase the power parity at a local level to their advantage.

Kurdish tribes and their role in the political representation of the Kurds in Turkey

Tribes and tribal relations is an area receiving considerable academic interest. The pioneering early sociological and anthropological studies conducted by İsmail Beşikci, Martin van Bruinessen and Lale Yalçın-Heckmann have provided detailed descriptions of tribes and the tribal system in the Kurdish society.[1] The subsequent studies on the subject have further elaborated on the role they play in Kurdish politics and society in Turkey.[2] The existing literature has examined tribes as social organizations, the perseverance of tribal bonds and identities and the role tribes play in structuring the social, political and economic relations in Kurdish society. Martin van Bruinessen defines the Kurdish tribe as 'a socio-political and generally also territorial (and therefore economic) unit based on descent and kinship, real or putative, with a characteristic internal structure'.[3]

Tribes contain within themselves smaller units of clans and lineages and the belief that all its members share a common descent is generally held by all tribes but often disputed by scholars. Tribes came into existence because of alliances formed among several clans and lineages in a certain region or, in some cases, by two distinct tribes uniting. This was a process shaped by many local factors, such as the need to share access to land and pastures and the threat caused by rival groups and other tribes. Also, the membership of tribes was subject to fluctuation and change depending on factors such as tribes' ability to provide security and prosperity for their members.[4] Hence, it was common to find tribes ceasing their existence and new ones emerging to replace them. Also, it was common for tribes to be part of larger tribal confederations for political or security reasons, but the membership of a tribal confederation did not mean that tribes had to cease their distinct status or privileges associated with it.

Before the nineteenth century, numerous tribes and tribal confederacies were brought together under the rule of Kurdish emirates, which were the centres of Kurdish power and culture. These included the Bitlis emirate in present-day eastern Turkey, the Botan emirate in present-day south-east Turkey, the Ardalan emirate in present-day north-west Iran and the Baban and Soran emirates in the present-day Kurdistan Region of Iraq. Kurdish emirates became economically prosperous and maintained a significant degree of autonomy. The Bitlis emirate was abolished by the Ottoman Empire in the mid-seventeenth century and the remaining Kurdish emirates were abolished by the Ottoman authorities in the mid-nineteenth century as part of the Empire's administrative centralization reforms, known as the Tanzimat. The abolishment of emirates meant that in the subsequent period, tribes gained more power and influence and gained an opportunity to position themselves as the dominant form of social and political organization within the Kurdish society.[5]

Tribes have a strong association with a specific region and territory and every tribe claims a territory as its own; it is often the case that regions are named after the tribes inhabiting it.[6] The territorial concentration and the claims over land have been a source of rivalry and conflict between different tribes throughout history. However, it must be emphasized that some of the tribes remained nomadic until as late as the early 1980s, migrating between several locations throughout the year. Many others were based in a particular area permanently but maintained a semi-nomadic lifestyle and migrated to different pastures to graze their livestock from early spring to late autumn every year.

It would be a cumbersome task to provide a list of all Kurdish tribes in Turkey.[7] However, the following list can be provided of the well-known tribes: İzol, Bucak, Şeyhanlı, Pinyanişi, Ertuşi, Jirki, Doski, Bruki, Kikan, Metinan and Omeriyan. These are the tribes that managed to survive in the changing socio-economic context and have risen to prominence in the politics of the region during the twentieth century. Some of them have a significant number of members and wield a considerable amount of power. During the past fifty years, almost all the tribes lost connection to some of their members and the fact that they continue to have a high number of members is due to population increase rather than keeping their membership intact. However, some tribes have been more successful at adapting to the changing social realities of the twentieth and twenty-first centuries.[8]

A number of other recent studies have broadened the boundaries of research on tribes by examining the changing nature of tribal ties and affiliations in light of the significant socio-political transformation that the Kurdish majority regions have been experiencing in the past fifty years.[9] The role tribes play in the political representation of the Kurds in Turkey has also been subjected to close scrutiny in this new and developing research stream. These studies have been conducted as graduate and doctoral dissertations and have focused on a particular region or province to examine a number of questions relating to the political implications of the changing tribal relations.

Factors such as the increasing rates of urbanization and the spread of education among the Kurdish population in Turkey, economic development in the region and the rise of the Kurdish national movement have all contributed to the weakening and, in some cases, dissolving of tribal ties and affiliations. Of these factors, the rise of the Kurdish national movement since the 1970s and the conflict during the 1980s and 1990s, which resulted in a significant political mobilization of the Kurds in Turkey, should be emphasized. The past thirty years have witnessed a strengthening of Kurdish political identity among the Kurds in Turkey and a weakening of the tribal identities and ties that came with it. Many of the leading families that were politically active in centre-right parties lost their prominence as the Kurdish national movement gained more power. While this has not deterred the tribal elite from continuing to take part in politics in centre-right parties, some have chosen to change their allegiance to the pro-Kurdish political parties during the past decade.

The role of tribes in Kurdish politics in Turkey

As mentioned, prior to the rise of the Kurdish national movement in Turkey from the 1970s onwards, tribal and religious elite were the most influential and politically active group within the Kurdish society. This began after Turkey held its first competitive election in 1950 and was initiated by the DP, which was keen to consolidate its support base in the Kurdish majority regions. During the 1930s, many Kurdish tribal chiefs and religious leaders were exiled by Kemalists to southern and western Turkey to prevent the recurrence of Kurdish revolts. The DP government allowed their return from exile, which subsequently played an instrumental role in mobilizing the Kurds' electoral support for the DP during the 1950s and other centre-right parties in the later years. With this move, the traditional Kurdish elite became co-opted into centre-right Turkish political circles and a new patron–client relations came into being, which, in some form, continues into the present day.

A common practice employed by the political parties to win the tribal vote was to choose locally influential Kurdish tribal leaders from populous tribes as their parliamentary candidates. This practice enabled tribal leaders to be elected as MPs and was the dominant trend throughout the second half of the twentieth century. In her case study of tribes in the Hakkari province, Lale Yalçın-Heckmann argues: 'The leading families of Hakkari, with their tribal followers, still dominate party politics in Hakkari.'[10] She also discusses in detail the role tribal ties and relations play in local politics, especially in the selection and election of candidates for national parliament or the municipal council. Tribes often cooperated to get a common candidate elected but, on many occasions, cooperation was not possible. For example, in the 1983 national election, the candidate supported by the Pinyanişi tribe in Hakkari did not win, despite serving as the MP for the province, because the rival Ertuşi tribe mobilized behind its own candidate.[11]

The establishment of the YTP in 1961 was a significant historical development for Kurdish representation in Turkey because numerous Kurdish politicians who were former members of the DP were among its ranks and it gained significant support from the Kurds. It managed to obtain 13.73 per cent of the national vote in the 1961 general elections, winning fifty-four seats in the parliament and serving as a junior coalition partner in the government between 1962 and 1965.[12] The party was in charge of six ministries and the Minister of Health, Yusuf Azizoğlu (1917–70) was a Kurd who made various statements to the media about the disparity between the east and the rest of Turkey and the need for more state investment to correct the imbalance.[13] He was a medical doctor from a landholding family in Silvan, Diyarbakır and was active in DP prior to his involvement in the YTP.

Another leading Kurdish political actor active in centre-right politics was Kinyas Kartal (1900–91) who was an MP from the Justice Party (AP) for the Van province between 1965 and 1980 and a leading figure in the Bruki tribal hierarchy. His son, Nadir Kartal, was an MP for the Van province from the centre-right True Path Party (DYP) between 1991 and 1995. His nephew, Remzi Kartal, was also elected an MP in 1991 for the Van Province as part of the pro-Kurdish list under the SHP. The Zeydan family in Hakkari of the Pinyanişi tribe have played an important role in the politics of the Hakkari province over the past fifty years: Ahmet Zeydan was an MP for the CHP during the 1960s and 1970s; Mustafa Zeydan was the mayor of Yüksekova district from 1969 to 1989 and an MP for the DYP during the 1990s and for the AKP between 2002 and 2007; and Rüstem Zeydan was an MP for the AKP between 2007 and 2011.[14] In the 2015 general election, the tribe seem to have changed its allegiance to the HDP with a leading figure in the tribal hierarchy, Abdullah Zeydan, elected as the MP for the Hakkari province from the HDP. However, subsequently, at the 2019 local elections, Teoman Zeydan, the older brother of Abdullah Zeydan, was a candidate for the mayoral election in Yüksekova district for the AKP but he could not win.

The leader of the Şeyhanlı tribe, Ömer Cevheri was elected as a DP MP for the Şanlıurfa province in 1950. In the subsequent years, other members of the Cevheri family have also been influential in the politics of Şanlıurfa province and served as MPs. These include Necmettin Cevheri who served as an MP for the AP from 1963 to 1980 and subsequently for the DYP from 1991 to 2002; and Sabahattin Cevheri who was an independent MP for the Şanlıurfa province between 2002 and 2007 and an MP for the AKP between 2007 and 2011. Another leading figure in the Şeyhanlı tribe, Seyit Eyyüpoğlu, was active in the ANAP and served as an MP for the Şanlıurfa province from 1991 to 1999. In 2007, he was elected as an independent MP but later joined the AKP and in 2011 was re-elected from the AKP.

Similarly, a leading figure in the Kirvar tribe, Abdulrahman Odabaşı, served as an MP for the DP in the Şanlıurfa province between 1957 and 1960. Another leading figure of the tribe, Ahmet Karavar, was elected an MP from the Islamist RP in 1995 and again from the FP in 1999. The chief of the İzol tribe, another influential tribe in the Urfa province, was an MP from Islamist political parties between 1995 and 2011. Mehmet Celal Bucak and Sedat Edip Bucak, leading figures in the Bucak tribe in the Siverek district of Şanlıurfa province, were active in the national politics: the former was an MP for the AP during the 1970s and the latter an MP during the 1990s for the DYP.

Abdulkadir Timurağaoğlu, a leading figure in the Kikan tribe in Mardin, was elected as an MP at the 1977 general election from the National Salvation Party (MSP). He served until 1980 but other members of the family have been active in other Islamist political parties subsequently, such as the FP and the SP in the 1990s and the People's Voice Party (Halkın Sesi Partisi, Has Parti) during the 2010s, including serving as the presidents of the local party branch and standing as candidates in the general elections.[15] Members of the other leading families of the tribe have been elected as MPs in other mainstream political parties, including Mahmut Duyan from the DYP and

Ömer Ertaş from the ANAP in the general elections held on 24 December 1995. Ömer Ertaş was re-elected as an MP from the ANAP in the general elections held on 18 April 1999. Mahmut Duyan was elected as an MP from the CHP in the general elections held on 3 November 2002.[16] The leader of the Delmamikan tribe, Süleyman Çelebi was an MP for the AKP from the Mardin Province between 2007 and 2011.[17] The Ensarioğlu family in Diyarbakır have been active in the centre-right parties during the past three decades. Salim Ensarioğlu was an MP for the DYP and served as a state minister in the mid-1990s. His nephew, Galip Ensarioğlu, has been active in the various employers' associations in Diyarbakır, including being the president of the Diyarbakır Chamber of Commerce and Industry, and he was an MP for the AKP representing the Diyarbakır province between 2011 and 2018.[18]

While Kurds supporting centre-right political parties has been the dominant trend until the 2015 election, it is worth highlighting that many Kurdish political actors have also taken part in the left-wing political parties. The rise of Turkey's left-wing movement during the 1960s and later the Kurdish movement in Turkey from the 1970s onwards further weakened the power of the Kurdish elite and reduced their influence over Kurdish society. A Kurd active in left-wing political parties is Ahmet Türk, who is a tribal leader in the Mardin area and has been active within the CHP between 1974 and 1980, the SHP between 1987 and 1991 and within the HEP and other pro-Kurdish political parties since then serving as an MP between 1991 and 1994 and again between 2007 and 2014. From 2014 until his removal in 2017, he was the co-mayor of the Mardin province. He was re-elected the co-mayor in March 2019 but was again removed from his position and replaced by the governor of Mardin province in August 2019. It is also quite common to find tribes changing their party affiliation frequently because of the changing local and national political dynamics. For example, the Metinan tribe was supporting CHP in the early 2000s but subsequently changed its affiliation to the AKP, with its leader Hatip Durmaz becoming a member of the AKP in 2007.[19]

In addition to their political influence at a national level, it is common that the leading families from the tribal hierarchy maintain significant commercial and political influence in their region and provincial city. Many of the local-level party representatives at district and provincial levels, mayors or other local representatives were also selected from the leading tribal families. This has been one of the main reasons that tribes have continued to exist and in some cases been able to recreate their role to strengthen their power and influence over their members.[20] Through political engagement, the tribal leaders have been able to centralize the power and distribute the political offices accordingly. With the rise of the pro-Kurdish political parties in Turkey and its success at the local elections, tribes have not been as successful in determining the outcomes of the local elections.

The state–tribe relations took a new dimension with the establishment of the village guard system in 1985 as a paramilitary group to fight the PKK. The state began to work with the leading tribal families and offered them concessions and money to persuade them and the members of their tribe to join the village guard system. Formally, the participation in the village guard system was voluntary but those who refused became victims of intimidation and widespread oppression. These ranged from barring the villagers from the use of grazing lands to food embargoes and to coercing people to leave their villages. Initially, tribal leaders signed to become village guards and through the tribal leader people from lower levels of tribal hierarchy were recruited into the scheme. Some of the well-known tribes that were recruited as village guards include the Bucak, İzol and Karakeçili tribes in Urfa, the Ertuşi tribe in Van and Hakkari, and Pinyanişi and Jirki tribes in Hakkari. The concessions included forgiving the crimes committed by the tribal leaders – a good example would be that of the leader of the Jirki tribe in Hakkari, Tahir Adıyaman, being pardoned for several crimes he was charged with or investigated for in exchange of accepting and persuading the members of his tribe to join village guards.[21]

Animosity towards the PKK due to tribal allegiance and issues connected to local tribal rivalries were amongst the reasons tribes chose to become village guards.[22] Participating in the village guard system has been an important source of tribes' income and has been used to enhance their political power and influence in the region. For tribes, the village guard system provided an additional source of income and enhanced their power at a local level to enable them to maintain their influence in the region and amongst their members. Many of the heads of the village guards have also served as district mayors or local heads of various mainstream Turkish political parties.[23] For example, Kamil Atak, who was the head of the village guards in the Cizre district of Şırnak province, was elected as the mayor of Cizre town in the 1994 and 1999 local elections.

The number of village guards has risen steadily since the system came into existence and in 1995 it stood at 62,186.[24] Between 1985 and 2009, a total of 123,476 people served as village guards with a high number still under duty.[25] According to the Ministry of Interior figures, on 31 November 2012, the number of temporary village guards stood at 45,596. In addition, there were 19,413 voluntary village guards in that period.[26] However, the current number of temporary village guards is likely to be higher after the government recruited more in September 2015.[27] The village guard system was spread across the Kurdish majority regions but the biggest concentration has been in the provinces of Batman, Bingöl, Bitlis, Diyarbakır, Hakkari, Mardin, Siirt, Şırnak, Urfa and Van.[28] Between 1985 and early 2014, a total of 1,401 village guards were killed and a further 2,066 were maimed in combat with the PKK guerrillas.[29] During the late 1980s, the PKK carried out numerous attacks against village guards, including against their family members. While the armed clashes between the village guards and the PKK guerrillas have occurred regularly throughout the conflict, on some occasions, the PKK declared amnesties for the village guards to dissuade them from fighting for the state. At times, the PKK took actions not to antagonize village guards and there were informal deals agreed with certain tribes to reduce the tensions.

The HDP's success in incorporating tribes into its structure and organization, especially during the campaign for the 2015 general election, was significantly aided by the transformation in Turkey's Kurdish conflict in the past decade. The most significant aspect of this transformation was the dialogue process involving the leader of the PKK, Abdullah Öcalan, the state officials and a delegation comprising HDP MPs, and it achieved some milestones such as the unilateral ceasefire the PKK declared on 21 March 2013 and the PKK's subsequent promise to pull its guerrilla forces out of Turkey. Also, the reduction in violence during the past fifteen years has made a positive contribution to the reinvigoration of civil life in Kurdish majority areas of Turkey. During the mid-2010s, there was an increasing attempt to incorporate the tribes into the ranks of the pro-Kurdish parties and, consequently, they have nominated several candidates from tribes for the local or the general election. As mentioned above, Abdullah Zeydan of the Pinyanişi tribe was selected as the candidate and was subsequently elected as an MP for the Hakkari province. The HDP has successfully canvassed many other tribes in the region that have been supporting the AKP in the past decade.[30]

Ethno-linguistic groups in Kurdish majority regions

Kurdish majority regions have been historically home to other ethnic and religious groups, but the demographic composition of the region has changed significantly during the early twentieth century. The genocide against Armenians and other Christian minorities in 1915 has significantly decreased the size of their population. In the contemporary period, there are several ethnic groups in Kurdish majority regions with the Arab minority being the main one. The Arab population is mainly concentrated in the provinces of Mardin, Şanlıurfa, Batman and Siirt with smaller communities residing in the provinces of Bitlis, Muş and Şırnak. The population of the Arab minority in Turkey is estimated at around two million but the population of the Arab minority in Kurdish majority regions is estimated at 650,000.[31] The biggest concentration of the Arab population in Kurdish majority regions is in the Şanlıurfa province where an estimated 400,000 Arabs are based. A small population of historic Christian minorities in Kurdish majority regions, such as the Armenian, Chaldean and Assyrian communities, continue to exist but their number has been decreasing throughout the twentieth century and is currently estimated at less than 50,000. There are several Assyrian churches and seminaries that are open and continue their activities. The St Giragos Armenian Church in Diyarbakır was restored and opened to religious service in 2012 and it also frequently organized cultural events until it was heavily damaged in 2016 as a result of the conflict in Diyarbakır's Sur district.

In addition, there are minorities such as the Zazas that are culturally and linguistically close to the Kurds. The population of Zazas is estimated at 1.8 million and around 10 per cent of the Zazas are adherents of the Alevi faith, with the remainder being Sunni Muslims.[32] Most Zazas are integrated into Kurdish society and identify themselves as Kurds.[33] However, in some cases, Zazas have contested being labelled as Kurds and see themselves as a distinct ethnic group. Many Zazas hold important political positions and the HDP represents a cross-section of the Kurdish population in Turkey. There are ethnic Turkish populations residing across the Kurdish majority regions. In some of the regions, these communities constitute a majority or a significant minority and have settled in the region after the Armenian Genocide.

Much like the Kurdish tribes, the Arab population in regions with a Kurdish majority have also been mobilized by the centre-right political parties since the 1950s. Many people of Arab origin have been elected as MPs from the AKP and risen to prominence in national politics. These include Halil Özcan who has been an MP for the Şanlıurfa province since 2011; Yahya Akman who was an MP for Şanlıurfa province between 2002 and 2015; and Yasin Aktay who has been an MP for the Siirt province between 2015 and 2018. In contrast with the centre-right political parties, the pro-Kurdish political parties have not been very successful in mobilizing the Arab minority. They have increased the number of candidates of Arab origin in the recent elections and a well-known public figure and professor of Law at Ankara University, Mithat Sancar, was elected in the Mardin province in the 2015 general elections. The pro-Kurdish political parties have also increased their efforts to increase the political representation of Christian minorities and in the local election held on 30 March 2014, a Syriac woman Februniye Akyol was elected as the co-mayor of Mardin province.[34] A human rights lawyer from the Syriac community, Erol Dora, has been an MP for the pro-Kurdish political parties since 2011 and was re-elected at the general elections held in 2015. Armenian community activist Garo Paylan was elected from the HDP list in Istanbul in the general election held in 2015 and again in the 2018 general election from the Diyarbakır Province.

Political attitudes and engagement of tribes and the tribal population

In this section, I analyse the results of the survey to find out more about the political behaviour and attitudes of people who strongly associate with a Kurdish tribe. In total, seventy Kurdish individuals, all of whom identified themselves as a member of a tribe, completed the survey. Seventeen of the respondents were residing in Diyarbakır, seventeen in Mardin, nineteen in Şanlıurfa and seventeen in Van. A total of 72.5 per cent of the respondents identified themselves as supporters of the HDP and 21.7 per cent as supporters of the AKP. Some 76.6 per cent of the respondents stated that the current institutional set-up in Turkey is not suitable for making their voice heard. Special effort was made to devise a sample that accounts for the diverse nature of the Kurdish tribal structures. However, given the high number of tribes and the differences in terms of the strength of tribal connections, it would be very difficult to produce a representative sample that could be generalizable to the whole tribal population. Twelve of the respondents were between the ages of 18 and 29, fifteen were between the ages of 30 and 40, nineteen were between the ages of 40 and 50, and twenty-four were aged 50 and above. The data gathered during field research together with other available information was used to inquire into the political behaviour and attitudes of tribal Kurds and assess the role tribes play in their political representation.

The analysis of the survey reveals that several actors are identified as representatives of tribe members. Political parties and elected representatives are identified as the main representatives with 32.5 per cent of the respondents choosing a political party, 7.3 per cent an MP and 6.5 per cent local governments as their representative. The tribal and family dimension also plays an important role in political representation with 20.3 per cent identifying the chief of the tribe and a further 8.9 per cent a family connection as their representatives. Some 16.3 per cent see state functionaries as their representatives, 3.3 per cent see clerics and 4.9 per cent other actors. The other actors range from professional associations, cabinet members and non-governmental organizations.

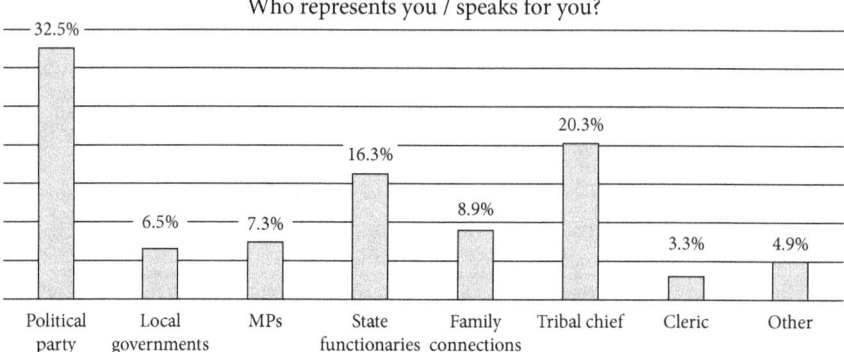

Figure 3.1 Members of Kurdish tribes' political attitudes.

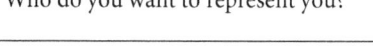

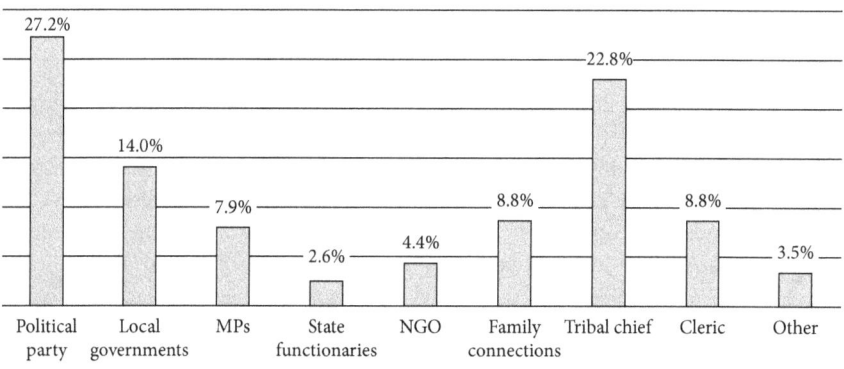

Figure 3.2 Members of Kurdish tribes' desired political representatives.

The above figures roughly correspond with the respondents' desired representatives but there are also significant differences: 27.2 per cent identified a political party, 7.9 per cent an MP, 14 per cent local governments and 2.6 per cent functionaries as their desired representatives. As to their desired representatives, 14 per cent of the respondents answered local governments, which is significantly higher than the actual proportion of respondents who sees them as their representatives. Conversely, a significantly lower proportion of the respondents (2.6 per cent compared to 16.3 per cent) identified state functionaries as their desired representative. The proportion of respondents who identified clerics as their desired representative is also higher than the number who sees them as their representative (8.8 per cent compared to 3.3 per cent).

The results of the survey confirm the strong association tribes have with a political party and the important role political parties and MPs play in their political representation. As mentioned above, a large section of the tribes has been involved in the political parties at local and national levels since the 1950s and it is not surprising to discover that a large section of tribe members see them as their representatives. Tribes' involvement in political parties is strong and certain parties in a province are often associated with certain tribes. In general, tribes often behave in a pragmatic way and make choices to support a political party on the conditions of the time. Generally, tribes tend to remain loyal in their support for a political party if an established political relation continues to serve their interests and especially if they are happy with the selected candidates in a general election. However, there are numerous examples of tribes shifting their support from their preferred political party to a different party because their leader is not selected as a candidate at a general election. A well-known example is tribes in Şanlıurfa province withdrawing their support from the DP in the general election held in 1957 and supporting the CHP instead, which went to win all nine seats for the province. In the general election held in 1954, the DP won eight out of the nine seats in the province.[35] This was at a time when tribes were quite powerful and able to persuade their members to vote as a block. It is doubtful that such a result would be possible in the current period. There are other examples where a tribal leader has stood as an independent candidate after being refused by a political party and was elected as an MP. In general, however, the established patterns of political association between tribes and political parties tend to continue over many years. A significant number of the respondents described themselves as AKP supporters and, alongside the good relations the AKP has with tribes, this is also because of tribal people being quite religious and being drawn to the AKP because of its Islamist outlook. Hence, party ideology and policies also play an important role in determining people's strong affiliation with a political party.

More than two-thirds of the respondents identified themselves as a supporter of the pro-Kurdish HDP. The HDP and other pro-Kurdish political parties before it in the past decade have been able to generate strong support and appeal amongst the Kurds irrespective of their tribal background. Political ideals and demands promoted by the pro-Kurdish political parties' appeal to a wide section of Kurdish society and transcend the tribal bonds and allegiance. In addition, many of the members of the pro-Kurdish political parties and their leaders are drawn from the local population, which further strengthens the bond between the Kurdish population and the pro-Kurdish political parties. With the rise of the pro-Kurdish political parties in Turkish politics, those members of tribes who are mobilized by nationalism have a political party advocating the political values that they can choose to support and are no longer dependent on mainstream Turkish political parties. As discussed above, in recent years, the pro-Kurdish political parties have also increased their efforts to win the support of tribes that do not support them and have struck deals and alliances at a local level.

Several tribal leaders have stood as independent candidates in local and national elections but have not been successful, which points to the decreasing influence and importance of tribes in political representation. It may be also due to divisions within the tribes and because not all members are mobilized by their tribal identity and affiliation. It is now widely accepted that the tribal elite's influence does not translate to delivering block votes to a political party. Despite this, the domination of politics by several tribal families in Kurdish majority regions continues but there are differences between provinces and regions. In Şanlıurfa province, the dominance of tribes is higher and more tribal families are represented in national and local politics. This is because the tribes in Şanlıurfa are more organized and have maintained their central internal structure. In other provinces such as Diyarbakır and Van, tribal dominance is less visible but still present. In the 2011 general election, several tribal leaders such as Ahmet Ersin Bucak and Zülfikar İzol stood as independent parliamentary candidates but neither was elected. It is also increasingly the case that there are divisions in the tribal hierarchy about which party to support and often different parties select candidates from the different leading families of populous tribes to win the electoral backing of tribes. Hence, in addition to the tribal elite losing their ability to influence their members, divisions within tribes or their leading tribal families cause fragmentation in the tribal vote.

Some 20.3 per cent of the respondents consider a tribal chief to be their representative, and a further 8.9 per cent consider it to be family connections. As discussed above, due to the socio-political and economic developments many tribes lost their territorial concentration and the influence over their members. This decline in the influence of tribes is reflected in cases of tribal leaders standing as independent candidates in local and national elections but failing to win. The decreased ability of tribes to get their preferred candidates selected as a candidate in a general election has created a situation where tribes focus on consolidating their power at local, district or neighbourhood levels. In the 2014 local elections, Ali Murat Bucak of the Bucak tribe ran as the candidate of the Democratic Party (DP) for the Siverek district and came second in the race with 28,881 votes.[36] This result is a good reflection on the electoral strength of the Bucak tribes as the DP has failed to establish a notable presence in local and national politics in Turkey since it was established in 2007.

The development of modern communication technologies, socio-economic development and modernization and the rise and influence of the Kurdish national movement has meant that other influences have also been important in determining the voting choices that people make. Because of the politicization of Kurdish identity in Turkey, tribe members have become more aware of the political context and are in a better position to choose a political party that appeals to their views and values. Tribal leaders and elders were very influential over the voting patterns of the tribe members during the 1950s and 1960s, but in recent years their influence has declined considerably. With the spread of education and the increase of urbanization, the strong connection between tribal leaders and political representatives started to weaken. In rural areas, it may be easier to convince tribe members to vote for a particular party due to the denser tribal relations, but this ability is likely to be lower in urban centres. There is also a generational difference between the younger people who can navigate their way through the modern life and have a lesser reliance on the tribal networks and the older generation who need the support of the tribal network to solve their legal or bureaucratic problems and rely more on the tribal network in their day-to-day life.[37] In addition, tribal leaders and elders are involved in dispute resolution and reconciliation between tribal families and individuals, which further enhances the tribe's importance to its members. In some cases, people may identify with a tribe and think that it fulfils an important function in their social lives, but their tribal affiliation is not so strong that it determines their political attitudes or behaviour.

A significant percentage of respondents identified state functionaries as their representatives but the percentage that identified them as their desired representatives is much lower. Though many tribes have forged close relations and ties with the state and state representatives, this relationship is developed out of the necessity rather than choice. Also, tribes do not have strong leverage against the state representatives, and on most occasions the relationship involves demands placed on them which create significant risks to the members and leaders of the tribes. In the case of tribes taking part in the village guard system, for example, it requires armed conflict with the PKK, which led to many losing their lives. The village guard system is also frowned upon by the Kurdish population in general and often leads to social exclusion and stigma.

Conversely, a much larger proportion of the population identified local governments as their desired representative, which is much higher than the proportion of the respondents who sees them as their representative. Some tribes have lost their ability to influence the selection process in the general elections and, as a result, have increasingly targeted the local governments as part of their strategy to remain influential in politics. In addition, the increase in the number of the local councils under the control of the pro-Kurdish political parties has enabled them to build their power base in the local level and the attitudes of the tribes reflect that development.

As to their desired representatives, 4.4 per cent of the respondents identified NGOs, in comparison to 1.6 per cent who see them as their representatives. There has been an increase in the number of civil society groups and associations that operate in the Kurdish majority regions of Turkey. These range from human rights NGOs, women rights groups, groups that target poverty elevation and religiously motivated groups. In the past decade, we have also witnessed the establishment of numerous associations by tribes that function as support networks for their members and offer several other services. These associations offer financial aid to members who need it and a range of other services, such as scholarships for university students, advice and mentoring and social activities to strengthen community relations. Through such associations, tribes continue to maintain a connection with their members who have settled in urban areas in Turkey. Most tribes have their own association and the number of such associations has been increasing in the past decade.

In 2011 in Mardin and the surrounding area, the Kalenderi tribe opened such an association which aimed at increasing the communication among the members of the tribe and also to offer support and financial aid to its members.[38] Community associations for the İzol tribe have been established in a number of provinces during the past twenty years and a range of services are offered to the tribe members, including regular events across Turkey and a newsletter to inform the members about developments and as a means of regular communication.[39] There are many similar associations in Van, Diyarbakır, Batman and other major cities in the region. In addition, there are associations established to represent the village guards. These are organized at district and province levels and nationally under the Confederation of Security Guards and Martyrs' Families.

Concerning the issue of in what types of activities the respondents will involve themselves to be represented by their desired representatives, 49.7 per cent of the respondents prefer political mobilization as a way of participating in the political

What would you do to achieve your desired representation?

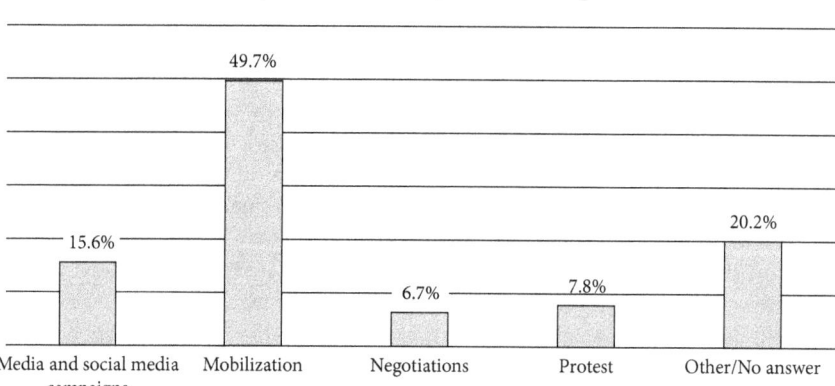

Figure 3.3 Action Kurdish tribe members take to achieve desired representation.

When you feel like no one is representing you, what do you do or feel like you should do?

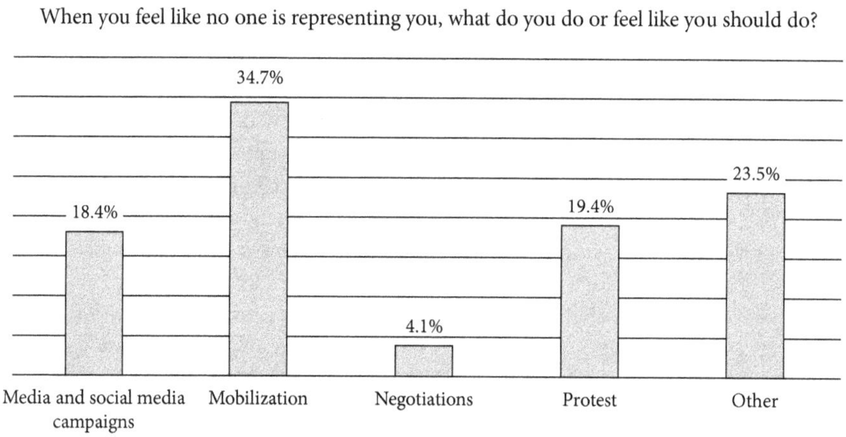

Figure 3.4 Action Kurdish tribe members take when no one is representing them.

processes and choosing the actors they wish to represent them. These activities range from casting votes to canvassing for votes and in some cases standing as a candidate at the elections. As discussed previously, a tribal leader standing as an independent candidate at the general elections has been a tactic frequently used. Due to the decline in the influence of tribes, they often do not get elected. Additionally, tribes have focused their efforts on consolidating their power at a local level and tribal leaders have stood as candidates for the position of the district mayor. Some 15.6 per cent of the respondents expressed a willingness to participate in media and social media campaigns, 6.7 per cent rely on negotiations and 7.8 per cent on protest to make their voice heard. The influential tribal leaders have access to state functionaries and politicians which allows them to negotiate to represent their interests. However, this may not be available to everyone, hence the percentage of people who use other methods to make their voice heard. The respondents who answered 'other' was 20.2 per cent, with the majority of them not specifying what they would do. This may be due to the survey being completed at a time when there was an active and accelerating conflict between the PKK and the state, thus, the respondents may have not expressed an opinion to protect themselves.

Similar responses were given to the question 'When you feel like no one is representing you, what do you do or feel you should do?' Mobilization seems to be the more preferred option with 34.7 per cent expressing support, followed by protest and then media and social media campaigns favoured by 19.4 per cent and 18.4 per cent of the respondents, respectively. Around 18 per cent of the respondents did not express an opinion and the remainder of the respondents stated that they will attempt to represent themselves, including through casting their vote, complaining to representative authorities and engaging with the tribal hierarchy directly. A small percentage of the respondents stated that they would accept the situation and take no action when they felt no one was representing them.

4

Religious groups and political representation

This chapter provides an analysis of the role religious orders, clerics and other religious organizations play in the political representation of Kurds in Turkey. In part one, I provide a discussion on the role of religion in Kurdish politics and society and chart the main trends and developments in the twentieth century and in the early twenty-first century. I also unpack the main developments via a discussion of the types of political activities that Islamist groups and movements foster among the Kurds in Turkey and highlight important aspects of the Islamist-Kurdish public political debate. In part two, I discuss the results of the survey conducted to further explore the religion–politics relationship and highlight the way it affects people's political participation and representation.

Islam had a strong influence in Kurdish society throughout the twentieth century and its social influence had strong political dimensions. From 1950 onwards, the Kurdish religious elite began to take part in Turkey's centre-right political parties and played a leading role in these parties' attempts to mobilize Kurdish voters. The Sufi religious orders (*tariqas*) and individual clerics have been instrumental in the right-wing political parties' increasing their support base in Kurdish majority regions in Turkey. However, as a corollary to the spread of education and secularization of society in Turkey in the past fifty years, Islam's appeal and influence in Kurdish society have been declining.[1] This process has weakened Islam's appeal and influence, but Islamic identity has demonstrated a strong resilience against the modernizing forces and secular political ideologies. In the recent past, a significant number of Kurds have been mobilized by Islamist political parties, such as the RP during the 1990s and the AKP since the early 2000s. Islam's influence at the societal level in the Kurdish majority region is highly visible and a large section of Kurds continue to remain devout and practising Muslims. The fact that positions of religious authority continue to be held in high esteem among Kurds is indicative of Islam's continual influence.

With the rise of the Kurdish national movement in Turkey, the power of the religious-political actors that have been traditionally representing the Kurds has been declining in the past three decades. Currently, the Kurdish Islamist political landscape in Turkey is highly complicated with a diverse number of groups and movements active. The Sufi orders, such as the Naqshbandiyya or Qadiriyya, and Islamist groups continue to currently play a significant role in the Kurdish society and politics in Turkey. More specifically, we can identify the Kurdish Islamist political groups and religious orders, their Turkish equivalents and the radical violent Islamist organizations as the main groups and movements that religious Kurds support. Kurdish Islamist religious groups include those that have a predominantly Kurdish outlook, such as the locally organized religious orders and political movements, including the Azadi Movement, Hüda-Par (Free Cause Party) and Democratic Islam Congress (Demokratik İslam Kongresi, DİK). There are also a wide variety of Turkish Islamists groups and movements that were and are active among the Kurds, such as the Gülenist religious network. In addition, radical violent Islamist groups such as Hizbullah and Al-Qaida have also managed to find a following among the Kurds in Turkey. In recent years, ISIS has also managed to find followers among the Kurds, particularly in the Adıyaman and Bingöl provinces, and most of the terror attacks that it carried out in Turkey in 2015 against the pro-Kurdish movement and Turkey's peace network were carried out by its Kurdish recruits.

The role of religion in Kurdish politics and society

Islam has been a source of political and economic power in Kurdish society for a long period of time.[2] Saladin, the much-revered twelfth-century Muslim warrior and founder of the Ayyubid dynasty, was a Kurd and his Kurdish origins are often emphasized by Kurdish Islamists to enhance the claim that the Kurds played a significant role in the spread of Islam and in the development of Islamic civilization. It is quite popular for some Kurdish people to identify themselves as *Sayyid* and trace their origin to Prophet Mohammed to enhance their position in society.[3] The reverence such an association generates shows the importance of Islam among the Kurds and the deep influence it has had on Kurdish culture. Religious scholars have played a key role in the development of Kurdish classical literature and these include poets Melayê Batê, Melayê Cizîrî and Ahmedi Xanî.[4] There are many other religious figures in Kurdish history who contributed to the development of Kurdish culture and the influence of religiously motivated Kurds on Kurdish cultural production continue in the current period.

Several religious figures have played an important role in Kurdish politics, particularly from the second half of the nineteenth century onwards and were involved in Kurdish nationalist rebellions.[5] This came about because of the abolishment of Kurdish emirates in the mid-nineteenth century by the Ottoman state, which created more space for religious leaders in the subsequent decades to become influential and establish themselves as the leading force in Kurdish politics. The well-known Kurdish religious-political leaders include Sheikh Ubeydullah, who led the first Kurdish revolt in 1880–1, and Sheikh Said, who led the first major Kurdish revolt against the newly established Turkish republic in 1925. Both sheikhs were leading figures in the Naqshibandiyya order and had widespread influence among the Kurdish tribes at the time. Ottoman authorities exiled Sheikh Ubeydullah to Mecca where he died in 1883 but his son, Seyyid Abdülkadir, returned to Istanbul after the Young Turk Revolution in 1908 and continued to be active in Kurdish political circles. He was one of the founders of Kürt Teavün ve Terraki Cemiyeti (Kurdish Society for Mutual Aid and Progress) in 1908 and Kürdistan Teali Cemiyeti (Society for the Rise of Kurdistan) in December 1918. The Sheikh Said rebellion was supported by other religious figures and many Kurdish tribes, and after the rebellion was suppressed, Sheikh Said and forty-six of his comrades, including Seyyid Abdülkadir, were executed by hanging in Diyarbakır and other Kurdish cities. In the period following the defeat of the rebellion, Sheikh Said's extended family and many other Kurdish religious dignitaries were exiled to western Turkey, where they remained until 1929. They were then exiled again to western Turkey and remained there between 1934 and 1947.

Historically, the Sufi orders or *tariqas* such as the Naqshibandiyya and Qadiriyya have been very influential in Kurdish society in Turkey.[6] Concerning the role these Sufi orders played in Kurdish society, Martin Van Bruinessen argues:

> Sufi orders have been prominently present in Kurdistan, and the Sufi shaykh is perhaps more representative of Kurdish Islam than the legal expert. Most of the best-known ʻulama in Kurdish history were sufis, and many of these sufis acquired considerable political influence. Various sufi orders were present in Kurdistan at one time or another, but for the past few centuries, the scene has been dominated by the Qadiriyya and the Naqshibandiyya.[7]

Sheikhs and mullahs (*mele* in Kurdish) were the main religious positions in the Kurdish majority regions that have retained their influence in the twentieth century. The religious orders managed many *madrasas* (Islamic educational institutions that provided religious education) in the Kurdish majority regions and built an organizational network around them. There were several Sufi lodges (*dargah* or *tekke*) in which religious teaching was also carried out. For example, the Küfrevi Sufi lodge in Bitlis was a well-known and well-established institution that educated numerous Kurdish religious scholars and sheikhs. However, the organizational form and traditional structures of Kurdish Islam were disturbed by the restrictions placed on religious education during the 1920s and 1930s in Turkey. These restrictions resulted in the dismantlement of Kurdish *madrasas* in the early republican period and meant that the age-old way of training religious scholars and clergy came to an end. While many of the *madrasas* were abolished, some of these institutions managed to survive well into the 1960s and continued to deliver religious education in less formal contexts. These institutions played a significant role in the continuation of Kurdish Islamic traditions and their transmission to the new generations.[8] As a result, Kurdish Islamic practices survived in enduring circumstances and maintained a strong presence, especially in the rural areas of the majority Kurdish regions, where most of the Kurdish population in Turkey lived until the 1980s.

In the contemporary period, some of the individuals who trained in Kurdish *madrasas* as religious scholars have, through their political writings and prose, contributed to Kurdish cultural and political awakening during the 1960s. These include Mehmet Emin Bozarslan who authored important works during the 1960s on the social problems of the Kurds in Turkey and thereby contributed to the public political debates on the Kurdish question taking place in Kurdish society.[9] Another example is the poet Cigerxwîn (Sheikmous Hasan) in Syria who abandoned religion in favour of Marxism and became one of the best-known modern Kurdish poets. Recently, attempts have been made to re-introduce the *madrasa* education in Kurdish majority regions and currently an institution that provides religious education in the Kurdish language to around 300 students is active in Diyarbakır.[10] The establishment is officially described as a venue that provides Qur'an instruction but the education it provides is based on the traditional Kurdish *madrasa* curriculum.

Sufi religious orders were banned in 1925 and the state seized all their property and endowments. The ban was applied strictly during the 1930s and 1940s, but the restrictions were relaxed after 1950 when Turkey became a multiparty electoral democracy.[11] This was because the newly elected AP government was keen to get the backing of the religious masses and the easing of the restrictions served that purpose. Similar recruitment methods to those used for mobilizing the Kurdish tribal elite were followed for recruiting the religious figures:

> The political parties soon discovered that it was impossible to win elections in the Kurdish provinces without the support of shaikhs or powerful chieftains. In exchange for delivering the votes of their followers, the shaikhs could claim various favours from the central, provincial or local government. This in turn helped them to dispense patronage and build up a stronger following.[12]

Such efforts by the political parties integrated sheikhs and other religious figures into the political networks, which was used by the religious elite to further empower themselves in society. From the 1950s onwards, they began to directly represent their constituents and, alongside tribal leaders, established themselves as the main political actors in Kurdish society. The promise of support and distribution of funds have played a key role in enhancing the religious orders' ability to fulfil its patronage role. This system of representation was well entrenched and many of the well-known sheikhs and religious leaders were elected as MPs.

Hence, since the 1950s, many of the religious orders and dignitaries were involved in political parties or at least established relations with them and became incorporated into the existing patron-client relations. Many sheikhs or junior members of sheikh families were active in politics from 1950 onwards. For example, Kasım Küfrevi, who was a member of the family that manages the Küfrevi Sufi lodge, was an MP for the DP from the Ağrı province between 1950 and 1960. He was re-elected in 1965 from the YTP list and again in the 1969 election from the Republican Reliance Party (Cumhuriyetçi Güven Partisi, CGP). Another dominant figure in Kurdish politics was Abdulmelik Fırat, the grandson of Sheikh Said, who served as an MP for the DP between 1957 and 1960 and for the DYP between 1991 and 1995. Muhyettin Mutlu was an MP for the Bitlis province from the ANAP between 1987 and 1991 and Abdulhaluk Mutlu served as an MP for Bitlis between 1995 and 1999, both of whom are members of the Tağiler family who have a strong connection to the Naqshibandiyya order in the town of Norşin, Bitlis province. Another member of a sheikh family, Abdulkerim Zilan, served as an MP for the Siirt province from the CHP between 1973 and 1980 and subsequently as an MP for Batman province from the SHP between 1991 and 1995.

The Gaydalı (also known as İnan or İnan Gaydalı) family has been quite dominant in the politics of Bitlis province and a number of its members served as MPs. The family's origins are traced to a well-known Naqshibandiyya Sheikh Sibgatullah Arvasi who played a significant role in the religious life of the region in the nineteenth century. The family's involvement in politics began when Selahattin İnan Gaydalı was elected as an MP for Bitlis in 1950 from the DP list. He was re-elected on two occasions and remained as an MP until 1960. From the 1970s onwards, his sons began to become involved in politics. His older son, Abidin İnan Gaydalı, was elected an MP for the Bitlis province in the 1969 general election from the Justice Party (AP). He was re-elected in the 1973 general election after the return of civilian rule following the military coup of 1971 and once more in the 1977 general election. Selahattin İnan Gaydalı's younger son, Kamran İnan, was elected as an MP from the ANAP list for Bitlis province at the 1983 election and served until 1999. Between 1999 and 2002, he was elected to parliament from the Van province. Other members of the family who played an active role in the politics of the province include Edip Safter Gaydalı who was an MP between 1991 and 2007 for the ANAP and then between 2002 and 2007 as an independent. The family's involvement in politics continues with the election of Mahmut Celadet Gaydalı as an MP for the province from the HDP list in the 2015 general election. He has been re-elected in the November 2015 and June 2018 general elections.

Religious orders continue to play an important role in the politics of the region. Like the centre-right political parties in the second half of the twentieth century, using the existing tribal and religious networks to win the support of the electorate in the Kurdish majority regions has been utilized effectively by the AKP throughout the past fifteen years. This has strengthened the power and influence of religious orders in Kurdish society but the AKP's approach to providing greater recognition of Kurdish identity seems to have also had an impact on winning the support of the religious orders. However, the AKP's turn towards Turkish nationalism seemed to have pushed some of the Kurdish sheikhs away from it. This has become more prominent especially after its authoritarian turn after the 2011 general election. The AKP's support for the Syrian opposition in the Syrian conflict and negative attitude towards the Kurdish movement in Syria has led to a greater number of Kurdish religious leaders and dignitaries removing their support. For example, in an interview published in the pro-Kurdish *Özgür Gündem* newspaper in Turkey, Seyit Hayrettin Merci, a Kurdish sheikh from the Seyidoğlu branch of the Naqshibandiyya order, openly called for Kurdish Muslims to withdraw their support from the AKP, claiming it supported the jihadist groups, such as the Al-Nusra, which attacked Kurds in Syria.[13]

As discussed above, the Naqshibandiyya and Qadiriyya religious orders have a long history in Kurdish society in Turkey. In their study of the social impact of religious orders in Diyarbakır, Yanmış and Aktaş claim that there are six religious groups that are connected to the Naqshibandiyya and five groups that are connected to the Qadiriyya order in Diyarbakır. Some of these groups comprise of a core membership of thirty to forty people but others have a membership that numbers hundreds.[14] These include the Sultan Şeymus Ezzuli group and the Münir Baba group. One of the biggest Sufi orders is the Haznevi group, which is a part of the Naqshibandiyya order and is organized in all of the Kurdish majority provinces as well as in the main Turkish cities and in Syria. However, it is impossible to provide the number of Kurds who are active in these religious orders as there are no statistics and such networks remain quite secretive. What is certain is that they continue to have a strong appeal in provinces such as

Adıyaman and Bingöl and perform religious ceremonies and offer courses to study the Qur'an. Currently, a well-known Kurdish sheikh belonging to the Naqshibandiyya order is Abdulbaki Erol, who resides in the Menzil village in Adıyaman province.[15] The group is known as Menzilciler and currently operates across many Turkish cities, including Istanbul and Ankara. It has established civil society organizations, including the Semerkand Cultural Centre, educational institutions under the auspices of Biltek Okulları (Biltek Schools), a university, a media network consisting of a TV station, a radio station and a monthly magazine, and also several business enterprises, including a passenger transportation company. The Menzil group has been a staunch supporter of the AKP and has urged its members to vote for it in several elections, including the June 2018 general and presidential elections.[16]

In addition to the Sufi religious orders, some Kurdish religious scholars have risen to prominence in Turkey. Of these, Bediüzzaman Said Nursi needs special emphasis as his ideas have had a deep impact on the revival of Islam in Turkey. Nursi was a religious scholar born in 1877 in Bitlis and is known for authoring the *Risale-i Nur Külliyatı*, which is his interpretation of the Qur'an written between the 1910s and 1950s. He died in 1960 but his ideas have continued to retain their appeal and influenced the creation of several religious orders, including the well-known and influential Gülen Cemaat (Religious Community) and other less influential religious orders, such as the Med-Zehra group, which was led by Sıddık Şeyhanzade until his death in 2017. The Med-Zehra group was formed in and has been active since 1971, and during the 1990s it published a monthly newspaper *Dava* in irregular intervals from 1989 to 1998. The Nûbihar publishing house, which has Kurdish–Islamic inclinations, continues to be active and publishes a magazine by the same name.[17] The group is also organized in the form of community centres in Diyarbakır, Van and Batman and organizes research on Kurdish history, language, literature and religion and regularly holds panels and seminars on these topics. These community centres also run Kurdish language courses.[18] These two publications have been the main outlets for the dissemination of Kurdish Islamist groups inspired by Nursi's ideas. Other religious orders inspired by Nursi include Okuyucular (the Readers), Yazıcılar (the Writers), Zehra group, Maşveret group (also known as Kırkıncılar group, named after its founder cleric Mehmet Kırkıncı (1928–2016), and Yeni Asya group. These groups are collectively described as the Nur Movement (Nurculuk or Nur Cemaati). In contrast with these groups, the Med-Zehra group openly advocates Kurdish rights in Turkey and seeks to develop an Islamic solution to the Kurdish question.

The Islamist discourse has been a source of ideological challenge against Kurdish nationalism and the Kurdish movement in Turkey, and in addition to the Hüda-Par and Hizbullah that I discussed in Chapter 1, this challenge has been provided by other groups, such as the Gülenist network and other Turkish Islamist political groups and organizations. The Gülen network has been expanding its organization network in Kurdish majority regions of Turkey since the late 1980s onwards.[19] Named after Turkish cleric Fethullah Gülen (b. 1941), the Gülenist network consisted 'of autonomous units including associations of workers and businessmen, private schools, and media outlets such as Samanyolu TV, Burç FM, and Zaman daily. The movement established cultural organizations, lobby groups, college student bodies, and hundreds of educational centres in 160 countries around the globe'.[20] Its education activities, including the teaching of Islam and Qur'an, carried out through its widespread network of private schools and educational institutions, such as those that trained students to pass university entrance exams (*dershane*), were used to recruit members and disciples. It also forged ties between the business community in the urban centres and developed regular and frequent outreach activities to build itself a popular base among the Kurds.

As a result, the Gülenist network has spread across the towns and cities in the Kurdish majority region rapidly throughout the 1990s and the rise of the AKP in 2002 has accelerated this process as Gülenists were able to continue their activities in the open and disencumbered by interference from state institutions.[21] In particular, its ability to enhance the career prospects of its disciples was another 'pull' factor that influenced people's decisions to join the Gülenist network. Maintaining good relations with the government enabled the Gülenist network to facilitate the entry of its members into positions at the state bureaucracy, universities, the army and the police force. In addition, the opportunities that being part of a larger and well-organized network afforded persuaded many business people to join the Gülen network. The business network of the Gülenists was organized under TUSKON (Turkish Confederation of Businessmen and Industrialists) that brought together the small and medium businesses close to or owned by Gülenists under one representative organization. It was established in 2005 and remained active until it was closed down in 2016 as part of the government's crackdown on the activities of the Gülenists following the attempted military coup on 15 July 2016.

Another avenue through which the Gülenist network organized was the civil society organization and the charities sector. In fact, the number of charities, associations and civil society organizations has significantly increased in the past decade and this trend was facilitated mainly by the democratization reforms the government introduced after 2004 to meet the EU membership conditions.[22] A number of new civil society organizations were established and used as a means to distribute provisions to the poor and rations during Ramadan and the Feast of Sacrifice (Eid al-Adha). It has become common practice to organize communal dinners in urban centres at the end of the fasting period throughout Ramadan.[23] Such activities have proved useful for Islamist charity organizations to build networks in poor neighbourhoods and mobilize religious Kurds.

Several other lesser-known groups have emerged and operate across the Kurdish majority regions of Turkey. Of these, Şahımerdan Sarı and his Vasat (Medium) Cemaati have been gaining some attention in recent years. He was born in Adıyaman Province in 1960 and worked as an imam between 1978 and 1995 when he resigned to establish and lead his own religious order. He received a life imprisonment sentence in 1997 for carrying out a terror attack in Gaziantep that targeted a bookstore that sold the Bible and resulted in a death and injury to twenty-five people. He was in prison for ten years and released in 2007, but soon after his group was listed as a terror organization and in 2011 he was declared guilty of founding a terror organization and imprisoned for twelve years. He was captured in the Kurdistan Region of Iraq (KRI) and was imprisoned until February 2018, when he was returned to Turkey. He has consistently claimed that the legal cases against him were politically motivated and orchestrated by Gülenist prosecutors.[24]

An Islamist-leaning human rights organization, the Association for Human Rights and Solidarity for the Oppressed (MAZLUMDER), has also been active in the Kurdish majority regions since the early 1990s. Former HDP MP for Kars province and the current mayor of Kars Municipality Council Ayhan Bilgen was a former chairman of the MAZLUMDER between 2006 and 2007. The current HDP MP for Kocaeli province, Ömer Faruk Gergerlioğlu, also served as the organization's chairman between 2007 and 2009. As well as hosting public events and seminars, it has conducted fact-finding and observation missions to investigate and produce reports of human rights violations that took place in the Kurdish majority regions. As a result, it established itself as an important and respected human rights organization. However, following a disagreement between its members concerning the Kurdish Question in Turkey and the failure to hold its extraordinary general meeting, Ankara Civil Court appointed a trustee to MAZLUMDER and at its general meeting, which took place on 19 March 2017, the decision was taken to close sixteen branches of the organization. The majority of the closed branches were based in the Kurdish majority regions and included the branches in the provinces of Diyarbakır, Şanlıurfa, Van, Muş, Batman, Bitlis, Bingöl, Şırnak and Hakkari.[25] Subsequently, the predominantly Kurdish former members of MAZLUMDER established Rights Initiative (HAK İnsiyatifi) in April 2017 to continue their activities.[26]

Several new religious groups and networks have been established in the Kurdish majority regions and are currently active and contest the AKP, Gülenist network and other Islamist groups as the representative of Kurdish Muslims. These include the Union of Scholars of Kurdistan (Kürdistan Alimler Birliği), the Democratic Islam Congress (DİK) and the Religious Leaders' Assistance and Solidarity Association (Din Alimleri Yardımlaşma ve Dayanışma Derneği, DİAYDER). These are representative organizations that bring together Kurdish religious scholars and practitioners and through their activism challenge the dominance of religion by the state. They have been opposing the dominance of mainstream Turkish Islamist organizations in Kurdish society and instead have been trying to revive the influence of traditional forms of Kurdish Islam. For example, on numerous occasions since 2011 and as a form of passive resistance, the DİAYDER performed the Friday prayers in Diyarbakır in open public places. This was popularly described as *Sivil Cuma* and was organized as a protest against the domination and use of religion by the state for its political objectives.

As I have argued elsewhere, from the early 1990s onwards, the PKK was keen to show its acceptance of the religious diversity within the Kurdish society and, in particular, it increasingly showed its willingness to embrace some aspects of Islam.[27] The PKK's appropriation of some elements from Islam into its discourse was a pragmatic move on its part as it coincided with the growth of the Islamist movement in Turkey during the late 1980s and early 1990s. The Islamist Welfare Party (Refah Partisi, RP) managed to generate strong support from the Kurds and increased its votes in the Kurdish regions throughout the 1990s. During the 1995 general election, it managed to win more than thirty MPs from the regions predominantly populated by the Kurds, which established them as the main rival to the pro-Kurdish HADEP. The strength of the RP showed the force of the appeal of Islam and its potential to mobilize the Kurds.[28]

A number of recent studies on the Kurdish conflict in Turkey have examined how the Kurds and Turks' shared religious heritage influenced the conflict, how the level of religiosity in Kurdish society has been affected by the ongoing conflict and the impact religiosity has on support among Kurds for the PKK and its ongoing insurgency.[29] In the discourse of the Islamist actors in Turkey, the origins of Kurdish conflict are often traced to the imposition of a secular Turkish identity by the Kemalist elite and they argue that nationalist antagonisms can be overcome by an appeal to a shared Islamic identity.[30] As I discussed in Chapter 2, during the 2000s, in its ideological contest with the secular Kurdish national movement, the AKP leaders often invoked Kurds' Islamic heritage and presented themselves as the representatives of the religious Kurdish people in Turkey. While appealing to a certain section of Kurdish society, this approach did not completely manage to overcome the ethnic antagonisms and depoliticize Kurdish identity. According to Mehmet Gurses, the AKP's appeal to Islam could not succeed in uniting the Kurds and Turks for the following four reasons: (1) Kurdishness and Kurdish identity played an important role in the lives of religious Kurdish Muslims; (2) the Islamic identity it put forward as the replacement of the secular Turkish identity was not free 'from the heavy dose of nationalism'; (3) rather than being a genuine attempt to resolve the conflict, the AKP's use of Islam as an overarching identity was mainly motivated by the need to diffuse the domestic and external pressure it was under to address the Kurdish demands and rights and consequently it failed to develop a clear policy framework; and (4) the deep social and political cleavages in the Kurdish and Turkish societies in Turkey prevented the development and imposition of an Islamic identity as a supra-identity.[31]

The importance of Kurdishness for the identity of religious Kurdish Muslims shows the level of religiosity in Kurdish society has been declining. The PKK's insurgency had a significant socio-political impact on the lives of Kurds in Turkey, including on their attitudes towards religion. This complex process is summarized neatly by Mehmet Gurses, which is worth quoting at length:

> The three-decades-long armed struggle for greater rights for the Kurds in Turkey has transformed traditional Islamic values predominantly among the Kurds and resulted in redefining Islam's role in Kurdishness. Islam is no longer a substitute for Kurdish identity but rather has been subordinated to secular ethnonationalist demands. War experiences along with secular ideology have created an environment that has given rise to detachment from religious identity and a growing identification with ethnic nationalism.[32]

Attempts to use Islam to undermine the popular support the Kurdish movement has been receiving from the religious Kurds have not been able to ideologically marginalize it. Consequently, since the early 1980s, the PKK has been the dominant actor in Kurdish society in Turkey and the state's instrumentalization of Islam in its policies to 'distance Kurds from the PKK' has not worked as intended.[33] Also, throughout the 2000s and 2010s, the pro-Kurdish political parties support base among the religious sections of Kurdish society increased.[34]

The Kurdish Alevis and Yazidis in Turkey

Although most of the Kurds in Turkey are Sunni Muslims, a significant percentage of the Kurds are Alevis and there is also a smaller Yazidi community. Different estimates of the Alevi population have been provided ranging from 10 per cent to 40 per cent of Turkey's total population and their exact number is unknown. A conservative estimate of the Alevi population in Turkey would cite a figure of between 10 and 12 million. In addition to Kurdish Alevis, which are estimated to constitute 20 per cent of the Alevis in Turkey, Turkish and Arab Alevi communities also exist. Many Kurdish Alevis self-identify as Turkish which creates further difficulties for estimating the Kurdish Alevi population.[35] Because of migration to western Turkey and Europe since the 1960s, the Kurdish Alevi population in the Kurdish majority regions have been decreasing. As part of the restrictions placed on religious activity and the practices of religious groups in the early years of the republic, the Alevi worship and learning centres such as dervish lodges were closed. This disrupted the religious organizations and practices of Alevis in the subsequent decades.[36]

The Alevi Kurds tended to be concentrated in provinces with a mixed Turkish and Kurdish population and were often subjected to repression and intimidation throughout the twentieth century. On occasions, this oppression took the form of massacres and pogroms committed by Turkish nationalists and Sunnis against Kurdish Alevi communities, such as the Maras Massacre in December 1978, which resulted in the death of 100 people and many more injured.[37] On 2 July 1993, Alevi intellectuals and community leaders who were in the city of Sivas to attend an Alevi cultural festival were killed after a Turkish nationalist and Sunni fundamentalist mob set fire to the Madımak hotel, where the event was due to be held. The protestors targeted the hotel because Aziz Nesin was amongst the participants, who had caused widespread anger in Turkey for translating Salman Rushdie's *The Satanic Verses* into Turkish.[38] Previously, a more organized and systematic massacre was carried out by the state in Dersim (Tunceli) in 1937–8. There were numerous other smaller-scale attacks against Alevis in western Turkey during the 1970s, 1980s and 1990s.

Several Kurdish Alevis have been active in early Kurdish uprisings and nationalist activities. One of the leaders of Koçgiri rebellion, Nuri Dersimi, had a strong association with Kurdish nationalist organizations. He took part in Kurdish resistance in Dersim and, following the defeat of the Kurdish forces, he escaped to the French mandate of Syria and Lebanon and continued his activities there until his death in 1973. The leader of the Dersim resistance, Seyyit Rıza, was executed in 1937. Kurdish Alevis activism continued during the 1960s when the Kurdish national movement began to re-emerge. For example, one of the leading figures of the 1960s Kurdish activism in Turkey, Sait Kırmızıtoprak, was an Alevi Kurd from Dersim. He was one of the leaders of the TKDP and was killed in Iraqi Kurdistan in November 1971.

Starting in the early 1970s, Alevis have been involved in Turkish left-wing organizations in large numbers and the political experience Alevi activists gained in such organizations has been useful for conceptualizing and challenging their experience of oppression in Turkey leading to the politicization of Alevi identity in the 1990s and onwards. This process has taken place in the cities in western Turkey and in Alevi Diaspora communities in Western Europe, where a well-connected Alevi network of community centres and associations has been in existence since the 1990s. These are mainly Alevi place of worship (*cemevi*) which also function as community organizations. Throughout the 1990s, similar organizations have come into existence in Turkey and through such organizations many Alevis have taken part in cultural and religious activities.

A major Alevi cultural organization is the Istanbul-based Republican Education and Culture Centre Foundation (Cumhuriyetçi Eğitim ve Kültür Merkezi Vakfı, Cem Vakfı), which was established by Izzettin Doğan in 1995 and continues to function as a platform for the promotion of Alevi identity and culture. Another organization that is actively involved in the promotion of Alevi rights is the Alevi-Bektaşi Federation (Alevi-Bektaşi Federasonu), which was established in 2002 as a representative organization for the Alevi community centres and associations in Turkey. Another significant Alevi organization is the Pir Sultan Abdal Cultural Centre (Pir Sultan Abdal Kültür Merkezi), which is named after the fifteenth-century Alevi poet and was established in 1988. This organization has grown over the years and currently has over seventy-five branches across Turkey. A new organization with a mainly Kurdish-Alevi membership, the Democratic Alevi Associations (Demokratik Alevi Dernekleri, DAD) has been active in Turkey in the past decade and has around thirty-five centres across Turkey. Several Alevi organizations are active in the diaspora in Europe and have created representative bodies that lobby for Alevi rights in Europe and in Turkey.

Also, many *cemevis* and cultural centres that offer Alevi religious service were opened in Turkey and in western Europe since the late 1980s. Festivals and other cultural activities have further strengthened the ties among Alevi communities and have helped stabilize the meaning of Alevism in modern times. As a result, a vibrant Alevi political and cultural community has emerged and mobilized around the recognition of Alevi religious and cultural identity and the removal of all restrictions placed on Alevi identity. Media and television broadcasts by Alevi groups have become a part of the repertoire of Alevi mobilizations in the past decade and strengthened the sense of Alevi identity.[39] In recent years, in addition to channels that cater for the Turkish Alevi community, such as Cem TV and Yol TV, a new channel, TV10, that caters for the Kurdish Alevi community, was established in Istanbul in 2011. Its broadcasts could be watched in Turkey and Europe via satellite and it regularly broadcasted in the Kurmanji and Zazaki dialects of the Kurdish language. Since 2016, as Turkey's authoritarian turn accelerated, TV10 was closed down by a government legislative decree. A news agency, Pir Haber Ajansi (PİRHA), was established in November 2016 that provides regular news reports on issues affecting the Alevi Kurdish community, and Can TV was established in Germany in May 2018 to continue the mission of TV10.

In 1966, the Unity Party (Birlik Partisi, BP) was established by Alevi political figures and the party won eight seats in the parliament at the 1969 general election. It changed its name in 1973 to the Unity Party of Turkey (Türkiye Birlik Partisi, TBP) and won one seat at the parliament at the general elections held in the same year. In the subsequent years, it did not manage to grow into an established political party and was dissolved in 1981. In recent years, a higher number of political actors have been vying to represent the Alevis in Turkey. Alevis have traditionally supported the CHP and has been supportive of the secular order built in the republican period. During the 1970s, Alevi Kurds voted in large numbers for the CHP. The politicization of Islam and its instrumentalization in politics by the centre-right political parties seems to have played a role in Alevi Kurds' gradual turn towards the CHP during the 1960s and 1970s. During the 1980s and early 1990s, Alevi Kurdish voters mainly supported the Social Democratic Populist Party (SHP) and then, following its re-establishment in 1992, the CHP. In provinces where a significant Kurdish Alevi minority exists such as Erzincan, Kahramanmaraş, Kayseri, Malatya, Tunceli and Sivas, a high percentage of Kurdish Alevi voters still tend to vote for the CHP. The CHP has a notable Kurdish support base also among the Alevi Kurds living in the urban centres in Turkey's west. The rise of political Islam in Turkey has strengthened the Alevi's association with the CHP and the party's defence of secular order has found strong resonance among the Alevis.[40] In fact, the rise of Islamist parties in Turkey has become a key concern for the Alevis who fear that Islamist encroachments will target their way of life and see Turkey's secular order as a protective shield. The CHP retains a strong appeal among Alevi Kurdish voters and the CHP's current leader, Kemal Kılıçdaroğlu, is an Alevi and influences the choices of Alevi Kurdish voters, particularly the older generation.

Many of the organizations and Alevi religious leaders active within the Kurdish Alevi communities have been supporting the HDP in the recent elections. In the June 2015 and November 2015 elections, several Alevi community leaders were elected as MPs in the HDP's list, which has further strengthened the relations between Alevis and the HDP. Also, a range of Alevi demands has been articulated by the HDP and other political parties that represented the pro-Kurdish political movement in Turkey in the 1990s and 2000s.[41]

As mentioned above, the HDP has worked closely with the Alevi community organizations to identify Alevi political representatives for its electoral lists. Several candidates directly nominated by Alevi organizations have been elected to the parliament as MPs under the HDP's list. In 2015 in western Turkey, the HDP had several Alevi community leaders such as Turgut Öker and Ali Kenanoğlu in Istanbul and Müslüm Doğan in Izmir elected as MPs. In addition, several Alevi Kurds were elected such as Alican Ünlü in Tunceli. This trend continued with the 2018 election, with several of the Alevi community leaders being re-elected to the parliament as part of the HDP's list. In addition to Turgut Öker and Ali Kenanoğlu who were re-elected in Istanbul, Alevi rights activist Kemal Bülbül was elected an MP for Antalya province. The analysis of the HDP's voter profile provided by KONDA for the June 2015 election reveals that Alevis constitute 7 per cent of the HDP's voters and 12 per cent of all the Alevis voted for the party.[42] According to the analysis of the 2018 election, 16 per cent of the Alevis voted for the HDP.[43] It is likely that the majority of the HDP's Alevi voters are Kurdish, but due to the difficulties with estimating Alevi Kurdish population it is difficult to know the exact proportion.

The Yazidis are another significant Kurdish-speaking ethnoreligious group. Most of the Yazidis are based in Iraq and there are also significant Yazidi populations in Russia and other former Soviet republics in the Caucasus, particularly in Armenia. Turkey had a sizeable Yazidi community but, throughout the twentieth century, the population of the Yazidis has been decreasing significantly with many migrating to Germany and other Western European countries. Currently, it is estimated that only 3,200 Yazidis remain in Turkey.[44] Despite the decrease in population, the pro-Kurdish political parties have been keen to provide representation to Yazidis, and in the 2015 general election two Yazidi politicians, Feleknas Uca and Ali Atalan, were elected as MPs for the Diyarbakır and Batman provinces, respectively.

Political attitudes and engagement of religious groups, sects and Sufi communities

This section analyses the survey results and inquires deeper into the political behaviour and attitudes of Kurds who are part of religious networks or take part in the activities of religious groups and organizations. In total, seventy-two such Kurdish individuals completed the survey in the autumn of 2016, and of these, seventeen were residing in Diyarbakır, nineteen in Mardin, nineteen in Şanlıurfa and seventeen in Van. The respondents were drawn from diverse educational and occupational backgrounds, and all identified themselves as Sunni Muslims. Extra effort was made to include people belonging to different religious orders, religious organizations and Islamist social movements and different levels of the hierarchy of their respective organization were selected. The sample included people from most of the main religious orders and groups active in the Kurdish majority regions, except the Gülen movement, who – owing to the security situation and the conflict between the Gülenists and the governing AKP since 2013 – could not be reached. Sixteen of the respondents were between the ages of 18 and 29, thirty-two were between the ages of 30 and 40, and twenty-five were aged 40 and above. The data gathered during field research together with other available information is used to inquire into the political behaviour and attitudes of the religious Kurds and assess the role religious orders and groups play in their political representation. Some 53.3 per cent of the respondents identified themselves as supporters of the HDP and 42.2 per cent as supporters of the AKP. The remaining respondents identified themselves as supporters of other Islamist parties such as the Hüda-Par and a small section did not disclose their political affiliation. A total of 72.1 per cent of the respondents stated that the current institutional set-up in Turkey was not suitable for making their voice heard.

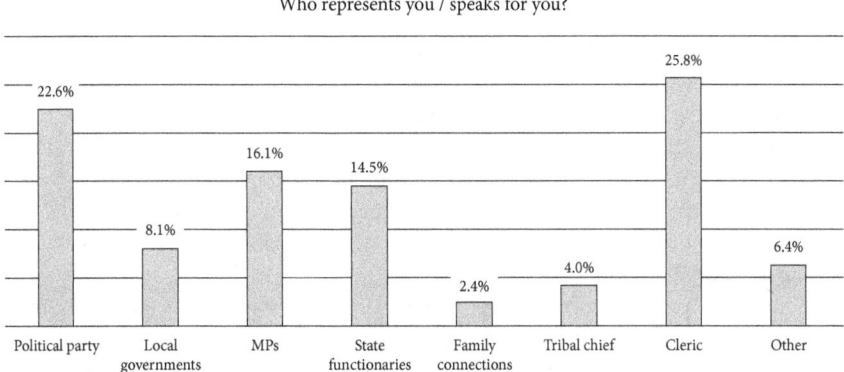

Figure 4.1 Religious Kurds' political representatives.

Like the patterns of representation among tribes, a diverse number of actors are actively involved in the representation of religious Kurds in Turkey. Some 25.8 per cent of the respondents identified a cleric, such as a sheikh or an imam, as their representative. As discussed previously, there is a long list of religious figures in Kurdish majority regions that took part in national politics through the centre-right political parties from the 1950s onwards and such patron–client relationships continue in the modern period. As a result, through their own involvement or their political networks, these religious figures can directly represent their supporters or followers. A further 2.4 per cent identified family connections as their representatives and 4 per cent identified tribal leaders. Although tribal leaders have their own social base in Kurdish society, it is also not uncommon for them to be part of the religious orders and groups. Hence, in some cases, tribal leaders can hold leading positions in religious orders and identifying them as their representative can be due to a religious connection rather than a strictly tribal one.

As to their representatives, 22.6 per cent of the respondents identified a political party and a further 8.1 per cent and 16.1 per cent identified the local governments or MPs as their representatives, respectively. Political parties have increased their efforts to represent the religious voters and increasingly in the past few years appeal to them directly rather than through intermediaries. This is especially the case in areas where the religious orders are not very strong. The local governments in three of the cities the surveys were carried out were held by the HDP at the time of the completion and in Şanlıurfa it was held by the AKP. The representation of many religious–political actors in the HDP and the AKP is also significant. Even though the pro-Kurdish movement has been quite successful in mobilizing religious Kurds, this has been done partly through the inclusion of popular religious actors and representatives in its ranks. These include Altan Tan who has been an MP for Diyarbakır since 2011 and was previously active in Islamist political parties during the 1990s. Nimettullah Erdoğmuş was elected as an MP from Diyarbakır province in the 2015 general election, and before his election he was the mufti of Diyarbakır between 2011 and 2015. In fact, he has been a cleric all his life and served as the mufti of Elazığ and Kilis before his appointment to Diyarbakır. Other figures popular among the religious voters were also elected as MPs in the 2015 general election, including the academic Kadri Yıldırım and the Mahmut Celadet Gaydalı, who was elected from the Bitlis province and, as discussed above, is from a well-known and established family connected to the Argas sheikhs of the Naqshibandiyya order. The inclusion of these figures in the HDP has further strengthened the relations between the party and the religious voters. The AKP has been using the religious networks as intermediaries to mobilize Kurdish voters, and in the past decade it too established a widespread grassroots party network in the Kurdish majority regions. In addition, it has used numerous civil society organizations and charitable trusts to reach out to a wider section of the Kurdish voters to consolidate its strong position in the Kurdish majority regions.

Some 14.5 per cent of the respondents identified state functionaries as their representatives and the reasons for such a high level is because the imams of the mosques are appointed by the Presidency of Religious Affairs and are thus considered as state employees. These are the main officials that many religious people would engage with frequently and have a strong connection to. In general, however, religious people do not feel very close to the state or state functionaries because, since the declaration of republic in 1923, the state–religion relations in Turkey have not been very cordial and for long periods in its history the Islamist reaction to secularism (*irtica*) has been viewed as a significant security threat to the country's republican regime. In the survey, 6.4 per cent of the respondents failed to identify any actor as their representatives or identified themselves as their own representatives. It is possible that these respondents did not wish to reveal their representative or, if the respondents took part in the activities of the Gülen movement or had links to it, they would be unwilling to express it on grounds that such a disclosure may endanger their safety and security.

As to their desired representative, 40.4 per cent of the respondents identified this as a cleric, which is significantly higher than the percentage of respondents who identified clerics as their actual representatives. Individuals who are part of religious orders, such as sheikhs and imams (*mele* in Kurdish) are grouped together under the label 'cleric'. Religious orders and groups have been quite active in the past thirty years in promoting and developing religious networks in Kurdish society. There has been a further increase in the activities of the religious orders and organizations especially during the AKP rule over the past fifteen years. Organizations linked to Hizbullah, the Gülen movement and the AKP, such as charitable trusts and community networks, have enabled these political actors to reach a large section of Kurdish society. In the past decade, the AKP has been particularly keen to promote and empower religious actors as a counterbalance against the pro-Kurdish movement in Turkey. The Gülen movement has also been highly active in the Kurdish majority regions and through its educational activities has recruited many Kurds. However, as part of the government's crackdown on Gülen activities since 2013 and particularly since July 2016, the operations of the Gülenists network has weakened in Turkey.

The Hüda-Par and other Islamist orders are likely to be the beneficiaries of the crackdown on the Gülenist network and the pro-Kurdish political movement. In the case of the Hüda-Par, it has established a strong network that provides charitable

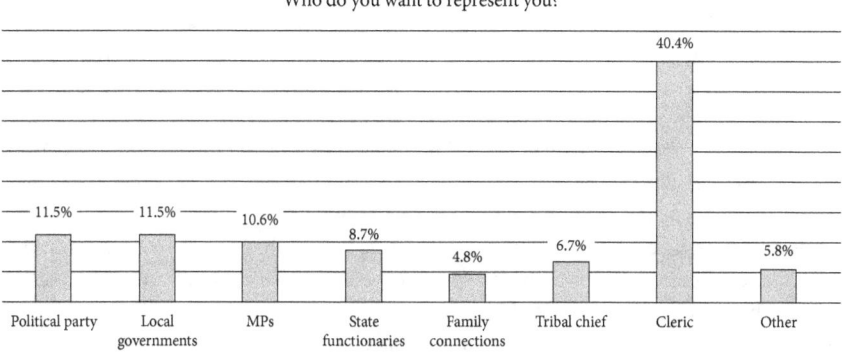

Figure 4.2 Religious Kurds' desired political representatives.

services to its core constituency and to the families of the members who died during Hizbullah's conflict with the PKK in the 1990s. Clerics and other religious dignitaries also put people in touch with larger religious networks which they can use to find jobs, resolve legal issues and benefit from the services. The religious actors do not only operate in the religious sphere but have influence in politics and economic matters and have the ability to put their followers in touch with a wider network. People may be drawn to religious orders or organizations for many different reasons but their ability to provide their members and followers with a social and support network can be identified as one of the main reasons. Members who need financial help or depend on charity, such as food and clothes, can approach religious orders or organizations that either provide help or can put them in touch with other organizations if they cannot provide help themselves.

In addition, religious or spiritual reasons should not be overlooked. Religious orders and organizations enable their followers or members to study the religious texts in greater depth and take part in religious ceremonies and rituals that enhance the religious experience and strengthen Islamic identity.[45] Religious orders play a spiritual function in the lives of their members and provide them with a social network and connections that increase social capital, and a sense of security and identity that helps them overcome the isolation and alienation in a rapidly changing social world.[46] Given the conflict had a huge impact on the social and economic life of the region and that many people suffer the consequences of poverty, networks that strengthen the social ties and support the community can play a significant role in helping the forcibly displaced people to integrate into their new surrounding and rebuild their lives.

Some 33.6 per cent of the respondents identified a political party, local government or MPs as their desired representative, which shows the continuing relevance of political parties in the lives of religious Kurds. However, this is a significant decrease in the percentage of individuals who identified a political party, local government or MPs as their actual representatives. As mentioned above, through intermediaries and incorporating religious–political actors into their structures, the HDP has been quite successful in representing the religious sections of the Kurdish population. In addition, the AKP's Islamist discourse strongly resonates with the religious Kurds and, as a result, they have been able to draw the support of Kurdish voters. A significant decrease in the percentage of respondents who identified state functionaries as their representatives is also recorded. This shows that a significant section of Kurds who strongly identify with Islam prefer a representative that derives their authority or influence from religion.

A large section of the respondents, 34.5 per cent and 38.7 per cent, respectively, identified mobilization as the approach they would take to be represented by their desired representatives or when they feel no one is representing them. There are several organizations that are involved in the political mobilization of religious Kurds. Regular events that attract large crowds such as the Blessed Birth Week have also been important in recent years. There are other smaller instances of mobilization led by organizations and networks close to Hizbullah and the Hüda-Par. A wide range of methods, such as media and social media, are used in their attempt to reach out to a wider audience. It is not only Hizbullah and related organizations that are active in the Kurdish majority regions, but other Kurdish and Turkish Islamic groups and organizations are involved

Religious Groups and Political Representation 89

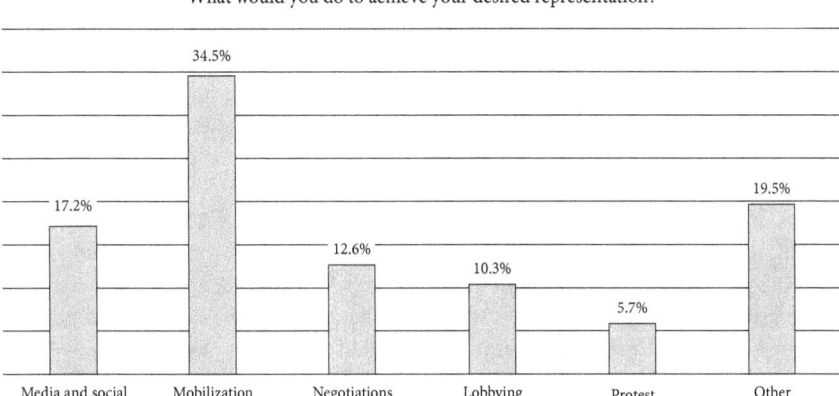

Figure 4.3 Action religious Kurds take to achieve desired representation.

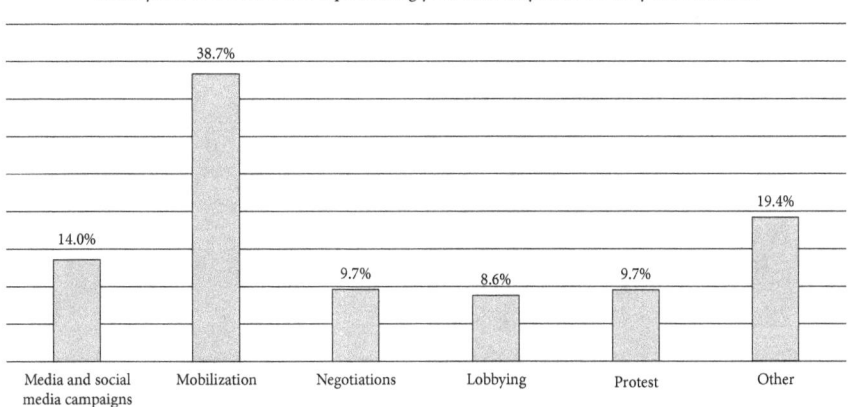

Figure 4.4 Action religious Kurds take when no one is representing them.

in mobilization. As mentioned, Islamic organizations such as DİAYDER and religious orders have been quite active in mobilizing religious Kurds, particularly in Diyarbakır.

Some of the Kurdish Islamic organizations are part of larger Islamist networks and use them to access political actors, government representatives and state officials. These larger networks are activated especially when religious groups and organizations negotiate and lobby to empower or reach out to their desired representation or to make their voice heard. A significant number of the respondents identified protest as an activity in which they would take part to achieve their desired representation or to make their voice heard when no one is representing them. Widespread protests are regular events in the Kurdish majority regions of Turkey and these are organized by the Islamist as well as the pro-Kurdish movement. A significant section of the respondents rely on the media and social media to make their voice heard. The survey also revealed that 19.5 per cent of the respondents rely on other methods to be represented by their desired representatives or when they feel they are unrepresented. A significant section of the respondents stated that they will do something else in order to achieve their desired representatives or when they feel they are not represented. Of these, a small section answered 'nothing' and 'peaceful protests', and a large section stated that they would pray to Allah when faced with such a situation.

Praying may be considered as a sign of respondents' hopelessness and may imply that they do not have a choice other than divine intervention. However, praying can also be considered a sign of the respondents' strong belief in Islam and their conviction that Islam provides a solution for such situations. A large section of Muslims who practice Islam believe that the rules and guidance offered in the Qur'an or other religious texts are very important and shape the actions they take in the choices and situations they confront. For example, verse 45 of chapter two of the Qur'an (*Al-Baqarah surah*), commands Muslims to pray to Allah when confronted with a difficult situation: 'And seek help through patience and prayer, and indeed, it is difficult except for the humbly submissive [to Allah].'[47] Hence, praying symbolizes an individual's submission to Allah and the respondents' action may be due to their religious practice and belief in Islam rather than a symbol of their hopelessness.

5

The modern classes and political representation

This chapter inquires into the role Kurds from modern social classes play in Kurdish political representation. The data obtained about the representation of Kurdish modern classes from the field research together with other available information is used to inquire into the complex issue of political representation of Kurds belonging to modern socio-economic classes. In part one, I provide an overview of the Kurdish business, middle- and working-class people in Turkey and the types of business activities they engage in. In part two, I analyse the results of the survey conducted with Kurdish business, professional and working classes in Istanbul, Ankara, Diyarbakır and Van and interpret the trends and attitudes that the survey data reveals.

It is quite common to come across Kurds in almost any business sector or profession in Turkey. However, to avoid possible or likely discrimination, individuals may not identify themselves as Kurds or emphasize their Kurdish identity. Also, being active within Kurdish political circles in Turkey brings with it many risks, including job loss and even prosecution, particularly when political tensions in the country are high. Hence, whether due to assimilation or a desire to avoid the possible adverse reactions, many Kurds in Turkey choose not to identify themselves publicly as Kurds, which creates a major difficulty for academic research as it is very difficult to provide numbers or percentages of business, professional or working-class people who are Kurdish. Many people choose to identify as Turks or Muslims for ideological, political and economic reasons. For example, Cüneyd Zapsu, who was a close associate of President Erdoğan, is of part-Kurdish descent but has grown up in Istanbul and does not identify with Kurds even though he does state that he is part-Kurdish. He was involved in the formation of AKP in 2002 and acted in its executive council for many years.[1] Similarly, the famous singer and businessman İbrahim Tatlıses is also of Kurdish descent, but he too underplays his Kurdish heritage. The current leader of the CHP Kemal Kılıçdaroğlu is rumoured to be of Kurdish descent and was born in a Kurdish-Alevi majority province of Tunceli but he publicly denies that he is a Kurd. He has described his ethnic origin as Turcoman several times, but according to his wife, he is of Zaza Kurdish origin.[2] Hence, there are many Kurds who are active in national politics and in business who tend to publicly de-emphasize their Kurdish identity and origin. There have been many Kurdish musicians who have been successful in Turkey and some of the most famous Turkish artists and film directors are Kurdish. For example, the famous singer Ahmet Kaya was a Kurd, as was the world-renowned film director Yılmaz Güney. However, both had to flee Turkey to avoid prosecution or imprisonment in 1999 and 1981, respectively. The conceptual artist Ahmet Güneştekin is also Kurdish and continues to work in Turkey.

While the size of Kurdish business and professional classes has increased over the years, it is impossible to quantify their number or what percentage of the business community is Kurdish. The mechanization of agriculture and expansion of capitalist economic relations into Kurdish majority areas from the 1950s onwards led to an increase in the migration of Kurds to western Turkey. Many settled in cities such as Istanbul and Izmir and became part of the growing working classes there. Also, in the same period, the spread of education and the establishment of more schools in the Kurdish majority areas has increased the number of educated Kurds who have subsequently taken professional positions, such as teachers and civil servants. The Village Institutes that were established in 1940 and were transformed into teacher training schools in 1950 played a major role in this process in the early years. Later, during the early 1960s, there was a significant increase in boarding schools in the Kurdish majority regions, which led to an increase in the number of Kurds receiving an education. Gradually, with the expansion of higher education in Turkey, the number of Kurds receiving university degrees has increased, particularly from the mid-1980s onwards. Consequently, the number of Kurds working in education and health sectors and in the civil service has increased significantly in recent decades.

In addition to a steady stream of Kurdish migration to western Turkey since the 1950s, the conflict between the PKK and the state security forces during the 1980s and 1990s led to the forced displacement of a significant number of Kurds who have subsequently settled in the western and southern cities in Turkey and joined the ranks of the working class. Istanbul has been one of the main recipients of the forcibly displaced people who have settled in the working-class districts of the city with many working in the construction sector and in the textile sweatshops or in other unskilled jobs such as market vendors. There has also been an increase in the number of working-class people in Kurdish majority regions as a result of the conflict and depopulation of the rural regions. Due to insufficient employment opportunities in the Kurdish majority regions, seasonal migration of Kurdish workers is also widespread, with many moving to other areas of Turkey for jobs in agriculture, tourism and construction sectors. Often local and family connections play an important role in this type of temporary migration for work and it is mainly men involved. In the case of the agricultural sector, seasonal migration often involves whole families and occurs mainly during spring and summer seasons.

Overview of the economy of the majority Kurdish provinces of Turkey

Historically, the economy of Kurdish majority provinces in Turkey has been mainly agrarian with small industrial output and mining. These provinces tend to be less developed and poorer, and a quick glance at the key socio-economic indicators reveal the scale of regional inequality.[3] For example, the GDP per capita in Turkey in 1998 was equal to US$3,176 but the figure for the provinces with a Kurdish majority population was far below this level. In Van it was US$1,212 and in Diyarbakır it was US$1,875.[4] In 2014, the GDP per capita in Turkey rose to US$10,404.[5] However, the GDP per capita in the Kurdish majority provinces continues to lag far behind and is between US$3,500 and US$4,000.[6] Also, the unemployment rate in the majority Kurdish eastern and south-eastern provinces is much higher than the national average. According to the Household Labour Force Statistics 2011 published by Turkish Statistical Institute, in 2009, the unemployment rate was 16.6 per cent in the predominantly Kurdish populated eastern region and 17.4 per cent in south-eastern region while the national figure was 14 per cent. Similarly, in 2011, unemployment in Turkey stood at 9.8 per cent but, in the eastern and south-eastern regions, it was at 11.2 per cent and 11.7 per cent, respectively.[7] In 2010, the unemployment rate was 13.5 per cent in the Diyarbakır province and 17.2 per cent in the Van province.[8] In 2013, it rose to 18.7 per cent in Diyarbakır, reaching almost twice the rate of Turkey's average of 9.7 per cent.[9] The situation in other predominantly Kurdish-populated provinces is far worse with a rate of 24 per cent recorded in Mardin, Batman, Şırnak and Siirt.[10]

There are pockets of industrial development in Kurdish majority regions such as in Batman due to the discovery of oil in the 1960s and the subsequent development of the oil industry there. Attempts to develop the region were made in the past but so far it has not managed to resolve the deep-rooted regional inequality. In the 1980s, the Özal government intensified the efforts to develop the Kurdish majority provinces with the commencement of the Southeastern Anatolian Project (GAP) which involved building hydroelectric power plants and dams on the Tigris and Euphrates rivers and a widespread irrigation system. It sought to develop the region's infrastructure, increase the agricultural output and serve as a catalyst for socio-economic development. However, despite some progress, the project is yet to be completed and, more importantly, it is yet to make the expected impact on the region's economic development. This is despite recent efforts to revive the project with an action plan for the period 2008–12 that involved increased government investment to diversify the production and increase output and industrialization in the region.[11]

Throughout the past twenty-five years in Turkey, the share of the agriculture and industry sectors have been in decline while the share of the services sector has been on the rise. In 2011, of the total employed people 25.5 per cent were employed in the agricultural sector, 26.5 per cent were employed in the industry sector and 48.1 per cent in the services sector.[12] There is an over-concentration of employment in Turkey's western regions: in 2009, 32.5 per cent of the employment was based in the north-west corner (Istanbul and the surrounding provinces) and 14.1 per cent in the Aegean region (around Izmir). In contrast, only 3.9 per cent and 6.2 per cent of the employment was based on the majority Kurdish eastern and south-eastern regions, respectively.[13] In the eastern region, 39.6 per cent of the employed people were in the agricultural sector, 18.3 per cent in industry and 42 per cent in the services sector. The corresponding figures for the south-eastern region were 23.3 per cent, 25.7 per cent and 51 per cent while the national average for Turkey was 25.5 per cent, 26.5 per cent and 48.1 per cent, respectively.[14] Being the two main cities in the Kurdish majority region, I now turn my attention to the economic conditions of Diyarbakır and Van.

Diyarbakır's economy continues to be predominantly based on agriculture (industrial meat and cotton production), with small-scale industry and tourism also providing a significant source of income. There are 342 industrial business enterprises registered in the Diyarbakır province employing 8,198 people. Some 27 per cent of the workers employed in the industry are in the area of mining and 18 per cent in food processing.[15] Of the registered industrial business enterprises, 27 per cent are in food processing, 23 per cent in mining, 8 per cent in non-metallic mineral production, 8 per cent in chemicals, 5 per cent in forestry and 4 per cent in textiles. However, only 5 per cent of the workforce is employed in industry. Limestone production is Diyarbakır's main industrial output and there are nineteen companies in total active in limestone extraction, processing and sales.[16] Some of these companies have been in operation over a long period of time but others are new.[17] Over the past decade, there has been a steady increase in the export of goods produced in Diyarbakır. In 2005, the amount of goods Diyarbakır exported totalled US$57 million but this figure increased to US$281 million in 2013.[18] In 2014, the figure stood at US$264 million, with the decline attributed to the regional instability. While there is a significant increase in Diyarbakır's exports, the percentage Diyarbakır contributes to Turkey's total exports remains quite low at 0.2 per cent. Domestic and foreign tourism is a growing activity and it is likely to increase more in future with the newly completed Thermal Village in the district of Çermik.[19]

Similarly, Van's economy is also based predominantly on agriculture with small-scale industrial development. In addition to the economic disruption due to the conflict between 1984 and 1999, the earthquake in 2011 caused further difficulties. However, in recent years economic activity has returned to normal. This is reflected in the significant increase in the number of domestic and foreign tourists visiting Van, which reached 609,257 in 2013 and increased to 847,375 in 2014 and 912,610 in 2015.[20] In 2012, there were 115 industrial business enterprises registered in Van but only 16 per cent of them are classified as industrial. The province's biggest enterprises are the cement factory, which was established in 1969, and the sugar refinery in Erciş; food processing and mining companies are the other significant businesses.[21] The total number of people employed in these business enterprises is 3,026 and 40 per cent of the business enterprises are in food processing (meat and poultry), employing 54 per cent of the industry workforce.[22]

Overall, with the significant decline in violence due to the conflict between the PKK and Turkish army during the past fifteen years, the economy of the Kurdish majority regions has seen growth and diversification. This is reflected in the increase in the number of business enterprises in the past decade, especially in small and medium-sized businesses. At the end of 2014, the total number of business enterprises in Diyarbakır was 7,273 and 4,845 in Van.

However, the sudden escalation of the conflict since July 2015 in the majority Kurdish regions has reversed much of the positive developments of the past fifteen years. Many of the small and medium-sized businesses in Diyarbakır's Sur district have been unable to carry out their operations and, consequently, have temporarily closed down or ceased operations permanently. The conflict in Mardin's Nusaybin district has also had a significant negative effect on the economic activity and

Table 5.1 Types of business enterprise in 2015 in Diyarbakır[23] and Van.[24]

Type of firm	Diyarbakır	Van
Joint stock company	534	356
Limited company	4,544	2,666
Sole proprietor	1,909	1,194
Cooperative	282	158
Other	4	14
Total	7,273	4,388

caused widespread disruption to the transportation of exported goods into the Kurdistan Region of Iraq.

The Kurds in Turkey's economy

Due to the lack of reliable statistics and the high numbers of Kurdish workers and professionals in Turkey, it is very difficult to provide a detailed and accurate description of their jobs and professions. Such an account can only be possible if countrywide surveys are conducted with a high number of people. It is within this background that an account of the Kurdish working class and professionals in Turkey is provided. However, in comparison to the working-class Kurds and those employed in professional occupations, the Kurdish business community is much better known mainly because it is much smaller. In this section, I firstly provide a brief account of the spread of the Kurdish working class and professionals before moving on to discussing the Kurdish business community and the types of business activities they engage in.

As discussed above, the Kurdish majority regions have been underdeveloped throughout the past century which has meant very little industrial development has been taking place in these regions. Factories belonging to the state-controlled tobacco and alcohol beverages company (TEKEL in Turkish) in Adıyaman, Batman, Diyarbakır, Urfa, Muş, Bitlis and Malatya provinces created employment opportunities for the Kurdish working class there. Additionally, several cement factories have been in operation in the Kurdish majority regions which has increased the number of jobs for the working class. Another significant economic enterprise is the Ceylanpınar Agricultural Enterprise, which is publicly owned and managed by the Agricultural Business Enterprise General Directorate (TIGEM in Turkish). However, the overall availability of jobs in the Kurdish majority regions has not been high enough to provide jobs for the growing population and, as a result, from the 1960s onwards, many Kurds migrated to western Turkey in search of better employment opportunities. The number of Kurds in western and southern Turkey significantly increased after the forced displacement of Kurds as part of the state's counter-insurgency measures against the PKK. Therefore, in terms of characteristics, the Kurdish working class in Turkey is quite diverse. There are well-established Kurds employed in skilled and relatively more secure jobs as well as many who are employed in more unstable jobs in informal sectors. Kurds have a strong presence in the services sector, in the construction industry, textiles, shipbuilding and retail and hospitality sectors.

Despite its relatively large population, the percentage of people in paid employment in Turkey is low compared to developed countries. In 2007, only 49 per cent of working-age people were in paid employment. This low participation rate is partly due to the lower percentage of women in employment. In 2014, the labour participation rate for women was 30.3 per cent while it was 71.3 per cent for men.[25] In 2007, there were 22.64 million people in employment in Turkey of which only 22.2 per cent were women. In 2010, the number of employed people in Turkey stood at 22.594 million and in 2011 it rose to 24.11 million of which 61.7 per cent were described as regular employees.[26] The number of people in some kind of employment is likely to be higher than the official figure as there are many unregistered workers in the informal sectors of the economy as well as seasonal workers who are mainly Kurdish and migrate to areas of Turkey to work in agricultural jobs, such as cotton picking in Adana, during the summer. The total number of workers employed in the informal economy is estimated to be 3.5 million.[27] Although it is impossible to provide statistics on the ethnic composition of the workers employed in the informal economy and working in unstable jobs, a high number are thought to be Kurds who have been forcibly displaced to western Turkey and the urban centres in the Kurdish majority regions during the 1990s.[28]

In 2011, the number of employed people in the Kurdish majority eastern and south-eastern regions were 1.02 million and 1.555 million, respectively.[29] The labour participation rate in 2011 in Malatya, Elazığ, Bingöl and Tunceli was 48.1 per cent for the total workforce, 72.1 per cent for men and 25.4 per cent for women. For Van, Muş, Bitlis and Hakkari, the figures were 47.3 per cent for the total workforce, 72.9 per cent for men and 22.9 per cent for women. The labour participation rate in the provinces of Şanlıurfa and Diyarbakır was even lower at 32.8 per cent for the total workforce, 59.6 per cent for men and 7.9 per cent for women. A similar rate was recorded in Mardin, Batman, Şırnak and Siirt provinces: 33.9 per cent for the total workforce, 61.9 per cent for men and 8.2 per cent for women.[30] Similar to the situation of the working classes, it is also very difficult to state with certainty how many Kurds are employed in professional jobs in Turkey. The number of Kurds who are employed in the public sector has increased significantly in the past two decades, especially in the education and health sectors, but despite that, the Kurds are under-represented in the public sector in Turkey. It is difficult to know what percentage of public sector employees are Kurdish.

The Kurdish business community

A US$2 million donation made by the US-based Kurdish businessman Hamdi Ulukaya to help the Kurdish refugees fleeing ISIS assault on Kobani in autumn 2014 generated ample attention to the Kurdish business community.[31] Ulukaya's brand, Chobani Yoghurt, has turned him into a billionaire in less than a decade after he established his business in 2005 following the purchase of an ailing plant with a small business loan.

His experience is unique as far as the success and scale of business operations are concerned. However, there are many other lesser-known successful Kurdish business people who have risen through the ranks to establish themselves in their respective sectors.

Rather than focusing on medium and small businesses, this section will focus on the relatively bigger business enterprises. First, an account of the Kurdish business community in Turkey's west is provided, then I move on to discussing those based in the majority Kurdish provinces. In addition, there is a growing Kurdish business community in European countries and growing ties with Kurdish majority regions in Turkey.[32] Both among the Kurds in western Turkey and among those in the Kurdish majority regions, there is an over-concentration of Kurdish business activity in the construction sector. Many of the Kurdish upper businesses also have significant presence in the tourism sector. Over the past fifty years, the number of Kurdish-owned business enterprises based in western or southern Turkey has been steadily increasing, and almost all the major Kurdish business enterprises are based there. In contrast, the business enterprises in Kurdish majority regions have been established more recently.

Due to the low levels of economic developments in the Kurdish majority region, the Kurdish business community emerged and developed in Turkey's western cities. Additionally, with the increasing economic activity in the Kurdish majority regions during the past fifteen years because of the significant decline in conflict, the number of upper Kurdish business people based in the Kurdish regions has also been increasing. Currently, the Industrialists and Business Peoples Association of Diyarbakır (Disiad) has 107 people registered as members and significant numbers of people have been registered in the Diyarbakır and Van branches of the Independent Industrialists and Businessmen Association (Müsiad).[33] Being a member of the Islamist-leaning Müsiad is likely to provide significant benefits in terms of business networks and connections. There are various other business organizations active in the Kurdish majority provinces.[34] While it is impossible to give an exact figure for the size of the Kurdish business community or the exact scale of their business activities, below I discuss some of the Kurdish owned upper-business enterprises that operate in Turkey to give an overview of the emergence and development of the Kurdish business community in Turkey.

Most of the Kurdish-owned business enterprises started in the construction sector but over the years have diversified into the tourism, manufacturing, energy, logistics, financial and mining sectors. The headquarters of many of the upper-business enterprises are based in Istanbul or Ankara but they carry their operations across Turkey. Yenigün İnşaat (Construction) was established in Istanbul in 1973 and currently conducts business across Turkey and internationally. It also operates within the tourism sector with hotels in western and southern Turkey.[35] İçkale İnşaat was established in Ankara in 1971 by Mehmet İçkale who was a Kurd from Diyarbakır and has substantial business interests in the areas of construction and tourism. Likewise, Ceylan Holding was established in 1960 in Ankara and has been doing business in the areas of construction, tourism, services and finance. Kolin Group also started in the construction sector in 1977 in Ankara but subsequently also moved into the logistics and energy sectors.[36] Toprak Holding is Istanbul-based and was started by Halis Toprak in 1979, who is a Kurd from Lice, Diyarbakır. It started as a construction business and subsequently moved into industry, import–export and tourism. The owners of Süzer Holding (headquartered in Istanbul) are Kurds and they too started in construction and later moved into other sectors. Another example of successful upper-level Kurdish businessman is Şeyhmuz Tatlıcı who was a Kurd from Diyarbakır and has even made the list of richest people in Turkey.[37] He started in construction in 1965 in Istanbul and later diversified into other areas such as mining, tourism and real estate.

Another major conglomerate is Limak Holding, which was established in 1976 and it is currently headquartered in Ankara. It is managed by its founder, Nihat Özdemir, who is a Kurd from Diyarbakır, and his business partner Sezai Bacaksız.[38] The group's primary areas of operation are construction, mining, tourism, energy and the aviation industry. It has been managing the Sabiha Gökçen airport in Istanbul and was involved in the building of Istanbul's new airport, which became operational on 29 October 2018. Its construction operations are international and highly diversified, including roads and infrastructure projects such as airports. Currently, it is involved in the building of several major projects such as the Blaise Diagne International Airport in Dakar, Senegal, the Pristina Airport in Kosovo and in the expansion of Kuwait International Airport.[39] The group also operates in the area of cement production and owns several factories around Turkey. It is involved in the building of several new hydroelectrical power plants across Turkey and also owns numerous hotels in popular Turkish holiday resorts. The group's operations have grown phenomenally in the past decade, and it is known to be very close to the AKP.

The textile sector is another area of business in which the Kurds have a strong presence. Textiles workshops were one of the areas that the Kurdish migrants found work in upon arrival in western Turkey, particularly in Istanbul. The sector experienced a significant boom during the 1980s as the availability of cheap labour and Turkey's export promotion policies provided a suitable environment to increase production. Over the past decade, due to increased competition, the sector has experienced a decline but despite that it remains an important area. At the end of 2013, the textiles and clothing sector employed 1,416,000 people across Turkey and accounted for 18.3 per cent of the country's exports.[40] There are many small and medium business enterprises in the textiles sector that are managed by Kurds and specialize in the production of fabrics and clothes. Many also have wholesale units based mainly in Istanbul's Laleli district, which has become a hub for textile exporters, especially to Russia, Ukraine and other Eastern European countries. Predominantly, their factories and production units are based in cities and towns near Istanbul, such as Çorlu.

The most well-known companies include Balizza Tekstil, Nude Giyim, Porto Tekstil, Kalkan Tekstil, Arya Tekstil, Kılıç Tekstil and Dosso Dossi Tekstil. There are many other lesser-known Kurdish-owned textile companies in Turkey. Many of the well-known companies were established during the 1990s but some date back to the early 1970s. Dosso Dossi Tekstil has expanded its operations in the recent years and currently owns a large hotel in Istanbul's old city as well as organizing the Dosso Dossi Fashion Show that brings textile together companies involved in wholesale and export with their customers. Zar û Zeç Kids is also a Kurdish-owned textile business, which has its headquarters in Laleli and specializes in the production and sale of children's clothing, with Russia and Ukraine being their main markets. Other large Kurdish-owned textiles businesses include Asya Tekstil, which specialize in importing machinery used in the textiles industry. Another Kurdish-owned firm is Roza Tekstil, which was established in 1994 and specializes in the production of zips for a variety of products, and according to the company's own estimates has a 20 per cent market share in Turkey.[41] In addition to the above-mentioned companies, there are many other Kurdish-owned companies based in different regions of Turkey that specialize in the production and sale of other textile products such as socks and towels for the domestic and export markets.

It is important to emphasize that, over the past decade, the size of the upper Kurdish business community has been growing, including in both the cities of Diyarbakır and Van. However, the business enterprises located in the region are mainly newly established. In Diyarbakır, new businesses operating in the production and sale of limestone blocks and other materials have made significant progress, which includes companies such as Dimer and Dibaz. Similarly, several construction firms such as Diyor, Dengiz İnşaat and Tankay İnşaat have been showing strong growth in the past two decades. The biggest business enterprise in Diyarbakır is Ceylan Karavil Group, which has a significant business interest in the construction and retail sectors and currently owns a factory producing plasterboards, and the Ceylan Karavil Shopping Mall just outside Diyarbakır city. Additionally, the number of upper-business enterprises operating in the sector of auto sales and the production of auto parts is also on the rise. Several companies operate in food production, processing and distribution (dairy, poultry, meat and agriculture). Textile firms have also been increasing their operations in Diyarbakır in the past decade.

In Van, the tourism sector has been growing in the past decade. Agriculture remains the main sector with foodstuffs accounting for 40 per cent of the industrial output in the province.[42] Similar to Diyarbakır, food production, processing and distribution companies have been growing in Van in the past decade. Also, several construction firms have been growing their operations, such as Doğu Şirketler Grubu, which started as a construction firm in 1986 but subsequently moved into other areas such as mining, cement and insurance. In May 2016, there were a total of 4,388 business enterprises registered in Van and their combined capital stood at US$1.145 billion (3.377 billion Turkish lira).[43] The number of Kurdish business people has been increasing in other Kurdish majority provinces mainly in the agriculture and construction sectors.

Overall, the Kurdish business community in the provinces with a Kurdish majority population is relatively new but growing. It is dominated by construction, agriculture and food-processing sectors and, in the case of Diyarbakır, mining is also a significant economic activity. Due to the adverse economic conditions caused by years of underdevelopment and the conflict, industrial development has been minimal, and the economic life of the region has been severely disrupted. As a result, the Kurdish business community has not been able to accumulate significant capital to invest and grow their operations. During the past fifteen years, Turkey has witnessed significant economic growth and in recent years the government has increased public investment in the region and established regional development agencies to address and coordinate the investment in the region. The Action Plan for the Southeastern Anatolian Project

(GAP) in 2014 and the 'New Incentive System' (Yeni Teşvik Sistemi) that came into being in 2012 have been used by the government to increase public investment and encourage private investment in the region. The GAP aims mainly to develop and improve the infrastructure and transport links in the region while the incentives provided by the state include tax reductions, allocation of land to business enterprises and investment credit.

Many of the Kurdish business people have cultivated and maintained strong relations with the AKP governments in the hope that such a connection will provide economic benefits for them, and the government has used state investment and economic incentives to gain the support of the Kurdish business community.[44] In fact, many of the Kurdish business people in the majority Kurdish regions support the AKP rather than the pro-Kurdish movement. However, the government's attempts have not been wide enough to revitalize the region's economy and the incentives the region received were lower than western Turkey. In addition, the improving economic ties between the Kurdistan Region of Iraq (KRI) and Turkey have also had a positive impact on the region. However, the AKP's nationalist character is cited as a major barrier to developing stronger ties with the Kurdish business community. This is stated by several Kurdish businessmen who claim that the government has taken a negative attitude to greater integration of the economies of Kurdish provinces in Turkey with that of the KRI. In fact, a view common among the Kurdish business community in the majority Kurdish regions is that the AKP has prevented stronger economic ties to develop between the two Kurdish regions, fearing that it may increase support for Kurdish separatism.[45] Instead, the government has provided support for Turkish firms to export goods to the KRI and bid for infrastructure projects.

Political attitudes and engagement of the modern classes

In this section, I analyse the results of the survey to find out more about the political behaviour and attitudes of the Kurdish business, middle and working classes. I will also highlight the specific conditions that affect the political behaviour and attitudes of different classes. In total, 152 Kurdish individuals completed the survey, and the respondents were drawn from Kurds residing in Ankara (35), Diyarbakır (40), Istanbul (39) and Van (38). The dispersion of Kurdish population and the concentration of economic activity in western parts of the country necessitated that we include Kurds residing in the main cities and economic centres of Turkey as well those that are based in the main cities of the Kurdish majority region. The respondents belonged to one of the five groups (upper business, medium business, professional strata, professional associations and the working classes) with at least seven people selected in each category in each city. Thirty-four of the total number of respondents were women. Thirty-six of the respondents were between the ages of 18 and 29, sixty-two between the ages of 30 and 40, thirty-four between the ages of 40 and 50, and twenty were aged 50 and above.

All but one of the respondents in Ankara had moved there from the Kurdish majority provinces and on average they have resided there for 21.5 years. Respondents from the business community have lived in Ankara the longest, with the number of years resident in Ankara higher than the average. The average time the working class and professional respondents resided in Ankara was considerably lower than the average. In total, five of the respondents from Istanbul were born there and, like the situation in Ankara, the respondents from the business community had lived there the longest, on average for twenty-five years. The average years the respondents in Istanbul had lived there were 18.6 years. Around 65 per cent of people were supporters of the pro-Kurdish movement or other Kurdish political parties/groups. The number of AKP supporters was also significant but they tended to be from the business community. A considerable number of respondents did not reveal their political affiliation. The number of people supportive of the pro-Kurdish movement or other Kurdish political parties was highest amongst the respondents from working-class or professional backgrounds. This is not surprising because HDP has established itself as the representative of the Kurdish people and it performed particularly well in areas of western Turkey where the Kurds are based, particularly in the working-class districts. In Kurdish majority areas, it has been drawing strong support since 1999 at a local level and it significantly increased its support base in Kurdish majority areas in the 2015 elections.

The analysis of the survey reveals that a diverse set of actors, such as political parties, state officials, local governments and non-governmental organizations (NGOs) are involved in the representation of Kurds. This is most evident in the behaviour and attitudes of the business classes, which has maintained ties with the governing AKP as well as the pro-Kurdish political parties. In addition, they have established several civil society organizations to further their interests. The Kurdish business community based in Istanbul and Ankara become part of the existing organizations rather than establishing their own. The upper-business community have the necessary connections to access different political parties and the means to establish and manage organizations. Also, given that the Kurds have been active in Turkish politics from the 1960s onward and have been politically mobilized during the past three decades, it is perhaps unsurprising that there exists a complex Kurdish political and civil society network in Turkey that the Kurdish individuals use to represent themselves and further their interests.

However, almost 90 per cent of the respondents (134 out of 152) see the current institutional set up in Turkey as not suitable for their representation. The demands for institutional reform and decentralization of power in Turkey have strong currents among the Kurds and in recent years the idea of transferring power from central government to local governments has been gaining more centre stage in the public discussion. The importance of political parties for the Kurds' political and public life is also confirmed by the findings of the survey. The percentage of respondents who identified political parties as representative of their interest range from 22.1 per cent in the case of medium business respondents to 39.4 per cent in the case of the upper-business respondents. The corresponding figures for the professional strata, professional associations and the working classes are 33.4 per cent, 32.2 per cent and 33.7 per cent, respectively.

The dynamics involved in business people's engagement with political parties is quite complex and needs further analysis. In the past decade, the Kurdish business community have been getting more powerful and becoming more visible in Kurdish

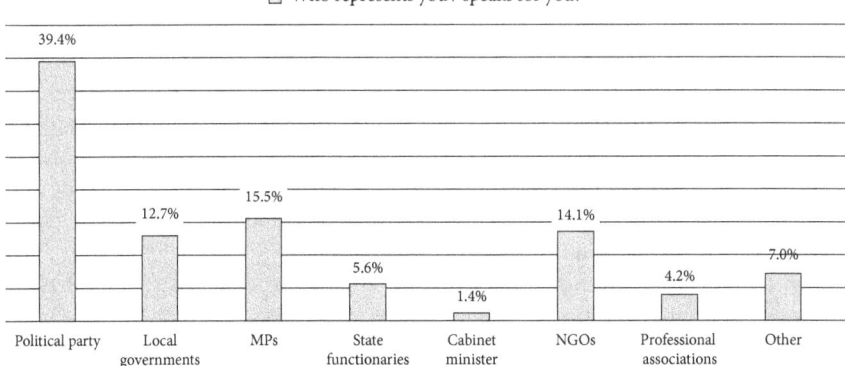

Figure 5.1 Political representatives (upper business).

politics. This has been aided by the increased integration of Turkey into the world economy and trade, and the empowerment of the Kurdish political movement at a local level. However, many of the business enterprises located in the Kurdish majority regions are newly established and achieve a yearly turnover of between between US$9 million and US$130 million (between 25 and 400 million Turkish lira).[46]

On the one hand, the Kurdish business community in majority Kurdish provinces needs to maintain a good relationship with the government to be seen as favourable for state-sanctioned bids and contracts as well as to be able to benefit from state subsidies and incentives. On the other hand, the pro-Kurdish movement has control of the local governments in most of the majority Kurdish provinces which necessitates that the business community have a relationship with the pro-Kurdish parties as well. Also, they may share the demands for greater Kurdish rights that the pro-Kurdish parties advocate but benefit from the neoliberal policies that the AKP government has been pursuing. This situation creates problems for the Kurdish business community as the pro-Kurdish movement and the AKP are rivals and at times their rivalry turns into a tug-of-war. However, due to reasons I discuss below, the business community is not able to fully form strong ties with either of the two political parties in the Kurdish majority regions.[47] A meeting took place between Kurdish businessmen and the leader of the CHP, which shows that the Kurdish business community is willing to engage with other political parties.[48]

Having good relations with the governing party also enables the business community to take part in bigger business networks. For example, the Müsiad is close to the AKP and through such a strong organization the Kurdish business community can represent their interests with the government. Also, through such business organizations, they can develop new business opportunities and connections that can further aid their development. The patron–client relationship that has become a key feature of Turkish politics appears to be continuing under the AKP rule. Several high-profile AKP politicians who have a strong local connection, such as Hüseyin Çelik in Van and Mehmet Mehdi Eker (2002–15) and Galip Ensarioğlu (2011–18) in Diyarbakır, play an instrumental role in drawing the support of the local business community for their party and linking the business community with the political party. Eker was the Minister of Food, Agriculture and Livestock between 2003 and 2015 and Çelik was the Minister of Education between 2003 and 2009.

Also, there is a growing relationship between the state officials and the business community through organizations such as the development agencies. The business community is represented on the board of the Karacadağ Development Agency in Diyarbakır and Eastern Anatolia Development Agency in Van. Being able to benefit from the subsidies and other financial help the state provides can significantly enhance the capacity of businesses to grow and increase their activities. As part of the action plan for the GAP, state incentives and subsidies have further strengthened the Kurdish business community's ties with the AKP.[49] However, AKP's Turkish nationalism has prevented a closer tie and has been cited as the reason behind the discriminatory attitude towards the Kurdish businesses especially when it comes to the relations between Kurdish business community in Turkey and the KRI. The Kurdish business community has complained that they have not been allowed to fully participate in the government-sponsored initiatives to develop trading relations with the KRI.[50]

Over the past two decades, the pro-Kurdish parties' power base has been increasing significantly and they now control the local governments in many of the majority Kurdish regions. Having a stronger local base in the Kurdish majority regions has brought the business community and the pro-Kurdish movement closer and also it means that the business community needs to cultivate good relations with the pro-Kurdish political parties.[51] Additionally, instances of collective mobilization occur regularly in Kurdish majority regions and the business community may seek to influence the developments via liaising with the Kurdish representative organizations such as the Democratic Society Congress (DTK). The business community would be using their influence within the Kurdish representative bodies to prevent action that adversely affects the business community, such as shop closures as a form of protests that most businesses are obliged to participate. However, according to a recent study of the Kurdish economic elite, the left-wing discourse that the Kurdish movement has used in its articulation of the Kurdish demands in Turkey has prevented the mobilization of Kurdish economic elite who tend to favour more market-friendly economic policies.[52]

The normalization that the Kurdish majority regions witnessed during the past fifteen years has created more space for the Kurdish business community. In this time, the Kurdish business community has been developing stronger ties with Turkey-wide business associations and use them to represent their interest. As already mentioned, Müsiad is quite active in the majority of Kurdish regions with offices in Diyarbakır and Van. Because of the reduction in violence and improvement of the economic conditions during the 2000s and the first half of the 2010s, we have seen a rise in the number of the organizations representing the business community during the past decade.

Various business organizations exist in the majority Kurdish regions with the Industrialists and Business People's Association of Diyarbakır (Diyarbakır Sanayici ve İş İnsanları Derneği, Disiad) and Industrialists and Businessmen's Association of the Southeast (Güneydoğu Sanayici ve İş Adamları Derneği, Günsiad) being the prominent ones. Disiad was established in 1996, is currently the biggest association with

107 members and has links to Turkish Industrialists' and Businessmen's Association (Türk Sanayicileri ve İş İnsanları Derneği, Tüsiad). They have been quite active in recent years in campaigns that support the peace dialogue between the PKK and the government.[53] A further example is the Business Women's Association of East and Southeast (Doğu ve Güneydoğu İş Kadınları Derneği, DOGUNKAD), which was established in May 2011. It aims to increase women's employment in Kurdish regions and supports campaigns to achieve that objective. It is Diyarbakır-centred but is a regional organization.[54] In addition, the Diyarbakır Chamber of Commerce and Industry (DATSO) is active and brings the business people of the Diyarbakır province together. In April 2014, an attempt was made to form the Association of Industrialists and Businessmen of Kurdistan (Kürdsiad) and the application was launched with the provincial governor's office in Diyarbakır but, subsequently, the application was refused on the grounds that the name and statutes of the association contained a reference to Kurdistan.[55] These business associations are active in civil society initiatives and seek to influence government policies or political developments at local government level.

In Van province, Van Chamber of Commerce and Industry (Van Ticaret ve Sanayi Odası, VANTSO) is active and one of the main organizations for business people in the province. In addition, a number of other business organizations have been established over the years and are currently active, including the Van Organized Industry Businessmen's Association (Van Organize Sanayicileri İş Adamları Derneği, VOSIAD) and Van Entrepreneurial Young Businessmen's Association (Van Girişimci Genç İşadamları Derneği, VANGGIAD). The Istanbul-based Van Businessmen's Association (Van İşadamları Derneği, VİŞAD) also has a presence in the Van Province.

The relatively peaceful environment between 2000 and 2015 coupled with minor reforms to broaden Kurdish rights in Turkey has all contributed to a more positive discussion regarding the Kurdish question in Turkey. For many Kurdish business people in Turkey, involvment in supporting Kurdish charitable activities is not particularly straightforward and can land them in trouble. Being involved in Kurdish politics had far worse consequences then discrimination for Kurdish businesses during the early 1990s, when the Kurdish business community were targeted as part of the Turkish state's counter-insurgency actions. On 4 November 1993, the then PM Tansu Çiller declared that the government was in possession of the list of Kurdish businessmen who gave support to the PKK and soon after the declaration a number of prominent Kurdish businessmen were abducted and killed by unknown assailants.[56] These include Behcet Cantürk whose dead body was discovered on 15 January 1994 and Savaş Buldan, Hacı Karay and Adnan Yıldırım who were killed on 4 June 1994.[57] These murders generated significant fear amongst the business community and led to many publicly dissociating themselves from any Kurdish-related activism. In 2013, the government passed the '6415 Numbered Law on the Prevention of Terrorism Financing' (6415 Sayılı Terörizmin Finansmanının Önlenmesi Hakkında Kanun), which has again raised tensions within the business community. The law contains widespread measures including freezing company assets and accounts based on reasonable doubt and it is been feared that the state may use the measures to unfairly target Kurdish businesspeople. Hence, the trauma caused by the state actions against the Kurdish businessmen during the 1990s is still very much fresh in the minds and the business community fears that they may yet again become the target of the state's actions.[58]

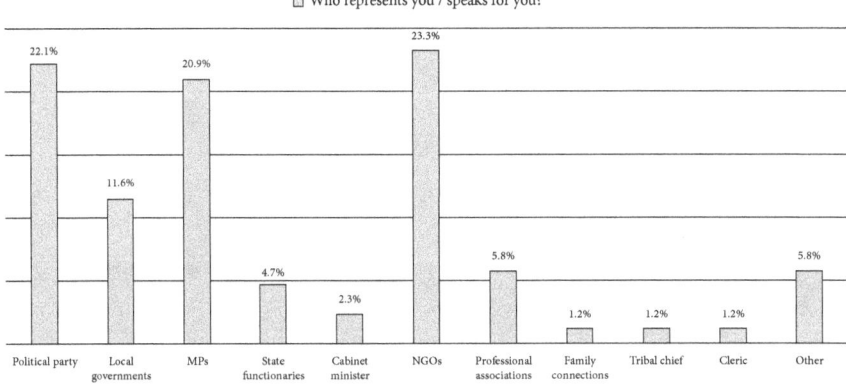

Figure 5.2 Political representatives (medium business).

In comparison with the other groups, a relatively lower level of the medium business respondents see political parties as their representative. For example, the percentage of medium business respondents who see local authorities as their representatives is at a similar level to the population average but the percentage that identified MPs as their representatives is slightly higher than any other group. The fact that businesses rely on local governments for the many services and events taking place at a local level affects their economic welfare which is why upper and medium businesses engage with local governments on a more regular basis. Open support for the Kurdish movement is likely to generate animosity particularly in areas where Kurds form a minority. Turkish nationalist lynching attempts against Kurds and mob attacks on Kurdish business premises have been occurring frequently in western Turkey, which is likely to affect medium businesses more than upper-business enterprises.

However, in terms of political attitudes, there is not much difference between the upper- and medium-level businesses. Both groups tend to prefer negotiations and lobbying when it comes to seeking representation. The medium-level business community is less likely to seek representation through mobilization in contrast to the upper-business community. The upper business tends to use lobbying and negotiation to further their interests and this is because they have access to people and means to do it. The establishment of organizations to represent themselves is also important for lobbying/negotiation practices because they could pool the resources together and have a bigger impact on the political representatives. This is likely to have a local as well as national dimension. At a local level, it involves the pro-Kurdish party representatives and other pro-Kurdish representative bodies such as the DTK. At a national level, they are likely to approach the government ministers or the local MPs of the governing party. It is highly likely that state institutions such as the Development Agencies could be approached for lobbying and negotiations. The medium business community is more likely to take part in protests to further its representation. This is because the medium-business community contains a wider section of Kurdish society who are likely to have political attitudes that are like those prevalent within the Kurdish society in general.

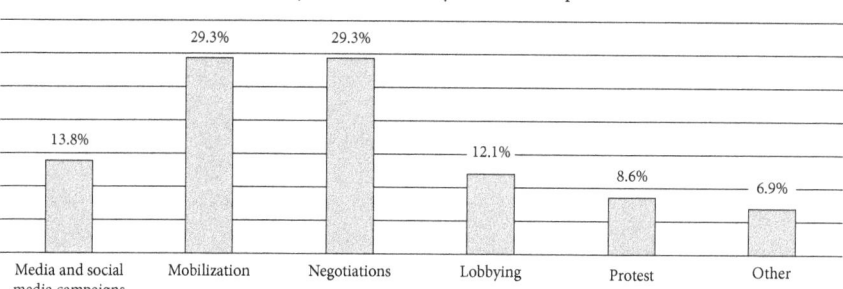

Figure 5.3 Action taken to achieve desired representation (upper business).

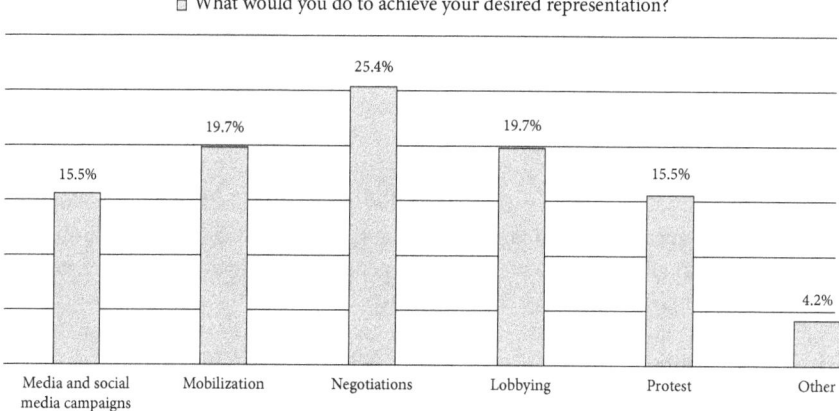

Figure 5.4 Action taken to achieve desired representation (medium business).

Unlike the upper businesses who could influence the political parties more due to the relative power positions, the medium businesses are not able to influence the decisions of the political parties and, as such, feel they are not very responsive to the demands of the medium-level businesses. Thirdly, the medium-sized businesses are more likely to be represented by an NGO that has a narrower sectional interest, such as an employer's organization or the trader's association. This is similar to the figures for the professional strata and professional associations and confirms the view that the middle classes are more likely to engage in NGOs to represent themselves. Also, currently, the dominant view within the Kurdish movement is to resolve the Kurdish question through democratization and decentralization. This view finds considerable acceptance among the population and, consequently, it is not surprising that many Kurds see the local governments as their representatives. More importantly, the number of people who wish they were represented by the local governments is higher than the number who feels they are represented by the local governments. This is further evidence of the popularity of the idea of local-level representation among the Kurds.

During the past fifteen years, people from the professional strata have been increasing their role and influence in the Kurdish movement.[59] The middle-class professional strata have increased their participation in the pro-Kurdish political parties and many of the leading figures of the HDP, such as its former co-president Selahattin Demirtaş and former mayor of Diyarbakır Osman Baydemir, who are both lawyers and were active in the Human Rights Association (IHD) of Diyarbakır. There are the local branches of Turkey-wide civil society organizations, and Kurds use such organizations to pursue their interests. For example, recently the Union of Chambers of Turkish Engineers and Architects (TMMOB) played a significant role in the Kurdish community's challenge of the state's decision to build residential buildings in the Hevsel Gardens area of Diyarbakır, which has been used for many years as agricultural land. TMMOB took the legal challenge against the state's decision and succeeded in preserving the area as agricultural land.[60] The professional organizations such as the Turkish Medical Association (TTB) and the Bar Association of Diyarbakır have been active in raising Kurdish democratic demands and acting against human rights abuses that Kurds suffer in Turkey. Its late president Tahir Elçi was a prominent human rights lawyer who on numerous occasions headed research teams to investigate instances of human rights violations by the state and publish reports that document such abuses.[61] Additionally, individual lawyers connected with the Bar Association of Diyarbakır or the Human Rights Association represent Kurdish individuals in their legal claims and use national as well as the international mechanisms, such as the European Court of Human Rights, in their pursuits. Recently, new representative organizations that have a predominantly Kurdish membership have been established, such as the Mesopotamia Lawyers' Association in the majority Kurdish regions and the Libertarian Lawyers' Association in western Turkey. Hence, a diverse number of civil society organizations in Kurdish majority areas are active in putting forward the demands of the Kurdish society in Turkey.

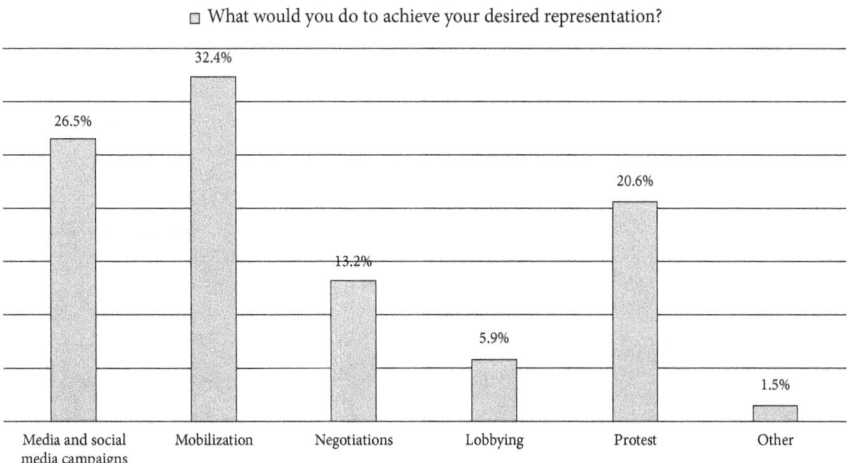

Figure 5.5 Action taken to achieve desired representation (professional strata).

The professional strata are likely to be involved in various forms of mobilization and protest, but they also use the media and social media campaigns, negotiations and lobbying in order to raise their voice. Many of the Kurdish professional strata were active in pro-Kurdish and leftist student circles at universities during the 1990s and 2000s and their political experience during their student days seems to have left a mark on their political attitudes and behaviour.

This tendency to engage in protests and mobilization is more manifest among the working classes in comparison to other social classes. Although a broad set of actors are involved in the representation of Kurds, the degree to which the system is responsive to their demands is an open question. The political activism by the working class tends to take the form of protests and mobilization, which shows that the institutions of the state are not accessible to them. They are also more likely to use media and social media campaigns to raise their voice through organized collective action. The use of social media as a tool for political expression has become more widespread in Turkey especially after the Gezi Park protests and to challenge the narrative the state and pro-government media networks were disseminating. Some of the professional organizations that are active in the majority Kurdish regions have also been active in raising broader democratic demands, which has put them in opposition to the AKP government. The government during the last few years has ignored popular demands and on numerous occasions has resorted to suppressing protests. Hence, the nature of the demands raised by each social class has a bearing on the method used to raise that demand publicly.

In the post-1980s context, trade unions have become less active and influential but some trade unions such as the KESK and Eğitim-Sen have been responsive to the articulation of Kurdish demands in Turkey, particularly education demands. This has led to these trade unions taking a more pro-Kurdish stand and, in some cases, becoming more active in peace activism as well as in raising the demands of Kurds such as mother-tongue education.[62] The visible increase in the activism of trade unions around the Kurdish demands reflects the increase in Kurds' activism and rising influence within the trade unions. Kurds are represented in the trade-union movement including many in the leadership capacity. During the past few years,

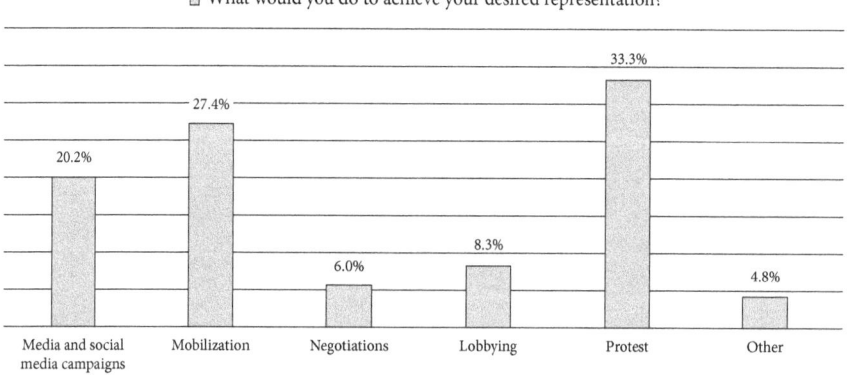

Figure 5.6 Action taken to achieve desired representation (working class).

The Modern Classes and Political Representation

trade unions have come under government pressure for their activities regarding Kurdish rights and many of their members arrested as part of the KCK (The Union of Kurdistan Communities) operations in 2009–12.[63] In early September 2016, Turkish Prime Minister Binali Yıldırım declared that Kurdish teachers will be removed from their positions on suspicion of supporting terror organizations.[64] Subsequently, the government passed a delegated decree that suspended around 11,000 teachers, mainly the members of the Eğitim-Sen trade union and those who took part in strike action on 29 December 2015 to demand, amongst others, the end to state's military operations in the Kurdish majority region that had a devastating effect on many of the region's cities and towns. Although some teachers could resume their duties subsequently, many remain still suspended from their duties. This is just one of the examples that demonstrate how Kurdish professionals use existing representative organizations to raise collective Kurdish demands in Turkey.

The Kurdish business community is quite active and vocal when it comes to making their voices heard when they feel no one is representing them. Among the actions taken, media and social media campaigns seem to be their preferred choice with 23.2 per cent expressing their support for such action. Negotiations are also a favoured approach with a quarter of the respondents showing support of this. Surprisingly, taking part in protests and other forms of mass-mobilization, which is favoured by the working class and the professional strata, is also seen by the upper-business community as an effective method to make their voice heard. Mobilization includes getting involved in a political party and taking part in activities such as canvassing and forming political or advocacy networks that bring like-minded people together. Finally, 13 per cent of the respondents from the upper-business community expressed lobbying as a preferred approach to make their voice heard when they feel no one is representing them.

A similar pattern emerges for the respondents from the medium-business community, with protest and lobbying used more compared to the upper-business community. They are less likely to rely on media and social media campaigns and negotiations compared to the upper-business community.

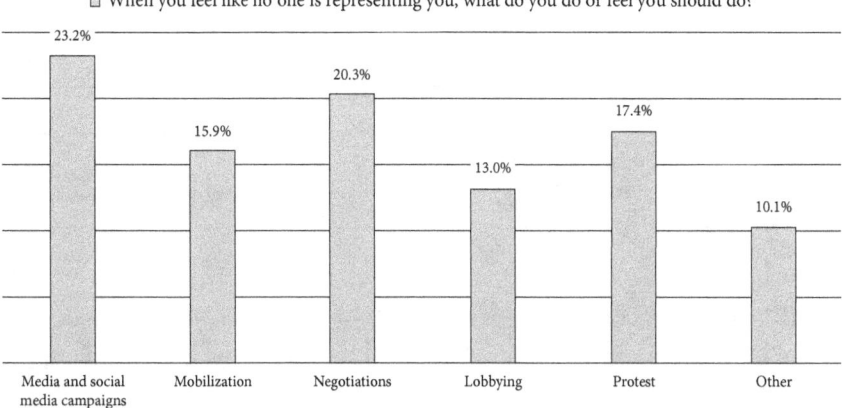

Figure 5.7 Action taken when no one is representing them (upper business).

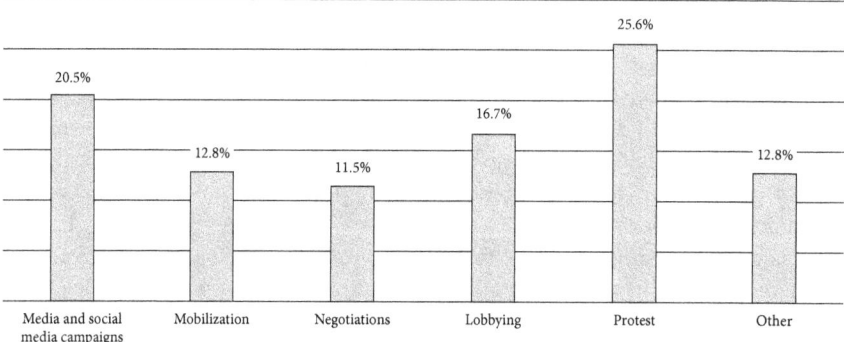

Figure 5.8 Action taken when no one is representing them (medium business).

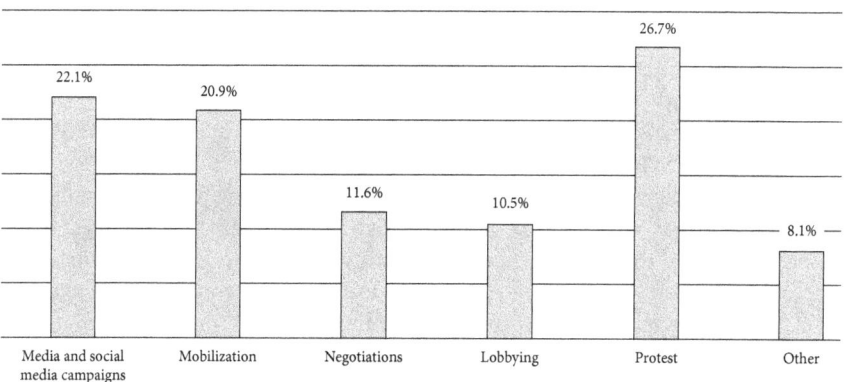

Figure 5.9 Action taken when no one is representing them (professional strata).

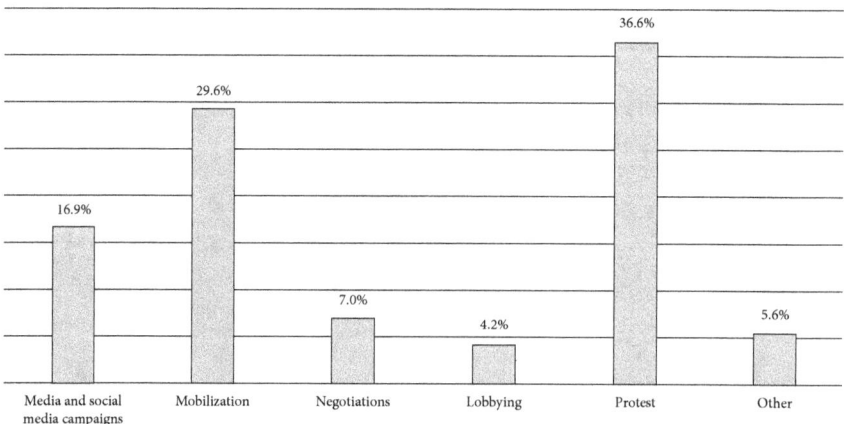

Figure 5.10 Action taken when no one is representing them (working class).

The responses from the professional strata also show a similar per cent of the group support each repertoire of actions. The percentage of the respondents who stated protest as their preferred choice was 26.7 and media and social media campaigns was 22.1. Political mobilization was supported by 20.9 per cent of the respondents and negotiation and lobbying by 11.6 per cent and 10.5 per cent, respectively, as the preferred actions to make their voice heard when no one was representing them.

In addition to the five main actions, a number of other actions have also been stated by the respondents from each category. These range from doing nothing to using violent or non-violent means to make their voice heard. Seeking support from like-minded people or forming groups to advocate their cause was also listed by several respondents.

For the Kurds from a working-class background, protests and mobilization is the preferred action to make their voice heard, with 36.6 per cent and 29.6 per cent of the respondents expressing their support for such action, respectively. This is unsurprising as the Kurdish majority regions have been the sites of many mass protests during the 2000s and 2010s. Lobbying and negotiations are the least chosen approach with only 7 per cent and 4.2 per cent expressing their support for such action, respectively.

6

Women and youth and political representation

This chapter first discusses local- and national-level political activities that Kurdish women take part in to highlight their activism in political parties and civil society organizations that have a feminist/women's rights agenda. Second, the activities that Kurdish youth and students take part in at local and national levels and issues that are specific to youth and student representation are discussed. The background on the role women and youth and students play in Kurdish politics offered in the first and second sections, respectively, are used to contextualize the results of the survey conducted among women and youth and students in Diyarbakır, Van, Ankara and Istanbul, which I analyse in sections three and four.

Many of the Kurdish political organizations that came into existence during the 1970s were established by Kurdish students, and throughout the past thirty years of the Kurdish struggle, Kurdish youth and students have been actively taking part in politics in large numbers. The nucleus of the group that established the PKK was exclusively comprised of students studying at the universities in Ankara in the mid-1970s and most of its early activists were recruited from universities and teacher training colleges. University students also constituted a significant section of the people who joined the PKK during the late 1980s and early 1990s, when the PKK's membership grew rapidly. Similarly, Kurdish women have been taking an active role in the PKK's activities from its early years onwards, and during the past thirty years many have joined the PKK's guerrilla force. Kurdish women have also been actively mobilized by the pro-Kurdish democratic movement over the past thirty years. In the current period, both Kurdish women and youth and students continue to take part in politics in large numbers.[1] Although the two groups will be covered in a single chapter, the account provided highlights each group's distinct experiences.[2]

In terms of the numbers involved and the impact generated, Kurdish women's mass mobilization in Turkey is unprecedented in Kurdish history. Initially, during the early 1980s, women started to actively take part in the support networks for the political prisoners that were in detention following the military coup of 12 September 1980. Although women were involved in the PKK from the onset, they have increased their activism significantly from the late 1980s onwards. Since its emergence in 1990, the pro-Kurdish movement has also played a significant role in facilitating Kurdish women's political participation. A historic moment took place when Leyla Zana was elected as an MP in Diyarbakır for the HEP in the 1991 Turkish general election and subsequently she became a symbol for Kurdish rights in Turkey. During the early 1990s, women have participated in large numbers in the numerous instances of *serhildan* (uprisings), which have been significant events with widespread consequences. Mobilization by Kurdish women has continued in the past decade with many new women's rights organizations established in the main Kurdish cities and towns that represent Kurdish women and their interests.

In the early years of the PKK's insurgency during the mid-1980s, many young Kurdish men from rural backgrounds were recruited as guerrilla fighters. With the increasing numbers of Kurds attending universities in Turkey during the late 1980s and early 1990s, the PKK also began to recruit many Kurdish students into its ranks. Similarly, Kurdish youth and students have been taking part in the activities of the pro-Kurdish political parties, which had a well-organized and active youth branch from the mid-1990s onwards. Increasingly over the past decade, protests by Kurdish youth and the occasional clash with the police have been occurring regularly in the urban areas in the majority Kurdish regions and in the cities in western Turkey that have a significant Kurdish population. Additionally, Kurdish students have been active in campaigns for Kurdish educational rights in Turkey, and during the 2000s and more recently, Kurdish youth and students have taken part in significant numbers in Kurdish mobilization in Syria to fight against ISIS, particularly from 2014 onwards.

Kurdish women's political activism

Political engagement and activities by Kurdish women have increased significantly during the past three decades and contributed to the discursive transformation and political practices of the Kurdish national movement in this period. The number of Kurdish women active in politics in elected positions before the 1980s was very low. The case of Zekiye Midyat, who was the mayor of Midyat district in Mardin province between 1957 and 1960, is an exception. Despite the absence of political representation, Kurdish women did participate in public life and a few of them have risen to prominence in the cultural field. These include the famous singers Meryem Xan and Eyşe Şan.[3] Many other women have risen to prominence in the field of arts during the 1980s and 1990s. As briefly mentioned above, from the 1980s onwards, with the gradual increase in the activities of the Kurdish national movement, many Kurdish women started to engage in politics. This has made women more visible publicly and has also meant that their interests and demands started to be articulated within the Kurdish movement's political discourse.

In her pioneering research, Handan Çaglayan highlights the discursive strategies that the PKK deployed in mobilizing women. The PKK's approach centred on challenging the prevailing notion of women's position within the Kurdish society. During the 1980s, the PKK's discourse untangled the dominant interpretation of 'honour' as the protection of women's chastity and the purity of her body by articulating it more broadly as the defence of Kurdistan's land.[4] By attempting to free men from the burden of defending their honour, the key objective of this re-articulation of honour was the mobilization of men. However, from the early 1990s onwards, there was a major shift in the PKK's discourse as it started to construct a new women's identity, which increasingly identified women with acts of *heroic* resistance and sacrifice for the nation.[5] During the early 1990s, women started to be the performers of resistance acts and acquire a central stage in the PKK's representation of its struggle to its target groups.

Women have been identified as a key social and political group that will lead the democratic development and renewal in the region and the democratization of the society. Consequently, steps have been taken to establish the women's movement as an autonomous organization within the national movement. This led to the establishment of a women's party, the Party of Free Women (Partiya Jina Azad, PJA) in 2000, which changed its name to Partiya Azadiya Jin a Kurdistan (PAJK – the Freedom Party of Women of Kurdistan) in 2004. Additionally, there is a women's armed group Free Women's Units (Yekîneyen Jinen Azad ên STAR, YJA Star) operating as part of the PKK's guerrilla forces, the People's Defence Forces (Hêzên Parastina Gel, HPG). Whilst the mobilization of women has been a significant new development, and women do occupy high positions within the PKK hierarchy and their mass participation in politics has contributed significantly to the spread of notions of gender equality in Kurdish society, the organizational autonomy of the women's movement has not been achieved.[6]

The pro-Kurdish political parties have been especially active in mobilizing Kurdish women and over the past thirty years, they have become one of the main channels for Kurdish women's representation.[7] The election of Leyla Zana to the parliament in October 1991 was a watershed moment in the political representation of Kurdish women but the pro-Kurdish movement's subsequent progress in women's representation was gradual:

> However, until the end of 1990s pro-Kurdish political parties failed not only in promoting egalitarian gender values and policies, but also in supporting women's inclusion in politics. Kurdish women's participation and representation in political parties have substantially changed numerically with the passing of time. In comparison with the general picture of women's representation in politics in Turkey, women's representation in pro-Kurdish politics has significantly advanced especially since the year 2000.[8]

Hence, throughout the 2000s, the number of Kurdish women in elected positions increased significantly and, with the return of the pro-Kurdish parliamentary group in 2007, the number of Kurdish women MPs has also been on the rise. In 2007, seven of the pro-Kurdish party's twenty-two MPs were Kurdish women. In 2011, the number increased to eleven and most of them were Kurdish. After the November 2015 election, the number increased to twenty-three. Currently, many of the leading figures in the pro-Kurdish movement are women. These include the former co-mayor of Diyarbakır Municipality Gültan Kışanık, the former co-president of the HDP Sebahat Tuncel and the former co-chair of the DBP Emine Ayna. In addition, many other women including the above-mentioned Leyla Zana have been active in the HDP. In 1994, she was imprisoned for fifteen years along with fellow Kurdish MPs Orhan Dogan, Hatip Dicle and Selim Sadak for her political activities, but was released in 2004 and since then she has been active in politics. Pervin Buldan, who has been an MP since 2007, is another leading figure in the pro-Kurdish movement and is currently the co-chair of the HDP. She was part of the HDP's delegation that facilitated the dialogue process between the PKK and the Turkish government between 2013 and 2015.

Hence, Kurdish women hold many leadership positions of the pro-Kurdish political parties and women's rights are incorporated into the political programme of such parties and their discourse. This is one of the reasons why the HDP and its predecessors have been successful in mobilizing Kurdish women. Additionally, the pro-Kurdish political parties constructed a women's branch at the grassroots level, which has continued with the HDP and they use positive discrimination policies such as a 40 per cent gender quota and the co-chair system to increase women's elected representatives in political positions. The co-chair system requires that all the elected positions such as mayors, and party leaders at district, province and national levels need to be shared by a man and a woman.

Kurdish women have been also represented in the parliament by the AKP in the past decade. AKP's Kurdish women MPs include Oya Eronat and Mine Lök Beyaz, who were MPs for the Diyarbakır Province between 2011 and 2015, and Gülşen Orhan, who was an MP for the Van province between 2007 and 2015. However, their participation in the AKP needs to be seen within the AKP's overall strategy of articulating Kurdish identity within its conservative religious political project, which has been challenged by women for reinforcing patriarchal norms and preserving the existing gender inequality in society. As a result, the Kurdish women MPs in the AKP have not been very effective in pushing forward either Kurdish rights or women's rights agenda. Nevertheless, the AKP has a women's branch in each of the Kurdish majority provinces and continues to mobilize a significant number of Kurdish women through the appeal of its Islamist discourse.

In the past decade, the pro-Kurdish political parties have significantly increased their support base in the Kurdish-populated region and have consistently been performing well at the local elections. They controlled the municipal councils in many of the majority Kurdish regions until September 2016 when they were taken over by the state and elected mayors were replaced by trustees. Having a strong base at a local level in majority Kurdish regions has meant that many of the local governments at district or provincial levels have adopted policies to empower women and increase their representation in politics and society. This has led to the development of diverse practices such as campaigns against domestic violence, campaigns to raise public awareness about other forms of gender-based violence and inequality, legal advice and social support for women experiencing various difficulties. Women were organized as part of the pro-Kurdish political network with their own representative organizations. They were also organized under the Democratic Free Women's Movement (DÖHK) but in February 2015 it transformed itself into the Congress of Free Women (KJA), although it continues to be active in the majority Kurdish regions.[9]

An important development that took place in majority Kurdish regions in the past decade was the establishment of organizations that work to improve women's position in society and that offer several services to women, such as legal advice, psychological counselling, social integration projects for forcibly displaced women and their children and advice relating to domestic violence. These included Selis Women's Advice Association, Women's Centre (Kamer), Diyarbakır Women's Platform, Günışığı

Women's Association, Diyarbakır Municipality's Centre for Research and Application of Women's Problems (Dikasum), Ekin Ceren Women's Centre and Amida Women's Centre. Similarly, the following organizations, Van Women's Association (VAKAD), Saray Women's Association and Bostaniçi Maya Advice Centre for Women, were established in Van during the past decade and offered services and ran projects to improve women's lives in Van. However, since the autumn of 2016, as part of the state's repression of the Kurdish movement, all of the above-mentioned women's rights organizations in the majority Kurdish regions have been closed down by government's delegated decrees and their property seized by the state. The state interpreted the activities of the women's rights groups as promoting the objectives of the PKK.

It is worth pointing out that services for women in Kurdish majority regions are provided by a diverse network of organizations. For example, legal advice on domestic violence is provided by the Diyarbakır Bar Association and such activism has led to the establishment within its structures of a women's centre that is engaged in raising awareness about women's right amongst the society. The Human Rights Association (IHD) has been carrying out a campaign to combat the sexual harassment and assaults that women face in detention. In addition, numerous trade unions have specific units for activism on women's rights and employment issues. The two unions that have a strong presence in Kurdish majority areas are the KESK and Eğitim-Sen. Also, these trade unions have a significant number of Kurdish members in western Turkey.

A different type of organization that recently came into existence is the DOGUNKAD. It was established in Diyarbakır in May 2011 but aspires to represent businesswomen from Kurdish majority regions. It aims to increase women's employment in Kurdish majority regions and has so far been involved in various campaigns to achieve that objective. In western Turkey, Kurdish women take part in feminist organizations such as the Istanbul Feminist Collective, Istanbul Socialist Feminist Collective and Women for Peace Initiative. Similarly, in Ankara, Kurdish women take part in organizations that cater for a cross-section of society rather than Kurds specifically. In fact, the feminist movement in Turkey has been able to bring together women from different backgrounds and to a certain extent transcend the nationalist antagonisms that continue to prevail and restrict Kurds' ability to represent themselves in Turkey. An organization that has a presence in many of the cities in Turkey is the Women's Initiative for Peace. Additionally, many Kurdish women have been taking part in the ongoing campaign to uncover the fate of the forcefully disappeared people in the conflict. Collectively, they have become known as the 'Saturday Mothers' and they organize a sit-in protest and vigil every Saturday in front of Istanbul's Galatasaray High School. Another civil society organization founded and led by Kurdish women is Peace Mothers, which promotes a peaceful end to the conflict and carries out numerous activities.

In the past decade, we have also witnessed the establishment of many women's cooperatives in Kurdish majority regions, which aim to improve Kurdish women's economic welfare but also seek to bring about a transformation in social relations and gender equality.[10] Women's cooperatives offer services for mothers and educational activities for their children. Women's cooperatives have been established to increase women's participation in the labour market and help them to become economically independent, which in turn is expected to increase their participation in social and political life. It is a measure designed to combat economic inequality that women suffer disproportionately by empowering them to take a more active role in resolving problems that they face. Such measures aim to alleviate the impact of restrictions placed on women's participation and create mutually supportive relations among women. As an example, DOGUNKAD provided financial support to women's cooperatives and helps the cooperatives with technical know-how and expertise.[11] The cooperatives aim to improve women's skills sets and link up with networks and thereby increase their social capital. As an additional measure to encourage and increase women's participation in the economy, a market for women vendors in Diyarbakır was set up.[12] Although the negative impact of the conflict on women's lives, such as forced displacement, has been greater, the major changes that came about as a result of the political activism in the past three decades have also created opportunities for women to organize and assert their collective agency. Increasingly in the past decade, women began to assume a central stage in efforts to address numerous forms of inequalities that affect them disproportionately and became an 'active agent of change for themselves and for the "Kurdish struggle"'.[13] Through their activities, actions to end different forms of gender oppression, such as child marriage, polygamy and honour killings, have become more widespread.

Youth and students' political activism and participation

Political activities by Kurdish youth and students during the past two decades have been a key feature of Kurdish politics in Turkey. As mentioned before, Kurdish youth and students were recruited into the PKK's fighting force in large numbers during the late 1980s and early 1990s. The contact that the PKK guerrillas established with the Kurds in the rural areas played an important role in this process. Student organizations close to the PKK played a key role in the recruitment of students as members of the PKK, particularly during the early 1990s. Although the Kurdish youth in Turkey have been in the news frequently because of violent events and riots, their political activism is more diverse, and many other non-violent activities and practices have also been used. In fact, the youth and student activism is wide-ranging and is organized via several associations, and associations with a pro-Kurdish agenda at local and national levels.

The activism of Kurdish youth and students involves a complex network that includes organizations operating across high schools and universities and numerous local groups set up at a neighbourhood level but upwardly connected to the larger networks of the pro-Kurdish movement. Local-level groups operate as part of larger national-level groups and their activities are organized in conjunction with the overall objectives of the national-level group. Their activism is predominantly political in nature, but cultural organizations are also a part of the overall youth and student networks of Kurdish political movement in Turkey. The activities that youth and students take part in include protests, voting, canvassing and meetings as well as cultural work, language tuition, sports activities and music classes and performances.

Throughout the 2000s, hundreds of Kurdish youth were arrested at demonstrations and protests by the Turkish police and security forces. The youth were involved in clashes with the police and the mainstream Turkish media described them as 'stone-throwing children'.[14] On many occasions, they were tried under the country's anti-terror laws and given heavy sentences. Subsequently, the abuse and harassment they have experienced while in detention became part of the national debate and has generated much anger amongst the Kurdish population in Turkey.[15] Many Kurdish young people and students have been arrested for being part of the youth branch of the KCK and put on trial since 2008. An organization in which Kurdish youth play a central role that has been frequently mentioned in the press in the past years is the YDG-H (Patriotic Revolutionary Youth Movement).

Active since 2013, the YDG-H has frequently been involved in riots and protests in cities in western Turkey and the majority Kurdish regions. Some of its members have used firearms on occasions and set up checkpoints in the Kurdish majority cities purportedly to protect their communities and neighbourhoods from police violence. The YDG-H is made up of Kurdish youth and it is seen as a front organization for the PKK in the urban areas. It is particularly active in the cities in the Kurdish majority regions and has a notable presence in Istanbul's working-class districts that house a large Kurdish population. During the summer of 2015, the YDG-H took a leading role in the attempts by communities in many of the towns in the majority Kurdish regions to exercise local autonomy.[16] It is an underground organization and we do not know exactly its internal dynamics or how they are managed and mobilized. However, looking at its past practice, it has a capacity to mobilize many young people in western parts of Turkey and in Kurdish majority regions. On occasions, they have acted as a vigilante force and acted against drug sales and trafficking and prostitution in certain neighbourhoods in Istanbul and in the cities and towns in majority Kurdish regions. During the winter of 2015 and spring of 2016, many YDG-H members lost their lives in the clashes with the state security forces in the Kurdish majority regions. From the beginning of 2016, the members of the YDG-H in the majority Kurdish regions have been organized under a new name, Civilian Protection Units (Yekîneyên Parastina Sivîl, YPS). These units are organized at district or province levels and aim to be a self-defence force for the Kurds.

Overall in the past three decades, Kurdish youth has radicalized along the ethnic–nationalist lines and there are studies that show the attitude of the Kurdish youth is more radical than the older generations.[17] Consequently, in the past two decades, there have been many instances of Kurdish youth taking part in mass protests in many of the cities such as Istanbul, Adana and Mersin as well as the urban centres of the majority Kurdish provinces of Turkey. An example of this type of mobilization was the Kobani protests that took place in many of the cities in Turkey on 6–8 October 2014.[18] This seems to have propelled a wider mobilization to join the Kurdish forces in Syria in their fight against ISIS. There were several other occasions in which Kurdish youth participated in large-scale protests and clashes with the police, such as the wave of protests that took place in Istanbul and other cities on the occasion of the Roboski massacre in which thirty-four smugglers and their mules were killed on 28 December 2011.[19] Numerous protests took place on the anniversary of the massacre in subsequent years.

Kurdish youth groups, particularly those that are affiliated with the PKK, have been targeted by the state security forces since the summer of 2015. The state crack-down intensified on 24–5 July 2015, with mass arrests in Istanbul and other major Turkish cities following the ISIS terror attack on 20 July 2015, and continued throughout 2015. Although ISIS and Turkish left-wing groups were also targeted, the majority of those arrested were close to the PKK on the suspicion that they were members of its youth branches.[20] In the autumn of 2015, military operations focused on the Kurdish majority regions, particularly in the Sur district of Diyarbakır, Nusaybin, Sirnak and Cizre, and according to International Crisis Group a total of 2,712 people lost their lives, including 921 security forces, 1,215 PKK militants, 393 civilians and 219 youth who could not be definitively identified as civilians, or members of the PKK or the YPS.[21]

In addition to the YDG-H, the pro-Kurdish political parties have an active and wide youth network organized as a branch of the party. Both the HDP and DBP have youth branches and they carry out political activities amongst the youth. The HDP's election manifesto included numerous pledges to the youth and that shows that the youth is one of the main target groups for the party. In addition to the parties' youth branches, there are other organizations that offer services for the youth such as the Youth Cultural Centres. These are associations that are established to carry out cultural and social activities for the youth and are run by the municipal councils governed by the pro-Kurdish political party. The services offered by such centres include music, folk dancing, drama and art classes and sports activities.

More recently, the youth branches of the pro-Kurdish movement have been organized within a national structure known as the Democratic Youth (Dem-Genç).[22] This is a new organization that came into being in April 2015, and brings together the youth branches of the HDP, DBP, the Youth Cultural Centres, the Youth Assembly of the Democratic Society Congress and the student and university associations that I discuss below. Hence, there is a wide network of civil society organizations that takes the task of representing Kurdish youth and students. The establishment of the sports club Amedspor under the auspices of the Diyarbakır Municipality is another example in which the local authority in Diyarbakır attempts to engage the youth in different activities.

Both Dicle University in Diyarbakır and Yüzüncü Yıl University in Van have a predominantly Kurdish student population. There are other universities in the Kurdish majority regions and in addition, there are many Kurdish students that attend the universities in western Turkey. Hence, the Kurdish student population is dispersed across Turkey and most of the universities have a student association sympathetic to the Kurdish movement, which is organized under the Federation of Democratic Students Associations (DÖDEF). Both the Dicle University Student Association (DÜÖDER) and the Van Yüzüncü Yıl Student Association (YÜDER) are members of the DÖDEF. Many of the pro-Kurdish student associations complain about widespread police harassment and pressure from the university administration and have been accused of being a recruitment ground for the PKK.[23] As well as activities that are related to the issues students face, these associations are also involved in general political activism sympathetic to the Kurdish movement. For example, they have played a significant role in the campaign to save the Hevsel Gardens in Diyarbakır that were threatened with destruction when it was designated by the central government as a site for construction of residential buildings.[24] Some of the DÜÖDER activities attract as many as 3,000 students and they publish a monthly magazine titled *Tigris*.

As part of the KCK trials, from 2009 onwards, many students were arrested and incarcerated in prisons while awaiting trial. Many Kurdish students escaped to Europe without completing their studies in order to avoid arrest and imprisonment. Kurdish student activism takes place also in Turkey's private universities and the Kurdish student's organization of an annual conference on Kurdish culture and history at the Istanbul Bilgi University is a good example of the broad range of activities in which Kurdish university students engage.

The other groups to which Kurdish youth and students belong include the Gülenist network, which was particularly active in majority Kurdish provinces during the 2000s and early half of 2010s and has managed to establish a wide network within the Kurdish populated provinces that has links to even more remote villages. One of its primary activities was to operate university preparation courses (*dersane*) through which it has reached many Kurdish students and their families. The Gülenist network provided houses for Kurdish students to stay and offered scholarships and through such actions recruited and kept many Kurdish students within their ranks. It is primarily the material benefits that draw Kurds towards the Gülenist network. In fact, the movement maintained a hard-line attitude and continues to do so towards a political settlement in the conflict and sees the Kurdish movement as a rival in controlling the Kurds. The deterioration of the relations between the AKP and the Gülenist network from 2013 has resulted in a significant decline in its activities in the Kurdish majority provinces of Turkey. In the same period, the AKP intensified its efforts in the Kurdish majority areas to recruit and mobilize Kurdish youth through its youth branches and through several social assistance programmes, such as student dormitories, that it manages via the affiliated charities and civil society organizations.

Additionally, in recent years, the Kurdish youth have been recruited by the Islamist Salafist groups, particularly in the majority Kurdish provinces of Adıyaman and Bingöl. The recent ISIS attacks carried out in Turkey were undertaken by Kurdish youth radicalized by Islamist Salafist ideology.[25] However, it is very difficult to find out more about how these ISIS cells operate or recruit new members.[26] As discussed in Chapter 1, during the late 1980s and early 1990s, Hizbullah managed to attract and recruit many Kurdish youths to its ranks who have subsequently taken part in its violence against the pro-Kurdish political activists and the PKK sympathizers. This trend of recruiting youth to its ranks has continued in the past two decades and the Hüda-Par has a dedicated youth branch that carries out activities to mobilize Kurdish youth and students. In the past decade, frequent fights between students sympathetic to Hizbullah and the pro-Kurdish movement have broken out in Diyarbakır and Van universities.[27] In fact, Turkish universities have been a site of radical political activism over a long period of time and fights between student's groups continue to occur regularly. Kurdish youth and students are also involved in various Turkish socialist political groups, particularly in western Turkey.

Attitudes and political behaviour of Kurdish women

This section analyses the results of the survey to unpack the political behaviour and attitudes of Kurdish women. The survey was completed by twenty-eight respondents representing women NGOs, with seven women from each city of Istanbul, Ankara,

Diyarbakır and Van. The first two cities were chosen as they are the main cities in Turkey with a Kurdish population and the latter two cities because they are the main cities in the Kurdish majority region. As a result, a diverse number of respondents were included in the sample and an account of their experiences is included in the research. The mean age of respondents was 31 years and those who resided in Ankara and Istanbul have been settled there for fifteen years on average. Nineteen respondents described their political affiliation as HDP, four described as feminist, three as socialist and two did not declare their political affiliation. The overview provided in section one highlighted that the pro-Kurdish political movement and the PKK has played a key role in Kurdish women's participation and representation in politics during the past thirty years but more recently with the establishment of numerous women's organizations, we are witnessing growing autonomy of the Kurdish women's movement. This recent development can be seen as a new stage in women's activism and its development and evolution towards a more independent trajectory.

The analysis of the survey reveals that the pro-Kurdish political parties play a central role in women's representation. The survey also reveals that a high proportion of Kurdish women feel that they are represented by local governments and women's civil society organizations. A high number of Kurdish women have been taking part in the activities of the pro-Kurdish movement in Turkey during the past two decades both at the grassroots level and in a leadership capacity and their continued centrality for women's representation as confirmed by the survey is unsurprising. The participation of women in the pro-Kurdish movement indicates that they are mobilized by Kurdish demands for greater freedom and rights in Turkey as well as gender equality:

> These mobilizations resulted in an intersection of ethnic and gender identities, which drove women's activism for gender equality in politics in the end of 1990s and began positively effecting changes in their representation at the beginning of 2000s. Thus mobilization, via intersecting identities, was an influential factor in improving the representation of Kurdish women in politics.[28]

The participation of women in Kurdish politics, via the PKK and the pro-Kurdish political parties, has, as discussed in section one, led to the incorporation of women's rights into their political programme, and they have become one of the main advocates of women's rights in Turkey.[29] Women's participation has facilitated the Kurdish movement's adoption of such discourses and practices. The establishment by the HDP of an all-women parliamentary group to campaign against gender discrimination in Turkey is indicative of the continued importance attached to gender equality. The co-chair system and 40 per cent gender quota have seen women being elected to the positions of MPs and mayors of the councils. Therefore, women are playing a significant role in politics also at the local level in majority Kurdish regions.

With the establishment of women's organizations at a local level, there is now more action from the local council to support women and empower them in their struggle against gendered forms of violence. While we may not be able to quantify the exact impact these organizations are making on women's lives, they are an important source of support that women can rely on in times of hardship. Although many of the

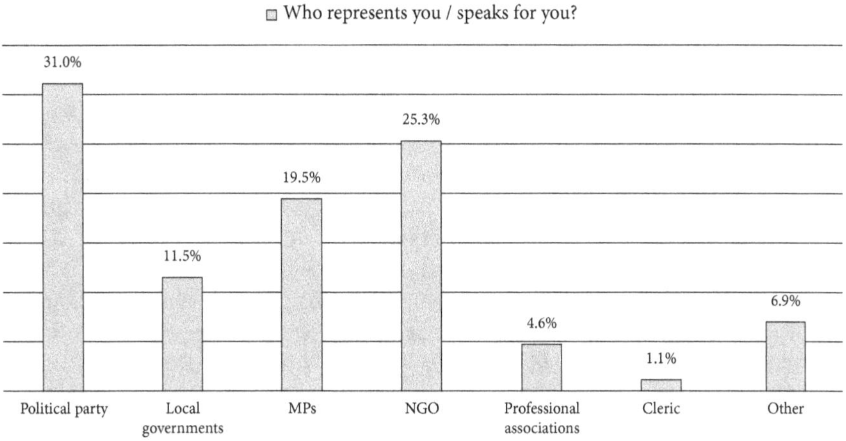

☐ Who represents you / speaks for you?

- Political party: 31.0%
- Local governments: 11.5%
- MPs: 19.5%
- NGO: 25.3%
- Professional associations: 4.6%
- Cleric: 1.1%
- Other: 6.9%

Figure 6.1 Women's political representatives.

women connected with the women's organizations are likely to be supporters of the pro-Kurdish movement, it is also important to mention that not all of the women's organizations are part of the pro-Kurdish political network.

In addition to broader Kurdish rights-based mobilizations, women have also been mobilized around particular issues. Specific instances include mobilization as part of national-level activism and against the violence that women experience. Campaigns to combat gendered forms of violence have managed to bring together Kurdish and Turkish women and feminist organizations and have engendered a post-national form of mobilization in Turkey. In the past five years, it is reported that at least 1,134 women have been murdered by their ex-husband or partner and this has been an issue high on the agenda of women's rights organizations, both Kurdish and Turkish.[30] Hence, it is not specifically the Kurdish national demands that have motivated Kurdish women's mobilization and some have taken part in the violent forms of mobilization particularly as part of the Kurdish military campaign against ISIS in Syria. The survey results show that it is predominantly women who feel that they are represented by the pro-Kurdish political parties at local and national levels but, in addition, various other political actors are involved in representing them, including the NGOs and the PKK.

With the increase in the influence of the pro-Kurdish political parties, services for women have increased. Many of these services are facilitated by women's organizations at the grassroots level with support from the local council. The services are holistic solutions to the social problems that women face, and they aim to empower women. With the increasing representation of the pro-Kurdish political parties in local governments, many more services for women were introduced, such as courses designed to improve women's employability.[31] Also recently the local authorities took a stronger stand against domestic violence. As part of the Diyarbakır City Consultative Council (Diyarbakır Kent Konseyi)'s structure, Women's Assembly was active, and it acts as a platform for women to directly raise their demands and represent themselves.

The number of women who wanted to be represented by the local governments is higher than the number who feel they are represented by the local governments. This can be explained by the fact that the pro-Kurdish parties have very little representation in western Turkey and for many of the participants in western Turkey having pro-Kurdish representation at a local level will benefit their lives. Also, women feel that if they have representation at a local government level, they can be more effective at addressing their concerns. All but one of the women respondents stated that Turkey's current form of government is suitable for their representation. The number of women who saw NGOs as their representatives is 25.3 per cent and, given the increasingly important role that women's NGOs have been playing, it is not surprising. Some of the women's NGOs came under pressure from the state and were closed down. The number of women who wanted the local governments to represent them is high and that shows the positive impact the local governments are making through their work and activism.

Kurdish women in western parts of Turkey are likely to have different experiences as the organizations in which they engage mainly carry out campaigns around post-national issues. In fact, Turkey's feminist movement has, to a certain extent, been successful in bringing diverse women's rights organizations around common demands. There are two specific feminist organizations that attract Kurdish women in some numbers: the Istanbul Feminist Collective and the Istanbul Feminist Socialist Collective. There has also been a visible increase in peace activism in recent years with Women for Peace being particularly active. Additionally, trade unions have also been quite active in raising Kurdish demands and working against gendered violence. There has been growing activism against gender violence around the cases of women who were murdered by their former partners or were the victims of rape, for example, the case of Özgecan Aslan in 2014.[32] There are also human rights organizations that have also been involved in representing women's demands such as violence under detention. The number of women who feel they are represented by NGOs is also high because, through the numerous organizations that women have created, they have been able to

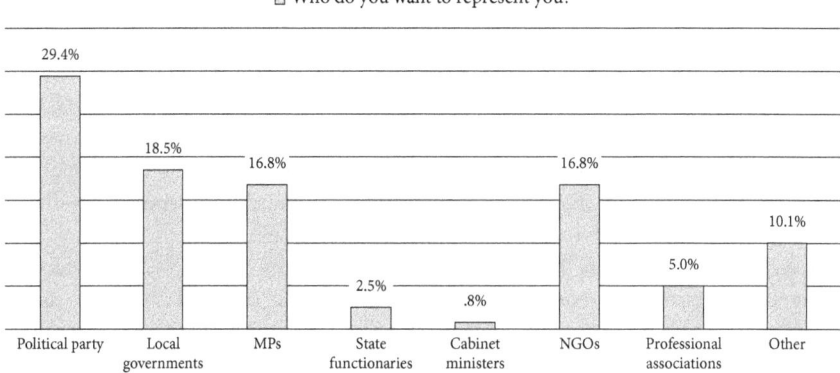

Figure 6.2 Women's desired political representatives.

make a difference, at least locally. Also, they have created a network of support that provides them access to a wider community, which is an important resource to have.

The use of media and social media to raise their demands, political mobilization and protests are the most popular forms of activism by Kurdish women. Many women connected with the pro-Kurdish movement are likely to be used to such forms of political activities and have the necessary skills for the organization of such activities as well as access to a greater number of the pool of activists. Being a movement that is very much at the margins of Turkey's mainstream politics, women's organizations and individual women actors are likely to have very little access to insiders in the government and state and, as a result, seeking to raise awareness through street protests and mass mobilizations are the only choice left for them. The nature of the demands seems to be important here as well as many of the demands raised cannot be easily accommodated without widespread reforms and changing social norms and prevailing attitudes. The government has not been very receptive to women's demands for equality and its social conservatism has been challenged by women's organizations for undermining the cause of gender equality in Turkey.[33]

In terms of action taken to achieve desired representation, mobilization, protests and media and social media campaigns also appear as the most frequently used methods by women. As discussed above, women have been mobilized by the Kurdish national movement as part of its activities and we have also witnessed a gradual move by women activists towards greater autonomy. Women activists have played a central role in the pro-Kurdish democratic movement making gender equality in political representation one of its key political objectives. The prominence of the use of media and social media to raise awareness of their concerns is reflected in the organization of a number of high-profile social media campaigns in the past decade. In contrast with the popularity of the use of media and social media, negotiation and lobbying are not used as frequently by women. The low number of women who use negotiation and lobbying to represent themselves shows that the women's associations are not very

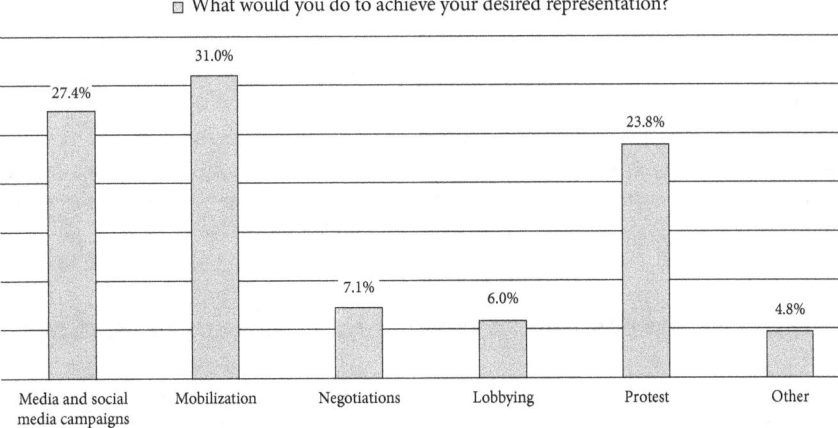

Figure 6.3 Action women take to achieve desired representation.

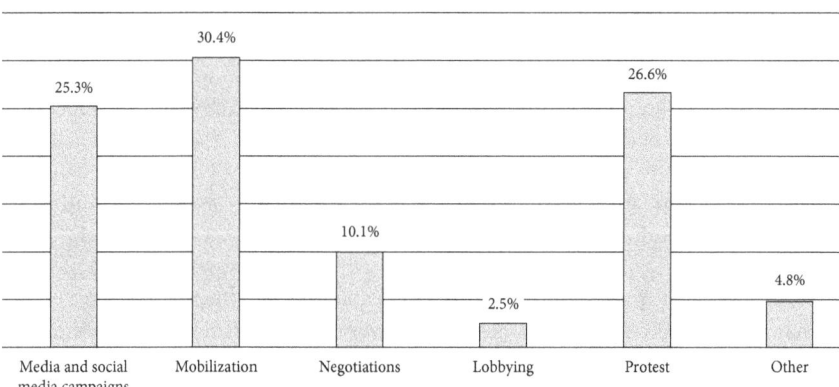

Figure 6.4 Action women take when no one is representing them.

well integrated institutionally with the government and the state structures. However, they are well integrated into the pro-Kurdish political networks and organizations and have received support from the municipal councils in order to continue their activities.

We witness a similar pattern of activism when we analyse action taken by women when they feel no one is representing them. Mobilization, protest and media and social media campaigns are frequently used by women to express their concerns and make their voice heard. Some 10 per cent of women identified negotiations as a method to get their voices heard when they feel no one is representing them. These negotiations could be with political parties that they feel a close bond with or other civil society organizations who could be receptive to women's political demands and the issues that they face. The fact that women's rights groups and organizations came under severe state repression as a result of Turkey's authoritarian turn since 2016 indicates that state and government officials are likely to take a hostile attitude to attempts by women to make their voices heard. The use of riot police and tear gas to forcefully disperse the International Women's Day march in Istanbul in 2019 is an example of the government's hostility towards collective action by women.[34] The HDP won back many of the municipal councils that the government took over in 2016 and has begun to reverse the policies the government-appointed trustees pursued, such as reopening women's centres and restarting the support services for women. However, since August 2019 onwards, the state has continued with its policy of removing Kurdish elected representatives and appointing a trustee as their replacement.

Attitudes and political behaviour of Kurdish youth and students

In this section, I analyse the results of the survey conducted with twenty-nine Kurdish youth and students to find out more about their political behaviour and attitudes. The respondents resided in Istanbul, Ankara, Diyarbakır and Van participated and extra care was taken to reflect the diversity of the Kurdish society in the sample. Ten of the respondents were women and on average the respondents from Ankara and Istanbul have resided there for five years, with one of the respondents born in Istanbul. The mean age of respondents was 23 and in total twenty-one respondents described their political affiliation as HDP and eight described themselves as supporters of the PKK. Fourteen of the respondents were students and fifteen belonged to youth associations. Youth political activism as part of Kurdish political activism continues, but in the past decade, we are seeing the spread of protest amongst the youth as they take part in instances of mass mobilization in increasing numbers in majority Kurdish regions and in cities of western Turkey. Previously, much of the violence in the conflict between the PKK and the Turkish army took place in the rural areas and in the past decade urban centres have become sites of widespread protests, unrest and activism. Kurdish youth have been at the centre of protests in the urban contexts and the ongoing trend indicates an increasing role for the youth in Kurdish resistance in Turkey.

As discussed above, the PKK and the pro-Kurdish political parties have been successful in mobilizing the Kurdish youth and students. This is facilitated by the existence of a widespread network in Kurdish majority regions as well as in western Turkey. The finding of the survey confirms the centrality of the political parties to the representation of Kurdish youth and students with 33.3 per cent citing political parties as their representatives. A further 19.5 per cent cite MPs as their representatives, 17.2 per cent cite NGOs and 10.3 per cent cite local governments. Some 13.8 per cent of the respondents cited 'other' as their representatives and this predominantly refers to the PKK, the KCK, Abdullah Öcalan and the PKK's guerrilla forces.

It is therefore not surprising that a higher number of student and youth respondents have identified a strong connection with the PKK and sees it as representing them and their interests. The number of respondents citing state functionaries, family connections, tribal chiefs and clerics is less than 10 per cent. In the case of students, the ties to their local family network and the tribal community are strengthened via

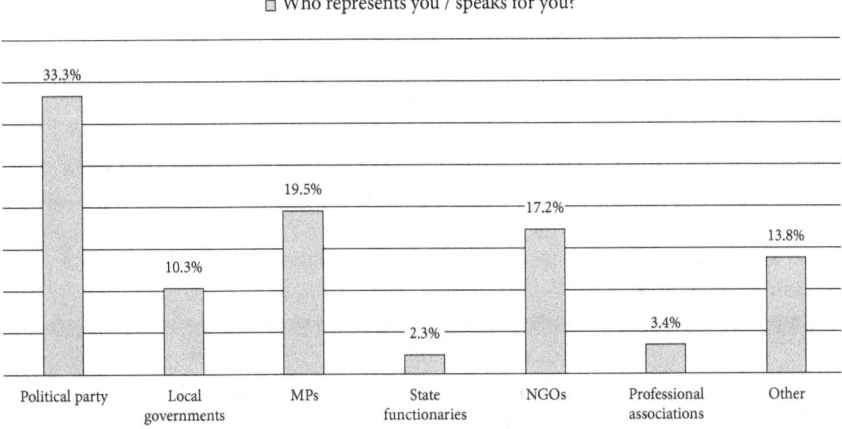

Figure 6.5 Youth's and students' political representatives.

support offered by local organizations such as financial assistance. In most cases, financial support for students is financed by businessmen and tribal chiefs and family connections play a role in obtaining them. Additionally, the role of the university-based networks and student organizations play a role in the types of political activities Kurdish students take part in. This is evident in their participation in campaigns for student's educational rights and demands for a more democratic education system. In fact, there have been ongoing campaigns for more democratic and inclusive higher education in Turkey since the establishment of the Council of Higher Education (YÖK) in 1982 resulted in undemocratic practices and removal of many left-wing and dissident academics in Turkish universities. In addition to the general democratic demands, Kurdish students have been mobilized around Kurdish language rights in Turkey and have been demanding education in Kurdish.

Turkish universities have been sites of political activism since the 1970s and on numerous occasions fights involving large numbers of students have broken out. There are many examples of these and in 2015 in Izmir Ege University a fight between student groups resulted in the death of one student and injury to another.[35] Many Kurdish students are active within the Turkish left-wing students' groups and as discussed above there also exists a widespread pro-Kurdish student network. Through such extensive networks, Kurdish students continue to be mobilized by the pro-Kurdish political movement in Turkey. Given the highly polarized and politicized university environment, many Kurdish students are likely to engage with the pro-Kurdish student networks in Turkish universities and be politicized while at university. Many Kurdish students have taken part in activities in support of a peaceful solution to the Kurdish conflict in Turkey and of the Kurdish struggle against IS in Syria.

Additionally, we need to consider the negative experiences of many of the Kurdish youth who grew up in the majority Kurdish provinces in Turkey during the years of the conflict. Kurdish society in Turkey has experienced a major dislocation in Turkey during the past twenty years and the generation of youth and students has been directly affected by the experience of displacement in Turkey. Many have the first-hand experience of oppression and have witnessed discrimination and rejection by the mainstream Turkish society. Consequently, the hostile environment in which the Kurdish youth have grown up has shaped their views and attitudes and pushed them towards radical political practices. The Kurdish youth are portrayed negatively in the mainstream media as trouble-makers and criminals which is likely to create resentment amongst them and validate the feelings of discrimination and rejection. Given they often come across police and state security forces, the level of trust they have in the state officials is low and consequently very few of them see state functionaries as their representatives. Additionally, the low level of social capital and connectivity to the wider society amplifies the conditions of poverty and discrimination to create a spiral of radicalism and protests.

In terms of political inclinations, we can observe a similar trend with 32.4 per cent of the respondents stating that they want to be represented by a political party. Some 18.3 per cent of the respondents stated they wanted to be represented by NGOs, 15.6 per cent by local governments, 14.7 per cent by MPs and 11 per cent by others. A very high number, 96.4 per cent, of youth and students think that the

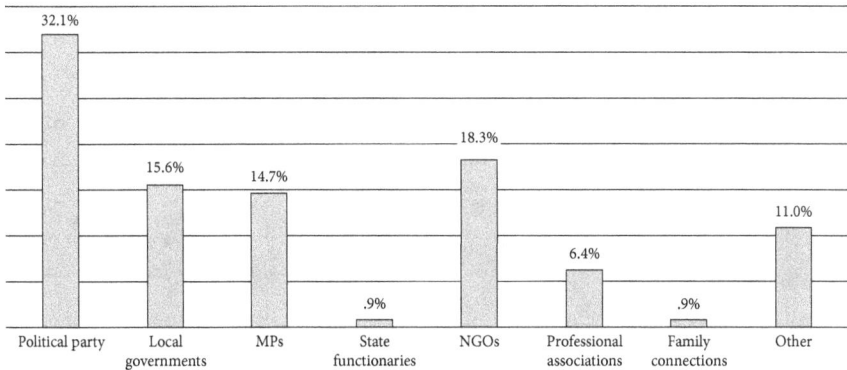

Figure 6.6 Youth's and students' desired political representatives.

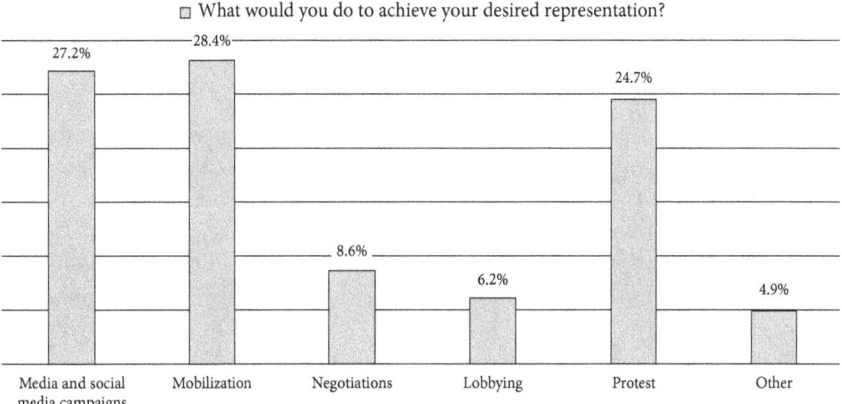

Figure 6.7 Action youth and students take to achieve desired representation.

current form of government does not allow them to make their voice heard. Despite such a high percentage of youth and students expressing disagreement with Turkey's institutional set-up, many cite the pro-Kurdish party or its MPs as their representatives who operate within the current political system. However, this should not be seen as an indirect assent of the political system in Turkey because the pro-Kurdish parties advocate reforming Turkey's political system and rebuilding it according to the model of democratic autonomy, which is an alternative institutional framework based on decentralization and democratization.[36]

The survey reveals a trend towards the involvement in more than one form of political activity and organization, and the types of networks and practices that the youth and students are involved in are quite diverse. Protesting and other forms

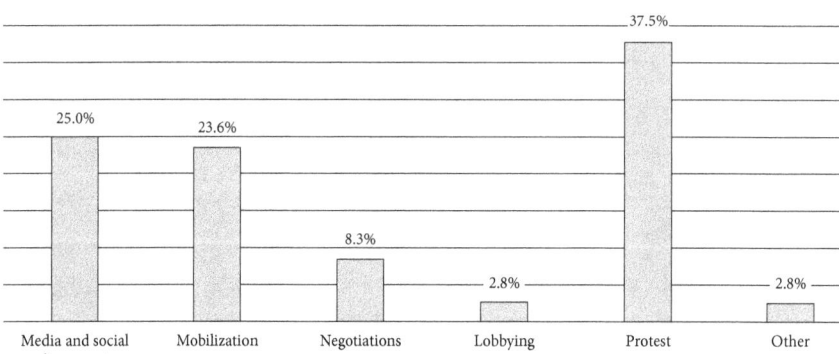

Figure 6.8 Action youth and students take when no one is representing them.

of collective mobilization can be singled out as the most common type of political activity that youth and students engage in. During the past few years in Turkey, Kurdish youth and students have participated in large numbers in popular protests during October 2014 against Turkey's inaction in the siege of Kobane by ISIS and during the Gezi Park protests during June 2013. The percentage of youth and students who are likely to support or engage in protests is higher than any other group. The number of youth and students who use media and social media campaigns to raise their demands is also significantly high. This is unsurprising given social media's popularity with young people. In contrast, the number who will resort to negotiation and lobbying is quite low, which shows that Kurdish youth and students are mainly part of dissident networks with very little access to government or state representatives and consequently collective action and protest are more common.

Mobilization, protest and media and social media campaigns also take a centre stage when youth and students want to make their voices heard when they feel no one is representing them, with 37.5 per cent of the respondents stating protest, 25 per cent media and social media campaigns and 23.6 percent mobilization as the action they are most likely to take. Some 8.3 per cent of youth and students identified negotiations as a method to get their voices heard when they feel no one is representing them. Similar to the situation of women, these negotiations are likely to be with political parties or civil society organizations who would be accessible to youth and students. Collective action by youth and students has been especially targeted by the police and security services since the summer of 2016 and many participants have been arrested. The police frequently use force to disperse Kurdish protesters and, as a result, there has been a significant decline in the number of protests taking place in the Kurdish majority regions in recent years. However, there were events in the past few years, such as election meetings and Newroz celebrations, that drew a large crowd and it is likely that if the restrictions are eased, protests and other forms of collective action could return in the Kurdish majority regions.

7

Representative democracy and the democratic confederal project: Reflections on the transformation of the Kurdish movement in Turkey

Thomas Jeffrey Miley with Luqman Guldivê

The context of state terror

The text by Cengiz Gunes provides an exhaustive overview of successive attempts to represent Kurdish identities, interests and aspirations in the party system of the Republic of Turkey. The legal obstacles and often harsh persecution that these would-be representatives have faced are a testimony to the limits on political freedom imposed by the constitutional order, which enshrines and promotes an aggressive, assimilationist, integral Turkish-nationalist conception of the Republic. Such a conception is incompatible with democracy in a context like that of the Republic of Turkey – a context characterized by 'deep diversities', associated with multiple communities of language and religious belief; a context with a long and bloody history of salient conflicts amongst citizens divided by alternative, competing and resilient conceptions of group belonging and political loyalty.[1]

Nor is it a coincidence that anti-democratic forces in the Republic of Turkey have so consistently and so vehemently insisted upon – even frequently rallied around – the imperative to repress the Kurdish minority. Recourse to tyranny in the name of the Turkish national majority against a mobilized and defiant Kurdish minority has proven a most effective formula for legitimating authoritarian rule, and indeed for countering any and all emergent challenges to existing relations of hierarchy. Nationalist belligerence as the antidote to the toxic threat of solidarity among the marginalized, the exploited, the oppressed.[2]

Human rights atrocities and state terror have been, and continue to be, inflicted upon the Kurdish minority by Turkish security forces, most brutally in the early 1990s, and now again with increasing intensity since the breakdown of peace negotiations in July of 2015. All-out war against the Kurdish Freedom Movement, both inside Turkey and across the border in Syria, has been the centrepiece of President Erdoğan's alliance with the far-right. Now, more than ever perhaps, the struggle for democracy in Turkey is thus intimately intertwined with the urgent need for a peaceful resolution to the so-called 'Kurdish question'. The alternative, as we have seen, is spiralling violence, tyranny and chaos.[3]

So too has the historical trajectory of the Kurdish Freedom Movement been profoundly influenced by the context of militarism, authoritarianism and paramilitary violence in which and against which it initially emerged and has never ceased to be in conflict. The Republic of Turkey was on the frontlines of the Cold War, a NATO member, and its security apparatus was armed to the teeth, and consistently permitted, encouraged, to be ruthless in its efforts to eradicate threats to capitalist social-property relations.

Torture and extra-judicial killings of leftist and pro-Kurdish militants propelled a process of polarization and radicalization that took place from the late 1960s, which escalated after successive coups in 1971 and 1980; coups that were intended to crush the left, and that reduced the legal channels for mobilizing anti-capitalist opposition to a bare minimum. A lethal combination of legal and extra-legal repression which together contributed to the emergence of the very kind of violent opposition whose eradication apologists for such measures claimed was the state's purpose and goal. A spiral of violence and repression was thus conjured, one that continues to this day.

The state and the guerrilla

The Kurdistan Workers' Party (PKK) was born in this maelstrom. From the outset, it was structured in accordance with the Marxist-Leninist principle of democratic centralism and conceived simultaneously as a vanguard political party and as a para-military force, a guerrilla committed to waging a 'prolonged people's war' for national liberation. Its goal was the attainment of a Kurdish nation-state, indeed, a state-communist utopia which would unite Kurds from Turkey, Iraq, Iran and Syria in a Greater Kurdistan.[4] A utopian dream, no doubt, equal to, if not even exceeding in ambition, the dystopian project against which it was struggling, that of the Kemalist Republic, with its intransigent goal of assimilating, if need be annihilating, all traces of Kurdish identity into a homogenized Turkish national imaginary.

The PKK acts in the name of the Kurdish nation. But as a proscribed guerrilla, it cannot be said to *represent* a Kurdish constituency, at least not in the same way that a legally recognized political party can.[5] In point of fact, even a legally recognized political party cannot be said to represent a nation, at least not in the same way that it can be described as representing a constituency. This is because, as Max Weber noted long ago, the nation belongs to the sphere of values, not to the realm of facts.[6] The common conflation between nation and state, terms treated so often as synonymous categories in discourse and praxis, must not be reproduced in social-science and political theory; for doing so contributes to the perpetuation of reified and essentialist notions of the nation which cover over and conceal the dynamics of power relations.[7]

Strictly speaking, it is citizens of the state who are represented by parliamentary assemblies, be it at local, 'regional' or 'national' (i.e. state-wide) levels. Elected representatives *represent* electoral constituencies, the boundaries of which, and electoral rules for, are established by laws whose compliance is guaranteed by the judiciary, and ultimately backed by the coercive force of the state. Likewise, the division of competences among different elected assemblies, as well as the balance of power between the legislative, executive and judicial branches of government are determined by constitutional norms, again, overseen by the judiciary, and ultimately backed by the coercive force of the state.

The state is thus the institutional arena within which claims to representation by politicians (elected or otherwise) are grounded, that is, recognized by law and guaranteed by force. Indeed, the state, to cite Max Weber again, has been famously defined as an organization, or complex of organizations, whose 'administrative staff (successfully) claims the monopoly of the legitimate use of physical force within a given territory'.[8]

Like all social-scientific definitions, Weber's one is, of course, contentious – but the intimate link he draws between *stateness* and violence is most certainly perceptive. It helps explain, for example, why the term 'terrorist' is most frequently reserved for non-state actors alone.[9] It also helps explain why state authorities tend to treat often relatively minor dangers posed to the general citizenry by so-called 'terrorist' organizations as if they were existential threats. For indeed, by challenging the state's monopoly on violence, such organizations effectively pose a challenge to what is commonly understood to be the very essence of *stateness*.[10]

Though in practice, not all paramilitary organizations are perceived as equally threatening by authorities of the state, as the experience of the Republic of Turkey confirms. In fact, state authorities have most often turned a blind eye, even collaborated with, paramilitary guerrilla forces committed to terrorizing individuals and communities suspected of actively plotting against 'territorial integrity' and/or against existing capitalist social-property relations, or simply sympathizing with those who do.[11] Good cop, bad cop, even worse cop.

It is worth emphasizing that Weber does not simply refer to the state as claiming a monopoly on violence, but rather, refers to a monopoly on *legitimate* violence.[12] The exercise of *illegitimate* violence, by contrast, we are led to assume, is the domain of the *criminal*, the *gangster*, the *bandit*, the *terrorist*. Though, of course, it can be objected that legitimacy, like beauty, is in the eye of the beholder – as reflected in the relevant, relativist maxim, that one person's terrorist is another person's freedom fighter. Though it would perhaps be more prudent to leave such objections to the cynics, the believers in, and practitioners of, *realpolitik*. After all, Socrates made Thrasymachus blush.

The term *terrorism* has a relatively straightforward definition, definitely more straightforward than Weber's difficult definition of the state. According to Wikipedia, '*terrorism* is, in the broadest sense, the use of intentionally indiscriminate violence as a means to create terror among masses of people in order to achieve a financial, political, religious, or ideological aim'. Though the web's most famous free encyclopaedia is quick to add, in a bout of online epistemic humility that stands in striking contrast to the boldness with which it dares to define the state, that 'there is no commonly accepted definition of terrorism'.[13]

In the context of the ongoing, Orwellian 'War on Terror', the impulse to embrace such reflexivity, to acknowledge the normative dimension and contested nature of the term *terrorism*, is understandable.[14] For the term is wielded with worrisome effectiveness by scaremongers cum warmongers in the political arena and the mass media in an extremely demagogic fashion, serving simultaneously to silence dissent and mobilize support for draconian measures at home and illegal wars of aggression abroad. A dose of relativism might indeed appear a useful antidote against such mass intoxication by neo-fascist propaganda techniques.

And yet, as Darnell Stephen Summers has cogently stressed, recourse to this type of relativism in debates about the nature of terrorism has one most unfortunate consequence for defenders of civil liberties and critics of tyranny: namely, it lets the biggest culprits of terrorism off the hook.[15] Who are these biggest culprits? Without a doubt, state actors. Indeed, according to the common-sense definition provided by Wikipedia, the United States of America is by far the most lethal terrorist organization on the planet. Its NATO partner, the Republic of Turkey, also ranks among the worst offenders. As do all of the US's fellow members on the UN Security Council.[16]

The PKK, as a paramilitary guerrilla force, has from the time of its inception been considered by the state authorities of the Republic of Turkey to be a terrorist organization. Indeed, Turkish authorities have consistently treated the PKK as public enemy number one; and as a result, those suspected of belonging to the organization, or even sympathizing with it, have been the victims of successive waves of brutal state terror. At the height of the war between the Turkish state and the PKK in the early 1990s, thousands of Kurdish villages were forcefully evacuated, tens of thousands murdered, a mass exodus provoked. More recently, since the breakdown of peace negotiations in 2015, another brutal wave of state terror has been unleashed, this time including urban settings, leaving another bloody trail of thousands killed and hundreds of thousands forcibly displaced.[17]

There is, of course, blood on the hands of the PKK, too, though not nearly as much as that on the hands of the Turkish security forces with which it has been at war for over four decades now.[18] Still, as PKK founder Abdullah Öcalan has come to lament, the organization has on too many occasions been guilty of behaving like a state.[19] This state-like behaviour on the part of the guerrilla cannot be treated lightly, or dismissed as a mere aberration; instead, it merits social-scientific analysis and theoretical reflection, as Öcalan himself has attempted, from the confines of his lonely prison cell on Imrali Island.

The right to rebel

Why the resemblance between the guerrilla and the state? There are many aspects to this question that must be addressed if we are to provide an adequate explanation. Let us begin with the matter of violence. The PKK launched its military offensive against the Turkish state in 1984, four years after the 1980 coup had triggered a bout of severe state repression, two years after the 1982 Constitutional reform had further entrenched military prerogatives, effectively confining and constricting the terrain of civilian politics. In a word, the PKK's offensive was a product and response to this context of state aggression and denial of basic civil liberties.

One need not be an anarchist to be able to understand and willing to apologize for, or even advocate, violent resistance in the face of such conditions of state tyranny. On the contrary, the theoretical tools of classical liberalism should in this regard suffice. After all, the canonical English liberal political philosopher John Locke famously justified the so-called 'Glorious Revolution' of the late seventeenth century, in which he took part, along the following lines:

> *Whenever the Legislators endeavor to take away, and destroy the Property of the People*, or to reduce them to Slavery under Arbitrary Power, they put themselves into a state of War with the People, who are thereupon absolved from any farther Obedience, and are left to the common Refuge, which God hath provided for all Men, against Force and Violence. Whensoever therefore the *Legislative* shall transgress this fundamental Rule of Society; and either by Ambition, Fear, Folly or Corruption, *endeavor to grasp* themselves, *or put into the hands of any other an Absolute Power* over the Lives, Liberties, and Estates of the People; By this breach of Trust *they forfeit the Power*, the People had put into their hands, for quite contrary ends, and it devolves to the People, who have a Right to resume their original Liberty.[20]

To put the point simply, for Locke, and for classical liberal political theory, when the state has declared war upon the people, the people are justified in taking up arms against the state.[21] To translate these terms of Enlightenment-era liberal philosophy into the language of post-Enlightenment Weberian social science, this means that, in conditions of authoritarian encroachments upon civil liberties and infringement of basic human rights, state actors risk losing their ability to exercise a monopoly on the use of legitimate violence.[22]

But it is one thing to be justified in taking up arms against state tyranny; another to be successful. Which brings us to the matter of survival. The PKK, of course, never came close to its original goal of establishing a state-communist Greater Kurdistan; and yet, it has achieved a feat that is rather remarkable nevertheless. Up against NATO's second-largest army, it has managed to survive, even to thrive, to maintain a plausible claim to represent a broad constituency of Kurdish people, for over forty years now. How has this virtual stalemate with the Turkish state been possible?

There is an old Kurdish saying that the Kurds have no friends but the mountains. Certainly, the region's mountainous terrain has helped the guerrilla to survive, rendering it logistically difficult for the Turkish security forces to eradicate it. Even so, the many decades of survival would have clearly been impossible if the guerrilla did not count on significant levels of popular support among the Kurdish public.[23]

The racism and systemic discrimination that Kurds have long faced at the hands of the Turkish state, intertwined and combined with the poverty and exploitation that characterizes the lives of so many Kurds, in both rural villages and urban shanty-towns, provides an objective basis, a reservoir of material and symbolic grievances, underpinning popular attitudes, helping to account for propensities to support insurrection.[24]

Multiple Kurdish constituencies

The PKK's efforts and success in recruiting a high proportion of proletarian and *lumpen* members among its early cadres, along with its aggressive pursuit of class warfare in the Kurdish countryside from the outset of its military campaign, earned it respect and revolutionary credentials, and clearly distinguished it from all other previous and contemporary rival pro-Kurdish organizations, which had been composed of, and catered nearly exclusively to, middle-class activists and sensibilities.[25]

But such respect and support have been by no means unanimous among Kurds. The PKK's ongoing military campaign has also earned it much enmity and fear among certain segments of the Kurdish population, especially those who, for diverse motives, have opted for collaboration with the Turkish authorities.[26] Such 'collaborationism' has been frequent not only among the wealthy few, the large-holding landowners who for generations have been integrated into the Republic's clientelistic networks; but also among less wealthy Kurds who over the course of the war have been co-opted or coerced into the village guard system, as well as among others who have been pulled into the orbit of reactionary forms of political Islam. And, of course, between the supporters and the collaborators, there are those with mixed feelings, the ambivalent, the a-political.

The relative success of Erdoğan's ruling AKP in general elections in Kurdish-majority provinces is well documented by Cengiz Gunes. The evidence he presents should be more than enough to correct over-simplified and binary accounts that would divide the Kurdish population into an overwhelming patriotic and revolutionary majority, on the one side, and a collaborationist and reactionary minority, on the other. The spectrum of political identities, opinions and behaviour among Kurds is certainly more complicated than that.

Unfortunately, there is a scarcity of survey research on patterns of national identification in the Republic of Turkey.[27] The formal restrictions on freedom of expression, combined with informal taboos, especially on matters related to Kurdish identity, have to date rendered such research for the most part unfeasible. Survey research would allow us to measure the diffusion of competing or complementary conceptions and sentiments of national belonging across diverse segments of the population; to see how these conceptions and sentiments relate to aspirations for the recognition of cultural rights, and for various degrees of political autonomy and/or independence; to verify how such conceptions, sentiments and aspirations relate to a host of different political attitudes and behaviours; to locate this variety of individual identities, attitudes and behaviours within existing constellations of material and social power relations; even to observe with some precision how these patterns evolve over time. The copious public opinion research on nationalisms in Spain, since the time of the transition to democracy in the late 1970s until the present, is exemplary in this regard.[28]

One of the great virtues of the comparative research project spearheaded by Faleh Jabar, of which the text by Cengiz Gunes is a part, is the systematic effort built into the research design to analyse how political representatives in the Kurdish regions of Turkey, Iraq, Syria and Iran respond to such questions. However, in Bakur, the context of intense repression following the breakdown of peace negotiations in July 2015, and especially in the aftermath of the attempted coup in July 2016, rendered conducting this research exceedingly difficult. The researchers commissioned by Jabar's team to do the work in Turkey are to be commended for their bravery. For indeed, many of the questions they posed to representatives of the different political parties are very sensitive. Keep in mind that many HDP representatives, including co-chairs Selahattin Demirtaş and Figen Yüksekdağ, have been imprisoned and charged with treason for making public statements articulating demands for political autonomy.[29]

The literature on nationalism in general, and on Turkish and Kurdish nationalisms in particular, is rich in detail when it comes to tracing the biographies and worldviews of nationalist activists and leaders, as well as the histories and programs of nationalist parties; but we know much less about the perspectives and sentiments of the people in whose names these leaders, activists and parties speak, that is, who they claim to represent.[30]

We can infer some things about the level of acceptance of these elite and activist perspectives among the general public from records of electoral performance. Yet, there are limits to our ability to infer from such records. For starters, because political parties present policy bundles or packages for competition in electoral campaigns.[31] Issues associated with national identity and aspirations are only part of the political programmes between which voters choose on election day. So, for example, a voter might opt for the AKP in a general election despite disagreeing with the party's stance on the so-called 'Kurdish question', because s/he approves of the ruling party's neoliberal development agenda and/or track record, or more likely because s/he approves of the AKP's version of political Islam. Indeed, post-election surveys are good tools for helping researchers decipher the meaning of electoral outcomes.

To make matters worse, in the case of the Republic of Turkey, the history of constitutional and legal proscriptions and restrictions on pro-Kurdish parties further complicates our ability to infer from electoral outcomes alone the contours of public opinion on matters related to national identity.

A comparison between Turkey and Spain

In Spain, the rich history of public opinion survey research on national identities, a tradition that can be traced back to the efforts of Juan Linz, has been usefully supplemented by an albeit smaller corpus of elite survey research, which allows us to compare and contrast the attitudes, identities and aspirations of parliamentarians with those of the constituencies who they represent.[32] This allows for crucial insights into the nature and limits of political representation regarding such matters in the country.[33] No equivalent scholarly corpus exists for Turkey, despite the valiant in-roads made by Faleh Jabar and his associates, including this important text by Cengiz Gunes.

Since the outbreak of the war between the PKK and the Turkish state in the 1980s, there has been an impressive proliferation of scholarly research on the so-called Kurdish question. And yet, we still know very little about what it means for ordinary people to call themselves Kurds. In Spain, to give but one important example, we know that for a clear majority of those who identify as Catalans or Basques, registering such identification does not preclude them from identifying as Spaniards as well. If asked the question, 'How do you identify yourself?' and given five options, 'Turkish, More Turkish than Kurdish, Equally Turkish and Kurdish, More Kurdish than Turkish, or Kurdish', what would the patterns of responses in Bakur be? Or, for that matter, what would the patterns of responses be among migrants from the Kurdish region living in the metropolitan regions of Istanbul and Ankara? Of course, no question is neutral, and how a question is framed can certainly condition responses. But survey research can also shed light on how the same people respond to differently framed questions.

As Juan Linz has explained, such survey research was very difficult to carry out before the transition to democracy in Spain. The fact that this type of research is virtually non-existent in Turkey is indicative of the level of authoritarian restrictions on political freedom in the Republic.

The comparison between the restrictions on freedoms in Franco's Spain and those in the Republic of Turkey raises an interesting question: how should the Republic of Turkey be classified in terms of the typology of political regimes?[34] The transition from a single-party state to competitive party politics occurred alongside, and was spurred on by, the Republic's incorporation into NATO, at the onset of the Cold War, right after the Second World War.[35] However, the space of permissible party competition remained severely constrained by Kemalist criteria embedded in the constitutional order, with entrenched military prerogatives reinforced after the 1980 coup. The tradition of coups – in 1960, 1971, 1980 and 1997 – long rendered emphatically clear the military's determination to make use of its prerogatives when deemed necessary to ensure the perpetuation of Kemalist ideals, rendering them beyond the scope of permissible political competition.[36] A 'guarded democracy', at best, with a long track record of constitutional and legal restrictions on representation for anti-capitalist, anti-secular and pro-Kurdish political organizations, as well as a bloody history of endemic political violence, state terror and human rights atrocities.

A crisis of Kemalist hegemony?

Since the ascension of Erdoğan and the AKP to power in 2002, Kemalist hegemony has increasingly given way to what Cihad Hammy has evocatively dubbed 'a marriage between Turkish nationalism and authoritarian Islam'.[37] Against the backdrop of ongoing accession talks with the European Union, there was much hope that Erdoğan might usher in a more democratic era of politics in the country; but by now, such hopes have given way to fears of neo-fascist involution, especially after the successive, escalating developments of (1) the demise of prospects for membership in the EU; (2) the breakdown of the alliance between Erdoğan and the Gülen movement, and the subsequent struggle for control over the state apparatus; (3) the end of peace negotiations and the reignition of all-out war against the Kurdish Freedom Movement; (4) the massive purges and political repression that followed the July 2016 failed coup; and (5) the hyper-presidentialist reform of the constitution. The constantly looming threat of coups may, for now, have been vanquished; however, the result is far from the liberal democratic 'end of history' once promised, but rather the emergence of yet another case of an increasingly frequent form of hybrid regime – which some scholars have termed 'participatory competitive authoritarianism', others 'electoral authoritarianism' and yet others 'electoral hegemony'.[38]

Robert Dahl famously distinguished 'polyarchies' (his preferred term for liberal, representative democracies) from other types of regimes, based on two dimensions or criteria: (a) the level of 'liberalization' or public contestation permitted; and (b) the level of inclusiveness in political participation permitted. Based on these two dimensions, he came up with a useful four-fold typology of political regimes: (1) closed hegemony (low liberalization, low inclusiveness); (2) inclusive hegemony (low liberalization, high inclusiveness); (3) competitive oligarchy (high liberalization, low inclusiveness); and (4) polyarchy (high liberalization, high inclusiveness).[39] According to this, the Republic of Turkey has long qualified as a regime of inclusive hegemony.

Dahl's choice of terms is in some respects confusing. For those familiar with Gramsci, especially, the distinction Dahl draws between 'hegemony' and 'polyarchy' (or 'liberal democracy') will most certainly seem counter-intuitive.[40] Likewise, for those familiar with the long and bloody history of human rights abuses by state authorities, to consider it 'inclusive' would appear the wrong term.

However, there is one important sense in which it makes sense to refer to the Republic of Turkey as an 'inclusive' regime. Unlike the regime of segregation during the Jim Crow era in the United States, or the regime of apartheid in South Africa, or under colonial regimes, the Republic of Turkey does not have any formal restrictions on the franchise; nor does it make any formal distinction between citizens and subjects. The regime is not formally 'exclusionary', but rather, 'assimilationist'.[41] Indeed, the term long officially used to describe its citizens of Kurdish descent was 'Mountain Turks'.[42]

Even so, though the regime is not exclusionary in principle, it has indeed proven exclusionary in practice. As I have described the Republic of Turkey elsewhere:

> A nationalizing state, dominated by an 'integral' brand of nationalism, assimilationist in principle, exclusionary more often than not in practice (Brubaker 1996). A nationalist mentality captured well by the famous words of the then-Prime Minister, Ismet Inönü, whose father was a 'Turkified Kurd', and who was destined to succeed Kemal as president after Kemal's death in 1938. He would insist, in 1925, in the midst of the wave of brutal repression: 'In the face of a Turkish majority other elements have no kind of influence. We must Turkify the inhabitants of our land at any price, and we will annihilate those who oppose the Turks or *'le Turquisme'*. A supremacist and ultimately exclusionary mentality captured even more bluntly by Kemal's Minister of Justice, who would boast in 1930: 'We live in a country called Turkey, the freest in the world. As your deputy, I feel I can express my real convictions without reserve. I believe that the Turk must be the only lord, the only master of his country. Those who are not of pure Turkish stock can only have one right in this country, the right to be servants and slaves' (Özcan 2006, p. 70).[43]

The nationalizing state versus the Kurdish project of 'national revival'

An 'integral' nationalism, the Turkish one. Why, we may ask, has its assimilationist project failed? Undoubtedly, a significant part of the explanation has to do with the dynamics of what Trotsky called 'combined, uneven development'. The systemic discrimination faced by people of Kurdish descent is not reducible to, but certainly has a lot to do with, their poverty. The grinding poverty associated with Kurdishness has not only reinforced popular prejudices against Kurds; most likely even more importantly, it long prohibited the majority of Kurds from the opportunity to assimilate, even if they so desired. Indeed, levels of literacy in the Kurdish region have consistently been by far the lowest in the country; as late as 1960, the literacy rate stood at only 15 per cent; and as late as 1970, it remained only 30 per cent.[44]

Significantly, it was in the 1960s that Kurdish intellectuals took advantage of the trend of liberalization that characterized that decade both to mobilize in favour of public expression in the Kurdish language and, increasingly, over the course of the decade, to articulate the idea that the Kurdish region constituted an 'internal colony'. By the 1970s, Kurdish university students, including the young Abdullah Öcalan, came on the scene, committed to spreading the gospel of 'internal colonialism' among the Kurdish masses.[45]

Miroslav Hroch, in his classic book, *The Social Preconditions of National Revival in Europe*, documents the spread of national consciousness among minorities in Europe, and usefully distinguishes among three phases of mobilization: Phase A, in which a minority of intellectuals come to valorize and cultivate awareness about the worth of the minority group's language, culture and history; Phase B, in which a new generation of activists increasingly politicize this project, and begin evangelizing beyond intellectual circles, among broader segments of the minority group; and Phase C, in which a mass movement emerges.[46] The model he provides need not be interpreted in a deterministic or teleological manner, the transition from Phase A to Phase B to Phase C is not inevitable or unavoidable. However, as the movement gains momentum, with each successive transition among phases, the task for state authorities of assimilating the minority group into the majority nation is rendered increasingly difficult, if not utopian. Indeed, once a movement of 'national revival' has passed the threshold of gaining significant traction among members of a minority group, efforts at assimilation to fend off the emergent threat to the dominant nationalist imaginary, to the one propagated by the state, are likely to be counterproductive, to trigger polarization, even spiral like a boomerang.[47]

The plight of the Kurds in Turkey, however, is in important respects different from that of the 'national minorities' in Europe whose movements are so insightfully analysed by Hroch – the Norwegians, the Czechs, the Finns, the Estonians, the Lithuanians, the Slovaks, the Flemish and the Danes (in Schleswig). We emphasized above that the 'assimilationist', integral nation-building policies of the Turkish state distinguished the Kurdish plight from that of colonialism proper. But the crucial similarities between the Kurdish plight and that of colonized peoples should not be ignored either. Similarities associated with the sense of quasi-racial superiority propagated by the Turkish nationalizing-state, and reflected in widespread, popular prejudices among the Turkish-speaking national majority vis-à-vis the Kurds.

The plight of the Kurdish 'permanent minority'

Robert Dahl has emphasized the problem for democratic theory posed by the plight of permanent minorities.[48] Representative democracy tends to presuppose that groups that constitute minorities today can tomorrow become the majority. But for 'national' minorities, at least once the threshold of national consciousness among a critical mass has been crossed, their fate is that of a permanent minority, perpetually facing the threat of tyranny exercised in the name of the majority.

Federal or other 'consociational' arrangements can help ameliorate the plight of permanent minorities, but to institutionalize such measures democratically would require the consent of the majority. What's more, even after such measures are institutionalized, the arbiters of the new federal division of powers are likely to enforce the views of the hegemonic majority whenever push comes to shove. This might sound like an argument in favour of secessionism – if it weren't for the fact that 'national' groups are not hermetically sealed, and thus cannot be discretely divided. As such, the creation of new national states is capable of creating new national majorities, but much less likely to resolve the problem of permanent minorities.[49]

The problem for the Kurdish minority in Turkey has been further compounded by the constraints and constrictions, both legal and extra-legal, on political representation for perspectives and projects that would challenge hegemonic, integral Turkish-nationalist conceptions. It is not a coincidence that the 'revival' and mobilization of Kurdish national consciousness took place during the 1960s, a decade of relative liberalization. But the limits of the Republic's newfound toleration were soon reached.

The so-called 'coup by memorandum' of 1971 unleashed a crackdown on the anti-capitalist left, as well as on any and all expressions of pro-Kurdish sentiments – a crackdown that included proscriptions on political organizations accused of propagating Kurdish 'separatism', prosecution of prominent pro-Kurdish militants, among others, even more repressive police-state tactics, including widespread torture, as security forces combed the Kurdish countryside in an effort to hunt down leftists and 'separatist agitators'.[50]

The suppression of legal channels for expressing and mobilizing anti-capitalist dissent contributed to the proliferation of leftist guerrilla groups over the course of the 1970s, which in turn exacerbated the vehemence and the violence of the security forces, as well as that of far-right paramilitary groups with organic links to the 'deep state'. A spiral of violence had commenced, albeit one in which, it should not be forgotten, the torture and violence perpetrated by forces on the right far outweighed any human rights' violations by forces on the left. The repressive violence would be stepped up even further after the 1980 coup.[51]

Violence and national consciousness

This is the context in which the PKK emerged, something all-too-conveniently and often ignored or forgotten in moralizing, liberal condemnations of the paramilitary organization's means and ends. It is, as well, a context which renders the analogy between the Kurdish plight in Turkey and the plight of colonized peoples seem more plausible, indeed, that makes it impossible to dismiss such claims as mere rhetorical bluster or hyperbole.

Which brings us, again, to the matter of violence. For decolonization, as Fanon has famously insisted, 'is always a violent phenomenon'. More specifically, in his much-celebrated analysis of the dynamics of the Algerian anti-colonial struggle, Fanon brings to bear insights from psychoanalysis to emphasize the constructive aspect of violence, its ability to generate national consciousness. According to Fanon, this constructive, generative capacity of anti-colonial violence operates at both the collective and the individual levels. Collectively, '[t]he armed struggle mobilizes the people', binding them together, 'throw[ing] them in one way and in one direction'. Immersion in this process of armed struggle, in turn, has ramifications at the level of the individual psyche and consciousness. Not only does it 'introduc[e] into each man's consciousness the ideas of a common cause, of national destiny and of a collective history'; simultaneously, anti-colonial violence acts as 'a cleansing force'. It 'frees the native from his inferiority complex and from his despair and inaction', 'makes him fearless' and 'restores his self-respect'.[52]

Fanon's text has been frequently misconstrued as a one-sided, even reckless, celebration of anti-colonial violence – perhaps because people pay too much attention to the chapter 'Concerning Violence' and not enough attention to the chapter on 'Colonial Wars and Mental Disorders'.[53] Be that as it may, his point about the capacity of anti-colonial violence to generate national consciousness introduces an important element worthy of consideration in any discussion about representation and the 'national question'.

Hroch's model of 'revival' among national minorities in Europe is one that does not presuppose or require any causal role for violence – except to the extent that the context of the state, in which and against which these movements are mobilized, sets the parameters of peaceful politics, implicitly threatening to make use of its 'monopoly on legitimate violence' whenever the ruling class perceives a fundamental threat to its interests. But Hroch himself has very little to say about this.

Even so, from the standpoint of representation, it is worth noting that in the European cases Hroch studies, he finds national consciousness to have been invariably born amongst intellectuals, the 'national agitators' par excellence, and only subsequently spreads beyond this stratum to be taken up by broader segments of society. Hroch's observation is in line with Eric Hobsbawm's more general historical-materialist claim that national consciousness tends to arise most intensely and most consistently among the 'lesser examination-passing classes'.[54] Likewise, both Hroch's and Hobsbawm's observations square with those of Max Weber, who advanced a similar argument over a century ago. According to Weber:

> The significance of the 'nation' is usually anchored in the superiority, or at least the irreplaceability, of the culture values that are to be preserved and developed only through the cultivation of the peculiarity of the group. It therefore goes without saying that the intellectuals, as we have in a preliminary fashion called them, are to a specific degree predestined to propagate the 'national idea', just as those who wield power in the polity provoke the idea of the state.
>
> By 'intellectuals' we understand a group of men who by virtue of their peculiarity have special access to certain achievements considered to be 'culture values', and who therefore usurp the leadership of a 'culture community'.[55]

As such, the 'national ideal' does not arise spontaneously; nor does it necessarily even resonate among wide swathes of the toiling masses, among peasants or urban workers, at least, not initially. In some cases, the original core of intellectuals who serve as bearers of the national ideal manage to evangelize effectively, and their ideal takes root among the masses. But far from always.

Most often, the instrument used for the 'nationalization of the masses' has been the state itself. This is largely true even for the prototypical European cases of 'national unification', Germany and Italy. Indeed, as Guiseppi Mazzini, first prime minister of Italy, would emblematically declare: 'We have made Italy, now we must make Italians'.[56] In other cases, however, in opposition to a state, the instrument has been a party, including – as Fanon observed with the FLN – ones organized as guerrillas, engaged in armed struggle. Such has been the historic role of the PKK in the Kurdish region of Turkey.

The motifs of martyrdom and collective sacrifice

To insist upon the PKK's role in generating national consciousness among Kurds is not to deny pre-existing awareness, feelings or shared senses of Kurdishness beyond the core of revolutionary militants. Instead, it is to suggest that the guerrilla's intervention transformed the significance of such sentiments, rendering Kurdish subjectivity politically salient, increasingly defiant, infused with a collective will to struggle. Even if, in the process, it pits some Kurds against others, elevating a sanctified few to the status of heroes, while expelling others from the emergent imagined community.

The sanctified few are mostly militants killed in combat, revered as 'martyrs', their blood sacrifice commemorated in posters, as a sign of respect and as a means of strengthening resolve among the living. Their images represent and give meaning to the Kurdish struggle; the 'martyrs' provide a model for militant ethics, a vision of revolutionary virtue; they thus exercise a powerful influence over the contours and content of political imagination in and around the movement.[57] We shall prevail, we must prevail, the 'martyrs' did not shed their blood in vain. Such are the sentiments evoked. This is how courage is concocted, fortitude forged.

Imagined communities are also about imagined possibilities. About what people can imagine being possible; about what they imagine themselves to be capable of enduring and achieving; about what they can imagine themselves being willing to kill for and, more importantly, what they can imagine themselves being willing to die for. When pragmatic acquiescence to an unjust status quo comes to seem unbearable, when death comes to seem preferable, when resistance comes to seem the only option, this is when new political communities are born.

The 'martyrs', through their ultimate sacrifice, helped to create new horizons of imagination among the living. In this respect, they can be said to represent the Kurdish nation. Despite the fact that they are not 'representative' – indeed, in a way, precisely *because* they are not. They represent in a *generative* sense. Through their individual examples and deaths, they bring a new consciousness into being. They *prefigure* and *embody* the ideals of a revolutionary nation to come.

Öcalan as prophet

There are the 'martyrs'; and then there is the leader. The one whose appeal and authority is recognized and celebrated by virtually everybody in the movement, whose leadership is treated as indisputable, beyond question or contestation. A secular prophet, the nation in the flesh. Abdullah Öcalan. It is Öcalan for whom the 'martyrs' fell; his vision and will that inspires the struggle. The concept of charisma most certainly applies. Max Weber proves again useful for our attempt to comprehend. Weber defined charisma as:

> [A] certain quality of an individual personality, by virtue of which he is set apart from ordinary men and treated as endowed with supernatural, superhuman, or at least specifically exceptional powers or qualities. These are such as are not accessible to the ordinary person, but are regarded as of divine origin or as exemplary, and on the basis of them the individual concerned is treated as a leader ...[58]

The followers of Öcalan are bound by his charismatic authority. They recognize in him 'exceptional personal qualities' and 'extraordinary personal accomplishments', which together inspire their 'loyalty and obedience', very much in accordance with Weber's characterization of the phenomenon. But still, the phenomenon remains quite difficult to grasp, at least in purely secular terms. As Charles Lindholm has explained:

> Charisma as a term, of course, did not originate with Weber. It had a long history in Christian theological discourse, and signified the gift of grace, resembling in some senses the Greek idea of the 'divine man' or the Roman concept of *facilitas*, the hero's innate ability to project to success due to his connection with the divine. For Christians it meant the intuitive recognition by laypeople that a saint has intimate contact with God.[59]

There is something analogous at work in the relationship between Öcalan and his disciples, which is what makes it appropriate to refer to him as a secular prophet.

Among modern secular leaders, this charismatic relationship resembles in an important respect the reverence long accorded to figures such as Mao and Mandela. Indeed, it was from Mao, albeit inflected through the example of Che Guevara, that Öcalan had originally devised and sought to implement the PKK's initial strategy of a 'prolonged people's war'. And like Mao, Öcalan's tremendous popularity is linked to his recognition as a hero of the cause of national liberation. Though crucially, unlike Mao, Öcalan's movement was never victorious, though it has not been defeated either.

After Mao came to power, the Chinese Communist Party would instrumentalize and transform this popular reverence, making use of the state apparatus and of authoritarian controls over political communication to carefully cultivate 'the image of Mao as a saviour of the Chinese nation', as a means of increasing both 'internal cohesion and external appeal'. Even so, as Leese has emphasized, this image 'always bore the danger of being hijacked for contradictory purposes', at least unless it 'remained under firm party control'.[60] And in fact, in the mid-1960s, during the Cultural Revolution, Mao would consciously employ the cult 'to mobilize the masses against the party bureaucracy'.[61]

Of course, rather than coming to power, Öcalan was forced into exile in Syria, where he lived for close to two decades, before being forced out of that country, too, eventually apprehended and subsequently imprisoned on Imrali island, where he has remained, in virtual isolation, for two decades more. In this respect, his plight and charismatic appeal are more reminiscent of Nelson Mandela, whose decades-long imprisonment on Robben Island served to reinforce his moral authority, rendering him a living symbol of the oppression of his people.

In the end, Mandela, like Mao, also came to power. But, in contrast to Mao, he was elected into office, and successively and successfully incorporated into the liberal-democratic, capitalistic mainstream. His charismatic appeal managed to survive, for the most part untarnished, even beyond his death, though put to the service of decidedly reformist ends. Among the pantheon of domesticated myths, right next to Gandhi and Martin Luther King. Öcalan, instead, remains to this day a captive, confined to a lonely existence in conditions of extreme isolation, inside his prison cell, 'chained to the rock of Imrali'.[62] Though in a way he has been fortunate; for his captivity has allowed him thus far to avoid succumbing to either of the twin temptations, of tyranny or co-optation.

The paradox of democratic leadership

Charismatic leadership stands in considerable tension to the logic of representative democracy. As a type of authority, Weber contrasted it explicitly to 'traditional' modes of rule, on the one hand, and to 'legal-rational' ones, on the other. Weber conceived of charismatic authority as both a 'revolutionary and an unstable form of authority'. One of the distinguishing features of charismatic leaders, according to Ivan Szelenyi, a prominent interpreter of Weber, is their ability to 'promise change' and to radically alter 'people's attitudes and values'. This is both the source of charisma's strength as well as of its instability, since it tends to 'deteriorate if the leader cannot produce the promised changes'.[63] In the process, charismatic relationships are routinized, channelled and transformed into one of the other two modes of rule.[64]

The radical alterations in people's attitudes and values that charismatic leaders are capable of inducing renders them revolutionary. And yet, the difficulty of delivering on their promises renders their charismatic authority unstable – prone to dissipation, routinization or both. Öcalan's imprisonment, like that of Mandela, has resulted in a strengthening of his charismatic appeal, an intensification of devotion to him among his followers. But at the same time, his prolonged isolation has also induced a good dose of self-reflection – about the dangers of the twin temptations of tyranny and co-optation.

In fact, well before his arrest, from 1993, at the height of the war, in the midst of devastating human rights atrocities by the Turkish security forces, including mass village evacuations, Öcalan had begun to make calls for peace. Such calls were due in no small part to a pragmatic recognition of the impossibility of ever winning a 'prolonged people's war' against NATO's second-largest army, especially given the global balance of power in the post-Cold War world. But the end of the Cold War also got Öcalan thinking about the reasons for the defeat of state-communism.[65]

So began a long process of re-assessment, re-articulation and transformation, of both the means and the ends of the movement he had inspired. A process that would accelerate in the months and years after his arrest. Paradoxically enough, prison turned out to be a place of mental freedom for Öcalan who, despite very limited access to books, has produced a most impressive corpus of writings, both in terms of volume and ambition. In one of his most recent publications, Öcalan reflected explicitly on this paradoxically emancipatory impact of imprisonment on the parameters of his thought. In his words:

> Before prison, while I was able to develop both in theory and practical action, I did not have much of a chance to develop my perception of truth. For those who face grave challenges in life, the circumstances of a prison are highly educational. Maximum security prisons are not places for theoretical and practical struggle; instead, they are places where, if one's will is not crushed, one can develop a deep perception of truth and the means necessary to struggle for it. Prison allows those who fight for exceptional causes to strive daily to attain the truth. Prison time that is spent doing this is, I am certain, worthwhile.[66]

From seeker of power to seeker of truth. Such are the terms Öcalan chooses to depict the transition of his existential orientation while in captivity. His will to power kept in check. And a lot of time on his hands, to read, to think, to write. A monastic life of sorts, which would appear to have opened epistemic horizons previously denied him. Though unlike a monk or an ordinary prisoner, millions hang on his every word.

While in prison, Öcalan has used his charismatic authority to affect a paradigm shift in the Kurdish Freedom Movement – from a Marxist-Leninist conception of national liberation to a radical democratic critique of the state, and of patriarchy as the root of all hierarchy. Indeed, influenced by the framework of libertarian municipalism sketched by social-ecologist Murray Bookchin, Öcalan has elaborated a thoroughgoing critique of the tenets of democratic centralism, alongside a principled renunciation of the goal of a Kurdish nation-state. A 'democratic confederal' alternative, not just for Kurds, but for the broader Middle East.[67]

Quite an unexpected, radical-democratic turn coming from a charismatic guerrilla leader of a national liberation movement. Unprecedented even, perhaps. An attempt to channel his charismatic appeal and influence not towards the conquest of state power, but rather, to get his followers to embrace a comprehensive critique of all relations of hierarchy, oppression and domination. An exercise in democratic leadership, one is tempted to conclude.

The theory of democracy has a hard time dealing with leadership.[68] Indeed, to many, the very notion of 'democratic leadership' will probably sound like a contradiction in terms. If not a cynical catchphrase, like that of 'democratic centralism'. The Leninist conception of 'democratic centralism' served to legitimate a monopoly of power by the Communist Party; in turn, a monopoly of power within the Party by the Central Committee; in turn, most often, a monopoly of power within the Central Committee by the Party Chairman. In a word, autocracy, or dictatorship, couched in the language of democracy. All 'leadership', no democracy, if not in the theory, certainly in the practice, of 'democratic centralism'.

But what about the theory, and the practice, of multiparty, representative democracy? What is the space for democratic leadership in such regimes? This question is very much related to the concept of representation. Mainstream democratic theorists tend to measure the quality of representation, and even define democracy, first and foremost in accordance with the criterion of responsiveness. For example, as Robert Dahl would write on the very first page of *Polyarchy*, 'a key characteristic of a democracy is the continuing responsiveness of the government to the preferences of citizens, considered as political equals'.[69] Likewise, Adam Przeworski insists: '[a] collectivity governs itself democratically when decisions implemented on its behalf reflect the preferences of its members'.[70]

The limits and logic of 'representative democracy'[71]

Such is the theory. However, in practice, the empirical literature has demonstrated a high degree of autonomy, or lack of responsiveness, between the policy preferences of democratic constituencies and the policy views and choices of elected representatives. This can be attributed in no small part to the fact that political parties are hierarchical organizations susceptible to capture by privileged minorities and powerful interest groups.[72]

Competitive, multiparty elections are intended to secure a certain degree of responsiveness, by giving the electorate the opportunity to hold unresponsive representatives accountable – the chance 'to throw the bums out'. However, privileged groups can exercise their power to secure disproportionate influence among multiple parties across the party system, and thus get them to collude to disregard constituency preferences.

Most often the means by which establishment parties so collude is by changing the subject, that is, by 'mobilizing biases' and 'setting the agenda', so as to reduce the terrain or set of issues over which they compete, to begin with.[73] Such de facto reduction of the terrain of party competition means, in practice, that representative democracy most often come closer to Dahl's ideal type of 'inclusive hegemony' than to his ideal type of 'polyarchy'.

The constriction of the space of multiparty competition need not take place through explicit lobbying, direct capture or conscious collusion among political representatives and the state bureaucracy. Most emblematically, in the case of corporate capitalist interests, because of their control over crucial, productive resources, this minority almost always possesses a 'blackmail' power sufficient to limit the policy options that can be seriously considered, much less pursued, by any elected government, regardless of the profile or predilections of those who 'man the state apparatus'.[74] As Przeworski and Wallerstein have explained:

> [U]nder capitalism all governments must respect and protect the essential claims of those who own the productive wealth of society. Capitalists are endowed with public power, power which no formal institutions can overcome. People may have political rights, they may vote, and governments may pursue popular mandates. But the effective capacity of any government to attain whatever are its goals is circumscribed by the public power of capital. The nature of political forces that come into office does not alter these limits, it is claimed, for they are structural – a characteristic of the system, not of the occupants of governmental positions nor of the winners of elections.[75]

This 'blackmail' power is what Marxist scholars have dubbed 'the structural dependence of the state on capital'. It helps ensure the representation of the preferences of the capitalist minority above and beyond the representation of constituency preferences, and indeed, to encourage the pragmatic adaptation of constituency preferences, to get the majority to accept that catering to the particular interests of the capitalist class is at the same time in the interest of all. The implicit threat and 'blackmail' being that the capitalist minority will wreak general havoc on any government that jeopardizes its specific class interests in reproducing the basic parameters of capitalist social property relations.

The criterion of responsiveness that is built into the dominant definitions cum defences of representative democracy tends to depend upon a conflation of preferences with interests. Such conflation leads mainstream theorists to downplay the significance of the phenomenon of pragmatic acquiescence, and either to ignore or to explicitly deny the spectre of systematically distorted preferences. Otherwise put, they treat preferences as exogenous determinants of, rather than endogenous moments within, broader political processes.

Recognition of the endogenous nature of preferences, however, problematizes the reliance upon responsiveness as the sole or primary criterion for judging the quality of democratic representation. Political parties do not merely reflect, but in fact help shape citizen preferences, alongside a whole host of what Althusser termed 'ideological state apparatuses', including the state bureaucracy, the schools, the mass media, religious institutions and the family.[76] These institutions all tend to be organized hierarchically, and they all tend to perpetuate deference to hierarchically sanctioned values and authorities.

An authoritarian style of political leadership is one that actively seeks to reinforce such deference to hierarchy; by contrast, a democratic style of leadership is one that seeks to promote suspicion and critical reflexivity towards hierarchy in all its forms – including that of the relationship between leaders and followers. Truly democratic leadership is self-liquidating in that sense.

This is why democratic leadership stands in so much tension with the logic of representative democracy, which by its very nature perpetuates the dialectic of leaders and followers, institutionalizes submissiveness to elected authorities, indeed, delegates sovereignty to them. Or, perhaps better put, in representative forms of government, the citizens surrender their sovereignty to their alleged representatives – since, as Rousseau provocatively but perceptively argued a quarter of a millennium ago, in *The Social Contract*, sovereignty cannot be represented; it can only be exercised.[77] Though the genealogy of the notion of sovereignty itself should not be covered over or forgotten, descending as it does from the divine right of kings.[78]

The imperative of participation, the need to raise consciousness

As Bernard Manin has emphasized, representative government was originally considered an alternative to democracy, which was until only recently conceived as requiring direct and active citizen participation, that is, self-rule in a literal, not metaphorical, sense.⁷⁹ The passive, largely depoliticized, uninformed electorates in regimes that by contemporary standards qualify as democracies are perhaps more accurately described as subjects – at best, 'constituencies' – not citizens. Despite the formal legal protections contemporary 'citizens' enjoy, the fact remains, they do not govern themselves. Instead, their participation is limited to the candidate selection process, otherwise and increasingly known as the electoral circus.⁸⁰ A spectator sport, and not one of which most people are even big fans.

The adjectives 'passive', 'depoliticized', 'uninformed' are, of course, causally linked. Participation in decision-making processes clarifies, facilitating the acquisition of knowledge about issues and alternatives being decided upon; whereas exclusion from such processes mystifies, perpetuating ignorance and feelings of incompetence among those left out. This is the core insight of the theory of participatory democracy, as well as the related and still burgeoning body of literature on deliberative democracy.⁸¹

Participation in institutions of genuine self-governance is thus an educational experience. But it requires, in turn, a citizenry with the time, resources, energy and predisposition to participate. In other words, genuine self-governance requires a broader educational project, one committed to a radical critical pedagogical approach, in the tradition of Paolo Freire, as outlined in his highly influential contribution, *The Pedagogy of the Oppressed*.⁸² An educational project that aims to help people unlearn and deconstruct the ubiquitous, hegemonic lies and propaganda that serve to legitimate unjust, oppressive, hierarchical social relations.

For the purposes of initiating and guiding such an educational project, political organization and leadership prove indispensable. Leadership on the model of radical pedagogy. A project of *paideia*, to invoke and indulge for a moment the preferred terminology of the still-too-influential grecophiles.⁸³ A collective educational project, and one which includes more than just a de-constructive aim of inculcating a *hermeneutic of suspicion*.⁸⁴ Indeed, an exclusive focus on the art of deconstruction has an elective affinity with the nihilistic and hyper-individualistic pretensions so pervasive in the neoliberal university.

No, a truly radical and critical pedagogy needs positive commitments, too. It must include a reconstructive goal as well. A commitment to 'moral education and character building', albeit not of a traditional sort. An 'anti-morality', perchance. Or maybe 'faith/anti-faith' would be a better choice of terms. An education into an ethic of solidarity and egalitarian values. And a collective commitment to forging the capacity for sacrifice, indeed, the will to struggle, against the forces of exploitation, domination and marginalization, against injustice in all its forms.

The goals of critical pedagogy for radical democracy may seem contradictory; and indeed, to a certain extent, they may be. A healthy balance between a *hermeneutic of suspicion* and an *ethic of conviction* is certainly difficult, but not altogether impossible to achieve.⁸⁵ Given the urgent nature of the need for collective struggle to transform the systemically entrenched but suicidal, genocidal and 'eco-cidal' dynamics of global capitalism and neo-Imperialism, those of us who can *should* make an effort. From each according to their abilities, after all.

Contemporary political theory and dominant, narcissistic culture may be obsessed with the 'self' in self-determination; however, it has shockingly little to say about the concept of determination, except as the term is used in debates about causality. But determination, of course, has another meaning as well.

The competitive and consumerist ethos promoted by increasingly unfettered capitalism, combined with the thorough discrediting of capitalism's 'state-socialist alter-ego', have together contributed to the emergence of what Bookchin provocatively called *homo consumerans*.[86] Or what Stephen Casmier even more ironically dubbed, 'The New Reagan Man'.[87] A model that is highly influential across the globe, but perhaps most influential in the 'West', where the hegemony of capitalism is most deeply entrenched.

Guerrilla discipline as revolutionary discipline?

Which brings us back to the subject of the guerrilla. The guerrilleros were once lionized among some in the western New Left, perhaps most famously by Régis Debray, who, in *The Revolution in the Revolution?*, indicatively remarked:

> [A]ny man, even a comrade, who spends his life in a city is unwittingly a bourgeois in comparison with a guerrillero. He cannot know the material effort involved in eating, sleeping, moving from one place to another – briefly, in surviving.[88]

Though he forgot to mention the fact that the guerrillero is trained into a revolutionary discipline that includes, first and foremost, following orders; only a select few get to issue commands. A select few that is virtually always self-selected and that exercises a hierarchical authority which cannot be easily revoked or held accountable, at least not through electoral mechanisms.

In a word, the revolutionary guerrillero is made in the image and likeness of the very figure against whom s/he is trained to fight, the existential enemy, the state soldier. The dialectical resemblance between the ethic of the guerrillero and the ethic of the soldier, in turn, reflects the similarity in authoritarian command structures shared by the revolutionary guerrilla and the bourgeois military alike. A microcosm and a crucial example of what Bookchin had in mind when he referred to state socialism as capitalism's 'alter ego'.

Debray's champion and role model was, of course, Che Guevara, one of the last martyrs of the revolutionary pantheon of Marxism-Leninism. A man often held up as a shining example of heroic selflessness, even a prefiguration of the promise of a state-socialist 'New Man', who himself put some thought into the subject of the need for radical pedagogy, and to its links with revolutionary praxis. In Guevara's own formulation:

> The sermons of the past have been transposed to the present in the individual consciousness, and a continual labour is necessary to eradicate them. The process is two-sided: On the one side, society acts through direct and indirect education; on the other, the individual subjects himself to a process of conscious self-education.

> The new society being formed has to compete fiercely with the past. The latter makes itself felt in the consciousness in which the residue of an education systematically oriented towards isolating the individual still weighs heavily ...[89]

It is worth noting that the primary feature of the education into the 'old society' that Guevara chooses to stress is its orientation 'towards isolating the individual', not its tendency to perpetuate deference towards hierarchy. For indeed, the latter is a virtue in a soldier. Which again demonstrates the elective affinity between the guerrilla and the state. In this vein, from his jail cell, Öcalan has expressed some rather piercing, self-critical thoughts, at the same time implicitly directed at the operational commanders of the guerrilla organization he created and continues to inspire and even nominally to lead. In Öcalan's words:

> The PKK had been conceived as a party with a state-like hierarchical structure similar to other parties. Such a structure, however, causes a dialectic contradiction to the principles of democracy, freedom and equality, a contradiction in principle concerning all parties whatsoever their philosophy. Although the PKK stood for freedom-oriented views we had not been able to free ourselves from thinking in hierarchical structures.[90]

The guerrilla has not been disarmed or disbanded, a development which Öcalan has never advocated or foreseen, even at the height of the peace process, his calls for the organization to lay down its arms notwithstanding. This is the crux of the issue from the standpoint of the Turkish state or, for that matter, from the standpoint of any state. But what is more problematic, at least from the standpoint of a commitment to radical democracy: nor has the organization's hierarchical structure, its chain of command, been transformed, despite Öcalan's emphasis and efforts to encourage a 'paradigm shift'.

From democratic centralism to democratic confederalism

The Kurdish Freedom Movement, however, encompasses more than the PKK. Indeed, as Akkaya and Jongerden have insisted, from 2005, 'the PKK and all affiliated organizations' were restructured along the lines of the democratic confederal model, 'under the name of the Union of Kurdistan Communities (Koma Civaken Kurdistan, KCK)', and organized alongside the Democratic Society Congress (Demokratik Toplum Kongresi, DTK), conceived as 'part of the attempt to forge a new political paradigm, defined by the direct and continual exercise of the people's power through village, town, and city councils'.[91]

How has this transition from Marxist-Leninist, democratic centralist guerrilla party into a more decentralized, more horizontally networked movement taken place? What have been the main achievements, challenges and obstacles for this reorganization and reorientation, this 'paradigm shift'? And what have been the consequences of this process of transformation for the movement? These are very important questions, about which the literature on the Kurdish movement – in English, at least – remains equivocal, when not entirely silent. The equivocations, the awkward silences, of the literature are symptomatic of the taboos, contradictions and limits of human rights normative discourse exacerbated in the age of the war on terror. They also reflect what Dilar Dirik has perceptively termed the 'male state gaze' embedded in the methods and *epistemes* of mainstream social sciences.[92]

The devastation and trauma wrought upon the Kurdish people by the Turkish security forces, the systematic state terror, the total evacuation of thousands of villages, the killing of tens of thousands, the displacement and exile of millions, made it abundantly clear to Öcalan by the early 1990s that the Maoist cum Guevarista strategy of a 'prolonged people's war' by the PKK could not lead to military victory, to 'national liberation', to the creation of an independent socialist Kurdish nation-state. The military might of NATO's second-biggest army, exercised within its own sovereign territory, was simply too brutal, too overwhelming a force, to overcome. Faced with the realization of the impossibility of victory, even the prospect of total annihilation, Öcalan began to reach out to European politicians, from his refuge in the Beqaa Valley and in Damascus, in search of a way to end the war without sacrificing the dignity of the Kurdish people, in search of a way towards a peaceful and democratic resolution to the raging conflict.

The end of the Cold War undoubtedly also influenced Öcalan's burgeoning conviction that the party and the movement which he had brought into being was in dire need of reformation, indeed, of fundamental reorientation. The collapse of the Soviet Union meant the disappearance of a state-communist bloc capable of patronizing and protecting a 'liberated', single-party socialist Kurdish republic, inevitably wedged between hostile, neighbouring nation-states. It simultaneously signified the definitive death knell for the credibility of the state-communist ideal. In sum, it induced a crisis both at the level of *realpolitik* and at the level of principles.

There were also developments originating from the grassroots in Bakur, which were amplified, encouraged and promoted by the organized diaspora in Europe, operating within the orbit of the movement. These developments have been well documented by Gunes himself in his incisive 2012 monograph on *The Kurdish National Movement in Turkey*. They included the spread of 'public celebrations and mass protests', most emblematically around the annual *Newroz* festival, reconstrued as a myth of Kurdish resistance; as well as in events organized to commemorate the self-immolation of PKK prisoners and other 'heroic acts of sacrifice' among PKK 'martyrs'. Indeed, a whole repertoire of 'representation of resistance practices' emerged, congealing around the myth of *Newroz*, and also hoisting up a host of 'exemplars', a veritable pantheon of revolutionary martyrs, the public commemoration, even worship, of whom burst onto the streets in a wave of so-called *serhildan* (or 'rebellions').[93] From the early 1990s, such '[b]ourgeoning civil resistance' against the security forces came increasingly to complement the ongoing guerrilla campaign.[94]

One of the more remarkable aspects of the repertoire of 'representation of Kurdish resistance' that emerged from the early 1990s onwards was the prominent place of women. Not only did women 'participate in large numbers in numerous *serhildan*'; they also 'took an active role in the activities of the legal political Kurdish parties', indeed, they 'came to the forefront of the resistance' and were increasingly 'constituted' and commemorated 'as "exemplars"'.⁹⁵ Alongside and helping to propel such emergent symbolic and organizational prominence of women in the movement, over the course of the 1990s, Öcalan would formulate an elaborate theoretical critique of patriarchy. Indeed, he would come to consider women as the 'first colony', and even to 'redefine national liberation as first and foremost the liberation of women'.⁹⁶

Öcalan's emphasis on the primacy of the struggle against patriarchy was quite developed even before his abduction and imprisonment, and has featured prominently in his copious prison writings, perhaps especially in his original synthesis and articulation of the long history of hierarchy, his vision of the dialectic of domination and resistance. In Öcalan's account of patriarchy, its origins are intimately intertwined with the emergence of the state. And especially since his imprisonment, Öcalan's thought has taken a radically anti-statist turn. What began as a pragmatic, realistic appraisal of the impossibility of attaining a Kurdish nation-state through a guerrilla war against Turkish security forces, and as a compromise proposal calling for respect for human rights and cultural rights, alongside measures of decentralization or autonomy, developed, under the influence perhaps especially of Murray Bookchin, into a principled rejection of the state. In effect, Öcalan advanced a redefinition of self-determination, now understood as radical, direct democracy, against the state.⁹⁷

Under Bookchin's influence, Öcalan would also take up the theme of the urgent need for social ecology. Even so, as with the emphasis on the struggle against patriarchy, the sensitivity of the movement to ecological issues was not just born like Athena. It did not just spring spontaneously out of Öcalan's head. Instead, it was forged in concrete struggles, most emblematically, the struggle to save the ancient village of Hasankeyf in the province of Batman, set to be submerged underwater by the Turkish state's Ilisu Dam project. A struggle in which the European environmentalist movement would forge organic links with the Kurdish movement, thereby prefiguring the overlapping, decentralized networks of resistance envisioned by the democratic confederal ideal.⁹⁸

Öcalan's articulation of democratic confederalism grows out of a deep disenchantment with and critique of Marxism-Leninism, which, in quasi-confessional terms, in a series of penetrating self-criticisms of his own previous mentality, he accuses of reproducing the cult of hierarchy, of behaving as organizations like mini-states, acting in accordance with a logic of conquest and domination, rather than resistance and freedom. The emphasis on the struggle against patriarchy, the fostering of awareness of the urgency of social ecology, the thoroughgoing critique of the state, the promotion of popular assemblies and championing of radically decentralized, direct democracy, all of these components of the 'paradigm shift' are explicitly contrasted to the democratic-centralist model and mindset.⁹⁹

Likewise, Öcalan's critique of Marxism-Leninism includes a critique of its scientism, of its hostility to the realm of myth, of its bias in favour of secular-fundamentalism. In this latter vein, in recent years, Öcalan has urged the Kurdish movement to organize a Democratic Islam Congress, with the purpose of elaborating a liberationist interpretation of the ethical and political implications of professing and practising the authentic Islamic faith.¹⁰⁰ Whether, in practice, the tradition and perception of militant secularism among movement cadres and supporters has been transformed is another matter – certainly worthy of close empirical investigation, given not only the history of conflict with Kurdish Hezbullah to which Gunes's text refers but also in terms of countering the appeal of Erdoğan's AKP and its brand of patriarchal, neoliberal Islam, not to mention the ongoing struggle with reactionary jihadists in Rojava. The fact that the first Kurdish rebellions against the Kemalist republic were mobilized along the secular-religious divide, in the name of the community of believers, is not irrelevant in the present. Indeed, the proper relationship between religion and politics continues to be a source of dispute and contestation, capable of dividing contemporary Kurds. The movement's attempt to articulate a Democratic Islam is intended to transcend such divisions; how serious and successful this attempt is will no doubt condition the contours and horizons of support for the ambitious democratic confederal project advanced by the Kurdish Freedom Movement.

Finally, and crucially, the principled rejection of the strategy of 'national liberation', understood in terms of the pursuit of a Kurdish nation-state, has included a rather elaborate set of arguments against the insidious evils of what Öcalan refers to as 'feudal nationalism', most often in reference to the example of Barzani in South Kurdistan. The ideological and programmatic reorientation of the Kurdish Freedom Movement thus includes not just renunciation of the goal of a state, but more ambitiously, the aspiration to transcend altogether the confines of the 'nationalist imaginary'. A transcendence which should not be confused with repudiating pride in Kurdishness, but rather, with escaping the dialectic of 'majority' versus 'minority'. Indeed, as Öcalan has insisted, 'in democratic confederalism there is no room for any kind of hegemony striving'.[101]

Self-administration and autonomous organization of directly democratic assemblies, not to mention of self-defence militias, for all ethnic and religious groups as the alternative to the tyranny of the majority, to the 'hegemonic striving' deeply ingrained in the ideology of nationalism. A tall order to ask from a movement that has sacrificed so many lives for the dream of a Greater Kurdistan. An exercise in democratic leadership, if ever there was, on the part of Öcalan, his attempt to get his followers to dream internationalist dreams of radical democracy, to imagine forms of confederation that cut across and beyond the mental borders imposed by the cult of the national community. Easier to pronounce than to achieve. And so, again, a subject worthy of close empirical investigation, of which the survey of political representatives conducted by Guldivê and his colleagues for Gunes's manuscript, under very difficult conditions of state repression, provides a very partial but nonetheless important point of departure.

The struggle against patriarchy, the struggle for social ecology, the struggle against the nation-state, the struggle against sectarianism in all its forms, the struggle for radical, direct democracy – these are all significant departures from the original articulation of the struggle for 'national liberation' understood as the creation of a state-communist Greater Kurdistan. Indeed, ambitious aspirations, and a thoroughgoing reorientation of the goals of the movement, which mainstream social scientists interested in understanding the movement too often either ignore or downplay, and which advocates for the movement tend to take (or at least portray) at face value, when close empirical investigation of the terms of consciousness and praxis of the cadres and supporters of the movement is what the commitment to and search for truth ultimately requires.

Challenges for the 'new paradigm'

The organizational transformations undertaken since 2005 have been conceived and justified as means to decentralize and thus democratize – indeed, de-Leninize – the Kurdish Freedom Movement. But it would be a mistake to think that Öcalan's intention has been to unambiguously compromise or moderate the radicalism, the profound anti-capitalism, of the movement. On the contrary, if anything, the project of democratic confederalism, articulated as radical, direct democracy against the state, provides a more fundamental, more thoroughgoing critique and threat to the status quo assumptions of the international order in the age of globalized plutocracy and the Orwellian war on terror. Especially if the appeal of the program were to spread beyond the project's Kurdish constituency, if it were to be embraced en masse by Turks, by Arabs, by Persians, and beyond. The articulation and practice of self-determination as direct democracy, as collective action in accordance with the principles of social ecology, would indeed constitute a major threat for all the geopolitical alliances and local power blocs vying for influence and control across a bleeding region and burning globe. By contrast, the emergence of another independent, crony-capitalist or even state-communist cum state-capitalist petro-state would ultimately constitute a much less threatening prospect for the global system.

Though, of course, the discourse of democracy – even the discourse of radical, direct democracy – is sufficiently rife with ambiguity, *aporia*, even contradictions, to be simultaneously susceptible to opportunist as well as insurrectionist interpretations, intentions and derivations. The paradoxes of power in politics cannot be abolished by organizational fiat, programmatic pronouncement or ideological catchphrases alone. It is one thing to declare radical decentralization and horizontal-participatory organizational forms, another altogether to actually operate in accordance with such principles.

An egalitarian and participatory ethos capable of promoting both a deep respect for freedom and a will to struggle for collective justice, to the point of ultimate sacrifice, is indeed hard to come by. Even harder, perhaps, to create. The problems associated with *vanguardism* are difficult to avoid, even in the absence of explicit hierarchical organizational forms. Informal tyranny and effective concentration of power can occur without formal hierarchy; in fact, in some ways, and in some circumstances, 'structurelessness', or formally horizontal structures, may be even more conducive to tyranny and/or easier for a minority faction to control than organizations structured in accordance with more bureaucratized, formalized hierarchies.[102]

The spectre of tyranny cannot be so easily vanquished; it is inherent to the realm of politics. As Rosa Luxemburg rightly stressed in her own incisive, prophetic polemic against Bolshevism, dating back to 1904, organizational form itself ultimately reveals more about circumstances than it does about principles.[103] Particular historical trajectories and dynamics, concrete political contexts, tend to impose specific organizational forms. Moreover, most crucially, so long as only a minority of the population is mobilized and actively participating, regardless of formal organizational structure, the reality of *vanguardism* will remain: decisions affecting broad constituencies, and programmatic pronouncements made in their names, will, in fact, be made by small minorities.

A life-and-death example from the glorious, 'structureless' revolution of the anarchosyndicalists in Spain, in the summer of 1936, proves most illustrative in this regard. As Burnett Bolloten has explained in vivid detail, the anarchosyndicalist CNT-FAI refused to seize power, despite having protagonized the successful defence of the populous from the fascist assault on Barcelona, despite finding itself 'at the helm', it opted instead to share power with the constitutional, elected authorities, who ultimately rolled back the revolution. Even so, Bolloten proceeds to point out: 'Although opposition to dictatorship was the rationale most frequently used by the anarchosyndicalists to explain their decision not to impose their will in Barcelona, they nevertheless established in rural areas a multiplicity of parochial dictatorships with the aid of militia groups and revolutionary tribunals.'[104] In sum, radical decentralization, even 'structureless', is no guarantee against tyranny.

The anarchosyndicalists in Spain were notable for their outright rejection of participation in electoral politics. Theirs was a vision of direct democracy, organized primarily at the level of the factory and in self-defence militias, radically decentralized but confederated. Rousseau's objection to the idea of delegated sovereignty animated their bitter opposition to the parliamentary form of representation. The radically horizontal, seemingly 'structureless' anarchosyndicalists perhaps paradoxically converge with the hierarchically structured, centralized Marxist-Leninist guerrilla form in their mutual commitment to the conjuring of a new people, a new order, through acts of revolutionary insurgency, or, as Debray provocatively puts it, to the transubstantiation of 'the political word into flesh'.[105]

The 'democratic-confederal' reorientation of the Kurdish movement has, by contrast, facilitated a flourishing of pro-Kurdish, electoral party politics. Admittedly, as Gunes has well-documented both in this manuscript and in his previous book, there is a deeper history to pro-Kurdish party politics in the Turkish electoral arena, with precedents of victories of pro-Kurdish candidates in municipal elections in Batman and Diyarbakır dating back to 1977, though one of these candidates would be murdered, the other imprisoned.[106]

For its part, the 1982 Constitution 'strictly banned any mention of the existence of the Kurds and incriminated any political party or organization voicing Kurdish demands', thereby severely limiting the space of toleration for pro-Kurdish voices within the realms of municipal and parliamentary representation.[107] Even so, from the early 1990s, coinciding with the outbreak of the *serhildan*, the mass street rebellions, the 'bourgeoning civil resistance' that came to complement the ongoing guerrilla campaign, 'pro-Kurdish representation ... was able to return', as the movement 'managed to build an institutional base and endure the state's numerous attempt to suppress it', with a series of political parties emerging, then being suppressed, then emerging anew, to challenge 'the established order in Turkey to recognize Kurdish identity and cultural rights, and putting forward proposals for political reconciliation to end the cycle of violence'.[108] In the wake of the 'paradigm shift', initially against a backdrop of relative liberalization and efforts to converge with European norms, the advances of the movement in electoral politics, at both the municipal and the parliamentary levels, have been considerable, as Gunes has again well-demonstrated.

The prospects for peace, especially in the period between 2013 and 2015, contributed to unprecedented levels of electoral support for the pro-Kurdish HDP. In July of 2015, against a backdrop of escalating tensions, intimidation and harassment, the party nevertheless managed to pass the very high 10 per cent threshold to form for the first time a parliamentary group in the Grand National Assembly and did so again in the snap election in the autumn, amidst the wave of state repression that was unleashed after the breakdown of the peace process. All these developments are treated in considerable detail and with admirable sophistication by Gunes in the text.[109]

The literature on conflict resolution in the English language, which is highly influenced by the paradigmatic case of Northern Ireland, tends to employ a four-fold analytical distinction, ubiquitous in 'transitology' studies more generally: namely, the distinction between reformists and revolutionaries in the opposition, on the one side, and between moderates and hardliners in the state, on the other.[110] Through this lens, the art of conflict resolution is interpreted as mirroring the 'game' of representative democracy, as requiring the forging of a consensus amongst reformists and moderates, and the side-lining, or marginalization, of revolutionaries and hardliners.[111]

Partly overlapping with this distinction between reformists and revolutionaries is another distinction, between the 'political' and 'military' wings in opposition movements. The examples of Sinn Fein and the IRA, or Herri Batasuna and ETA, are especially relevant in this regard.[112] Integral to the process of side-lining revolutionaries are efforts to coax the 'political' wing into dissociating from, even to denounce, the armed struggle, in exchange for measures of compromise and accommodation. This means, in effect, the recognition of and adaptation to the state's monopoly of legitimate violence, in exchange for partial political concessions to the movement's demands. The definitive ceasefire, followed by full-fledged disarmament, are thus envisioned in the model. Incorporation into a state that promises to be more responsive. With the forging of trust the principle task, its absence the most difficult obstacle, on the road to peace and 'reconciliation'.

The Kurdish Freedom Movement's 'paradigm shift' to a certain extent can be understood through such a 'conflict resolution' frame – with the HDP in the role of Sinn Fein, and even Demirtaş in the role of Gerry Adams. But there are limits to this comparative lens, imposed not only by the extent and brutality of state terror on the part of Turkish security forces; but also, in terms of the state-centric terms of reference. The breakdown of the most recent peace negotiation proves illustrative in this regard. What caused the collapse of these negotiations were not so much events inside of Turkey, but rather, events in the north of Syria.

Kurdish people are divided across four states, their plight the incarnation of the contradictions of the dismemberment of the Ottoman Empire and the emergence of the nation-state form in the 'Middle East' at the end of the First World War. The Kurdish Freedom Movement may have given up on the goal of an independent nation-state encompassing the whole of Greater Kurdistan, but it has not surrendered its commitment to some form of political unity among all Kurds. Indeed, the project of 'democratic confederalism' explicitly institutionalizes forms of 'confederal' collaboration within a transnational 'Middle Eastern Union'.[113] To this degree, the movement has never ceased to object to the institutional legacies left by Sykes-Picot or Lausanne. Even if Öcalan has been emphatic that his 'paradigm shift' envisions transcending state borders, not creating new ones.

The establishment of a stronghold in the north of Syria by the Kurdish Freedom Movement against the backdrop of civil war and state collapse, the emergence and consolidation of a revolutionary space for constructing democratic confederalism in practice, has had tremendous ramifications for political dynamics inside of Turkey. The heroic resistance of the Kurdish forces in Kobane was instrumental in setting off alarms within the Turkish state's security apparatus. Moreover, the Turkish state's selective enforcement of its southern border, its complicity with the crossing of international *jihadis*, contrasted with the vigour and lethal force which it proved willing to exercise in order to prohibit Kurds from Bakur from crossing to help defend Kobane, only served to douse fuel on a simmering fire, especially after Erdoğan appeared on television to gloat about an imminent fall of the city. The window of opportunity, the prospects for peace, were thus undermined by developments beyond the Turkish borders. A spillover of the conflict in Syria, which ultimately precipitated and unleashed the ongoing, all-out war on the Kurdish Freedom Movement, now operative on both sides of the border, and in Iraqi Kurdistan as well.[114]

Amidst the polarizing dynamics of violent state repression and street mobilization across the Kurdish region of Turkey, in the broader context of the siege of Kobane, latent ambivalences and ambiguities in terms of tactics and strategy associated with the democratic confederal model were thrust to the surface. The detonator was the decision by some urban youth associated with the movement to dig trenches, to attempt to block the access of Turkish security forces from passing into certain neighbourhoods. A de facto declaration of democratic autonomy, intended as a display of collective self-defence, explicitly justified in terms of Öcalanist principles and goals, as an effort to construct democratic confederalism. Some months later, after the PKK had called off its ceasefire in the summer, dozens of pro-Kurdish municipal authorities would in turn issue declarations of democratic autonomy.[115]

First the trenches, then the full-fledged declarations of local autonomy. These actions were interpreted by Turkish security forces as nothing short of treasonous assaults on state sovereignty, and so triggered a swift escalation in the intensity and extent of state repression, including the imprisonment of thousands of political representatives and movement activists (HDP co-chairs and MPs, and BDP mayors and city councillors, among them); as well as the siege of close to sixty municipalities – a veritable human rights' atrocity.[116]

Which brings us back to Lenin. The fact is, the democratic confederal model, at least as articulated by Öcalan and his followers, may reject the Leninist principle of democratic centralism, and may even reject the Leninist conception of 'national liberation'; but it does not abandon the Leninist analysis of the situation of 'dual power'.[117] Nor does it renounce a willingness to engage in armed insurrection. Indeed, its vision is one of armed militias organized for the purposes of people's self-defence, a vision of democracy *against* the state. And so, in Turkey and in Syria, and increasingly in Iraq, too, the Kurdish Freedom Movement now finds itself at the crossroads, in a critical juncture for the future of the democratic confederal ideal – one predicted by none other than Murray Bookchin, with whose prophetic words we shall conclude:

Libertarian municipalists do not delude themselves that the state will view with equanimity their attempts to replace professionalised power with popular power. They harbour no illusions that the ruling classes will indifferently allow a Communalist movement to demand rights that infringe on the state's sovereignty over towns and cities. Historically, regions, localities, and above all towns and cities have desperately struggled to reclaim their local sovereignty from the state (albeit not always for high-minded purposes). Communalists' attempts to restore the power of towns and cities and to knit them together into confederations can be expected to invoke increasing resistance from national institutions. That the new popular-assemblyist municipal confederations will embody a dual power against the state that becomes a source of growing political tension is obvious. Either a Communalist movement will be radicalized by this tension and will resolutely face all its consequences, or it will surely sink into a morass of compromises that absorb it back into the social order that it once sought to change. How the movement meets this challenge is a clear measure of its seriousness in seeking to change the existing political system and the social consciousness it develops as a source of public education and leadership.[118]

Conclusions: Re-thinking Kurdish political representation in Turkey

Turkey's transformation to a multi-party system in the period 1946–50 created opportunities for Kurdish political representation, but as the discussion presented in this book demonstrates, the Kurds' experience of representing themselves and their interests in the institutions of the state has not been a smooth journey. As discussed in Chapter 1, following a two-decade hiatus, Kurdish political activism in Turkey re-emerged during the early 1960s and had begun evolving into a popular opposition movement during the mid-1970s. However, for Turkey's state elites and dominant political actors, the advocacy of Kurdish rights was seen as a case of separatism and proscribed in the name of defending the country's national unity and territorial integrity. Also, the Kurdish question became a source of political mobilization for Turkish nationalists from the early 1970s onwards, who interpreted the advocacy of Kurdish rights as part of a broader conspiracy to divide Turkey and spread communism. Hence, despite Turkey's relatively straightforward transition to electoral democracy in 1950, building inclusive political institutions that were able to respond in a constructive manner to the popular political demands of the country's culturally and politically plural society has been a challenge that Turkey is yet to overcome.

Since the transition to democracy, centre-right conservative parties have dominated Turkish politics and ruled the country either through single-party governments or as the largest parties in coalition governments. The centre-left has been mainly represented by the CHP, but its political programme throughout the twentieth century has been shaped by a resolute commitment to safeguarding the essence of the republican regime instituted by Mustafa Kemal Atatürk. From the 1970s onwards, Islamists and far-right Turkish nationalist political parties began to draw support from the electorate. In addition, the Turkish Armed Forces acted as the guardian of the republic and intervened in politics whenever it perceived the republic's Kemalist principles to be under threat.

Historically, the centre-right parties have been more open to engagement with Kurdish political actors. This began with the DP in 1950 and led to a significant increase in the *descriptive* representation of the Kurds, with Kurds being elected to a public office as MPs and district or provincial mayors. Responding to the demands of the popular masses and attempting to curb the excesses of the Kemalist regime were the main political objective for DP governments.[1] The DP won the 1950, 1954 and 1957 general elections with landslides but its ability to rule the country was compromised by its increasing authoritarianism and apparent disregard for the opposition and the sections of the society represented by it, which culminated in a military coup in May 1960 and the execution of Adnan Menderes in September 1961. The military's rule was short and new elections were held in autumn of 1961. Many of the DP's Kurdish MPs continued their activities within the newly established YTP, which managed to get 13.7 per cent of the vote. In the subsequent general election in 1965, the YTP lost much of its support base.

A similar approach to that of DP and Menderes was taken by Süleyman Demirel's AP during the second half of the 1960s. In 1971, the military carried out its second direct intervention and remained in power until 1974 when parliamentary elections were held. However, the second half of the 1970s was marked by political polarization, unstable coalition governments and growing violence between the left-wing guerrillas and right-wing Turkish nationalist groups, which further complicated the democratic consolidation and paved the way towards the coup d'état of 12 September 1980. After the 1980 coup, the military's influence grew considerably because the new constitution written under the guidance of the generals ensured a central role for it in the country's politics by empowering the National Security Council (Milli Güvenlik Kurulu, MGK) to became the key decision-making body.[2] Also, the rogue and criminal elements within the military and security establishment, popularly referred to as the 'deep state', influenced the political developments through politically motivated murders, massacres and assassinations.[3] Consequently, despite the counter-hegemonic challenges against Turkey's established political order, the political system shaped by Kemalism has been maintained and a programme for widespread democratization and liberalization capable of addressing Kurdish political demands could not be initiated or implemented by the country's governments.

A new constitution was drafted under the guidance of the military and approved in a referendum in June 1982. The new constitution created a rigid political framework and curtailed the space allocated for democratic politics. Elections were scheduled for November 1983, with Turgut Özal's ANAP emerging victorious and forming the government in December 1983. Özal was the dominant figure in Turkish politics throughout the 1980s and the early 1990s and formed single-party governments in 1983 and 1987 and served as the country's president from 1989 until his death on 17 April 1993. The 1990s were characterized by unstable coalition governments.

The AKP's leader Recep Tayyip Erdoğan emerged as the dominant figure in Turkish politics in 2002. Successive AKP governments carried out democratization reforms during the 2000s that increased Kurdish cultural rights in Turkey but many of these reforms have been marred by a lack of genuine desire for recognition of Kurdish identity and the requisite rights in Turkey. The piecemeal approach has failed to institute a pluralist democratic framework and, more importantly, is yet to result in full recognition of Kurdish identity and group rights in Turkey. The past two decades have witnessed an improvement in the substantive representation of the Kurds, leading to Kurdish political actors openly calling for widespread political reforms to broaden the political space available to the Kurds and for the state to recognize Kurdish identity and collective national rights, including Kurdish self-government and language rights in Turkey.

As Chapters 1 and 2 discussed in greater detail, currently, there are several Kurdish political actors involved in the representation of the Kurds in Turkey, but the main contest in the past decade has been between the political parties belonging to the pro-Kurdish democratic movement and the AKP. From the late 1990s onwards, the pro-Kurdish movement has managed to build a strong regional presence in Turkey's south-east where the Kurds constitute a majority of the population. Their efforts in the past decade have seen an increase in Kurdish representatives being elected in the western parts of Turkey too, especially in provinces where large Kurdish communities reside. The balance of power has been shifting in favour of the pro-Kurdish movement since 2011, and in the general elections held in June 2015, the current representative of the pro-Kurdish movement, the HDP, managed to establish itself as the undisputed representative of the Kurds in Turkey. The HDP's success is built on the advances the movement has made in the past decade but surpassed all previous efforts when it managed to win eighty seats in Turkey's parliament in June 2015.

Hence, the level of support the HDP obtained in June 2015 is unprecedented in Turkey's history and set the ideal context for political reforms to accommodate Kurdish rights in Turkey. However, rather than taking measures to move Turkey towards peace and recognition of national diversity and political pluralism, the governing AKP's response has been to intensify its repression and elimination of Kurdish representation, which has reversed the gains the pro-Kurdish democratic movement has made in the past decade. Many Kurdish elected representatives have been removed from their positions and are currently remanded in custody while the courts hear their cases. While repression of Kurdish political representatives in Turkey was always present to a certain degree, since the summer of 2015, we have witnessed an extraordinary level of repression of Kurdish political activities in Turkey. Once again, the state security discourse began dominating all aspects of Kurdish politics to leave very little room for alternative articulations of Kurdish political demands.

The study's main findings: multiple constituencies, multiple challenges

A quick glance at Kurdish politics in Turkey reveals that a number of political actors are active and contest the political representation of the Kurds. These include pro-Kurdish and Turkish political parties, actors connected to the tribal and religious elite, and Islamist movements. Throughout the twentieth century, legal and political barriers to the expression of Kurdish political demands in Turkey have effectively marginalized Kurdish political actors that advocated reform of Turkey's political system, demanded group rights for the Kurds in Turkey or sought constitutional recognition of Kurdish identity and difference. The rise of the Kurdish national movement in Turkey during the 1970s began the process of change in the form of Kurdish political representation. As I discussed in Chapter 1 and elsewhere in my previous research, during the 1960s Kurdish organic intellectuals played an important role in Kurdish cultural activities.[4] As Miley and Guldivê's discussion of Miroslav Hroch's phases of nationalism highlights, Kurdish politics in Turkey in the 1960s closely resembles the phase B of a nationalist mobilization, in which activist (organic) intellectuals undertook a range of activities to spread national consciousness among the Kurdish population in Turkey.

The late 1960s to the early 1970s was a period in which Kurdish activists and the political demands that they raised for the Kurds in Turkey radicalized, and many Kurdish activists who were active within Turkey's left-wing movement began to advocate the establishment of separate Kurdish political organizations to advance the Kurdish cause. In the 1970s, several Kurdish political groups and clandestine political parties emerged and took the cause of Kurdish liberation to a more organized form. The view that a forceful challenge of the state authority was needed to end the oppressive and assimilatory policies of the Turkish state began to gain widespread acceptance among the new generation of Kurdish political activists. Hence, from the late 1970s onwards, dissent-oriented political practices began to gain centrality in Kurdish politics in Turkey. The politicization of a larger section of the Kurds in Turkey during the 1970s and 1980s began to challenge the existing order in Turkey and questioned the genuineness of the Kurdish elite's ability to represent the needs or interests of the popular Kurdish masses. These parties and groups had to conduct their activities in an unstable and violent political environment during which the state's repression intensified. State repression turned into an entirely different dimension after the coup d'état on 12 September 1980 and many of these groups could not survive when their members and activists were incarcerated in prisons. The coup also brought an end to the pro-Kurdish provincial-level representation that Kurdish candidates had obtained in Diyarbakır and Batman at the local elections in 1977. Hence, from the early 1980s onwards, the PKK became the hegemonic force in Kurdish resistance in Turkey.

Relocating to Lebanon's Beqaa Valley presented the PKK with the opportunity to organize as a military movement and prepare for its military campaign to liberate Kurdistan from foreign domination, which began on 15 August 1984. From the mid-1980s onwards, the PKK began co-ordinating a network of community organizations and cultural centres in Europe. The Kurdish diaspora in Europe played an important role in the PKK's rise by providing financial support and human resources, enabling the PKK to establish an information and organizational network and form links with the socialist and human rights groups to harness diplomatic support. During the 1990s, the PKK established several representative organizations with the objective of mobilizing different segments of Kurdish society. Specific organizations were established for Alevis, Muslims, Yazidis etc., as well as for women, workers and youth.

Additionally, the PKK was involved in the establishment of Kurdish representative organizations in Europe, such as the Kurdish Parliament in Exile and the Kurdish National Congress (Kongreya Netawa Kurdistan, KNK), which strengthened the claim that the PKK was a national organization and able to attract Kurds from all backgrounds. Additionally, the existence of Kurdish cultural organizations in Europe enabled the facilitated Kurdish cultural renewal and the production and dissemination of Kurdish culture. In fact, the Kurdish cultural revival constituted a significant aspect of the PKK's mobilization and through mass communication the alternative Kurdish identity was represented. Images and symbols of Kurdistan, such as maps and flags, have created a sense of a unified homeland for the Kurds and helped the Kurds feel part of an imagined community.

Conclusions: Re-thinking Kurdish Political Representation in Turkey 165

In the Turkish state and popular media discourses, the PKK's struggle has been described as strictly a case of terrorism and banditry. Such a representation has been used widely to delegitimate the PKK as a movement and its advocacy of Kurdish rights in Turkey more broadly. As Miley and Guldivê highlight in their comment in this book, the link between representation and legitimacy is a central aspect of the debate on political representation. This issue is also at the heart of the debate on who are the Kurds' legitimate representatives in Turkey. Despite the state's representation of the PKK's struggle as a case of terror and separatism, the PKK managed to gain the support and backing of a significant number of Kurds and is seen as a legitimate actor.

The PKK's claim to represent the Kurds is self-authorized but widely accepted within the Kurdish community in Turkey. The PKK has been the main organization that has been struggling for Kurdish national demands and has been at the centre of Kurdish political developments since the early 1980s in Turkey. Also, the PKK's framing of Kurdish demands has a strong resonance among the Kurds, and it has managed to establish a strong base within the Kurdish community in Turkey as well as in the diaspora. Despite the many setbacks the PKK has experienced in the past two decades, it has maintained its support base and continuously managed to mobilize Kurds and recruit fighters into its ranks. Hence, among a large section of the Kurdish population in Turkey, it is seen as a legitimate actor and an organization that speaks on their behalf. A brief look at the way the PKK represents itself and its struggle to its target groups are needed to understand why this is the case.

To counter the state's representation of its struggle as terrorism, the PKK produced and disseminated its own representation of its struggle to its target groups. The PKK describes itself as a guerrilla movement committed to armed struggle to realize its political objectives and a national liberation movement. This representation strongly resonates among its constituency and the perceptions the Kurds have of the PKK's struggle are different than that of the state or the Turkish society at large. As I have argued elsewhere, the PKK reactivated the Newroz as a myth of Kurdish national resistance to construct a contemporary myth of resistance to represent its struggle, which is deployed in its discourse to enhance its appeal to Kurdish communities.[5] In the PKK's contemporary myth of resistance, the performers of resistance practices were constituted as exemplars. Initially, the myth was constructed around the performers of the PKK's early resistance practices in Diyarbakır Prison. Later, exemplars were broadened and included women. Many of the heroic acts of resistance were committed on 21 March – the Newroz festival – and during the early 1990s, organizing mass gatherings during the Newroz festivals and other important days in the Kurdish political calendar were seen as a symbol of Kurdish popular resistance in many Kurdish cities and towns. The significance of the construction of Newroz as a contemporary myth of resistance lay in the fact that it enabled the PKK to represent its struggle as the embodiment of Kurdish national struggle in Turkey.

The PKK took actions during the 2000s to move away from the use of violence towards a legitimate ground, but these have not resulted in a significant shift in the state's approach. As discussed in Chapter 1, the PKK's initial objective of an armed insurgency to overthrow the rule of Turkish state and unify the Kurds under a socialist republic gave way to the notions of 'democratic autonomy' and 'democratic confederalism', which proposes the accommodation of Kurdish rights within Turkey's territorial integrity and are developed as part of a broader framework for solving the Kurdish question in the Middle East. The PKK's ideological transformation began during the early 1990s, but from 1999 onwards it turned into a deeper-level transformation and changed entirely the movement's objectives and political demands for the Kurds. The capture of the PKK's leader Abdullah Öcalan in February 1999 precipitated its subsequent discursive and organizational transformation and, currently, the democratic transformation of Turkey, the constitutional recognition of the Kurdish identity and the democratization of society to enable the free development of Kurdish language and culture are the key demands articulated by the PKK. In this period, as well as redefining its political objectives, the PKK sought to transform itself into a legal platform. The PKK also attempted to transform its hierarchical structure by broadening its membership and including political figures within its structures. These include the co-president of the Kongra-Gel, Zübeyir Aydar, and the co-president of the KNK, Remzi Kartal, both of whom were initially elected as MPs for the HEP in 1991 but had to leave Turkey in 1994 to avoid imprisonment.

However, the PKK's attempts to transform itself into a legal and non-violent movement during the 2000s, including establishing numerous new political organizations, have faced further difficulties due to the global context and the 'war against terror', which limited the PKK's political space. The difficult international context meant that the PKK's strategic transformation has not successfully led to its acceptance as a democratic movement advocating political change through non-violent means. From 2004 onwards, a new violent phase in the conflict started but it did not reach its previous peaks and periodic ceasefires and dialogue with the state that explored a peaceful end to the conflict between 2009 and 2015 prevented an acceleration of the conflict. However, from July 2015, the conflict accelerated significantly, which reversed much of the progress made in the past decade. Violence has not been eliminated in the conflict and it resumed in July 2015 following a breakdown in the dialogue process. While the continuation of violence presents significant barriers to a peaceful resolution of the conflict, it is difficult to successfully transform the conflict towards non-violence without the state's firm commitment to improving Kurdish rights in Turkey.

The pro-Kurdish democratic movement is the other main Kurdish political movement in Turkey. Since the movement's formation in 1990, it has been represented by several political parties. The pro-Kurdish parties have campaigned for the recognition of Kurdish identity, political rights and a peaceful end to the conflict between the PKK and the Turkish state. Their articulation of Kurdish rights brought them under severe repression and several of these parties were forced to close down; many of their members and activists faced different levels of repression, including arrest, detention, torture and murder. The state and Turkey's mainstream political parties justified the severe repression the pro-Kurdish political parties faced on grounds that they were the political wing of the PKK.

The urgency of raising popular Kurdish demands for the recognition of their identity and culture as well as formulating a political solution to the conflict became the focal points in their discourse. Their emphasis on the need for a democratic and political solution to the conflict has been interpreted as support for PKK and Kurdish separatism. This has been the dominant view held by the state and key political actors in Turkey and the nationalist antagonisms generated by the PKK's guerrilla struggle has been channelled against the pro-Kurdish parties. Throughout their existence, they have been treated as outsiders and are not seen as legitimate political actors by the state elite and mainstream political parties in Turkey. The relations between the pro-Kurdish parties and the PKK has been a complex one. As Chapter 1 discussed, the leaders of the pro-Kurdish parties strongly deny that they are the political wing of the PKK and argue that the state and the dominant political forces in Turkey use such framing to justify the repression of their movement. They reject the use of violence and campaign for a peaceful resolution of the conflict, but they emphasize that they share the same social base with the PKK.

Despite the repression, the pro-Kurdish political parties have managed to continue their existence and campaign for a peaceful solution of the Kurdish question. The transformation experienced in the conflict between the PKK and the state security forces opened up more space for the pro-Kurdish parties to become more effective actors. The attempts by pro-Kurdish parties to broaden the space for Kurdish political representation and their articulation of the demands for democratic change in Turkey began to pay dividends after 2007 when the pro-Kurdish parliamentary representation returned. This created a platform for the pro-Kurdish parties to build a wider pro-democracy mass movement. The return of the pro-Kurdish parliamentary opposition brought new momentum to Kurdish politics in Turkey. The pro-Kurdish parties consolidated their position as the dominant political party in the Kurdish regions during the late 2000s and their success in local and general elections during 2014 and 2015 enabled them to further strengthen their position and campaign for the accommodation of Kurdish rights and demands.

The relatively peaceful period in the conflict during the 2000s and 2010s has enabled the pro-Kurdish parties to become a stronger political actor with the HDP managing to pass the 10 per cent electoral threshold in the general election on 7 June 2015. The HDP incorporated many actors popular with the religious and tribal Kurdish voters in the past decade that has enabled it to consolidate its support base within these constituencies. Having a local base and their representation in the national assembly created opportunities to *legitimately* raise Kurdish political claims through democratic channels. However, despite winning the backing of a significant section of the Kurdish electorate in the past decade, the pro-Kurdish political parties are not perceived as legitimate representatives of the Kurdish people by the state authorities in Turkey because they are seen as an extension of the PKK.

However, very little objective evidence is produced by the advocates of the claim that the HDP is the political wing of the PKK. The HDP's refusal to describe the PKK as a 'terror organization' despite the pressure from the state and mainstream Turkish political parties and advocacy of a political solution to the conflict is interpreted as implicit support for the PKK. The perception that HDP supports PKK is likely to have an impact on its ability to appeal to the wider Turkish society but not as much among the Kurdish society in Turkey. Given the popular support the PKK enjoys from the Kurdish people, it is conceivable that a section of the HDP voters also support the

PKK and it is likely that for a section of the Kurdish voters, particularly in the Kurdish majority provinces in south-east Turkey, the presumed connection between the HDP and the PKK is the reason they vote for it. Most Kurdish voters view the HDP as part of a greater Kurdish struggle for rights in Turkey and, for a large section of them, the HDP's advocacy of Kurdish rights is the source of its legitimacy rather than the existence of a connection between the PKK and HDP.

In addition to the PKK and the pro-Kurdish political parties, the Islamist political actors have also been active in Kurdish politics. Chapter 1 discussed the rise and evolution of Hizbullah and its conflict with the PKK during the 1990s. Hizbullah has been a very secretive organization and there is much that remains unknown about them. Its violent campaign seems to have come to an end with the death of its leader Hüseyin Velioğlu in 2000 and, subsequently, the group's influence has declined. However, it began to re-organize itself as a social movement during the 2000s and established its representative party, Hüda-Par, at the end of 2012; which continues to exist, but has so far been unable to challenge the dominance of the pro-Kurdish political parties at local or national levels.

Chapter 2 examined the Kurdish political actors' means of representation and evaluated the level of support that different political parties obtain in the Kurdish majority regions of Turkey. While a number of political actors have been contesting the representation of the Kurds in Turkey during the past two decades, the main rivalry has been between the AKP and the pro-Kurdish political parties. The AKP's main social base in the Kurdish majority regions is comprised of tribes and religious orders. In addition, in recent years, it has created an extensive network of Islamist charitable organizations and associations through which it reaches Kurdish voters. However, the AKP's Turkish nationalist leaning has become a source of friction within the Kurdish Islamist circles, who have begun to establish their own organizations to reach out to their target audience and separate from Turkish Islamist circles. The rise of the pro-Kurdish movement in the past two decades and winning the support of the majority of the Kurds since 2014 has enabled it to become the main representative of the Kurds in Turkey.

As Chapters 3 and 4 discuss, the findings of the study reveal that, despite losing their dominant position in Kurdish politics following the rise of the Kurdish national movement from the 1970s onwards, tribal and religious elites continue to maintain some influence. Competitive elections since 1950 created opportunities for Kurdish traditional elite to engage in politics and establish themselves as the dominant actors in Kurdish politics in Turkey. Many leading Kurdish tribal and religious figures have been active in Turkey's mainstream political parties as well as in the Islamist-leaning parties during the past seventy years. Throughout this period, the tribal and religious elite took advantage of their position in society to cultivate good relations with Turkey's political elite and in doing so further strengthened their dominant position within the Kurdish society. Their ability to act as intermediaries between the Kurdish population and the state and political parties placed them at the heart of Kurdish political representation in Turkey.

However, increasing levels of urbanization and the spread of education weakened the tribal ties and loyalties and reduced the tribal leaders' ability to mobilize the members of their tribes. Tribes have countered the consequences of these socio-economic transformations by developing new forms of organization to maintain and strengthen tribal ties and connections in urban contexts, such as through establishing community associations and creating support networks to retain their relevance to an increasingly urbanized and dispersed membership. The mainstream Turkish political parties continue to play a significant role in the representation of tribes in politics. The AKP and other centre-right political parties also maintain strong support among tribes and many tribal leaders continue to serve as MPs in the AKP. The village guard system also plays an important role in the tribes' ability to continue as significant political actors in the region as it gives them more resources and access to state dignitaries and government representatives. In recent years, the pro-Kurdish parties have increased their efforts to develop ties with tribes and include more tribal representatives in their ranks.

Religious groups and actors also continue to play an important role in the political representation of the Kurds in Turkey. Historically, they had a dominant position in Kurdish politics and society and their position can be traced back to the late nineteenth to early twentieth century when Kurdish religious elite established themselves as the leading political figures in Kurdish society and were involved as leaders in the early nationalist rebellions in Turkey. In the subsequent period, their influence has decreased significantly because of the secularization reforms the state carried out and also due to the dismantlement of the Kurdish religious networks. However, in the second half of the twentieth century, religious figures began increasing their influence in society because of their involvement in the centre-right political parties. This has led to their co-optation into Turkey's ruling elite and the political class.

The structural transformation Turkey and the Kurdish society has experienced in the past fifty years, including the modernization and secularization of society and increased urbanization, has transformed and in many respects reduced the appeal of religious groups and actors. As a reaction to the increasing influence of Kurdish national movement in Turkey in the past twenty years, religious groups and actors have increased their efforts to constitute themselves as important political actors within the Kurdish society. However, they have not been able to constitute themselves as independent actors and are dependent on a series of the centre-right or Islamist political parties. Their representation has been based on the existing patron–client relations that have been in place from the mid-twentieth century onwards and are used by Kurdish Islamic actors to increase their role and influence in the Kurdish society in Turkey.

Beyond the political parties and religious and tribal elites, the study identified a number of other actors and groups that are involved in the political representation of the Kurds. Chapter 5 focused on the political activities of Kurds belonging to modern social classes and examined the main forms of political engagement of the Kurdish business community as well as of individuals from middle-class, professional and working-class backgrounds. Due to the Kurdish population in Turkey being dispersed across the country and because many choose not to publicly identify themselves as Kurds, it has been very difficult to provide accurate figures for the size of the Kurdish business community and the types of business enterprises that they have created. The continuation of the conflict means tensions and episodes of ethnic violence targeting Kurds in western Turkey arise occasionally. The chapter noted that, due to frequent ethnic tensions, Kurdish businesses in western Turkey that cater to a predominantly Turkish clientele are more likely to de-emphasize their Kurdish identity. Kurdish small businesses operating in western Turkey, such as restaurants or small construction firms, are less likely to openly support the pro-Kurdish political parties as they are faced with a greater risk of being the targets of the mob violence. Even if the Kurdish businesses support the pro-Kurdish movement through financial donations, they are likely to do it in secret. Hence, the behaviour of the Kurdish business community and their attitudes need to be seen within the wider socio-political context in Turkey.

The reduction in violence during the 2000s and the first half of the 2010s made a positive contribution to the reinvigoration of civil life in Kurdish majority areas of Turkey. As a result, a number of organizations that represent the Kurdish business community have been established and are currently active. The normalization of political life increased investment and economic opportunities in the Kurdish majority regions. In addition, numerous trade unions and occupational associations have also become active in the representation of Kurdish political demands. A good example is trade unions active in the education sector advocating the demand for Kurdish mother-tongue education. Consequently, more avenues for the political representation of Kurds have become available in Turkey. Various other civil society organizations in the area of human rights, promoting the Kurdish language and poverty alleviation were also active in the Kurdish majority regions during the past decade. However, the repressive measures the government has adopted since the summer of 2015 have also targeted these civil society organizations and occupational associations and, as a result, the transformation and normalization experienced in the past two decades has been by and large reversed.

In Chapter 6, the focus turned to the political activities and attitudes of women and youth and students. It first provided an overview of Kurdish women's and youth and students' mobilization in Turkey from the late 1970s onwards. The discussion was situated within an historical context in order to interpret the experience of Kurdish women and youth and students in a longer time frame. Overall, a great majority of Kurdish women, youth and students take part in the political activities of the pro-Kurdish movement. This is expected as both of the groups have been active in the Kurdish movement and have to a certain extent internalized the attitudes and practices of the movement. This experience has enabled women and youth and students to initiate and develop new types of political practices. In the case of women, the past decade witnessed the establishment of organizations that campaign for gender equality and attempt to tackle specific problems women face, such as domestic violence. In the case of youth and students, they emerged as a force in Kurdish resistance in the urban centres and central actors in protests and other instances of collective mobilization.

Overall, Kurdish women are involved in the activities of a diverse set of organizations that have the specific aim of advancing women's rights in society or improving the conditions in which women are living. Women's political attitudes and behaviour resemble the political activism of the pro-Kurdish movement, which shows that they are influenced by the wider Kurdish movement. In the past two decades, many women have been elected as MPs and mayors and we have seen a significant increase in the number of women representatives. The presence of women within the PKK and the pro-Kurdish political parties has had a significant impact at a societal level. It has lessened the appeal and force of traditional values in Kurdish society, such as male domination, and brought about a gradual feminization of the Kurdish movement.[6] It has also increased women's visibility and participation in society, leading to a change in views and attitudes about what is expected from women, as well as women raising their political expectations and demands. Also, in the past two decades, the number of women's rights organizations that have been active in Kurdish majority areas has increased significantly. However, many of these organizations have been closed down by the government crackdown on Kurdish movement in 2016 and, as a result, the important progress made in the area of gender equality has been dented.

Youth and students are also involved in a wide array of activities and have been mobilized politically. In fact, recent developments suggest a new wave of activism by youth in urban settings that is likely to take centre stage in Kurdish political activism in Turkey. It is not only violence and political protests that Kurdish youth and students are involved in. The continuation of conflict and the increasing use of force to quell dissent by youth and students perpetuates the climate of tension and causes new waves of protest. The recent mobilization in Rojava to fight against the IS needs to be seen as part of a larger context of Kurdish youth and students being mobilized by the Kurdish movement. However, protest and violence are not the only means through which the Kurdish youth and students engage. On the contrary, they take part in a wide array of political and cultural activities in Turkey.

What's next for Kurdish political representation in Turkey?

The HDP thrived in a peaceful environment and its political activism between 2012 and 2015 contributed to the shift in the public debate on the recognition of Kurdish identity and accommodation of Kurdish rights in Turkey. The HDP's success in the June 2015 election boosted the hope that it will accelerate Turkey's search for peace and pave the way towards a negotiated end to the armed conflict between the state security forces and the PKK guerrillas. Since the summer of 2015, we have witnessed a process of re-securitization of Turkey's Kurdish question and the government's reliance on the use of military force on a massive scale to dismantle the pro-Kurdish opposition and repress any form of Kurdish dissent. In the first half of 2016, Turkish army and security forces targeted the PKK's urban strongholds in the south-east of Turkey, which led to huge destruction in Diyarbakır's old city, Şırnak, Cizre and Nusaybin, and resulted in many civilian casualties, widespread human rights violations and forced displacement of an estimated half a million Kurds.[7]

Since the mid-1980s, the PKK's insurgency has undergone a number of stages and the state's forced displacement of the Kurdish rural population during the 1990s managed to cut off the PKK's access to the people. The state's current counter-insurgency approach involves extensive use of aerial power and armed drones, which has made conducting a guerrilla struggle more difficult for the PKK. The Turkish army has also increased its army bases and presence in Iraqi Kurdistan to cut the PKK's supply routes between the Qandil Mountains where the PKK is based and Turkey. As a result, the human cost of the PKK's insurgency has increased, and its effectiveness decreased, which raises questions about the effectiveness of the PKK's strategy of using violence against the state security forces predominantly in rural contexts to further its political aims.

The Turkish government's approach to the management of the Kurdish question in Turkey since the summer of 2015 marks a significant departure from the policies adopted during the past decade. However, rather than an aberration, this needs to be seen as a return to the state's dominant policy, which it followed during much of the twentieth century. Even though the AKP started the dialogue process with the PKK and Abdullah Öcalan in January 2013 and continued it until April 2015, it did not significantly change its approach to the Kurdish question in this period and failed to develop a new policy framework for the accommodation of Kurdish rights in Turkey. For example, it remained opposed to the provision of education in the Kurdish language, refused to meet Kurdish demands for autonomy and self-government and the constitutional recognition of Kurdish identity in Turkey. Erdoğan and other senior AKP officials were keen to frame the objective of the dialogue process as the PKK's surrender rather than develop a new relationship with the Kurds in Turkey – as well as those in the neighbouring countries – that is based on recognising Kurdish identity and rights and facilitates the development of an institutional framework that fosters national pluralism and coexistence.

Instead, Erdoğan set out to build a new Turkish nationalist alliance with the ultra-nationalist MHP to eliminate Kurdish political representation at local and national levels. At the heart of this alliance lies the repression of the Kurdish movement and the Kurdish political representatives are targeted because they are the main opposition to the AKP's authoritarianism and the centralization of power in the hands of Erdoğan. The AKP has viewed the HDP as a barrier to its objective of designing a Turkish society in its Islamic conservative and Turkish nationalist image. It was prepared to tolerate a degree of pluralism but its accommodation of the Kurds is within the framework of Islamic unity and on the condition that it does not challenge the Turkish dominance.[8] As part of its redesign of Turkish politics and as a counterweight against the pro-Kurdish representatives, the AKP has been empowering Islamist and traditional Kurdish actors, such as the Hüda-Par, the tribal and religious elite and political groups affiliated with the Iraqi Kurdish KDP, which has emerged as a strong ally of Erdoğan and the AKP in the past decade.

The government's repression does not distinguish between the PKK and the HDP and its elected Kurdish political representatives. Government statements have frequently targeted all Kurdish political representatives and described them as a threat to Turkey's territorial integrity. Such language is also used widely by the pro-government and state media and by associating the HDP with violence and terrorism they aim to delegitimize Kurdish representatives in Turkey and dismantle the pro-democracy coalition that the HDP has built since 2012. As part of this strategy, the government has taken widespread measures to destroy the HDP's local and national institutional bases. The repression that the state used against the pro-Kurdish political parties during the 1990s and 2000s seems to have been reactivated once again against the HDP. On 20 May 2016, the Turkish parliament passed legislation to lift the immunity of MPs, which is a measure designed by the government to end or at least significantly weaken the HDP representation in Turkey's parliament. The government passed a delegated decree on 1 September 2016 to remove the elected pro-Kurdish mayors and replace them with appointed trustees.

Civil society initiatives and the pro-Kurdish media network that challenges the government's discourse on the Kurdish question have also become the target of state repression in the past year. İMC TV's broadcasts via the state's satellite television network were blocked on 24 February 2016 and the channel was closed down on 30 September 2016. A number of other TV channels and radio stations have also been closed down. The pro-Kurdish daily newspaper Özgür Gündem was closed down on 16 August 2016. Pro-Kurdish women's rights organizations and charities that worked in the area of poverty alleviation have also been closed. Turkey's authoritarian turn has further accelerated after the failed coup attempt on 15 July 2016, which is widely believed to be carried out by the supporters of the cleric Fethullah Gülen. The government has used the coup attempt to further weaken the centres of opposition and undermine the democratic institutions. Together with the support from the ultra-nationalist MHP, the AKP managed to get its constitutional amendment for an executive presidency through the parliament and put it to a referendum on 16 April 2017, which it won narrowly amidst widespread intimidation and irregularities.

The repression of the HDP has continued since the summer of 2015 and the future role it will play in Turkish politics depends on its resilience and ability to survive it. The HDP has built a strong political network since its foundation and managed to create a strong unity among diverse political movements. This deeper and denser unity makes the repression of the HDP more difficult and its repression is likely to face strong domestic and international opposition. Overall, the continuation of Turkish nationalist hegemony and its representation of Kurdish demands as a threat to Turkey's national and territorial integrity remains a significant barrier to Turkey's democratization and accommodation of Kurdish rights in Turkey.

The HDP's repression together with the securitization of the Kurdish question creates a hostile environment for the Kurds in Turkey and if continued will significantly weaken the Kurds' feeling of attachment to the country's political institutions. The long-term stability of Turkey's political system is only possible if Kurdish demands are accommodated. The main Kurdish political actors in Turkey conceive of a solution to the Kurdish question in Turkey in a way that does not threaten Turkey's territorial integrity. Overall, around 80 per cent of the survey respondents stated that they believed Turkey's current institutional set-up was unsuitable for the representation of the Kurds. In their study into Kurdish political attitudes in Turkey, Yeğen, Tol and Çalışkan identify popular support for the decentralization of political power and empowerment of local governments to enable forms of autonomy and self-government.[9] Also, their study demonstrates that around 80 per cent of their respondents supported the constitutional recognition of Kurdish identity and provision of education in the Kurdish language in public schools.[10] Hence, a form of territorial decentralization in Turkey and the recognition of Kurdish group rights can satisfy Kurds' political demands. However, Turkey's political parties have remained at best bellicose to the idea of the constitutional recognition of Kurdish identity and the associated rights.

In the past, Turkey's EU accession process was one of the main drivers of democratization and the improvement of Kurdish rights in the 2000s and, currently, Turkey remains a candidate for EU membership. Turkey–EU relations have a complex dynamic and, since 2015, the EU has been rather lenient with its criticism of the Turkish state's repression of the HDP, the widespread human rights abuses against Kurdish civilians and the alarming rate with which Turkish democracy has deteriorated since 2015 because Turkey has used the refugee crisis to increase its leverage over the EU and divert criticism from Turkey's anti-democratic turn.

The state's policy of repressing Kurdish opposition and curtailing its influence has a regional dimension and contains measures to prevent the development and consolidation of Kurdish representative institutions in Syria and Iraq.[11] Events and developments in Syria have had a huge impact on Turkey's domestic politics and Turkey frames its policy towards Syria's Kurds within its overall policy on the management of its Kurdish conflict. The Kurds' rising influence in Syria in the past four years has also influenced the government's approach to the Kurdish question in Turkey. The establishment of Kurdish de facto autonomy in Syria under the leadership of a political party that has an ideological affiliation with the PKK has become a key concern for Turkey in recent years. The Kurdish entity that is coming into being in Syria reduces the likelihood of moulding post-conflict Syria into a state shaped by Turkey's vision of the region.

The recognition of Kurdish identity and associated rights requires major changes in Turkey's identity as a state, but the public debate so far reveals the ideological rigidity of Turkish nationalism and its hesitation in accepting the legitimacy of Kurdish political demands and rights. Without the constitutional recognition of Kurdish identity in Turkey, it is difficult to address the many dimensions of the inequality Kurds as a group and Kurdish individuals from different segments face. Without the constitutional recognition of Kurdish identity, it is difficult to also effectively address Kurdish political demands as has been articulated by the main Kurdish representatives. While there is an urgent need for a wide public debate in Turkey about the specific steps needed to be taken to address Kurdish group rights, so far, the debate has been framed around the question of whether it is desirable to recognize Kurdish rights or not. The legal and political restrictions in Turkey have played a limiting role in the emergence of a constructive public debate on the Kurdish question in Turkey. Hence, there is an urgent need to identify specific steps or policies for the effective accommodation of Kurdish political demands.

For example, in the debate about the use of the Kurdish language in education, rather than focusing on the policies needed to effectively address Kurds' demands to educate their children in Kurdish language schools, the focus has centred on whether such a step would be desirable or not. An often-repeated argument against the use of the Kurdish language in education in Turkey centres on how it would disadvantage Kurdish students by decreasing their ability to use the Turkish language. Although this might be a legitimate concern for Kurdish parents who wish for the best opportunities for their children, it does not consider that with appropriate policies and resources, the present barriers to Kurdish language education can be overcome. In fact, the use of the Kurdish language in state schools can greatly contribute to educational achievements of Kurdish children as it would mean they would be educated in their mother language and not forced to learn a new language as a precondition of receiving an education. Furthermore, Kurdish language education can be introduced without creating adverse consequences to Kurdish children whose parents can no longer speak their mother tongue and can be an effective tool to reverse the effects of decades-long forced assimilation. Turkish language classes can be taught as part of the curriculum to enable Kurdish children to acquire the language. In addition, the removal of the legal restrictions on the use of the Kurdish language will likely increase job opportunities for the Kurdish-language educated as it would lead to the Kurdish language being widely used both in the public sector and in business.

Despite the persuasive case presented by philosophers and political theorists for the public recognition of group identities and rights, some scholars have argued against recognition on grounds that it can negatively impact the position of marginalized groups, such as the minorities within minorities and women.[12] However, empirical research seems to indicate that the recognition of group rights could improve the position of women and minorities within minorities, rather than marginalize it. For example, the existing research in Spain highlights the positive impact the regional governments of minority nations, especially in the Basque Country and Catalonia, has had on gender equality promotion in the past two decades.[13] Gender equality has also been gaining centrality in Kurdish politics in Turkey in the past decade. In the past decade, the equality demands of LGBT communities in Turkey has begun to be advocated by the pro-Kurdish political parties alongside the demands for the recognition of Kurdish group rights. Hence, the demand for the recognition of group rights need not result in the subordination of marginalized social groups and smaller minorities.

Similarly, minority demands for territorial autonomy, which requires the recognition of national minorities and their representation through self-governance structures within a given territory, has been challenged by dominant nations on grounds that its realization would lead to the ethnicization of the territory and territorial autonomy transforms into 'autonomy *for*' a national group.[14] This, too, is a legitimate concern for non-dominant groups living in a territory populated by a national minority. However, it is not a valid argument against the minority demands for autonomy and self-government because these concerns can be addressed through a more inclusive approach to the relationship between a territory and ethnic groups. In other words, inclusive autonomy arrangements that take the ethnic heterogeneity of the region into account can be developed and such an approach would create the potential for the better representation of all social groups in the decision-making processes.[15]

The dispersion of the Kurdish population across Turkey and the existence of large Kurdish communities in western Turkish cities, particularly Istanbul, poses additional difficulties for the realization of Kurdish autonomy. As I have discussed in my other work, this problem can be addressed via policies based on the Non-Territorial Autonomy (NTA) model, which has been used in Central and Eastern European countries to address the needs of ethnic groups that are dispersed across the country and do not constitute a majority in a region.[16] The NTA model was initially developed by Karl Renner and Otto Bauer at the end of the nineteenth century to accommodate the nationally diverse population of the Austria–Hungarian Empire within a democratic state, and its principal appeal to policymakers is that it proposes to accommodate national minorities without compromising states' territorial integrity.[17] NTA is suitable especially for national minorities that are territorially dispersed but its proponents argue that the model itself contains features, such as the accommodation of language rights and cultural self-governance, which will be useful for the territorially centred national minorities too and can, therefore, serve as an alternative model of accommodation.[18] Also, as stressed by Lapidoth and Kymlicka, NTA and TA are not mutually exclusive and can operate alongside one another.[19] NTA 'can be employed to supplement territorial autonomy, with the same minority benefiting from territorial autonomy in one region and cultural (personal) autonomy in another, depending on the demographics of different regions within a state'.[20] Hence, a hybrid autonomy system that combines territorial and non-territorial features could be suitable for addressing the cultural demands of all Kurds in Turkey.

In the past decade, despite the existence of significant opportunities to resolve the conflict, Turkey has failed to develop a new policy framework to transform and eventually end it. The widespread opposition against the accommodation of Kurdish rights in Turkey, particularly from the Turkish nationalist political parties and the public, needs to be first overcome before a consensus on a new political framework in Turkey can be developed. Turkey's excessively centralized political system took a new dimension with the constitutional reforms that were passed in a referendum on April 2017. This is likely to present barriers to the Kurdish representation as it further centralizes the decision-making process. The absence of a robust system of checks and balances in the new presidential system, the elimination of the opposition media and the deterioration of the power of the judiciary represents a backward step in terms of democratic standards and makes it more difficult for Kurds to put their message across. Hence, the future of Kurdish political representation depends on how they will adapt to Turkey's new realities and whether they will be able to carve political space to make their voices heard.

So far, the HDP has maintained its support base and, despite the repression it has faced, it has managed to gain most of the municipal councils in the March 2019 local elections. However, the elected HDP co-mayors face strong challenges in their efforts to exert their power. Around 2,000 officials of the municipal councils were removed from their positions by the trustees and replaced by AKP loyalists. The mismanagement of the municipal budgets by the trustees left many municipalities heavily in debt. Also, the HDP co-mayors will be under increased state scrutiny as Erdoğan promised to continue his policy of replacing them with appointed trustees. As discussed in more detail in Chapter 2, the process of removing the elected mayors and replacing them with state-appointed trustees is continuing and, as of November 2019, the co-mayors of twenty-four municipal, district and town councils have been removed, including Diyarbakır, Mardin and Van. The indications are that this policy will continue and the co-mayors of the remaining councils will also be removed. Nevertheless, in the short term, winning back the municipalities in the Kurdish region has boosted the morale of the party's support base and strengthen the HDP's efforts to counter the government's depiction of it as an illegitimate political movement. It has also increased the relevance of the HDP in the efforts to reverse the authoritarian turn in Turkish politics, particularly its supporters who helped the opposition beat AKP candidates in many of the country's urban centres. It proves that in future elections and through informal electoral alliances, the HDP can make a difference to the way Turkey is governed.

Notes

Introduction

1 Suzanna Dovi, 'Political Representation', *Stanford Encyclopaedia of Philosophy* (2017). Available online: https://plato.stanford.edu/entries/political-representation/ (accessed 6 April 2017).
2 Ibid.
3 Hanna Fenichel Pitkin, *The Concept of Representation* (Berkeley and Los Angeles: University of California Press, 1967), 38 and 55.
4 Ibid., 61.
5 Ibid., 92.
6 Ibid., 115.
7 Jane Manbridge, 'Should Blacks represent Blacks and Women represent Women? A Contingent "Yes"', *Journal of Politics*, 61:3 (1999), 628.
8 Ibid.
9 Susan A. Banducci, Todd Donovan and Jeffrey A. Karp, 'Minority Representation, Empowerment, and Participation', *The Journal of Politics*, 66:2 (2004), 534–56.
10 Michael Saward, *The Representative Claim* (Oxford: Oxford University Press, 2010), 43–4.
11 Michael Saward, 'The Representative Claim', *Contemporary Political Theory*, 5:3 (2006), 301–2.
12 Kendal Nezan, 'Kurdistan in Turkey', in *A People Without a Country: The Kurds and Kurdistan*, ed. Gerard Chaliand (London: Zed Books, 1992), 66–7.
13 Chris Kutschera, 'Kurdistan Turkey: Mehdi Zana, a Voice from behind the Bars' (1996). Available online: http://www.chris-kutschera.com/A/mehdi_zana.htm (accessed 8 October 2015).
14 Stanford J. Shaw and Ezel Kural Shaw, *History of the Ottoman Empire and Modern Turkey. Volume II: Reform, Revolution and Republic: The Rise of Modern Turkey, 1808–1975* (Cambridge: Cambridge University Press, 1977), 386.
15 Derya Bayır, *Minorities and Nationalism in Turkish Law* (London and New York: Routledge, 2013), 88.
16 Cenk Saraçoğlu, *Kurds of Modern Turkey: Migration, Neoliberalism and Exclusion in Turkish Society* (London and New York: I.B. Tauris, 2011), 59.
17 Bayır, *Minorities and Nationalism in Turkish Law*, 145–54.
18 Ioannis N. Grigoriadis, 'Türk or Türkiyeli? The Reform of Turkey's Minority Legislation and the Rediscovery of Ottomanism', *Middle Eastern Studies*, 43:3 (2007), 423.
19 For a discussion of the Turkish state's discourse on the Kurdish question, see Mesut Yeğen, 'Turkish Nationalism and the Kurdish Question', *Ethnic and Racial Studies*, 30:1 (2007), 119–51; Mesut Yeğen, 'The Turkish State Discourse and the exclusion of Kurdish identity', *Middle Eastern Studies*, 32 (April 1996), 216–29.
20 Bayır, *Minorities and Nationalism in Turkish Law*, 1.

21 Derya Bayır, 'The role of the judicial system in the politicide of the Kurdish opposition', in Cengiz Gunes and Welat Zeydanlioglu (eds), *The Kurdish Question in Turkey: New Perspectives on Violence, Representation and Reconciliation* (London and New York: Routledge, 2014), 27.
22 Derya Bayır, 'Representation of the Kurds by the Turkish Judiciary', *Human Rights Quarterly*, 35 (2013), 117 and 120.
23 Ibid., 120.
24 Ibid., 121.
25 T. Bahcheli and S. Noel, 'The Justice and Development Party and the Kurdish question', in Marlies Casier and Joost Jongerden (eds), *Nationalisms and Politics in Turkey: Political Islam, Kemalism and the Kurdish Issue* (London and New York: Routledge, 2011), 101–2.
26 Cengiz Gunes, *The Kurdish National Movement in Turkey: From Protest to Resistance* (London and New York: Routledge, 2012), 161.
27 Ibid., 163–4.
28 Bayır, *Minorities and Nationalism in Turkish Law*, 191–2.
29 Ibid., 165.
30 Ibid., 168.
31 Ibid., 170.
32 Derya Bayır, 'Turkey, the Kurds, and the legal contours of the right to self-determination', *Kurdish Studies*, 1:1 (2013), 18.
33 İbrahim Sirkeci, 'Exploring the Kurdish population in the Turkish context', *Genus*, 56:1–2 (2000), 154.
34 Tarhan Erdem, 'Türkiyeli Kürt ne kadar?', *Radikal*, 2013. Available online: http://www.radikal.com.tr/yazarlar/tarhan-erdem/turkiyeli-kurtler-ne-kadar-1130023/ (accessed 25 July 2018).
35 Mustafa Sönmez, 'Batı'ya Kürt Göçü ve G.Doğu'yu Kalkındırma Söylemi ... ', *Iktisat ve Toplum*, 31–2 (2015), 47–52.
36 Ibid., 47. The exact Kurdish population in Turkey is unknown, and estimates vary.
37 Geographically, Turkey is divided into seven regions: Aegean Region, Black Sea Region, Central Anatolia Region, Eastern Anatolia Region, Marmara Region, Mediterranean Region and South-eastern Anatolia Region. The historically Kurdish populated areas are predominantly in the Eastern and South-eastern Anatolia regions.
38 For a general discussion on internal displacement see Ayşe Betül Çelik, 'Transnationalisation of Human Right Norms and its impact on the Internally Displaced Kurds', *Human Rights Quarterly*, 27 (2005), 969–97; Joost Jongerden, 'Resettlement and reconstruction of identity: the case of Kurds in Turkey', *Ethnopolitics*, 1:1 (2001), 80–6.
39 Sönmez, 'Batı'ya Kürt Göçü', 49.
40 Ibid.
41 Türkiye İstatistik Kurumu, 'Adrese Dayalı Nüfus Kayıt Sistemi Sonuçları, 2015' (2016). Available online: http://www.tuik.gov.tr/PreHaberBultenleri.do?id=21507 (accessed 25 September 2016).
42 Türkiye İstatistik Kurumu, 'İlçelere göre şehir ve köy nüfusları – 1990 Genel Nüfus sayımı' (2015). Available online: http://rapory.tuik.gov.tr/16-05-2020-14:43:24-13297062243761754696787220081.html (accessed 20 September 2015).
43 Ibid.
44 Nufusu.com, 'Diyarbakır Nufusu' (2015). Available online: http://www.nufusu.com/il/Diyarbakır-nufusu (accessed 18 September 2015).

45 Türkiye İstatistik Kurumu, 'Adrese Dayalı Nüfus Kayıt Sistemi Sonuçları, 2013' (2014). Available online: http://www.tuik.gov.tr/PreHaberBultenleri.do?id=15974 (accessed 19 September 2015). The World Bank estimates that 73 per cent of Turkey's population resides in the urban areas (World Bank, 'Urban Population (% of total)' (2015). Available online: http://data.worldbank.org/indicator/SP.URB.TOTL.IN.ZS (accessed 19 September 2015)).
46 Milliyet, 'Diyarbakırın Nüfusu Açıklandı' (2015). Available online: https://www.milliyet.com.tr/yerel-haberler/diyarbakir/diyarbakir-in-nufusu-aciklandi-10593714 (accessed 22 October 2015).
47 Türkiye İstatistik Kurumu, 'Adrese Dayalı Nüfus Kayıt Sistemi Sonuçları, 2015' (2016). Available online: http://www.tuik.gov.tr/PreHaberBultenleri.do?id=21507 (accessed 26 September 2016).
48 www.Nufusu.com, 'Van Nufusu' (2015). Available online: http://www.nufusu.com/il/van-nufusu (accessed 18 September 2015).
49 Türkiye İstatistik Kurumu, 'Adrese Dayalı Nüfus Kayıt Sistemi Sonuçları, 2015' (2016). Available online: http://www.tuik.gov.tr/PreHaberBultenleri.do?id=21507 (accessed 26 September 2016).

Chapter 1

1 Russell J. Dalton, David M. Farrell and Ian McAllister, *Political Parties and Democratic Linkages: How Parties Organise Democracy* (Oxford: Oxford University Press, 2011), 3–5.
2 Susan E. Scarrow, 'Political Parties and Party Systems', in *Comparing Democracies: Elections and Voting in the 21st Century*, eds, Lawrence LeDuc, Richard G. Niemi and Pippa Norris (London: Sage, 2010), 45–6.
3 İlter Turan, *Turkey's Difficult Journey to Democracy* (Oxford: Oxford University Press, 2015), 82; Erik J. Zürcher, *Turkey: A Modern History* (4th Edition) (London and New York: I.B. Tauris, 2017), 211.
4 Igor P. Lipovsky, *The Socialist Movement in Turkey 1960–1980* (Leiden: Brill, 1992), 103.
5 For an account of the revival of Kurdish political activism in Turkey see Hamit Bozarslan, 'Political aspects of the Kurdish Problem in Turkey', in *The Kurds: A Contemporary Overview*, ed., Philip G. Kreyenbroek and Stefan Sperl (London and New York: Routledge, 1992); and Hamit Bozarslan, 'Kurds and the Turkish state', in *The Cambridge History of Turkey, Volume 4*, ed., Reşat Kasaba (Cambridge: Cambridge University Press, 2008).
6 Cengiz Gunes, 'Kurdish Politics in Turkey: Ideology, Identity and Transformations', *Ethnopolitics*, 8:2 (2009), 255–62.
7 Cengiz Gunes, 'The Kurdish Political Activism in Turkey: An Overview', in *Kurdish Issues: Essays in Honor of Robert Olson*, eds, Michael Gunter and Muhammed Ahmed (Costa Mesa: Mazda Publishers, 2016), 87. For an account of the treatment of the Kurdish political prisoners in Turkey in the early 1980s, see Welat Zeydanlıoğlu, 'Torture and Turkification in the Diyarbakır Military Prison', in *Rights, Citizenship & Torture: Perspectives on Evil, Law and the State*, eds, J. T. Parry and W. Zeydanlıoğlu (Oxford: Inter-Disciplinary Press, 2009).
8 Joost Jongerden and Ahmet Hamdi Akkaya, 'Born from the left: the making of the PKK', in *Nationalisms and Politics in Turkey: Political Islam, Kemalism, and the Kurdish Issue*, eds, Marlies Casier and Joost Jongerden (London: Routledge, 2011).

9 Abdullah Öcalan, *Kürdistan Devriminin Yolu (Manifesto)* (4th Edition) (Cologne: Weşanên Serxwebûn, 1992), 198.
10 PKK, *Politik Rapor: Merkez Komitesi Tarafindan PKK 1. Konferansina Sunulmuştur* (Cologne: Weşanên Serxwebûn, 1982), 136-7.
11 Cengiz Gunes, 'Explaining the PKK's Mobilization of Kurds in Turkey: Hegemony, Myth and Violence', *Ethnopolitics*, 12:3 (2013), 247-67.
12 Cengiz Gunes, 'Kurdish Mobilisation in Turkey during the 1980s and 1990s', in *The Kurdish Question Revisited*, eds, Gareth Stansfield and Mohammad Shareef (London: Hurst and Co., 2017), 190.
13 Gunes, *The Kurdish National Movement in Turkey*, 102.
14 *Berxwedan*, September 1987, 12.
15 Hamit Bozarslan, 'Foreword', in *The Kurdish Question in Turkey: New Perspectives on Conflict, Representation and Reconciliation*, eds, Cengiz Gunes and Welat Zeydanlioglu (London and New York: Routledge, 2014), v.
16 Gunes, *Kurdish National Movement in Turkey*, 35.
17 Ibid., 102.
18 Ibid., 136.
19 Abdullah Öcalan, *Savunma: Kürt Sorununda Demokratik Çözüm Bildirgesi* (Istanbul: Mem Yayınları, 1999), 22.
20 Abdullah Öcalan, *AİHM Savunmaları: Sümer Rahip Develtinden Demokratik Cumhuriyete (Cilt 2)* (Cologne: Mezopotamya Yayınları, 2001), 172-3.
21 Abdullah Öcalan, *Bir Halkı Savunmak* (Cologne: Weşanên Serxwebûn, 2004).
22 Ibid., 402-3.
23 For further reading on the PKK's ideological transformation and the democratic confederalism demands see Gunes, *The Kurdish National Movement in Turkey*, 124-51; Joost Jongerden and Ahmet Hamdi Akkaya, 'Democratic Confederalism as a Kurdish Spring: The PKK and the Quest for Radical Democracy', in *The Kurdish Spring: Geopolitical Changes and the Kurds*, eds, Mohammad M. A. Ahmed and Michael M. Gunter (Costa Mesa: Mazda Publishers, 2013), 163-85; Ahmet Hamdi Akkaya and Joost Jongerden, 'Confederalism and Autonomy in Turkey: The Kurdistan Workers' Party and the Reinvention of Democracy', in *The Kurdish Question in Turkey*, eds, Gunes and Zeydanlıoğlu, 186-204; Ahmet Hamdi Akkaya and Joost Jongerden, 'The PKK in the 2000s: Continuity Through Breaks?' in *Nationalisms and Politics in Turkey*, eds, Casier and Jongerden, 143-62.
24 Cengiz Gunes, 'Unblocking the Impasse in Turkey's Kurdish Question', *Peace Review: A Journal of Social Justice*, 24:4 (2012), 462-9.
25 PKK, *Program ve Tüzüğü*, (Cologne: Weşanên Serxwebûn, 2005), 13.
26 KCK, 'KCK Sözleşmesi (KCK Contract)' (2005), 2. Available online: https://storage.googleapis.com/google-code-archive-downloads/v2/code.google.com/bookstorer/KCK%20Sözleşmesi.pdf (accessed 1 June 2017).
27 Abdullah Öcalan, *Democratic Confederalism* (London and Cologne: Tansmedia Publishing, 2011), 33.
28 PKK, *Kürt Sorununda Çözüme Doğru Demokratik Özerklik* (Abdullah Öcalan Sosyal Bilimler Akademisi Yayınları, place not stated, 2009).
29 PKK, 'Demokratik Özerklik', *Serxwebûn* 301 (2007), 57.
30 Ibid.
31 Ibid.
32 PKK, *Kürt Sorununda Çözüme Doğru Demokratik Özerklik*, 94.
33 Ibid.

34 For a more detailed discussion of the PKK's democratic autonomy and democratic confederalism proposals see Cengiz Gunes, 'Unpacking "Democratic Confederalism" and "Democratic Autonomy" Proposals of the Kurdish Movement in Turkey', in *Autonomy as a Model for Minority Self Government: From Theory to European and Middle Eastern Perspectives*, eds, Olgun Akbulut and Elcin Aktoprak (Leiden: Brill Publishers, 2019); Cengiz Gunes and Çetin Gürer, 'Kurdish Movement's Democratic Autonomy Proposals in Turkey', in *Democratic Representation in Plurinational States: The Kurds in Turkey*, eds, Ephraim Nimni and Elcin Aktoprak (London: Palgrave McMillan, 2018).
35 For a more elaborated discussion of the pro-Kurdish movement in Turkey see Cengiz Gunes, 'Turkey's New Left', *New Left Review*, 107 (September–October 2017); Cengiz Gunes, 'The rise of the pro-Kurdish democratic movement in Turkey', in *Routledge Handbook on the Kurds*, ed., Michael Gunter (London and New York: Routledge, 2018).
36 A. Osman Ölmez, *Türkiye Siyasetinde DEP Depremi* (Ankara: Doruk Yayınları, 1995), 88–90; Eyyüp Demir, *Yasal Kürtler* (Istanbul, 2005), 92–3.
37 Ahmet Türk, *DEP Savunması* (Ankara, 1994), 7; Eyyüp Demir, *Yasal Kürtler* (Istanbul, 2005), 116.
38 Demokrasi Partisi (DEP), *Program*, 9 (date and place of publication not mentioned).
39 Bayır, *Minorities and Nationalism in Turkish Law*, 191–2.
40 'Eski DEP'lilerden Demokratik Toplum Hareketi', *Hürriyet*, 22 October 2004.
41 The BDP was the main pro-Kurdish party between 2009 and 2014 but subsequently it has changed its name to Democratic Regions Party (DBP). It is active only at local and regional levels and it supports the HDP at the parliamentary elections.
42 SecimHaberler.com, '2014 BDP Yerel Secim Sonuçları' (2014). Available online: https://secim.haberler.com/2014/bdp-secim-sonucu/ (accessed 26 July 2019).
43 DTP, *Demokratik Toplum Partisi'nin Kürt Sorununa İlişkin Demokratik Çözüm Projesi* (Ankara, 2008), 11.
44 Ibid., 12.
45 BDP, 'Barış ve Demokrasi Partisi Programı' (2008). Available online: https://bdpblog.wordpress.com/parti-programimiz/ (accessed 25 July 2019).
46 BDP, 'Democratic Özerklik Projesi' (2011). Available online: https://bdpblog.wordpress.com/2011/05/04/demokratik-ozerklik-projesi/ (accessed 25 July 2019).
47 DTK, *Kürt Sorununun Çözümü İçin Demokratik Özerklik* (Aram, Diyarbakır, 2012).
48 DTK, 'Demokratik Toplum Kongresi Bileşenlerince Hazırlanmış Olan, Demokratik Özerk Kürdistan Modelinin Taslak Sunumu' (2010). Available online: http://bianet.org/files/doc_files/000/000/179/original/demokratiközerklik.htm (accessed 25 July 2019).
49 Ibid.
50 HDP, *Büyük İnsanlık-Bizler Meclise* (Ankara, 2015), 10.
51 For further reading on the pro-Kurdish movement's democratic autonomy proposals see Çetin Gürer, *Demokratik Özerklik: Bir Yurttaşlık Heterotopyası* (Istanbul: Notabene Yayınları, 2015).
52 HDP, 'Parti Programı' (2012). Available online: http://www.hdp.org.tr/parti/parti-programi/8, (accessed 8 May 2017, author's translation).
53 Bianet, 'HDP'li Vekillere Tutuklama ve Gözaltıların Kronolojisi' (2017). Available online: http://bianet.org/bianet/siyaset/183856-hdp-li-vekillere-tutuklama-ve-gozaltilarin-kronolojisi (accessed 28 July 2018).
54 Hatice Kamer, 'HDP milletvekili İdris Baluken'e 16 yıl 8 ay hapis cezası', *BBC Türkçe* (2018). Available online: http://www.bbc.com/turkce/haberler-turkiye-42565573 (accessed 28 July 2018).

55 Bianet, 'HDP'li Vekillere Tutuklama ve Gözaltıların Kronolojisi'.
56 Isil Sariyuce and Ivan Watson, 'Turkey detains Kurdish politicians', *CNN* (2016). Available online: https://edition.cnn.com/2016/10/26/middleeast/turkey-detains-kurdish-politicians/index.html (accessed 28 July 2018).
57 The following report prepared by the DBP has provided a detailed account of the actions the trustees have taken since their appointment: Demokratik Bölgeler Partisi (DBP), *Demokratik Bölgeler Partisi Demokratik Ekolojik Katılımcı Kadın Özgürlükçü Yerel Yönetim Modeli ve Bir Gasp Aracı Olarak Kayyum Uygulamaları* (Diyarbakır, 2017), 30–5.
58 Bianet, 'HDP'li Vekillere Tutuklama ve Gözaltıların Kronolojisi'.
59 Gunes, *Kurdish National Movement in Turkey*, 166.
60 Süddeutsche Zeitung, 'Wir definieren die PKK nicht als eine Terrororganisation' (2016). Available online: https://www.sueddeutsche.de/politik/hdp-politiker-demirta-neue-friedensgespraeche-unter-erdoan-das-ist-nur-ein-leerer-traum-1.3146997-2 (accessed 1 August 2018).
61 HAK-PAR, 'İl Örgütleri' (2018). Available online: https://www.hakpar.org.tr/root/index.php?option=com_content&view=article&id=69&Itemid=66&lang=tr (accessed 2 August 2018).
62 HAK-PAR, 'Hak ve Özgürlükler Partisi Programı' (2013). Available online: https://www.hakpar.org.tr/root/index.php?option=com_content&view=article&id=60&Itemid=86&lang=tr (accessed 2 August 2018).
63 Kurdistan 24, 'HAK-PAR' ın vaadi federasyon' (2018). Available online: https://www.kurdistan24.net/tr/news/80a63019-4097-40da-b999-16c9fa2c514b (accessed 2 August 2018).
64 İ. Bagasi, *Kendi Dilinden Hizbullah ve Mücadele Tarihinden Önemli Kesitler* (2004). Available online: www.huseynisevda.biz/Dokumanlar/Kendi_Dilinden_Hizbullah/00.html (accessed 30 July 2018).
65 Mustafa Gürbüz, *Rival Kurdish Movements in Turkey: Transforming Violent Conflict* (Amsterdam: Amsterdam University Press, 2016), 139.
66 For an in-depth anthropological study of the Hizbullah see Mehmet Kurt, *Kurdish Hizbullah in Turkey: Islamism, Violence and the State* (London: Pluto Press, 2017).
67 Kurt, *Kurdish Hizbullah*, 22.
68 Ibid., 29.
69 Gareth Jenkins, *Political Islam in Turkey: Running West, Heading East?* (London: Palgrave MacMillan, 2008), 186.
70 Ibid., 187.
71 Ibid., 188.
72 Gürbüz, *Rival Kurdish Movements in Turkey*, 37; Kurt, *Kurdish Hizbullah*, 31–9.
73 Jenkins, *Political Islam in Turkey*, 190.
74 Risale Haber, 'Izzettin Yıldırım cinayetinde sır çözüldü' (2010). Available online: http://www.risalehaber.com/izzettin-yildirim-cinayetinde-sir-cozuldu-72968h.htm (accessed 24 February 2017).
75 Jenkins, *Political Islam in Turkey*, 191–2.
76 Milliyet, 'Gonca Kuriş neden öldürüldü?' (2011). Available online: http://www.milliyet.com.tr/gonca-kuris-neden-olduruldu–gundem-1341564/ (accessed 3 August 2018).
77 Hatice Kamer, 'Diyarbakır Emniyet Müdürü Gaffar Okkan öldürülmesinin 17'nci yılında anıldı' (2018). Available online: https://www.bbc.com/turkce/haberler-turkiye-42807355 (accessed 3 August 2018).

78 Ruşen Çakır, *Derin Hizbullah: İslami Şiddetin Geleceği* (Istanbul: Siyah Beyaz Metis Güncel, 2001), 76. The Hizbullah denies that it had any links with or was used by the state against the PKK. The account it presents of the conflict argues that its attacks against the PKK were in the spirit of self defence.
79 Jenkins, *Political Islam in Turkey*, 191.
80 Ibid., 194.
81 Mynet, 'Hizbullah'ın kilit adamı İsa Altsoy yakalandı' (2007). Available online: http://www.mynet.com/haber/guncel/hizbullahin-kilit-adami-isa-altsoy-yakalandi-277217-1 (accessed 3 August 2018).
82 Hüseyin Kaçar, 'Hizbullahçılar artık aramızda', *Hürriyet* (2011). Available online: https://www.sabah.com.tr/gundem/2011/01/05/hizbullahcilar_artik_aramizda (accessed 23 July 2019).
83 Hürriyet, 'Hizbullah'ın lideri Hacı İnan gözaltında' (2011). Available online: http://www.hurriyet.com.tr/gundem/hizbullahin-lideri-haci-inan-gozaltinda-16789783 (accessed 23 July 2019); Hürriyet, 'Hizbullahçıların kaçış planı' (2011). Available online: http://www.hurriyet.com.tr/gundem/hizbullahcilarin-kacis-plani-17547674 (accessed 23 July 2019).
84 Ahmet S. Yayla, 'Portrait of Turkey's ISIS leader Halis Bayuncuk: Alias Abu Hanzala', *International Centre for the Study of Violent Extremism* (2016). Available online: http://www.icsve.org/brief-reports/portrait-of-turkeys-isis-leader-halis-bayuncuk-alias-abu-hanzala/ (accessed 30 May 2017).
85 See Zeki Sarigil and Omer Fazlioglu, 'Religion and ethno-nationalism: Turkey's Kurdish issue', *Nations and Nationalism*, 19:3 (2013), 551–71.
86 Altsoy 2004, quoted in Gürbüz, *Rival Kurdish Movements in Turkey*, 139.
87 Gürbüz, *Rival Kurdish Movements in Turkey*, 140–1; Kurt, *Kurdish Hizbullah*, 16–17.
88 Gürbüz, *Rival Kurdish Movements in Turkey*, 157.
89 Kurt, *Kurdish Hizbullah*, 41.
90 Haber Türk, 'Muztazaf-Der'in Kapatılmasına Yargıtay'dan Onay' (2012). Available online: http://www.haberturk.com/gundem/haber/741601-mustazaf-derin-kapatilmasina-yargitaydan-onay (accessed 15 March 2017).
91 Jenkins, *Political Islam in Turkey*, 195.
92 Hüda also means God in Persian and Kurdish (Xweda) and Hüda-Par can be interpreted as the Party of God.
93 Hüda-Par, *Parti Programı* (2012). Available online: http://hudapar.org/Detay/Sayfalar/205/parti-programi.aspx (accessed 31 May 2017).
94 For a detailed discussion of the relevance and importance of non-probability sampling technique see Oisín Tansey, 'Process Tracing and Elite Interviewing: A Case for Non-probability Sampling', *PS: Political Science and Politics*, 40:4 (2007), 765–72.

Chapter 2

1 Fulya Atacan, 'A Kurdish Islamist Group in Modern Turkey: Shifting Identities', *Middle Eastern Studies*, 37:3 (2001), 111–44; Bulent Aras and Gokhan Bacik, 'The Mystery of Turkish Hizballah', *Middle East Policy*, 9:2 (2002). Available online: https://www.mepc.org/journal/mystery-turkish-hizballah (accessed 20 June 2017).
2 Mehmet Kurt, '"My Muslim Kurdish brother": colonial rule and Islamist governmentality in the Kurdish region of Turkey', *Journal of Balkan and Near Eastern Studies*, 21:3 (2019), 350–65; Serhun Al, 'Islam, ethnicity and the state: contested

spaces of legitimacy and power in the Kurdish-Turkish public sphere', *Southeast European and Black Sea Studies*, 19:1 (2019), 119–37.
3   Christopher Houston, *Islam, Kurds and the Turkish Nation State* (Berg: Oxford and New York, 2001), 136.
4   Erdem Yörük, 'Welfare Provision as Political Containment: The Politics of Social Assistance and the Kurdish Conflict in Turkey', *Politics & Society*, 40:4 (2012), 535.
5   Kurt, 'My Muslim Kurdish brother', 359–61.
6   Mehmet Yanmış, 'Diyarbakır Halkının Geleneksel ve Dini Değerlerdeki Değişime Yaklaşımı Üzerine Sosyolojik bir İnceleme', unpublished PhD thesis (Uludağ University: Bursa, 2015), 66.
7   Ibid.
8   Cuma Çiçek, 'Kurdish identity and political Islam under AKP rule', *Research and Policy on Turkey*, 1:2 (2016), 156.
9   Gül Arikan Akdağ, 'Rational political parties and electoral games: the AKP's strategic move for the Kurdish vote in Turkey', *Turkish Studies*, 17:1 (2016), 126–54.
10 Yörük, 'Welfare Provision as Political Containment', 535–8.
11 Cengiz Gunes, 'Political Reconciliation in Turkey', in *The Kurdish Question in Turkey: New Perspectives on Conflict, Representation and Reconciliation*, ed., Cengiz Gunes and Welat Zeydanlioglu (London and New York: Routledge, 2014), 271.
12 For a more detailed discussion see Gunes and Zeydanlioglu (eds), *The Kurdish Question in Turkey: New Perspectives on Conflict, Representation and Reconciliation*; Elcin Aktoprak, 'The Kurdish Opening and Constitutional Reform: is There Any Progress', 9 *EYMI* (2010), 243–67.
13 Hilmi Hacaloğlu, 'Erdoğan: Dolmabahçe Mutabakatı Doğru Değil', *VOA* (2015). Available online: https://www.amerikaninsesi.com/a/erdogan-dolmabahce-mutabakini-dogru-bulmuyorum/2690354.html (accessed 16 October 2018).
14 MyNet, 'Erdoğan ilk kez "Kürdistan" dedi' (2013). Available online: https://www.mynet.com/erdogan-ilk-kez-kurdistan-dedi-110100862637 (accessed 20 August 2018).
15 Cumhuriyet, 'Erdoğan, Barzani'yi kabul etti; Kürdistan bayrağı İstanbul'da göndere çekildi' (2017). Available online: http://www.cumhuriyet.com.tr/haber/dunya/685899/Erdogan__Barzani_yi_kabul_etti__Kurdistan_bayragi_istanbul_da_gondere_cekildi.html# (accessed 20 August 2018).
16 KONDA Araştırma ve Danışmanlık, *7 Haziran Sandık ve Seçmen Analizi* (Istanbul, 2015), 67.
17 YSK, 'Belediye Başkanlığı Seçimi Sonuçları' (1999). Available online: http://www.ysk.gov.tr/tr/18-nisan-1999-mahalli-idareler-genel-secimi/2805 (accessed 23 August 2018).
18 Gunes, *The Kurdish National Movement in Turkey*, 170.
19 See the website (in Turkish) of High Election Committee (Yüksek Seçim Kurulu (http://www.ysk.gov.tr/tr/29-mart-2009-mahalli-idareler-genel-secimleri/2820)) for the details of the local elections held on 29 March 2009.
20 The figures presented here are collated from the website http://secim.haberler.com/.
21 KONDA, *7 Haziran Sandık ve Seçmen Analizi*, 67.
22 For a more detailed discussion see Cengiz Gunes 'Turkey's New Left', *New Left Review*, 107 (2017), 9–30.
23 Cengiz Gunes, 'The ISIS Factor: The Kurds as a Vanguard in the War on the Caliphate', in *Kurdistan and the Middle East: New Challenges, New Balances?*, ed., Stefano Torelli (Rome: Italian Institute for International Political Studies, 2016).

24 Secim.Haberler.com, '31 Mart 2019 Yerel Seçim Sonuçları' (2019). Available online: https://secim.haberler.com/2019/yerel-secimler/ (accessed 2 May 2019).
25 The co-mayors of the following municipal and district councils were removed and replaced by a trustee: Diyarbakır, Mardin, Van, Hakkari, Bismil, Cizre, Derik, Erciş, Hazro, İdil, İpekyolu, Karayazı, Kayapınar, Kızıltepe, Kocaköy, Mazıdağı, Kulp, Nusaybin, Saray, Savur, Suruç, Yenişehir and Yüksekova. In addition, the co-mayors of the town Akpazar (Tunceli province) were removed.
26 Daniel Boffey, 'Turkey should investigate referendum vote "irregularities", says EU commission', *The Guardian* (2017). Available online: https://www.theguardian.com/world/2017/apr/18/turkey-should-investigate-referendum-vote-irregularities-says-eu-commission (accessed 16 October 2017).
27 The figures are collated from Secim.Haberler.com, '1 Kasım 2015 Genel Seçim Sonuçları' (2015). Available online: https://secim.haberler.com/2015/ (accessed 25 June 2019).
28 Milliyet, 'HÜDAPAR İstatistikleri' (2014). Available online: http://www.milliyet.com.tr/2014YerelSecim/hudapar/PartiDetay.htm (accessed 30 March 2017).
29 Time Türk, 'Hüda-Par'ın bağımsızları ne kadar oy aldı?' (2015). Available online: https://www.timeturk.com/huda-par-in-bagimsizlari-ne-kadar-oy-aldi/haber-11971 (accessed 19 August 2018).
30 The figures are collated from Secim.Haberler.com, '2018 Milletvekili Seçim Sonuçları' (2018). Available online: https://secim.haberler.com/2018/milletvekilligi-secim-sonuclari/ (accessed 25 July 2019).
31 InternetHaber, 'Mecliste kaç Kürt milletvekili var?' (2010). Available online: http://www.internethaber.com/mecliste-kac-kurt-milletvekili-var-230866h.htm (accessed 31 July 2017).
32 Cumhuriyet, 'Erdoğan: Yozgat milletvekili diye Kürt değil zannetmeyin, Bekir Bey Kürttür, Kürt' (2017). Available online: http://www.cumhuriyet.com.tr/haber/siyaset/796832/Erdogan__Yozgat_milletvekili_diye_Kurt_degil_zannetmeyin__Bekir_Bey_Kurttur__Kurt.html# (accessed 6 August 2017).
33 Youtube, 'World Economic Forum – Davos 2017 – Syria and Iraq: Ending the Conflict' (2017). Available online: https://www.youtube.com/watch?v=hX2NJbsh3Xs (accessed 4 April 2017).
34 The Turkish phrase '*Tek millet, tek bayrak, tek vatan, tek devlet*' is often used in Erdoğan's speeches and is defended as the boundaries of the AKP's approach to recognition of diversity.
35 See Zeki Sarigil, 'Curbing Kurdish ethno-nationalism in Turkey: an empirical assessment of pro-Islamic and socio-economic approaches', *Ethnic and Racial Studies*, 33:3 (2010), 533–53.
36 Mustafa Akyol, 'Why Erdoğan fired Turkey's top cleric', *Al Monitor* (2017). Available online: http://www.al-monitor.com/pulse/originals/2017/08/turkey-why-erdogan-dismiss-top-cleric.html (accessed 6 August 2017).
37 Personal communication with Dr Mehmet Kurt, 6 August 2017.
38 Bayır, 'The role of the judicial system in the politicide of the Kurdish opposition'.
39 KONDA, *7 Haziran Sandık ve Seçmen Analizi*, 67.
40 Cumhuriyet Halk Partisi (CHP), *CHP 2011 Seçim Bildirgesi* (place and publisher not stated) 2011; Cumhuriyet Halk Partisi, *Önce İnsan, Önce Birlik, Önce Türkiye* (place and publisher not stated), 2015.
41 Cumhuriyet, 'İşte CHP'nin Kürt sorununa yeni bakışı' (2015). Available online: http://www.cumhuriyet.com.tr/haber/siyaset/262581/iste_CHP_nin_Kurt_sorununa_yeni_bakisi.html# (accessed 31 July 2017).

42 HDP, 'Parti Programı' (2012). Available online: http://www.hdp.org.tr/parti/parti-programi/8 (accessed 30 August 2016, author's translation).

Chapter 3

1   İsmail Beşikçi, *Doğu'da Değişim ve Yapısal Sorunlar (Göçebe Alikan Aşireti)* (Ankara: Yurt Yayınları, 1992); Martin Van Bruinessen, *Agha, Sheikh and State: The Social and Political Structure of Kurdistan* (London: Zed Books, 1992); Lale Yalçın-Heckmann, *Tribe and Kinship Among the Kurds* (Frankfurt: Peter Lang publishers, 1991).
2   Martin Van Bruinessen, 'Kurds, states and tribes', in *Tribes and Power: Nationalism and Ethnicity in the Middle East*, eds, Faleh A. Jabar and Hosham Dawod (London: Saqi, 2002); Lale Yalcin-Heckmann, 'Kurdish Tribal Orbanisation and Local Political Processes', in *Turkish State, Turkish Society*, eds, Andrew Finkel and Nukhet Sirman (London and New York: Routledge, 1990); Hamit Bozarslan, 'Tribal Asabiyya and Kurdish Politics: A Socio-Historical Perspective', in *The Kurds: Nationalism and Politics*, eds, Faleh A. Jabar and Hosham Dawod (London: Saqi, 2006).
3   Van Bruinessen, *Agha, Sheikh and State*, 51.
4   Ibid., 58.
5   Bozarslan, 'Tribal Asabiyya and Kurdish Politics', 133; Bruinessen, *Agha Shaikh and State*, 133.
6   Van Bruinessen, *Agha, Sheikh and State*, 53–4; see also Yalçın-Heckmann, *Tribe and Kinship Among the Kurds*, 102.
7   For a more detailed list of Kurdish tribes see Mehrdad Izady, *The Kurds: A Concise Handbook* (London and Washington: Taylor Francis, 1992), 74–85.
8   For a discussion of the transformation of the Bucak tribe see Bozarslan, 'Tribal Asabiyya and Kurdish Politics'.
9   Although a number of social and cultural aspects of tribes are discussed in the existing literature, the following studies specifically examine the political role of tribes in Kurdish society: Safiye Ateş-Durç, 'Türkiye'de Aşiret ve Siyaset İlişkisi: Metinan Aşireti Örneği' (MA diss., Hacettepe University, Ankara, 2009); A. Vahap Uluç, 'Güneydoğu Anadolu Bölgesinin Toplumsal ve Siyasal Yapısı: Mardin Örnegi'nde Siyasal Katılım' (PhD diss., Istanbul University, Istanbul, 2010); A. Vahap Uluç, 'Kürtlerde Sosyal ve Siyasal Örgütlenme: Aşiret', *Mukaddime*, 2 (2010), 35–52; Faruk Sümer, 'Yerel Bir Güç Olarak Aşiretin Siyasal Fonksiyonu' (PhD diss., Hacettepe University, Ankara, 2009); Ahmet İlyas, 'Türkiye'de Aşiret Siyaset İlişkisi: Urfa Örneği (1950–2003)' (MA diss., Selcuk University, Konya, 2009).
10 Yalçın-Heckmann, *Tribe and Kinship Among the Kurds*, 70.
11 Ibid., 125.
12 Gunes, *The Kurdish National Movement in Turkey*, 53.
13 Kendal, 'Kurdistan in Turkey', 66–7.
14 Yüksekova Haber, 'Ahmet Zeydan Vefat etti' (2010). Available online: http://www.yuksekovahaber.com/haber/ahmet-zeydan-vefat-etti-26283.htm (accessed 19 September 2015).
15 Mardin Life, 'Mehmet Timurağaoğlu Kimdir?' (2015). Available online: http://www.mardinlife.com/Mehmet-Timuragaoglu-Kimdir-haberi-24508 (accessed 21 January 2017).
16 Uluç, 'Güneydoğu Anadolu Bölgesinin Toplumsal ve Siyasal Yapısı', 211.
17 Ateş-Durç, 'Türkiye'de Aşiret ve Siyaset İlişkisi', 43.

18 Radikal, 'Secimin en ilginc rekabeti: bir aile 3 rakip' (2015). Available online: http://www.radikal.com.tr/politika/secimin-en-ilginc-rekabeti-Diyarbakırda-bir-aile-uc-rakip-1312363/ (accessed 17 September 2015).
19 Ateş-Durç, 'Türkiye'de Aşiret ve Siyaset İlişkisi', 89.
20 Ibid., 3.
21 Ibid., 42; Bruinessen, 'Kurds, states and tribes', 175.
22 Semra Özar, Nesrin Uçarlar, and Osman Aytar, *From Past to Present a Paramilitary Organization* (Diyarbakır Institute for Political and Social Research (Disa), Diyarbakır, 2013), 143–58; Süreç Araştırma Merkezi, *Geçici Köy Koruculuğu Sistemi ve Barış Süreci* (Istanbul, 2015), 38–47.
23 Ateş-Durç, 'Türkiye'de Aşiret ve Siyaset İlişkisi', 43.
24 Özar, Uçarlar and Aytar, *From Past to Present a Paramilitary Organization*, 56.
25 Sabah, 'Türkiye'de Kaç tane Köy Korucusu var? Köy Korucularının görevi nedir?' (2016). Available online: http://www.sabah.com.tr/gundem/2016/05/17/turkiyede-kac-tane-koy-korucusu-var-koy-korucularinin-gorevleri-nelerdir (accessed 22 October 2016).
26 Türkiye Büyük Millet Meclisi İnsan Hakları İnceleme Komisyonu, *Terör ve Şiddet Olayları Kapsamında Yaşam Hakkı İhlallerini İnceleme Raporu* (Ankara, 2013), 128.
27 Hürriyet Daily News, 'Turkey set to recruit 5,000 village guards in anti-terror fight' (2015). Available online: http://www.hurriyetdailynews.com/turkey-set-to-recruit-5000-village-guards-in-anti-terror-fight.aspx?pageID=238&nid=88745 (accessed 23 October 2016).
28 For the numbers and the spread of the village guards see Özar, Uçarlar and Aytar, *From Past to Present a Paramilitary Organization*, 56.
29 Emrah Çelik, 'Koruculuk Uygulamalarının Terörle Mücadeledeki yeri: Geçici Köy Koruculuğu sistemi Örneği' (MA diss., Kara Harp Okulu Savunma Birimleri Enstitüsü, Ankara, 2014), 2.
30 See Fehim Tastekin, 'Kurds Abandon AKP', *Al Monitor* (2015). Available online: http://www.al-monitor.com/pulse/originals/2015/05/turkey-pious-kurds-abandon-akp-in-droves-hdp.html (accessed 1 February 2017).
31 Joshua Project, 'Country: Turkey' (2017). Available online: https://joshuaproject.net/countries/TU (accessed 22 January 2017).
32 Ibid.
33 See Mehmet S. Kaya, *The Zaza Kurds of Turkey: a Middle Eastern Minority in a Globalised Society* (London: I.B. Tauris, 2011).
34 Al Monitor, 'Mardin elects 25-year old Christian woman as mayor' (2014). Available online: http://www.al-monitor.com/pulse/originals/2014/04/christian-mayor-turkey-rights-bdp-mardin.html#ixzz4WUjzuJYX (accessed 22 January 2017).
35 İlyas, 'Türkiye'de Aşiret Siyaset İlişkisi', 63.
36 SeçimHaberler.com, 'Siverek Seçim Sonuçları' (2014). Available online: http://secim.haberler.com/2014/siverek-secim-sonuclari/ (accessed 25 January 2017).
37 Sıtkı Karadeniz, 'Aşiret Sisteminde Dönüşüm: Aşiretlerin Kentte Aldığı Yeni Şekiller – Batman Örneği' (PhD diss., İnönü University, Malatya, 2012), 226.
38 Mardin Life, 'Kalenderi Aşiretinin Derneğini AK Partili Akdağ açtı' (2011). Available online: http://www.mardinlife.com/Kalenderi-Asiretinin-Dernegini-AK-Partili-Akdag-acti-haberi-1056 (accessed 23 January 2017).
39 İzol Derneği, 'Anasayfa' (2017). Available online: http://izoldernegi.org/#!/Anasayfa (accessed 23 January 2017).

Chapter 4

1. Michiel Leezenberg, 'Political Islam Among the Kurds', in *The Kurds: Nationalism and Politics*, eds, Faleh A. Jabar and Hosham Dawod (London: Saqi books, 2006), 207.
2. Martin Van Bruinessen, *Agha, Sheikh and State: The Social and Political Structure of Kurdistan* (London: Zed Books, 1992), 205.
3. Ibid., 206-7.
4. Martin Van Bruinessen, *Mullahs, Sufis and Heretics: The Role of Religion in Kurdish Society* (Istanbul: The Isis Press, 2000), 47.
5. Kamal Soleimani, *Islam and Competing Nationalisms in the Middle East, 1876-1926* (New York: Palgrave Macmillan, 2016).
6. For a discussion of Naqshibandiyya in Kurdistan see Itzchak Weismann, *The Naqshibandiyya: Orthodoxy and Activism in a worldwide Sufi Tradition* (London and New York: Routledge, 2007), 101-5.
7. Van Bruinessen, *Mullahs, Sufis and Heretics*, 49.
8. Leezenberg, 'Political Islam Among the Kurds', 208.
9. See Metin Yüksel, 'A "Revolutionary" Kurdish Mullah from Turkey: Mehmed Emin Bozarslan and his Intellectual Evolution', *The Muslim World*, 99 (2009), 356-80.
10. Burhan Ekinci, 'Tekke, Tarikat, Medrese', *Al-Jazeera Turk Dergi* (2014). Available online: http://dergi.aljazeera.com.tr/2014/10/15/tekke-tarikat-medrese/ (accessed 13 March 2017).
11. Van Bruinessen, *Mullahs, Sufis and Heretics*, 26.
12. Ibid.
13. Hakan Yılmaz, 'Nakşibendi Şeyhi: Ak Parti'ye oy vermek Rojava'da Kürt kanının dökülmesine rıza göstermektir', *Hür Bakış* (2013). Available online: https://www.yuksekovahaber.com.tr/haber/s-hayrettin-merci-akpye-oy-vermek-111220.htm (accessed 13 March 2017).
14. Mehmet Yanmış and Ahmet Aktaş, 'Diyarbakır Sultan Şeyhmuse Ezzulli Dergahı Örneğinde Tarikatların Sosyal İşlevi', *International Journal of Kurdish Studies*, 1:1 (2015), 3.
15. Ekinci, 'Tekke, Tarikat, Medrese'.
16. Artı Gerçek, 'AKP'ye Menzilciler desteği' (2018). Available online: https://www.artigercek.com/haberler/akp-ye-menzilciler-destegi (accessed 29 August 2018).
17. Ufkumuz, 'Dava ve Nûbihar Dergileri' (2011). Available online: http://www.ufkumuzhaber.com/dava-ve-nubihar-dergileri-6385h.htm (accessed 27 February 2017).
18. Ekinci, 'Tekke, Tarikat, Medrese'.
19. Gürbüz, *Rival Kurdish Movements in Turkey*, 39.
20. Ibid.
21. Ibid., 42.
22. Ibid., 69.
23. Ibid., 84.
24. Şahımerdan Sarı (2019) 'Şahımerdan Sarı Hoca Kimdir'. Available online: https://www.mepanews.com/sahimerdan-sari-kimdir-27249h.htm (accessed 23 July 2019).
25. Cansu Kılınçarslan, 'MAZLUMDER'in 16 Şubesi Kapatıldı', Bianet (2017). Available online: https://m.bianet.org/bianet/insan-haklari/184643-mazlumder-in-16-subesi-kapatildi (accessed 3 July 2019).
26. Sema Kahriman, '27 Yıllık Deneyimli Yeni Bir Dernek: Hak İnisiyatifi', *Bianet* (2018). Available online: https://bianet.org/bianet/insan-haklari/200044-27-yillik-deneyimli-yeni-bir-dernek-hak-inisiyatifi (accessed 3 July 2019).

27　Gunes, *The Kurdish National Movement in Turkey*, 128–9.
28　See Zeki Sarigil, *Ethnic Boundaries in Turkish Politics: The Secular Kurdish Movement and Islam* (New York: New York University Press, 2018).
29　Mehmet Gurses, 'Is Islam a Cure for Ethnic Conflict? Evidence from Turkey', *Politics and Religion*, 8 (2015), 135–54; Mehmet Gurses, *Anatomy of a Civil War: Sociopolitical Impacts of the Kurdish Conflict in Turkey* (Ann Arbor: University of Michigan Press, 2018); Ekrem Karakoç and Zeki Sarigil, 'Why Religious People Support Ethnic Insurgency? Kurds, Religion and Support for the PKK', *Politics and Religion*, 13:2 (2020): 245–72.
30　Gurses, 'Is Islam a Cure for Ethnic Conflict?', 140.
31　Ibid., 150–1.
32　Gurses, *Anatomy of a Civil War*, 112.
33　Karakoç and Sarigil, 'Why Religious People Support Ethnic Insurgency?', 10.
34　Al, 'Islam, ethnicity and the state', 128.
35　For a more detailed discussion see Celia Jenkins, Suavi Aydın and Umit Cetin (eds), *Alevism as an Ethno-Religious Identity: Contested Boundaries* (London and New York: Routledge, 2018).
36　Bayır, *Minorities and Nationalism in Turkish Law*, 112.
37　Zürcher, *Turkey: A Modern History*, 267.
38　Ibid., 295.
39　For a more detailed discussion see Kumru Berfin Emre Cetin, 'Television and the Making of a Transnational Alevi Identity', *National Identities*, 20:1 (2018), 91–103.
40　Ioannis N. Grigoriadis, 'Political Participation of Turkey's Kurds and Alevis: A Challenge for Turkey's Democratic Consolidation', *Southeast European and Black Sea Studies*, 6:4 (2006), 455.
41　Gunes, C. 'Political Representation of Alevi Kurds in Turkey: Historical Trends and Main Transformations', *Kurdish Studies* (2020), 71–90.
42　KONDA, *7 Haziran Sandık ve Seçmen Analizi*, 68–9.
43　KONDA Araştırma ve Danışmanlık, *Siyasal ve Toplumsal Araştırmalar Dizisi* (Istanbul, 2018), 40.
44　Joshua Project, 'Country: Turkey' (2017). Available online: https://joshuaproject.net/countries/TU (accessed 22 January 2017).
45　Yanmış and Aktaş, 'Diyarbakır Sultan Şeyhmuse Ezzulli Dergahı', 6.
46　Ibid., 10.
47　Furthermore, verse 152 commands 'So remember Me; I will remember you. And be grateful to Me and do not deny Me.' And the related verse 153 commands 'O you who have believed, seek help through patience and prayer. Indeed, Allah is with the patient' (The Qur'an, 'Al Baqarah'). Available online: https://quran.com/2 (accessed 31 March 2017).

Chapter 5

1　Zaman, 'Cüneyd Zapsu: Kürt ve Rumeli kimliğimle övünüyorum', 25 May 2004.
2　Haberdar.com, 'Kılıçdaroğlu: Sol yüzde 35'ten fazla oy alamaz (Röportaj: Amberin Zaman)' (2011). Available online: http://www.haberdar.com.tr/roportaj/kilicdaroglu-sol-yuzde-35ten-fazla-oy-alamaz-h11810.html (accessed 15 September 2015).
3　For a more detailed discussion of the political economy of the Kurdish regions in Turkey, see Veli Yadirgi, *The Political Economy of the Kurds of Turkey: From the Ottoman*

Empire to the Turkish Republic (Cambridge: Cambridge University Press, 2017). See also Güllistan Yarkın, 'The Ideological Transformation of the PKK Regarding the Political Economy of the Kurdish Regions of Turkey', *Kurdish Studies*, 3:1 (2015), 26–46.
4 B. Ali Eşiyok, 'Kalkınmada Bölgesel Farklılıklar Büyüme Kutupları ve GAP (Tespitler ve Çözüm Önerileri)' (Türkiye Kalkınma Bankası, Ankara, 2002).
5 Türkiye İstatistik Kurumu, 'Statistical Bulletin' (2015). Available online: http://www.tuik.gov.tr/PreHaberBultenleri.do?id=18727 (accessed 18 September 2015).
6 Veysi Polat, 'Van, Hakkari, Muş ve Bitlis'in geliri Türkiye ortalamasının 4'te 1'i kadar' (2015). Available online: http://t24.com.tr/haber/van-hakkari-mus-ve-bitlisin-geliri-turkiye-ortalamasinin-4te-1i-kadar,292705 (accessed 25 September 2015).
7 Turkey Statistical Institute, *Household Labour Force Statistics 2011* (Ankara, 2012), 90.
8 Hamit Birtane, 'Diyarbakır'da Issizlik Orani Uzerine Bir Degerlendirme' (Karacadağ Kalkınma Ajansı, Diyarbakır, 2011), 4.
9 Erhan Demircan, 'TRC2 (Diyarbakır-Sanliurfa) Bolgesi Issizlik Rakamlarinin Degerlendirmesi' (2014). Available online: www.karacadag.gov.tr/Dokuman/Dosya/www.karacadag.org.tr_204_KK8K88TO_trc2_diyarbakir_sanliurfa_bolgesi_issizlik_rakamlarinin_degerlendirmesi.pdf (accessed 25 September 2015).
10 Bianet, 'Issizlik' (2015). Available online: http://bianet.org/bianet/ekonomi/162827-tuik-2014-issizlik-orani-9-9 (accessed 25 September 2015).
11 GAP, 'GAP Eylem Planı' (2010). Available online: www.gap.gov.tr/gap-eylem-plani-sayfa-25.html (accessed 10 October 2015).
12 Turkey Statistical Institute, *Household Labour Force Statistics 2011*, 11–12.
13 The eastern region includes the provinces of Bingöl, Bitlis, Elazığ, Hakkari, Malatya, Muş, Tunceli and Van. The south-east region includes the provinces of Adıyaman, Batman, Diyarbakır, Gaziantep, Mardin, Kilis, Şanlıurfa, Şırnak and Siirt.
14 Turkey Statistical Institute, *Household Labour Force Statistics 2011*, 103.
15 Türkiye Cumhuriyeti, Bilim, Sanayi ve Teknoloji Bakanlığı, *81 İl Durum Raporu* (Ankara, 2012), 137.
16 Mermer Şirketleri, 'Diyarbakır Mermer Firmaları' (2015). Available online: http://www.dimad.org.tr/index/firmalar/ (accessed 16 September 2015).
17 Of these, Mesut Mermercilik and Mimartstone have been in operation since 1972 while others such as Akmarsen Mermer and Çelik Mermercilik were established in the 1990s. Çelik Mermercilik and Mesut Madencilik are locally based with operations in surrounding areas of Diyarbakır, such as the bordering province of Adıyaman.
18 Hikmet Deniz, *Diyarbakır Dis Ticareti 2014 (Export of Diyarbakır 2014)* (Karacadağ Kalkınma Ajansı, Diyarbakır, 2014), 2.
19 Selman Delil and Armagan Tanrikulu, *Cermik Termal Turizm Raporu* (Karacadağ Kalkınma Ajansı, Diyarbakır, 2012).
20 Van Ticaret ve Sanayi Odası (VANSTO), *Van Sosyal ve Ekonomik Istatistikleri* (Van, 2016), 34.
21 Van Haber, 'Van Ekonomisi' (2015). Available online: https://www.wanhaber.com/ekonomi/van-ekonomisi-2-h255292.html (accessed 15 August 2015).
22 Türkiye Cumhuriyeti, Bilim, Sanayi ve Teknoloji Bakanlığı, *81 Il Durum Raporu* (Ankara, 2012), 447.
23 Diyarbakır Ticaret ve Sanayi Odası (DTSO), 'Faal Üye Sayısı (Firma Tipine Göre) – Number of Active Members (According to type of firm)' (2015). Available online: http://www.dtso.org.tr/2014/index.php/bilgi-bankasi/dtso/istatistik/uye-istatistikleri/faal-uye-firma-tipine-gore (accessed 25 October 2015). The latest available figure is for July 2013.

24 Van Ticaret ve Sanayi Odası (VANSTO) *Mayis Ayı Van İli Ekonomik İstatistikler* (Van, 2016), 13.
25 OECD, 'Employment Labour Force Participation Rate' (2015). Available online: http://stats.oecd.org/Index.aspx?DataSetCode=GENDER_EMP (accessed 30 March 2016).
26 Turkey Statistical Institute, *Household Labour Force Statistics 2011*, 10.
27 DİSK/Genel İş Sendikası, 'Emek Araştırması Raporu 7: Türkiye'de Emeğin Durumu' (2016). Available online: https://www.genel-is.org.tr/turkiyede-emegin-durumu-raporu,2,11091#.XsBkdkBFw2w (accessed 4 October 2016).
28 İsmat Kayhan, 'Türkiye'de işçi sınıfı Kürtleşti – Erdem Yörük ile söyleşi' (2009). Available online: https://sendika63.org/2009/-12/turkiyede-isci-sinifi-kurtlesti-erdem-yoruk-ile-soylesi-ismat-kayhan-anf-38732/ (accessed 4 October 2016).
29 Turkey Statistical Institute, *Household Labour Force Statistics 2011*, 88.
30 Ibid., 177.
31 Pinar Tremblay, 'An immigrant himself, Chobani yogurt founder becomes icon for refugees' (2014). Available online: http://www.al-monitor.com/pulse/originals/2015/10/turkey-usa-kurdish-immigrant-becomes-icon-for-refugees.html (accessed 28 September 2016).
32 In the past year, Kurdish businesses based in Europe increased their efforts to invest in Kurdish majority regions of Turkey (Milliyet, 'Avrupalı Kürt İşverenler DTSO'da Yatırım Brifingi Aldı' (2015)). Available online: https://www.milliyet.com.tr/yerel-haberler/diyarbakir/avrupali-kurt-isverenler-dtso-dan-yatirim-brifingi-aldi-10768228 (accessed 7 November 2015).
33 Disiad, 'Üyelerimiz' (2015). Available online: http://disiad.org.tr/uyelerimiz/ (accessed 15 September 2015). The numbers of members for Müsiad is not publicly available but since as an organization it has been active over a long period of time, it too has a similar number of members. It has regional offices in Diyarbakır and Van.
34 These include the following: GAIB (Union of Exporters of Southeast Anatolia, http://www.gaib.org.tr/); Günsiad (Industrialists and Business Peoples Association of Southeast); Vadsiad (Van Dynamic Industrialists' and Businessmen's Association).
35 Yenigun, 'Tarihce' (2018). Available online: https://www.yenigun.com.tr/tarihce/ (accessed 16 May 2020).
36 The Kolin group works very closely with Cengiz Holding, a pro-AKP business group, and has been involved in a number of joint construction projects together especially road and railway construction and irrigation dams (Sendika.org 'AKP'nin İhale Kralı Cengiz Kimdir' (2016)). Available online: http://politeknik.org.tr/akpnin-ihale-krali-cengiz-kimdir/ (accessed 26 July 2019).
37 Haber7, 'Kasiyerdi Türkiye'nin en zengini oldu' (2009). Available online: http://ekonomi.haber7.com/ekonomi/haber/421292-kasiyerdi-turkiyenin-en-zengini-oldu (accessed 18 October 2015).
38 Finans Gündem, 'Nihat Özdemir Kürtlere ne söyledi' (2013). Available online: http://www.finansgundem.com/haber/nihat-ozdemir-kurtlere-ne-soyledi/367667 (accessed 2 August 2017). See also Forbes, 'Sezai Bacaksiz' (2017). Available online: https://www.forbes.com/profile/sezai-bacaksiz/ (accessed 2 August 2017).
39 Limak, 'Limak Şirketler Grubu Faaliyet Raporu' (2017). Available online: http://www.limak.com.tr/docs/LimakFaaliyetRaporu2016.pdf (accessed 5 August 2017).
40 Türkiye Tekstil İşverenleri Sendikası, 'Tekstil ve Hazır Giyim Sanayiinin Türk Ekonomisindeki Yeri' (Istanbul, 2014), 9 and 13.

41 Roza, 'Biz Kimiz' (2016). Available online: http://www.rozazipper.com.tr/?dil=tr&sayfa=2&icerik=Hakkımızda (accessed 27 September 2016).
42 Van Ticaret ve Sanayi Odası (VANSTO), *Van Sosyal ve Ekonomik İstatistikleri* (Van, 2016), 19.
43 Van Ticaret ve Sanayi Odası (VANSTO), *Mayıs Ayı Van İli Ekonomik İstatistikler* (Van, 2016), 13.
44 Çiçek, *Ulus, Din, Sınıf*, 288.
45 Ibid., 189.
46 Ibid., 135.
47 Ibid., 257.
48 Hürriyet, 'CHP'den AK Parti'yi destekleyen iş adamlarıyla "gizli" görüşme' (2015). Available online: http://www.hurriyet.com.tr/chpden-ak-parti-yi-destekleyen-is-adamlariyla-gizli-gorusme-28559359 (accessed 19 October 2015).
49 Çiçek, *Ulus, Din, Sınıf*, 288.
50 Ibid., 136.
51 Ibid., 250.
52 Ibid., 78–9.
53 Disiad, 'Disiad'dan Toplumsal Uzlaşı ve Barış girişimleri' (2015). Available online: http://disiad.org.tr/haber-arsivi/disiaddan-toplumsal-uzlasi-ve-baris-girisimleri/ (accessed 11 October 2015).
54 Şeyhmuz Diken and Nurcan Baysal, *Kürdistan'da Sivil Toplum* (Istanbul: İletisim, 2015), 74–86.
55 Al Jazeera, 'Kürdsiad İsmine Veto' (2014). Available online: http://www.aljazeera.com.tr/haber/kurdsiad-ismine-veto (accessed 16 October 2015).
56 Milliyet, '20 yıl aradan sonra ortaya çıkan liste!' (2015). Available online: http://www.milliyet.com.tr/20-yil-aradan-sonra-ortaya-cikan-gundem-2089489/ (accessed 3 November 2015).
57 TİHV, *Türkiye İnsan Hakları Raporu 1994* (Ankara: TİHV Yayınları, 1995), 121–2, 125.
58 Resmi Gazete (Official Gazette), *Terörizmin Finansmanının Önlenmesi Hakkında Kanun* (Law No. 6415) (2013). Available online: http://www.resmigazete.gov.tr/eskiler/2013/02/20130216-3.htm (accessed 18 October 2015).
59 Çiçek, *Ulus, Din, Sınıf*, 188.
60 Yesilgazete, 'Hevsel Bahçeleri'ni kurtaran mahkeme kararı: Tarım alanlarında yapılaşmaya iptal' (2015). Available online: https://yesilgazete.org/blog/2015/05/07/hevsel-bahcelerini-kurtaran-mahkeme-karari-tarim-alanlarinda-yapilasmaya-iptal/ (accessed 16 May 2020).
61 Tahir Elçi was a popular and well-known figure who regularly commented on TV about the state of human rights in Turkey, and on 28 November 2015 he was killed during a press conference in Diyarbakır (*The Independent*, 'Tahir Elci: Kurdish human rights lawyer shot dead during press conference in Turkey' (2015). Available online: http://www.independent.co.uk/news/world/middle-east/tahir-elci-turkish-human-rights-lawyer-shot-dead-during-press-conference-turkey-a6753356.html (accessed 30 November 2015).
62 Eğitim-Sen, 'Laik, Bilimsel, Anadilinde Eğitim, Demokratik Yaşam ve Eşit Yurttaşlık İçin Mücadelemizi Kararlılıkla Sürdürüyoruz!' (2015). Available online: http://egitimsen.org.tr/laik-bilimsel-anadilinde-egitim-demokratik-yasam-ve-esit-yurttaslik-icin-mucadelemizi-kararlilikla-surduruyoruz/ (accessed 16 October 2015).

63 Bianet, 'KESK'e KCK Operasyonu' (2012). Available online: http://bianet.org/bianet/siyaset/139298-kesk-e-kck-operasyonu (accessed 17 October 2015).
64 Anadolu Ajansı, 'Başbakan Yıldırım: Terör örgütüyle ilişkili bütün öğretmenler açığa alınacak' (2016). Available online: https://www.aa.com.tr/tr/gunun-basliklari/basbakan-yildirim-teror-orgutuyle-iliskili-butun-ogretmenler-aciga-alinacak/640919 (accessed 24 October 2018).

Chapter 6

1 Joost Jongerden and Ahmet Hamdi Akkaya, 'Born From the Left: the Making of the PKK', in *Nationalims and politics in Turkey: political Islam, Kemalism and the Kurdish Issue*, eds, M. Casier and J. Jongerden (London: Routledge, 2011), 123–42.
2 There is a growing literature on activism by Kurdish women and youth, which includes the following: Handan Çağlayan, *Analar, Yoldaşlar, Tanrıçalar: Kürt Hareketinde Kadınlar ve Kadın Kimliğinin Oluşumu* (Istanbul: İletişim Yayınları, 2007); Necla Açık, 'Re-defining the role of women within the Kurdish national movement in Turkey in the 1990s', in *The Kurdish Question in Turkey: New Perspectives on Violence, Representation, and Reconciliation*, eds, C. Gunes and W. Zeydanlioglu (London and New York: Routledge, 2014); Melike Gül Demir, *1980'lerden 2000'lere Siyasal Kürt Kadınının İnşası* (Istanbul: Belge Yayınları, 2015); Dilar Dirik, 'The Revolution of Smiling Women: Stateless Democracy and Power in Rojava', in *Routledge Handbook of Postcolonial Politics*, eds, O. U. Rutazibwa and B. Shilliam (London and New York: Routledge, 2018); Isabel Käser, 'Mountain Life is Difficult but Beautiful!': The gendered process of 'becoming free' in PKK education', in *Kurds in Turkey: Ethnographies of Heterogenous Experiences*, eds, A. Çelik and L. Drechselová (Lanham: Lexington Books, 2019), 11–30; Haydar Darıcı,'"Adults see politics as a game": Politics of Kurdish Children in Urban Turkey', *International Journal of Middle East Studies*, 45:4 (2013), 775–90; Haydar Darıcı, 'Politics of privacy: forced migration and the spatial struggle of the Kurdish youth', *Journal of Balkan and Near Eastern Studies*, 13:4 (2011), 457–74; Zeynep Başer and Ayşe Betül Çelik, 'Imagining peace in a conflict environment: Kurdish youths' framing of the Kurdish issue in Turkey', *Patterns of Prejudice*, 48:3 (2014), 265–85.
3 Kakşar Oremar, *Eyşe Şan: Prensesa Bê Tac û Text* (Diyarbakır: Lis, 2012).
4 Çağlayan, *Analar, Yoldaşlar, Tanrıçalar*, 106.
5 Ibid., 107.
6 Gunes, *Kurdish National Movement in Turkey*, 143.
7 A detailed account of Kurdish women's mobilization in Turkey is also offered in the following studies: Salima Tasdemir, 'The Feminization of pro-Kurdish Party Politics in Turkey: The Role of Women Activists' (PhD diss., The University of Exeter, 2013); Zeynep Sahin, 'The Political Representation of Kurdish, Kemalist, and Conservative Muslim Women in Turkey (1990–2010)' (PhD diss., The University of Southern California, 2011); Lucie Drechselová, 'The Kurdish Women's Political Organizing from the Feminist Neo-Institutionalist Perspective' in *Kurds in Turkey: Ethnographies of Heterogenous Experiences*, eds, Çelik and Drechselová, 31–58.
8 Tasdemir, 'The Feminization of pro-Kurdish Party Politics in Turkey', 12.
9 Bianet, 'Kadınlar Kongra Jınên Azad'ı Kurdu' (2015). Available online: https://m.bianet.org/bianet/kadin/161974-kadinlar-kongra-jinen-azad-i-kurdu (accessed 30 August 2018).

10 These include the following: Mesopotamia Women's Cooperative (Urfa), Umutışığı Women's Cooperative (Diyarbakır), Van Yaka Women's Cooperative (Van) and Baglar Women's Cooperative (Diyarbakır).
11 Diken and Baysal, *Kürdistan'da Sivil Toplum*, 327.
12 İlke Haber, 'Diyarbakır'da sadece kadınların çalıştığı pazar açıldı' (2013). Available online: http://www.ilkehaberajansi.com.tr/haber/Diyarbakirda-sadece-kadinlarin-calistigi-pazar-acildi.html (accessed 10 November 2015).
13 Deniz Gökalp, 'A gendered analysis of violence, justice and citizenship: Kurdish women facing war and displacement in Turkey', *Women Studies International Forum*, 33 (2010), 263.
14 Pulitzer Center, 'Life After Prison: Kurdish Stone-Throwing Kids' (2011). Available online: http://pulitzercenter.org/projects/turkey-kurdish-kids-stone-throwing-jail-terrorists (accessed 16 October 2015).
15 Dorian Jones, 'Juvenile Detention Guards Sexually Abusing Minority Children in Turkey', *The Atlantic* (2012). Available online: http://www.theatlantic.com/international/archive/2012/03/juvenile-detention-guards-sexually-abusing-minority-children-in-turkey/255102/ (accessed 18 October 2015).
16 These include Varto in Mus province, Cizre in Sirnak province, Silvan and Surici in Diyarbakır. The police reacted by declaring week-long curfews leading to widespread protests and clashes with the police (*Financial Times*, 'Young Kurds take up arms as clashes increase in south-east Turkey' (2015). Available online: http://www.ft.com/intl/cms/s/0/d11a20a4-4a50-11e5-b558-8a9722977189.html#axzz3quSQYy8d (accessed 18 September 2015)).
17 The Christian Monitor, 'For Kurdish youth in Turkey, autonomy is no longer enough' (2015). Available online: http://www.csmonitor.com/World/Middle-East/2015/0817/For-Kurdish-youth-in-Turkey-autonomy-is-no-longer-enough (accessed 15 October 2015).
18 Cengiz Gunes and Robert Lowe, *The Impact of the Syrian War on Kurdish Politics Across the Middle East* (London: The Royal Institute of International Affairs, 2015), 10.
19 See Frederike Geerdink, *The Boys are Dead: The Roboski Massacre and the Kurdish Question in Turkey* (London: Gomidas Institute, 2015).
20 Bianet, 'Gözaltı Sayısı Beş Günde 1302'yi Buldu' (2015). Available online: https://m.bianet.org/bianet/insan-haklari/166393-gozalti-sayisi-bes-gunde-1302-yi-buldu (accessed 9 July 2019).
21 International Crisis Group, 'Managing Turkey's PKK Conflict: The Case of Nusaybin' (Brussels, 2017).
22 Diken, 'Kürt siyasal hareketinin gençlik yapıları, DEM-GENÇ çatısı altında birleşiyor' (2015). Available online: http://www.diken.com.tr/kurt-siyasal-hareketinin-genclik-yapilari-dem-genc-catisi-altinda-birlesiyor/ (accessed 16 October 2015).
23 Diken and Baysal, *Kürdistan'da Sivil Toplum*, 358.
24 Ibid., 363.
25 Noah Blaser and Aaron Stein, 'Islamic State's Network in Turkey' (2015). Available online: https://turkeywonk.wordpress.com/2015/10/30/the-islamic-states-network-in-turkey/ (accessed 12 November 2015).
26 BBC Turkish, 'IŞİD neden Adıyaman'da örgütlendi?' (2015). Available online: http://www.bbc.com/turkce/haberler/2015/10/151022_isid_adiyaman (accessed 17 November 2015).

27 Milliyet, 'Dicle Üniversitesi'nde öğrenci kavgası: 5 yaralı' (2013). Available online: https://www.milliyet.com.tr/gundem/dicle-universitesi-nde-ogrenci-kavgasi-5-yarali-1691072 (accessed 16 October 2015).
28 Tasdemir, 'The Feminization of pro-Kurdish Party Politics in Turkey', 289.
29 See also Mona Tajali, 'The promise of gender parity: Turkey's People's Democratic Party (HDP)', *OpenDemocracy* (2015). Available online: https://www.opendemocracy.net/5050/mona-tajali/promise-of-gender-parity-turkey-s-people-s-democratic-party-hdp (accessed 15 November 2015).
30 Sendika.org, 'Kadın cinayetleri haritası: 5 yılda en az 1134 kadın öldürüldü' (2015). Available online: https://sendika63.org/2015/11/kadin-cinayetleri-haritasi-5-yilda-en-az-1134-kadin-olduruldu-310904/ (accessed 25 Nobember 2015).
31 For example, the Kayapinar Municipal Council used to run a educational project where women could complete vocational courses.
32 BBC, 'Turkey rallies over murder of woman who 'resisted rape'' (2015). Available online: http://www.bbc.com/news/world-europe-31476978 (accessed 28 September 2015).
33 BBC, 'Turkey president Erdoğan: Women are not equal to men' (2014). Available online: http://www.bbc.com/news/world-europe-30183711 (accessed 28 September 2015).
34 Al Jazeera, 'Istanbul police use tear gas to disperse Women's Day marchers' (2019). Available online: https://www.aljazeera.com/news/2019/03/istanbul-police-tear-gas-disperse-women-day-marchers-190308193151561.html (accessed 9 July 2019).
35 Hürriyet, 'Ege Üniversitesi'nde kavga: Bir öğrenci öldü, biri ağır yaralandı' (2015). Available online: http://www.hurriyet.com.tr/ege-universitesinde-kavga-bir-ogrenci-oldu-biri-agir-yaralandi-28257188 (accessed 16 November 2015).
36 For a discussion of the Kurdish movement's democratic autonomy proposals see Cengiz Gunes, 'Accommodating Kurdish Demands in Turkey', in *The Challenge of Non-Territorial Autonomy: Theory and Case Studies*, eds, Ephraim Nimni, Alexander Osipov and David Smith (Oxford: Peter Lang International Publishers, 2013), 71–84.

Chapter 7

1 See Juan J. Linz and Alfred Stepan, *Problems of Democratic Transition and Consolidation* (Baltimore: The Johns Hopkins University Press, 1996), Chapter 2; and A. Stepan, J. Linz, and Y. Yadav. *Crafting State-Nations: India and Other Multi-National Democracies* (Baltimore: The Johns Hopkins University Press, 2011), Chapter 1; and Mark Redhead, *Charles Taylor: Thinking and Living Deep Diversity* (Lanham, MD: Rowman & Littlefield, 2002).
2 Indeed, the Republic of Turkey provides a prime example of the more general tension between 'nationalizing state policies' and democratic consolidation. Linz and Stepan have incisively characterized this tension as follows: '[I]n many countries that are not yet consolidated democracies, a nation-state policy often has a different logic from a democratic policy. By a nation-state policy we mean one in which the leaders pursue what Rogers Brubaker calls "nationalizing state policies" aimed at increasing cultural homogeneity. Consciously or unconsciously, the leaders send messages that the state should be "of and for" the nation. In the constitutions they write, therefore, and the politics they practice, the dominant nation's language becomes the only official language and occasionally the only acceptable language for state business and for public (and possibly private) schooling, the religion of the nation is privileged

(even if it is not necessarily made the official religion), and the cultural symbols of the dominant nation are also privileged in all state symbols (such as the flag, the national anthem, and even eligibility for some types of military service), and in all of the state-controlled means of socialization such as radio, television and textbooks. By contrast, democratic policies in the state-making process are those that emphasize a broad and inclusive citizenship where all citizens are accorded equal individual rights … The neglect in the literature on democratic transition and consolidation of the question of the legitimacy of the state is unfortunate because this variable, while not always of great importance for non-democratic polities, is of fundamental theoretical and political importance for democracies.' Juan J. Linz and Alfred Stepan, *Problems of Democratic Transition and Consolidation*, 25–6.

3   As we put the point in a report written in February of 2017: 'The events of the past year-and-a-half demonstrate very clearly that there can be no democracy in Turkey without a peaceful resolution of the Kurdish question. The political situation in the country has deteriorated dramatically over the past year-and-a-half, since the breakdown of the peace process in mid-June 2015, and especially since the failed coup in mid-July 2016. President Erdoğan has taken advantage of the state of emergency to escalate repression against all opposition, not just those groups allegedly implicated in the coup. The repressive measures include many clear violations of European and human rights norms to which Turkey is bound. These measures have targeted with special intensity the Kurdish Freedom Movement, but also extend to critical media and to dissenting voices in the press and academia, and to trade unions, human rights defenders and wider civil society. To make matters worse, the victims of these repressive measures have virtually no effective recourse to the judiciary, whose independence has been severely undermined. Indeed, the judiciary itself has experienced a massive and unlawful purge, as has the public administration and the educational system.' 'State Terror, Human Rights Violations, and Authoritarianism in Turkey. Report of the Third Imrali Peace Delegation Based on its Visit to Turkey, Feb. 13–19, 2017', in Thomas Jeffrey Miley and Federico Venturini (eds), *Your Freedom and Mine: Abdullah Ocalan and the Kurdish Question in Erdoğan's Turkey* (Montreal: Black Rose Books, 2018), 226.

4   On the roots of the Turkish–Kurdish conflict, see M. Angrist, 'Turkey. Roots of the Turkish-Kurdish Conflict and Prospects for Constructive Reform', in U. Amoretti and N. Bermeo, eds, *Federalism and Territorial Cleavages* (Baltimore: The Johns Hopkins University Press, 2004), 387–416; V. Eccarius-Kelly, *The Militant Kurds. A Dual Strategy for Freedom* (Santa Barbara, CA: Praeger, 2011); N. Entessar, *Kurdish Ethnonationalism* (London: Lynne Reinner Publishers, 1992); C. Gunes, *The Kurdish National Movement in Turkey. From Protest to Resistance* (London and New York: Routledge, 2012); M. Gunter, *The Kurds and the Future of Turkey* (London: Palgrave, 1997); J. Jongerden and A. Akkaya, 'Born from the Left. The Making of the PKK', in J. Jongerdon and M. Casier, eds, *Nationalism and Politics in Turkey. Political Islam and the Kurdish Issue* (London: Routledge, 2011), 123–42; D. McDowall, *A Modern History of the Kurds* (London: I.B. Tauris, 1996); T. Miley with C. Hammy and G. Yildiz, 'The Turkish-Kurdish Conflict in Historical Context', in T. Miley and F. Venturini, eds, *Your Freedom and Mine: Abdullah Ocalan and the Kurdish Question in Erdoğan's Turkey* (Montreal: Black Rose Books, 2018), 3–123; D. Natali, *The Kurds and the State. Evolving National Identity in Iraq, Turkey, and Iran* (Syracuse, NY: Syracuse University Press, 2005); E. O'Ballance, *The Kurdish Struggle, 1920–1994* (London: Palgrave MacMillan, 1996); A. Özcan, *Turkey's Kurds. A Theoretical Analysis of the PKK and*

Abdullah Öcalan (London: Routledge, 2006); D. Romano, *The Kurdish Nationalist Movement. Opportunity, Mobilization, Identity* (Cambridge: Cambridge University Press, 2006); S. Saeed, *Kurdish Politics in Turkey. From the PKK to the KCK* (London: Routledge, 2017); and P. White, *Primitive Rebels or Revolutionary Modernizers? The Kurdish National Movement in Turkey* (London: Zed Books, 2000).

5   This is not to claim that there is no representative relation between a guerrilla force and its purported constituency. In fact, as Che Guevara famously insisted: 'In the course of polemics those who advocate guerrilla warfare are often accused of forgetting mass struggle, almost as if guerrilla warfare and mass struggle were opposed to each other. We reject this implication. Guerrilla warfare is a people's war, a mass struggle. To try to carry out this type of war without the support of the population is to court inevitable disaster. The guerrillas are the fighting vanguard of the people, stationed in a specified place in a certain area, armed and prepared to carry out a series of warlike actions for the one possible strategic end – the seizure of power. They have the support of the worker and peasant masses of the region and of the whole territory in which they operate. Without these prerequisites no guerrilla warfare is possible.' *Guerrilla Warfare: A Method* (Peking: Foreign Language Press, 1964), 2. Notably, on the fiftieth anniversary of Guevara's death, PKK co-founder Duran Kalkan would refer to Che as 'our principal inspiration'. Available online: https://anfenglish.com/features/pkk-commanders-our-strongest-inspiration-was-che-guevara-22628. For a recent sophisticated conceptualization and defence of guerrilla violence as an 'imaginative technique of mobilization', at least in some instances, especially among those who suffer from an 'extreme lack of voice (representation)', see N. Chandhoke, *Democracy and Revolutionary Politics* (London: Bloomsbury Academic, 2015).

6   M. Weber, 'Structures of Power: The Nation', in H. H. Gerth and C.W. Mills, eds, *From Max Weber: Essays in Sociology* (Abingdon, Oxon: Routledge, 1991), 171–80.

7   As Linz and Stepan have emphasized: 'A nation does not have officials, and there are no defined leadership roles, although there are individuals who act as carriers, in the Weberian sense of *Träger*, of the national sentiment in movements or nationalistic organizations. There are no clear rules about membership in a nation and no defined rights that can be legitimately enforced (although nationalists often try to enforce behaviour on the part of those who identify with the nation or who they claim should identify with it). However, without control of the state, the desired behaviors cannot be legally or even legitimately enforced. A nation and nationalist leaders in its name do not have resources like coercive powers or taxes to demand obedience; only a state can provide those resources to achieve national goals in a binding way. The nation as such, therefore, does not have organizational characteristics comparable with those of the state. It has no autonomy, no agents, no rules, but only the resources derived from psychological identification of the people who constitute it. Whereas a state can exist on the basis of external conformity with its rules, a nation requires some internal identification. Benedict Anderson is quite right. Without "imagined communities" there are no nations.' Juan J. Linz and Alfred Stepan, *Problems of Democratic Transition and Consolidation*, 22. Likewise, from a distinctly post-colonial perspective, Homi Bhabha converges with Linz and Stepan when he insists: 'To write the story of the nation demands that we articulate that archaic ambivalence that informs modernity. We may begin by questioning that progressive metaphor of modern social cohesion – *the many as one* – shared by organic theories of holism of culture and community, and by theorists who treat gender, class, or race as radically

"expressive" social totalities.' 'DissemiNation: time, narrative, and the margins of the modern nation', in H. Bhabha, ed., *Nation and Narration* (London: Routledge, 1990), 294. For a persuasive warning against near-ubiquitous recourse to essentialism in discussions of the nation and nationalism, claims about 'social constructivism' notwithstanding, see R. Brubaker, *Nationalism Reframed* (Cambridge: Cambridge University Press, 1996).

8   M. Weber, 'The Fundamental Concepts of Sociology', in T. Parsons, ed., *The Theory of Social and Economic Organization* (New York: Free Press, 1964), 156.

9   In fact, as Henry Commager has argued: 'Even when definitions of terrorism allow for *state terrorism*, state actions in this area tend to be viewed through the prism of war or national self-defense, not terrorism.' Quoted in L. Donahue, 'Terrorism and the counter-terrorist discourse', in V. Ramraj, M. Hor and K. Roach, eds, *Global Anti-Terrorism Law and Policy* (Cambridge: Cambridge University Press, 2005), 20. For debates about the definition of terrorism, see the informative discussion by Alex Schmid, 'The Definition of Terrorism', in A. Schmid, ed., *The Routledge Handbook of Terrorism Research* (Oxford: Routledge, 2011), 39–157.

10 As Linz and Stepan have contended, in relation to violence and coercion exercised by 'non-state' actors associated with nationalist movements: '[A] nation crystallizing out of a nationalist movement, even when it does not control a state, can exercise power, use violence, or exact contributions without having yet gained statehood. But in a world system of states this means that the movement is taking over some of the functions of another state, subverting its order, so that a state is breaking down in the process. Nationalists can create private armies to enforce their aspirations and to challenge the authority of the state, which in some cases can lose control over a territory. In that case we are talking of the development of a civil war or a national liberation struggle, which might end in the creation of a new state.' Juan J. Linz and Alfred Stepan, *Problems of Democratic Transition and Consolidation*, 22.

11 For the sordid history of the so-called 'counter-guerrilla', much of which came to light during the Ergenekon trials, see D. Ganser, *Nato's Secret Armies. Operation Gladio and Terrorism in Western Europe* (London: Routledge, 2004); T. Miley with C. Hammy and G. Yildiz, 'The Turkish-Kurdish Conflict in Historical Context', in T. Miley and F. Venturini, *Your Freedom and Mine: Abdullah Öcalan and the Kurdish Question in Erdoğan's Turkey*; K. Yildiz and S. Breau, *The Kurdish Conflict: International Humanitarian Law and Post-Conflict Mechanisms* (London: Routledge, 2010). For information about the Ergenekon trials, see E. Zürcher, *Turkey. A Modern History* (London: I.B. Tauris. Fourth Edition, 2017).

12 The term legitimate is notoriously multi-faceted. In normative political philosophy, it tends to be used as an equivalent of fair or just. In empirical political sociology, by contrast, the focus is explicitly on perceptions and justificatory discourses, especially modes of legitimation (i.e. the justifications used by elites for the exercise of political authority). The realms of fact and of value are supposed to remain scrupulously separated, scholars working in this *sociological* tradition/discipline tend to believe, though of course, few if any social-scientific devotees of 'value-neutrality' manage to persuasively practice what they preach. In such an effort at 'value-free' sociology, Max Weber famously distinguished among three ideal types of legitimation – legal-bureaucratic, charismatic and traditional. If the discourse and ideology of the nation has proven so attractive to rulers in recent decades and centuries, perhaps this is because it combines a potent blend of Weber's three types of legitimation. The role of charismatic leadership in the 'founding' of nations is in this respect a phenomenon

that is difficult to deny. Charismatic leaders have often been worshipped as founders of nations, after all. The case of Öcalan is thus no exception in this regard. In point of fact, his figure and resonance paradoxically mirrors and simultaneously sublimates/ transvalues the cult of Atatürk, which, by the way, remains compulsory to this day in Turkey, even after close to two decades of hegemony of Erdoğan's brand of political Islam. Still, one might wonder, just why has state legitimacy proven so vulnerable to nationalist challenges over the past century, and what might this have to do with the spread of representative democracy, and relatedly, of democratic ideals? Nationalist conflicts pose a particularly thorny problem for state authorities concerned to legitimate their rule in accordance with democratic principles. This is because, as Sir Ivor Jennings famously emphasized, the notion of rule by (representatives of) the people, for the people – a notion which is arguably the very core of the democratic creed – tends to presuppose an answer to the question, 'Who are the people?' By extension, attempts to legitimate the exercise of authority by rulers elected to represent the people run into special difficulties in contexts where large segments of the population are not seen as, and/or do not see themselves as, belonging to the people, i.e. to the nation. Moreover, largely because of the fact that democratic politics tend to be confined within the boundaries of 'nation-states' (sic), peoplehood and nationhood are all too often conflated in the terms of contemporary political discourse, certainly but not only in Turkey, indeed, all around the globe. On the flip side, with respect to the question of violence in the phrase 'monopoly of legitimate violence', we know from the comparative study of nationalism that violent repression of ethno-cultural minorities more often than not seems to strengthen the cohesion of the victimized group, at least in the longer run, certainly in the contemporary period. The case of the Catalans and the Basques in Spain are quite exemplary in this regard. On the dilemmas for democratic theory posed by peoplehood, see I. Jennings, *The Approach to Self-Government* (Cambridge: Cambridge University Press, [1956] 2011); and, more recently, Rogers M. Smith, *Stories of Peoplehood* (Cambridge: Cambridge University Press, 2003). On the causal relation between violent Franquist repression and the subsequent strengthening of national identity in Spain, the work of Juan Linz on the subject remains worthy of close attention. See, in particular, his long essay from 1973, 'Early State-Building and Late Peripheral Nationalisms against the State: The Case of Spain', in Shmuel N. Eisenstadt and Stein Rokkan, eds, *Building States and Nations. Analysis by Region, Vol. II* (Beverly Hills: Sage Publications, 1973), 32–116, as well as the chapter on Spain in Juan J. Linz and Alfred Stepan, *Problems of Democratic Transition and Consolidation*.

13 https://en.wikipedia.org/wiki/Terrorism.
14 On the truly 'Orwellian' dimension of the ongoing war on terror, see the prescient 2003 volume published by the Campaign Against Criminalising Communities (CAMPACC), *A Permanent State of Terror?* (London). See also the special issue by the Institute for Race Relation's (IRR) journal, *Race and Class* on *The Politics of Fear: Civil Society and the Security State*. Available online. See also the incisive http://www.irr.org.uk/publications/issues/the-politics-of-fear-civil-society-and-the-security-state/; as well as the incisive article by the IRR's emeritus Director, A. Sivanandan, 'Racism, Liberty and the War on Terror' (Institute for Race Relations, 2006). Available online. http://www.irr.org.uk/news/racism-liberty-and-the-war-on-terror/. See, too, the recent book by the IRR's current Director, Liz Fekete, *Europe's Fault Lines: Racism and the Far Right* (London: Verso, 2017). For powerful criticism of the war on terror grounded firmly in a US constitutionalist perspective, see Bruce Ackerman, *Before the Next Attack:*

Preserving Civil Liberties in the Age of Terrorism (New Haven, CT: Yale University Press, 2007); and David Cole and Jack Dempsey, *Terrorism and the Constitution: Sacrificing Civil Liberties in the Name of National Security. Third Edition* (The New Press, 2006). For a critique of the war on terror paradigm from a perspective that nevertheless remains close to the US foreign policy establishment, see R. Malley and J. Finer, 'The Long Shadow of 9/11. How Counter-terrorism Warps U.S. Foreign Policy', *Foreign Affairs* (July/August 2018), 58–69. The consequences of the 'war on terror' for political expression and therefore representation are particularly grave. The banning of representative symbols such as flags or images of political leaders, and the prosecution of human rights defenders who seek to give legal and political advice to outlawed organizations/movements searching for ways to negotiate a democratic peace, are two pertinent examples of the anti-democratic core of the paradigm, its commitment to coercion over consensus, to weapons over words, its substitution of politics by war.

15 See D. Summers, 'Dancing with the Devil', as well as his sharp rejoinder to Michael Gunter in 'Consolidating Peace, Democracy and Human Rights after Raqqa: Prospects for the Region and the Kurds. Panel Discussion at the 14th Annual EUTCC Conference', in Miley and Venturini, eds, *Your Freedom and Mine: Abdullah Öcalan and the Kurdish Question in Erdoğan's Turkey*, 385–9, 396.

16 For a synoptic overview of the most blatant examples of US state terror in the past sixty years, see N. Chomsky, 'The Long and Shameful History of American Terrorism'. Available online: https://politics1660.wordpress.com/2017/01/22/noam-chomsky-the-long-shameful-history-of-american-terrorism/. See also the helpful reading list on state terror. Available online: http://www.chomskylist.com/category_page.php?category_id=97.

17 For details of the spiralling violence between the Turkish state and the Kurdish Freedom Movement and the human rights atrocities against the Kurdish population since the breakdown of peace negotiations in mid-2015, see T. Miley, 'State Terror, Human Rights Violations and Authoritarianism in Turkey', in Miley and Venturini, *Your Freedom and Mine: Abdullah Öcalan and the Kurdish Question in Erdoğan's Turkey*, 221–52.

18 According to most estimates, the number killed since 1984 exceeds 40,000; the number displaced, by now close to 4 million; the number of villages evacuated and destroyed, over 3,000. In 2001, a UN Special Rapporteur on extrajudicial, summary or arbitrary executions was provided by Turkish authorities with official figures in which these human rights atrocities are broken down further, since the declaration of the state of emergency in 1987. These figures help provide a sense of proportion in the balance sheet of suffering: 'over 23,000 suspected PKK militants killed, more than 4,400 unarmed civilians killed and 5,400 wounded, more than 5,000 police officers and gendarmes killed and 11,000 injured'. See K. Yildiz and S. Breau, *The Kurdish Conflict: International Humanitarian Law and Post-Conflict Mechanisms*, 6, 277 fn99.

19 See, for example, A. Öcalan, *War and Peace in Kurdistan. Perspectives for a Political Solution to the Kurdish Question* (Cologne: International Initiative, 2009), especially 28–30; and A. Öcalan, *Prison Writings. The PKK and the Kurdish Question in the 21st Century* (Cologne: International Initiative, 2011), 122–3.

20 J. Locke, 'The Right to Revolution', in *The Second Treatise on Government*, section 222. Available online: http://press-pubs.uchicago.edu/founders/documents/v1ch3s2.html.

21 See R. Aschraft, *Revolutionary Politics and Locke's Two Treatises of Government* (Princeton, NJ: Princeton University Press, 1986).

22   See the relevant conclusions in this regard reached by M. Manwaring, Professor of Military Strategy in the Strategic Studies Institute of the US Army War College, in his chapter, 'The Environment as a Global Stability-Security Issue', in M. Manwaring, ed., *Environmental Security and Global Stability. Problems and Responses* (Lanham, MD: Lexington Books, 2002). Manwaring contends on 168: 'Instability and violence are the general consequences of unreformed political, social, economic, and security institutions and concomitant misguided, insensitive, incompetent, and/or corrupt (i.e. illegitimate) governance. Thus, governance is the root cause and the central strategic problem in the current unstable security arena.' Translation from social-scientific cum military-speak into plain language: no justice, no peace.

23   As we have already noted above (in note 5), Che Guevara stressed the importance of popular support for determining the prospects of survival and ultimate success of the tactic of guerrilla warfare. In a similar vein, Mao Tse Tung famously insisted in his equally influential writings *On Guerrilla Warfare* (1937) that: 'The most important natural quality is that of complete loyalty to the idea of the people's emancipation. If this is present, the others will develop; if it is not present, nothing can be done.' Available online: https://www.marxists.org/reference/archive/mao/works/1937/guerrilla-warfare/ch05.htm.

24   For the most comprehensive and persuasive documentation of the objective, material conditions underpinning and fuelling the Kurdish insurgency in Turkey, see V. Yadirgi, *The Political Economy of the Kurds of Turkey: From the Ottoman Empire to the Turkish Republic* (Cambridge: Cambridge University Press, 2017). See also A. Ikduygu, et al., 'The Ethnic Question in an Environment of Insecurity: The Kurds in Turkey', *Ethnic and Racial Studies*, 22:6 (1999), 991–1010.

25   On the distinctive class composition of the cadres of the PKK, see D. McDowall, *A Modern History of the Kurds*, 418; D. Romano, *The Kurdish Nationalist Movement. Opportunity, Mobilization, Identity*, 89; M. Van Bruinessen, 'Between Guerrilla War and Political Murder: the Workers' Party of Kurdistan', *Middle East Report*, #153, July–August 1988, 42; and P. White, *Primitive Rebels or Revolutionary Modernizers? The Kurdish National Movement in Turkey*, 155–6.

26   On the role of the 'village guards' in the spiral of repression and violence in the Kurdish region, see D. McDowall, *A Modern History of the Kurds*, 422; D. Romano, *The Kurdish Nationalist Movement. Opportunity, Mobilization, Identity*, 83; and K. Yildiz and S. Breau, *The Kurdish Conflict: International Humanitarian Law and Post-Conflict Mechanisms*, 16.

27   An initial in-road into survey research that focuses on the Kurdish question in Turkey and is available in the English language was made by Z. Saragil, 'Curbing Kurdish Ethno-nationalism in Turkey: An Empirical Assessment of Pro-Islamic and Socioeconomic Approaches', *Ethnic and Racial Studies*, 33:3 (2010), 533–53. Unfortunately, Saragil's article relies on rather dubious extrapolations from the World Values Survey, a point made persuasively by F. Ekmeki, 'Understanding Kurdish Ethno-nationalism in Turkey: Socio-Economy, Religion, and Politics', *Ethnic and Racial Studies*, 34:9 (2011), 1608–17. For a rare example of original survey research conducted in Turkey that explores the political implications of Kurdish ethnicity on support for different political parties, see M. Toprak, et al., 'Transformations of Turkish Politics: Socio-Political, Economic and Ethnic Particularities', *bilig*, 50 (2009), 199–232.

28   The abundance of research about national identity in Spain that uses general population surveys and elite surveys is thanks in no small part to the research agenda

of Juan Linz, who from the mid-1960s produced a series of pioneering studies with FOESSA and DATA, and who, alongside some of his many students, would continue to pursue this agenda until the end of his life in 2013. For an excellent example of such research, see J. Linz, 'From Primordialism to Nationalism', in Edward A. Tiriyakian and Ronald Rogowski, eds, *New Nationalisms of the Developed West* (Boston: Allen & Unwin, 1985), 203–53.

29 Gunes's manuscript provides detailed information about the legal and extra-legal obstacles that pro-Kurdish political parties have faced in recent decades. One point worth mentioning in this regard is that the repression of parliamentary and local representation of pro-Kurdish voices has directly undermined peace negotiations on multiple occasions. For example, as I have explained elsewhere, after the murder of President Özal in 1993, '[a]longside stepped-up military assault, the Turkish government moved to ban the Kurdish political party HEP, which had emerged after a split with Turkey's Social Democratic Party (Gunes 2012, 56–164). Moreover, the Constitutional Court even decided to strip "one of the most moderate Kurds in the Assembly" of his parliamentary immunity. Further removals of parliamentary immunity soon followed. Moreover, such legal measures were complemented by extra-legal ones as well: assassinations of Kurdish politicians, bomb attacks on their headquarters and branch offices, and arrests of party members (McDowall 1996, 439). The window of opportunity for a negotiated, political solution to the ongoing human rights' tragedy in the Kurdish region was thus slammed shut.' See T. Miley with C. Hammy and G. Yildiz, 'The Turkish-Kurdish Conflict in Historical Context', in T. Miley and F. Venturini, eds, *Your Freedom and Mine: Abdullah Öcalan and the Kurdish Question in Erdoğan's Turkey*, 50. For details about the wave of state repression against the HDP since spring of 2015, and its contribution to the rapid deterioration of the human rights situation in the Kurdish region (and beyond) in Turkey, see T. Miley, 'State Terror, Human Rights Violations, and Authoritarianism in Turkey', in the same volume, 225–58. Available online: http://trise.org/2017/04/03/state-terror-human-rights-violations-and-authoritarianism-in-turkey/.

30 Indeed, as I have argued elsewhere: 'The social scientific literature on nationalism is plagued by empirical deficiencies. Despite the endless debates about how a nation should be defined, the abundance of general theories of nationalism, the extensive literature on nationalist ideology, movements and leadership, and even on nationalist parties and electorates, there remains a dearth of empirical data in the literature. The social groups in whose names nationalist ideologues speak are themselves poorly described. In most of the literature we find inadequate empirical data on the composition of these groups. There is little empirical research devoted to gauging the feeling of national identity. There is even less research relating patterns of different modes of national identification with the diffusion of different political attitudes.' See T. Miley, 'Against the Thesis of the "Civic Nation": The Case of Catalonia in Contemporary Spain', *Nationalism and Ethnic Politics*, 13 (2007), 1–37.

31 See I. Budge and D. McDonald, 'Choices Parties Define: Policy Alternatives in Representative Elections, 17 Countries 1945–1998', *Party Politics*, 12:4 (2006), 451–66; and J. Roemer et al., *Racism, Xenophobia, and Distribution: Multi-Issue Politics in Advanced Democracies* (Cambridge: Russell Sage Foundation Books, 2007). For an overview of the significance of this literature for the theory of representative democracy and for the theory of nationalism, see T. Miley, 'Democratic Representation and the National Dimension in Catalan and Basque Politics', *International Journal of Politics, Culture and Society*, 27 (2014), 291–322.

32 See X. Coller, et al., eds, *Political Power in Spain: The Multiple Divides between MPs and Citizens* (London: Palgrave Macmillan, 2018); as well as T. Miley, 'Democratic Representation and the National Dimension in Catalan and Basque Politics'.
33 For a good overview of the vast literature on representation in the social sciences, of the many related debates which have developed relatively autonomously, see S. Dovi, 'Political Representation', in E. Zalta, ed., *The Stanford Encyclopedia of Philosophy* (Stanford, CA: Stanford University Press, 2007). Available online: https://plato.stanford.edu/entries/political-representation/#PitFouVieRep. Several strands in the literature stand out as particularly pertinent to our discussion. First, there is a literature that has developed mainly in normative political philosophy, in which Hanna Pitkin's 1967 classic, *The Concept of Representation* (Berkeley, CA: University of California Press, 1967), still remains central, as exemplified by Gunes's references to it in this manuscript. For an overview of the reception of Pitkin's work, see S. Dovi, 'Hannah Pitkin: The Concept of Representation', in J. Levy, *The Oxford Handbook of Classics in Contemporary Political Theory* (Oxford: Oxford University Press, 2015). For a sophisticated critique of much of this normative literature from a perspective highly indebted to Hayden White's work in the fields of history and literary criticism, see F. Ankersmit, *Aesthetic Politics: Political Philosophy Beyond Fact and Value* (Stanford, CA: Stanford University Press, 1997). Among the most interesting developments in the normative literature in recent years has been the so-called 'constructivist' turn, which is in turn indebted to Carole Pateman's famous book from 1970 on *Participation and Democratic Theory* (Cambridge: Cambridge University Press). See, for example, the work of Lisa Disch, including her 2011 article, 'Toward a Mobilization Conception of Democratic Representation', *American Political Science Review*, 105:1, 100–14; as well as her more recent piece, 'The Constructivist Turn in Democratic Representation: A Normative Dead-End?' *Constellations*, 22:4 (2015), 487–99. As is evident in Disch's work, the normative literature has evolved in a more empirical direction, and is now convergent with debates in a second strand, that developed mainly within the tradition of empirical democratic theory, with its long-standing emphasis on the impact of institutional design on the type and quality of democratic representation. One of the most influential 'sub-strands' in this more empirically based literature on representation has been developed by feminist scholars, with Anne Phillips' book, *The Politics of Presence* (Oxford: Oxford University Press, 1995) being a canonical point of reference. There is likewise a related 'sub-strand' which focuses on the question of representation of ethnic and religious minorities. See the overview provided in Banducci, S.A., et al., 'Minority Representation, Empowerment, and Participation', *The Journal of Politics*, 66:2 (2004), 534–56. This feminist, critical race and multicultural contribution to the literature on representation in turn builds on related long-standing debates within empirical democratic theory, especially the debate about consociationalism, generated by Arend Lijphart's 1969 article, 'Consociational Democracy', *World Politics*, 25:2 (1969), 207–25; as well as the more recent debates about multinational federalism, of which Stepan, Linz and Yadav's 2011 book, *Crafting State-Nations: India and Other Multi-National Democracies*, is exemplary. See also the very recent volume by J. Cohen and A. Arato, *Forms of Pluralism and Democratic Constitutionalism* (New York: Columbia University Press, 2018), which includes an article by A. Stepan and J. Miley that explicitly addresses the relevance of the Öcalan-inspired, 'democratic confederal' Rojava revolution, 'Federacy and the Kurds: Might This New Political Form Help Mitigate Hobbesian Conflict in Turkey, Iraq, and Syria'. For the significance of all these convergent strands of abundant normative and

empirical literature for the theory of representative democracy, see the edited volume by A. Przeworski, et al., *Democracy, Accountability, and Representation* (Cambridge: Cambridge University Press, 1999); as well as J. Linz with T. Miley, 'Cautionary and Unorthodox Thoughts about Democracy Today', in Douglas Chalmers and Scott Mainwaring, eds, *Institutions and Democracy: Essays in Honor of Alfred Stepan* (South Bend, IN: University of Notre Dame Press, 2012), 227–52. Finally, there is yet another influential strand of literature on representation that deserves mention, which, however unfortunately, remains largely ignored by and in turn largely ignores the convergent debates in normative political philosophy and in comparative politics/empirical democratic theory, but dominates the discussion in cultural studies. Its canonical reference remains the work of Stuart Hall. See, for example, S. Hall, ed., *Representation. Cultural Representation and Signifying Practices* (London: SAGE, 1997).

34 The five-fold typology of political regimes provided by Juan Linz in *Totalitarian and Authoritarian Regimes* (Boulder, CO: Lynne Reinner Publishers, 2000) remains at the centre of debates in comparative political sociology on regime types. Nicos Poulantzas's *Fascism and Dictatorship: The Third International and the Problem of Fascism* (London: NLB, 1970) is probably still the most sophisticated contribution to the debate about regime types from within the Marxist tradition, though Göran Therborn also provides very pertinent reflections about regime types conceptualized as diverse 'bourgeois formats of representation' in chapter four of *What Does the Ruling Class Do When It Rules?* (London: NLB, 1978). For the controversy surrounding Linz's description of the Franco regime as an authoritarian regime, see T. Miley, 'Franquism as Authoritarianism: Juan Linz and his Critics', *Politics, Religion & Ideology*, 12:1 (2011), 27–50. For the relevant, more recent elaboration of the concept of 'competitive authoritarianism', see S. Levitsky and L. Way, *Competitive Authoritarianism: Hybrid Regimes after the Cold War* (Cambridge: Cambridge University Press, 2010).

35 See T. Miley with C. Hammy and G. Yildiz, 'The Turkish-Kurdish Conflict in Historical Context', 10–11.

36 See V. Yadirgi, *The Political Economy of the Kurds of Turkey: From the Ottoman Empire to the Turkish Republic*, 192.

37 See C. Hammy, 'Two Visions of Politics in Turkey: Authoritarian and Revolutionary', *Open Democracy*, 20 August 2016. Available online: https://www.opendemocracy.net/north-africa-west-asia/cihad-hammy/two-visions-of-politics-in-turkey-authoritarian-and-revolutionary.

38 For an overview of the burgeoning literature on 'hybrid regimes', see N. Ezrow, 'Hybrid Regimes', in F. Moghaddam, ed., *The SAGE Encyclopedia of Political Behavior* (London: SAGE Publications, 2017). For the elaboration of the concept of 'semiauthoritarianism', see C. Göbel, 'Semiauthoritarianism', in J. Ishiyame and M. Breuning, eds, *21st Century Political Science: A Reference Handbook* (London: SAGE Publications, 2011), 258–67. On the concept of 'competitive authoritarianism', see S. Levitsky and J. Loxton, 'Populism and Competitive Authoritarianism in the Andes', *Democratization*, 20 (2013), 107–36; and J. Loxton, 'Competitive Authoritarianism', in F. Moghaddam, ed., *The SAGE Encyclopedia of Political Behavior*. On the related concept of 'participatory competitive authoritarianism', see S. Mainwaring, 'Review: From Representative Democracy to Participatory Competitive Authoritarianism: Hugo Chávez and Venezuelan Politics', *Perspectives on Politics*, 10:4 (2012), 955–67. For the concept of 'electoralist hegemony', see C. Hacker-Cordón, 'Electoral Legitimation, Polyarchy, and Democratic Legitimacy', *American Political Science*

Association (Foundations Section, Washington, DC, 2001). Hacker-Cordón draws heavily on P. Anderson's important essay, 'The Antinomies of Antonio Gramsci', *New Left Review*, 100 (1976), 5–78.

39 See R. Dahl, *Polyarchy: Participation and Opposition* (New Haven, CT: Yale University Press, 1971).

40 For the elaboration of the Gramscian concept of hegemony, see P. Anderson, 'The Antinomies of Antonio Gramsci'; as well as his more recent, *The H-word: The Peripeteia of Hegemony* (London: Verso Books, 2017). For a penetrating critique of the Gramscian framework from an anarchist perspective, see J. Scott, *Domination and the Arts of Resistance: Hidden Transcripts* (New Haven, CT: Yale University Press, 1990), especially Chapters 3 and 4.

41 On the distinction between 'exclusionary' and 'assimilationist' nationalisms, see T. Miley, 'Against the Thesis of the "Civic Nation": The Case of Catalonia in Contemporary Spain'.

42 See C. Sagnic, 'Mountain Turks: State Ideology and the Kurds in Turkey', *Information, Society and Justice*, 3:2 (2010), 127–34.

43 T. Miley with C. Hammy and G. Yildiz, 'The Turkish-Kurdish Conflict in Historical Context', 8.

44 See D. Natali, *The Kurds and the State. Evolving National Identity in Iraq, Turkey, and Iran* (Syracuse, NY: Syracuse University Press, 2005), 97; and K. Ertur, *The Political Integration of the Kurds in Turkey* (Portland State University PhD dissertation, 1979). Available online: https://pdxscholar.library.pdx.edu/cgi/viewcontent.cgi?article=3897&context=open_access_etds.

45 See T. Miley with C. Hammy and G. Yildiz, 'The Turkish-Kurdish Conflict in Historical Context', 24–7.

46 See M. Hroch, *The Social Preconditions of National Revival in Europe* (New York: Columbia University Press, 2000).

47 For another important book in the literature on comparative nationalisms that makes ample use of the idea of 'thresholds', incorporated within a broader neo-Gramscian framework, see I. Lustick, *Unsettled States, Disputed Lands: Britain and Ireland, France and Algeria, Israel and the West Bank-Gaza* (Ithaca, NY: Cornell University Press, 1995). Lustick's account, unfortunately, follows Laclau and Mouffe's post-Marxist reading of Gramsci to excise the political-economic dimension almost entirely from the historical narratives that he weaves. For Laclau and Mouffe's highly influential post-Marxist take on hegemony, see *Hegemony and Socialist Strategy* (London: Verso, 1986). For cogent critiques of Laclau and Mouffe's framework in implicit defence of a more orthodox historical materialist perspective, see G. Therborn, *From Marxism to Post-Marxism?* (London: Verso, 2008), and P. Anderson, *The H-word: The Peripeteia of Hegemony* (London: Verson, 2017). See also T. Miley, 'Self-Determination in the Twenty-First Century: Beyond the Nation, against the State' (forthcoming).

48 See R. Dahl, *A Preface to Democratic Theory* (Chicago, IL: Chicago University Press, 1956), Chapter 4, 'Equality, Diversity, Intensity', 90–123.

49 See J. Linz, 'Democracy, Multinationalism, and Federalism', *Working Paper*, No. 103 (Madrid: Centro de Estudios Avanzados en Ciencias Sociales, Instituto Juan March de Estudios e Investigaciones, 1997).

50 See T. Miley with C. Hammy and G. Yildiz, 'The Turkish-Kurdish Conflict in Historical Perspective', 27–9.

51 Ibid., 35–6.

52 F. Fanon, *The Wretched of the Earth* (London: Penguin Classics, 2001), 74.
53 See E. V. Wolfenstein, *Psychoanalytic-Marxism. Groundwork* (Free Association Books, 1993), 432, n.3.
54 E. Hobsbawm, *Nations and Nationalism since 1780* (Cambridge: Cambridge University Press, 1990), 117–18.
55 M. Weber, 'Structures of Power: The Nation', in H. H. Gerth and C. Wright Mills, eds, *From Max Weber: Essays in Sociology*, 176.
56 Quoted in J. Linz, 'State Building and Nation Building', *European Review*, 1:4 (1993), 361. See also T. Miley, 'The Nation as Hegemonic Project', *Journal of Political Ideologies*, 23:2 (2018), 183–204.
57 See M. Koefoed, 'Martyrdom and Emotional Resistance in the Case of Northern Kurdistan: Hidden and Public Emotional Resistance', *Journal of Political Power*, 10:2 (2017), 184–99.
58 M. Weber, 'The Sociology of Charismatic Authority', in H. H. Gerth and C. Wright Mills, eds, *From Max Weber: Essays in Sociology*, 245–6.
59 C. Lindblom, *Charisma* (Oxford: Oxford University Press, 1993), 192.
60 D. Leese, *Mao Cult: Rhetoric and Ritual in China's Cultural Revolution* (Cambridge: Cambridge University Press, 2011), 20.
61 Ibid., 87.
62 A. Öcalan, *Manifesto for a Democratic Civilization. Volume One: The Age of Masked Gods and Disguised Kings* (Prosgrunn, Norway: New Compass Press, 2015), 21.
63 I. Szelenyi, 'Lecture 19: Weber on Charismatic Authority'. Available online: https://oyc.yale.edu/sociology/socy-151/lecture-19.
64 H. H. Gerth and C. Wright Mills, 'Introduction', in H. H. Gerth and C. Wright Mills, eds, *From Max Weber: Essays in Sociology*, 54.
65 T. Miley with C. Hammy and G. Yildiz, 'The Turkish-Kurdish Conflict in Historical Context', 51–64.
66 A. Öcalan, 'Seek the Truth', in T. Miley and F. Venturini, eds, *Your Freedom and Mine: Abdullah Öcalan and the Kurdish Question in Erdgoan's Turkey*, 315–16.
67 An increasing number of Öcalan's writings have been translated into English. See, for example, A. Öcalan, *The Roots of Civilization* (Transmedia Publishing Limited, 2007); *Prison Writings: The PKK and the Kurdish Question in the Twenty-First Century* (Cologne: International Initiative, 2013); *Prison Writings III: The Road Map to Negotiations* (Cologne: International Initiative, 2012); *Manifesto for a Democratic Civilization. Volume One: The Age of Masked Gods and Disguised* Kings; *Manifesto for a Democratic Civilization. Volume Two: The Age of Unmasked Gods and Naked Kings* (Prosgrunn, Norway: New Compass Press, 2017); and *The Political Thought of Abdullah Öcalan: Kurdistan, Women's Revolution and Democratic Confederalism* (London: Pluto Press, 2017).
68 See J. Linz with T. Miley, 'Cautionary and Unorthodox Thoughts about Democracy Today'.
69 R. Dahl, *Polyarchy: Participation and Opposition*.
70 A. Przeworski, *Democracy and the Limits of Self-Government* (Cambridge: Cambridge, University Press, 2010), 18.
71 This section draws substantially on T. Miley, 'Democratic Representation and the National Dimension in Catalan and Basque Politics'.
72 R. Miliband, *The State in Capitalist Society* (New York, NY: Basic Books, 1969).
73 P. Bachrach and M. S. Baratz, 'Two Faces of Power', *The American Political Science Review*, 56:4 (1962), 947–52.

74 N. Poulantzas, 'The Problem of the Capitalist State', *New Left Review*, 58 (1969), 67–78.
75 A. Przeworski and M. Wallerstein, 'The Structural Dependence of the State on Capital', *The American Political Science Review*, 82:1 (1988), 11–29.
76 L. Althusser, 'Ideology and Ideological State Apparatuses', in *On Ideology* (London: Verso, 2007), 1–140.
77 J. J. Rousseau, *The Social Contract*, Book 2.1. Available online: https://www.earlymoderntexts.com/assets/pdfs/rousseau1762.pdf.
78 See J. Bartelson, *A Genealogy of Sovereignty* (Cambridge: Cambridge University Press, 1993).
79 B. Manin, *The Principles of Representative Government* (Cambridge: Cambridge University Press, 1997).
80 For the conceptualization of elections as a 'candidate selection process', see G. W. Domhoff, *Who Rules America?* (McGraw Hill Education, Seventh Edition, 2013). For accounts of democracy that emphasize the primacy of participation, see C. Pateman, *Participation and Democratic Theory*; and, more recently, L. Disch, 'Toward a Mobilization Conception of Democratic Representation'. For the contrast between 'polyarchy' and 'popular democracy', see W. Robinson, *Promoting Polyarchy* (Cambridge: Cambridge University Press, 1996). For a vision of direct democracy conceived as an alternative to representative democracy that has had a strong influence on Öcalan, see M. Bookchin, 'Libertarian Municipalism', in J. Biehl, ed., *The Murray Bookchin Reader* (Montreal: Black Rose Books, 1999), 172–96; and M. Bookchin, *The Next Revolution: Popular Assemblies and the Promise of Direct Democracy* (London: Verso, 2015).
81 On 'deliberative democracy', see J. Cohen, 'Deliberation and Democratic Legitimacy', in J. Bohman and W. Rehg, eds, *Deliberative Democracy: Essays on Reason and Politics* (Boston, MA: MIT Press, 1997); J. Fishkin and P. Laslett, eds, *Debating Deliberative Democracy* (Wiley, 2008); A. Gutmann and D. Thompson, *Why Deliberative Democracy?* (Princeton, NJ: Princeton University Press, 2002); E. Leib, 'Can Direct Democracy Be Made Deliberative?', *Buffalo Law Review*, 54 (2006), 903–25; J. Mansbridge and J. Parkinson, eds, *Deliberative Systems* (Cambridge: Cambridge University Press, 2012); and C. Ross, *The Leaderless Revolution: How Ordinary People Can Take Power and Change Politics in the 21st Century* (London: Simon and Schuster, 2011).
82 P. Freire, *The Pedagogy of the Oppressed* (Continuum, 30th Anniversary Edition, 2000).
83 See M. Bookchin, *Urbanization without Cities* (Montreal: Black Rose Books, 1992), 299.
84 For the concept of 'the hermeneutic of suspicion', see P. Ricoeur, *Freud and Philosophy: An Essay on Interpretation* (New Haven, CT: Yale University Press, 1993).
85 For the concept of an 'ethic of conviction', see M. Weber, 'Politics as a Vocation', in H. H. Gerth and C. Wright Mills, eds, *From Max Weber: Essays in Sociology*, 71–128.
86 M. Bookchin, 'The Future of the Left', in *The Next Revolution: Popular Assemblies and the Promise of Direct Democracy*, 128.
87 S. Casmier and T. Miley, 'Subliminal Consciousness in the Killing Fields of Spain'. Unpublished paper delivered at the 16th Annual Conference of the Multidisciplinary Society, *The Space Between: Literature and Culture 1914–1945*, School of Advanced Study, University of London, 17 July 2014.
88 R. Debray, *The Revolution in the Revolution? Armed Struggle and Political Struggle in Latin America* (New York: Monthly Review Press, 1967), 70.

89 C. Guevara, 'Notes for the Study of Man and Socialism in Cuba' (Havana, 1965). Available online: http://www.sojust.net/essays/che_man_and_socialism.html.
90 A. Öcalan, *War and Peace in Kurdistan*, 28.
91 A. Akkaya and J. Jongerden, 'Confederalism and Autonomy in Turkey: The Kurdistan Workers' Party and the Reinvention of Democracy', in C. Gunes and W. Zeydanliogu, eds, *The Kurdish Question in Turkey. New Perspectives on Violence, Representation, and Reconciliation* (London and New York: Routledge, 2014), 186–204, quote from 193. See also A. Akkaya and J. Jongerden, 'Reassembling the Political: The PKK and the Project of Radical Democracy', *European Journal of Turkish Studies*, 14 (2012), 1–17; and S. Saeed, *Kurdish Politics in Turkey. From the PKK to the KCK*, 90–1.
92 D. Dirik, Competing Concepts of Freedom: Kurdish Politics between "Housewifization" and "Struggling Woman" (PhD diss., Department of Sociology, University of Cambridge, 2018).
93 Gunes, *The Kurdish National Movement in Turkey: From Protest to Resistance*, 116–18.
94 D. McDowall, *A Modern History of the Kurds*, 427.
95 C. Gunes, *The Kurdish National Movement in Turkey: From Protest to Resistance*, 119–20.
96 A. Öcalan, *Liberating Life: Woman's Revolution* (Cologne: International Initiative, 2013), 6. One of the institutional corollaries to this emphasis on the struggle against patriarchy is the movement's insistence upon establishing co-chairs and gender quotas for its political organizations and representative positions. This is exemplified not only in the statutes and practices of pro-Kurdish political parties in Turkey such as the Peoples' Democratic Party (HDP) and Democratic Regions Party (DBP), but also in the revolutionary arrangements that have been institutionalized in Rojava, in the North of Syria, since the middle of 2012. As Saleh Muslim Mohammed, the co-president of the Öcalan-inspired, Syrian-Kurdish Democratic Union Party (PYD) has explained: 'We established a model of co-presidency – each political entity always has both a female and a male president – and a quota of 40 per cent gender representation in order to enforce gender equality throughout all forms of public life and political representation.' Available online: https://kurdishissue.wordpress.com/2014/11/11/a-revolution-of-life-interview-with-saleh-muslim/.
97 See D. H. Matthews and T. Miley, 'Review of Abdullah Öcalan's *Manifesto for a Democratic Civilization*', in T. Miley and F. Venturini, eds, *Your Freedom and Mine: Abdullah Öcalan and the Kurdish Question in Erdoğan's Turkey*, 337–52.
98 See K. Geary, N. Hildyard and K. Yildiz, 'Holding Investors to Account: The Ilisu Dam Campaign', in E. Schmid, ed., *Listen to the Refugee's Story: How U.K. Foreign Investment Creates Refugees and Asylum Seekers* (London: Ilisu Dam Refugees Project, The Corner House, and Peace in Kurdistan, 2003).
99 As part of this 'paradigm shift', Öcalan has elaborated the concept of a 'democratic nation', which he insists can be institutionalized in one of two ways – either through compromise or unilaterally. In his words: 'The first is predicated on finding a compromise with nation-states. It finds its concrete expression in a democratic constitutional solution. It respects the historical-societal heritage of peoples and cultures. It regards the freedom of expression and organisation of these heritages as one of the irrevocable and fundamental constitutional rights. Democratic autonomy is the fundamental principle of these rights. The foremost conditions of this arrangement are that the sovereign nation-state renounces all denial and annihilation policies, and the oppressed nation abandons the idea of forming its own nation-state.

It is difficult for a democratic autonomy project to be implemented without both nations renouncing statist tendencies in this regard. EU countries took more than 300 years of nation-state experience before they could accept democratic autonomy as the best solution for solving nation-states' regional, national and minority related problems ... The second path for a democratic autonomy solution – one that does not depend on finding a compromise with nation-states – is to implement its own project unilaterally. In the broad sense, it recognises the Kurdish people's right to become a democratic nation through the implementation of democratic autonomy. It goes without saying that in this case conflicts will intensify with those sovereign nation-states who do not accept this unilateral implementation of becoming a democratic nation. If this happens, the Kurds will have no other choice but to adopt a full-scale mobilisation and war position in order to protect their existence and to live freely against the individual or joint attacks of nation-states (Iran, Syria and Turkey). They will not hold back from becoming a democratic nation with all its dimensions and to develop and realize their aspirations through their own efforts until they either reach a compromise or achieve independence amidst the warfare.' *Democratic Nation* (Cologne: International Initiative, 2016), 31–2.

100 See R. Dag, 'Democratic Islam Congress and the Middle East', *Open Democracy*, 13 June 2014. Available online: https://www.opendemocracy.net/north-africa-west-asia/rahman-dag/democratic-islam-congress-and-middle-east.
101 A. Öcalan, *Democratic Confederalism* (Cologne: International Initiative, 2011), 30.
102 See J. Freeman, 'The Tyranny of Structurelessness', *Berkeley Journal of Sociology*, 17 (1972), 151–65.
103 R. Luxemburg, 'Organizational Questions of the Russian Social Democracy' (1904). Available online: https://www.marxists.org/archive/luxemburg/1904/questions-rsd/index.htm.
104 B. Bolloten, *The Spanish Civil War. Revolution and Counterrevolution* (The University of North Carolina Press, 1979), 372.
105 R. Debray, *Revolution in the Revolution?*, 112.
106 C. Gunes, *The Kurdish National Movement in Turkey: From Protest to Resistance*, 152.
107 Ibid., 155.
108 Ibid., 152.
109 See also T. Miley with C. Hammy and G. Yildiz, 'The Turkish-Kurdish Conflict in Historical Context', 79–117.
110 For the original formulation of this four-fold distinction, see G. O'Donnell, P. Schmitter and L. Whitehead, eds, *Transitions from Authoritarian Rule: Tentative Conclusions about Uncertain Democracies* (Baltimore: The Johns Hopkins University Press, 1986). See also J. Linz and A. Stepan, *Problems of Democratic Transition and Consolidation*.
111 See, for example, A. K. Jarstadt and T. D. Sisk, *From War to Democracy: Dilemmas of Peacebuilding* (Cambridge: Cambridge University Press, 2008); and J. Tong, *Comparative Peace Processes* (Wiley, 2014).
112 See J. McGarry and B. O'Leary, 'Consociational Theory and Peace Agreements in Pluri-National Places: Northern Ireland and Other Cases', in G. Ben-Porat, ed., *The Failure of the Middle East Peace Process? A Comparative Analysis of Peace Implementation in Israel/Palestine, Northern Ireland, and South Africa* (London: Palgrave MacMillan, 2008), 70–96; T. White, ed., *Lessons from the Northern Ireland Peace Process* (Madison, WI: The University of Wisconsin Press, 2014); Robert P. Clark, *Negotiating with ETA. Obstacles to Peace in the Basque Country, 1975–1988*

(Reno: University of Nevada Press, 1990); and U. Aiartza and J. Zabalo, 'The Basque Country: The Long Walk to a Democratic Scenario', *Berghof Transitions Series No. 7*, 2010. Available online: https://www.berghof-foundation.org/fileadmin/redaktion/Publications/Papers/Transitions_Series/transitions_basque.pdf.
113 A. Öcalan, *Democratic Confederalism*, Part V, 35–44.
114 See T. Miley with C. Hammy and G. Yildiz, 'The Turkish-Kurdish Conflict in Historical Perspective', 96–100; and G. Yildiz, 'How Did Turkey's Peace Process with the PKK Rebels Fail? How Can It Be Resurrected?', MPhil thesis, Department of Sociology, University of Cambridge, 2017.
115 See T. Miley with C. Hammy and G. Yildiz, 'The Turkish-Kurdish Conflict in Historical Perspective', 100–16.
116 See T. Miley, 'State Terror, Human Rights Violations, and Authoritarianism in Turkey: Report of the Third EUTCC Imrali International Peace Delegation'.
117 V. I. Lenin, 'The Dual Power', (1917). Available online: https://www.marxists.org/archive/lenin/works/1917/apr/09.htm.
118 M. Bookchin, 'The Communalist Project', in *The Next Revolution: Popular Assemblies and the Promise of Direct Democracy*, 18–19.

Conclusion

1 İ. Turan, *Turkey's Difficult Journey to Democracy* (Oxford: Oxford University Press, 2015), 87–95.
2 See Turan, *Turkey's Difficult Journey to Democracy*, 110–40.
3 For a detailed discussion see Mehtap Söyler, *The Turkish Deep State: State Consolidation, Civil-Military Relations and Democracy* (London and New York: Routledge, 2015).
4 Cengiz Gunes, *The Kurdish National Movement in Turkey: From Protest to Resistance* (London: Routledge, 2012), 49–64.
5 Ibid., 101–23.
6 See also Salima Tasdemir, 'The Feminization of pro-Kurdish Party Politics in Turkey: The Role of Women Activists' (PhD diss., The University of Exeter, Exeter, 2013).
7 Ceylan Yeginsu, 'Turkey's Campaign Against Kurdish Militants Takes Toll on Civilians', *The New York Times* (2015). Available online: http://www.nytimes.com/2015/12/31/world/europe/turkey-kurds-pkk.html?_r=0 (accessed 30 December 2015).
8 D. Bayır, 'The role of the judicial system in the politicide of the Kurdish opposition', 23, in *The Kurdish Question in Turkey: New Perspectives on Violence, Representation and Reconciliation*, eds, C. Gunes and W. Zeydanlioglu, 21–46 (London and New York: Routledge, 2014).
9 Yeğen, Mesut, Uğraş Ulaş Tol and Mehmet Ali Çalışkan, *Kürtler Ne İstiyor? Kürdistanda Etnik Kimlik, Dindarlık, Sınıf ve Seçimler* (Istanbul: İletişim, 2016), 135.
10 Ibid., 126–30.
11 For a detailed discussion see Cengiz Gunes, *The Kurds in a New Middle East: The Changing Geopolitics of a Regional Conflict* (London: Palgrave MacMillan, 2019).
12 An excellent argument for the recognition of group rights and identities is provided in Charles Taylor, *Multiculturalism and The Politics of Recognition* (Princeton: Princeton University Press, 1992). For arguments that question the desirability of the recognition of group rights see Joshua Cohen, Martha Nussbaum and Matthew Howard, eds, *Is Multiculturalism Bad for Women?* (Princeton: Princeton University

Press, 1999); Leslie Green, 'Internal minorities and their rights' in Judith Baker, ed., *Group Rights* (Toronto: University of Toronto Press, 1994); Avigail Eisenberg and Jeff Spinner-Halev, eds., *Minorities within Minorities: Equality, Rights and Diversity* (Cambridge: Cambridge University Press, 2005); Chandran Kukathas, 'Are there any cultural rights?', *Political Theory*, 20:1 (1992), 105–39.

13   Alba Alonso and Tània Verge, 'Territorial Dynamics and Gender Equality Policies in Spain', *Fédéralisme Régionalisme* (2014). Available online: http://popups.ulg.ac.be/1374-3864/index.php?id=1365 (accessed 26 July 2019).

14   Francesco Palermo, 'Owned or Shared? Territorial Autonomy in the Minority Discourse', in Tove H. Malloy et al. (eds) *Minority Accommodation through Territorial and Non-Territorial Autonomy*, (Oxford: Oxford University Press, 2015), 17.

15   Ibid., 19–21.

16   Cengiz Gunes, 'Accommodating Kurdish Demands in Turkey', in E. Nimni, A. Osipov and D. Smith (eds), *The Challenge of Non-Territorial Autonomy: Theory and Case Studies*, 71–84 (Oxford: Peter Lang International Publishers, 2013); Cengiz Gunes, 'Approaches to Kurdish Autonomy in the Middle East', Nationalities Papers (2019, Forthcoming). See also Federica Prina, David Smith and Judith Sansum, 'National Cultural Autonomy in Central and Eastern Europe: Challenges and Possibilities', in *Democratic Representation in Plurinational States: The Case of Kurds in Turkey*, eds, Ephraim Nimni and Elcin Aktoprak (London: Palgrave Macmillan, 2018), 98–100.

17   David Smith and Karl Cordell, 'Introduction: The Theory and Practice of Cultural Autonomy in Central and Eastern Europe', *Ethnopolitics*, 6:3 (2007), 338; Ephraim Nimni (ed.), *National Cultural Autonomy and its Contemporary Critics* (London and New York: Routledge, 2005).

18   Ephraim Nimni, 'Introduction: The National Cultural Autonomy Model Revisited', in Ephraim Nimni (ed.), *National Cultural Autonomy and Its Contemporary Critics* (London and New York: Routledge, 2005), 1.

19   Ruth Lapidoth, *Autonomy: Flexible Solutions to Ethnic Conflicts* (Washington, DC: United States Institute of Peace, 1996), 39; William Kymlicka, 'National Cultural Autonomy and International Minority Rights Norms', *Ethnopolitics*, 6:3 (2007), 385.

20   Prina, Smith and Sansum, 'National Cultural Autonomy in Central and Eastern Europe: Challenges and Possibilities', 99–100.

Bibliography

Ackerman, B. *Before the Next Attack: Preserving Civil Liberties in the Age of Terrorism.* New Haven, CT: Yale University Press, 2007.
Aiartza, U. and Zabalo, J. 'The Basque Country: The Long Walk to a Democratic Scenario', *Berghof Transitions Series No. 7*, 2010.
Acik, N. 'Re-defining the role of women within the Kurdish national movement in Turkey in the 1990s'. In *The Kurdish Question in Turkey: New Perspectives on Violence, Representation, and Reconciliation*, edited by C. Gunes and W. Zeydanlıoğlu, 114–36. London and New York: Routledge, 2014.
Akkaya, A. H. and Jongerden, J. 'The PKK in the 2000s: Continuity Through Breaks?'. *Nationalisms and Politics in Turkey: Political Islam, Kemalism and the Kurdish Issue*, edited by M. Casier and J. Jongerden, 143–62. London and New York: Routledge, 2011.
Akkaya, A. H. and Jongerden, J. 'Reassembling the Political: The PKK and the Project of Radical Democracy', *European Journal of Turkish Studies*, 14 (2012): 1–17.
Akkaya, A. H. and Jongerden, J. 'Confederalism and Autonomy in Turkey: The Kurdistan Workers' Party and the Reinvention of Democracy'. In *The Kurdish Question in Turkey: New Perspectives on Violence, Representation and Reconciliation*, edited by C. Gunes and W. Zeydanlıoğlu, 186–204. London and New York: Routledge, 2014.
Al, S. 'Islam, ethnicity and the state: contested spaces of legitimacy and power in the Kurdish-Turkish public sphere'. *Southeast European and Black Sea Studies*, 19:1 (2019): 119–37.
Althusser, L. 'Ideology and Ideological State Apparatuses'. In *On Ideology*, 1–140. London: Verso, 2007.
Anderson, P. 'The Antinomies of Antonio Gramsci'. *New Left Review*, 100 (1976): 5–78.
Anderson, P. *The H-word: The Peripeteia of Hegemony.* London: Verso Books, 2017.
Angrist, M. 'Turkey. Roots of the Turkish-Kurdish Conflict and Prospects for Constructive Reform'. In *Federalism and Territorial Cleavages*, edited by U. Amoretti and N. Bermeo, 387–416. Baltimore: The Johns Hopkins University Press, 2004.
Ankersmitt, F. *Aesthetic Politics: Political Philosophy Beyond Fact and Value.* Stanford, CA: Stanford University Press, 1997.
Akdağ, G. A. 'Rational political parties and electoral games: the AKP's strategic move for the Kurdish vote in Turkey'. *Turkish Studies*, 17:1 (2016): 126–54.
Aschraft, R. *Revolutionary Politics and Locke's Two Treatises of Government.* Princeton, NJ: Princeton University Press, 1986.
Ateş-Durç, S. 'Türkiye'de Aşiret ve Siyaset İlişkisi: Metinan Aşireti Örneği'. MA diss., Hacettepe University, Ankara, 2009.
Bachrach, P. and Baratz, M. S. 'Two Faces of Power'. *The American Political Science Review*, 56:4 (1962): 947–52.
Bahcheli, T. and Noel, S. 'The Justice and Development Party and the Kurdish question'. In *Nationalisms and Politics in Turkey: Political Islam, Kemalism and the Kurdish Issue*, edited by M. Casier and J. Jongerden, 101–20. London and New York: Routledge, 2011.

Banducci, S. A., Donovan, T. and Karp, J. A. 'Minority Representation, Empowerment, and Participation', *The Journal of Politics*, 66:2 (2004): 534–56.
Bartelson, J. *A Genealogy of Sovereignty*. Cambridge: Cambridge University Press, 1993.
Bayır, D. *Minorities and Nationalism in Turkish Law*. London and New York, 2013.
Bayır, D. 'Representation of the Kurds by the Turkish Judiciary', *Human Rights Quarterly*, 35 (2013): 116–42.
Bayır, D. 'Turkey, the Kurds, and the legal contours of the right to self-determination', *Kurdish Studies*, 1:1 (2013): 5–27.
Bayır, D. 'The role of the judicial system in the politicide of the Kurdish opposition'. In *The Kurdish Question in Turkey: New Perspectives on Violence, Representation and Reconciliation*, edited by C. Gunes and W. Zeydanlioglu, 21–46. London and New York: Routledge, 2014.
Başer, Z. and Çelik, A. B. 'Imagining peace in a conflict environment: Kurdish youths' framing of the Kurdish issue in Turkey'. *Patterns of Prejudice*, 48:3 (2014): 265–85.
Beşikçi, İ. *Doğu'da Değişim ve Yapısal Sorunlar (Göçebe Alikan Aşireti)*. Ankara: Yurt Yayınları, 1992 [1969].
Bhabha, H. 'DissemiNation: time, narrative, and the margins of the modern nation'. In *Nation and Narration*, edited by H. Bhabha. London: Routledge, 1990.
Birtane, H. 'Diyarbakır'da Issizlik Orani Uzerine Bir Degerlendirme'. *Karacadag Kalkinma Ajansı*. Diyarbakır, 2011.
Bolloten, B. *The Spanish Civil War. Revolution and Counterrevolution*. Chapel Hill: The University of North Carolina Press, 1979.
Bookchin, M. *Urbanization without Cities*. Montreal: Black Rose Books, 1992.
Bookchin, M. 'Libertarian Municipalism'. In *The Murray Bookchin Reader*, edited by J. Biehl. Montreal: Black Rose Books, 1999.
Bookchin, M. *The Next Revolution: Popular Assemblies and the Promise of Direct Democracy*. London: Verso, 2015.
Bozarslan, H. 'Political aspects of the Kurdish Problem in Turkey'. In *The Kurds: A Contemporary Overview*, edited by P. G. Kreyenbroek and S. Sperl, 74–89. London and New York: Routledge, 1992.
Bozarslan, H. 'Tribal Asabiyya and Kurdish Politics: A Socio-Historical Perspective'. In *The Kurds: Nationalism and Politics*, edited by F. A. Jabar and H. Dawood, 130–47. London: Saqi, 2006.
Bozarslan, H. 'Kurds and the Turkish state'. In *The Cambridge History of Turkey, Volume 4*, edited by R. Kasaba, 333–56. Cambridge: Cambridge University Press, 2008.
Bozarslan, H. 'Foreword'. In *The Kurdish Question In Turkey: New Perspectives on Conflict, Representation and Reconciliation*, edited by C. Gunes and W. Zeydanlioglu, x-xv. London and New York: Routledge, 2014.
Brubaker, R. *Nationalism Reframed*. Cambridge: Cambridge University Press, 1996.
Budge, I. and McDonald, D. 'Choices Parties Define: Policy Alternatives in Representative Elections, 17 Countries 1945–1998'. *Party Politics*, 12:4 (2006): 451–66.
Çağlayan, H. *Analar, Yoldaşlar, Tanrıçalar: Kürt Hareketinde Kadınlar ve Kadın Kimliğinin Oluşumu*. Istanbul: İletisim Yayınları, 2007.
Çakır, R. *Derin Hizbullah: İslami Şiddetin Geleceği*. Istanbul: Siyah Beyaz Metis Güncel, 2001.
Casmier, S. 'Subliminal Consciousness in the Killing Fields of Spain.' Unpublished paper delivered at the 16th Annual Conference of the Multidisciplinary Society, *The Space Between: Literature and Culture 1914–1945*, School of Advanced Study, University of London, 17 July 17 2014.

Çelik, A. B. 'Transnationalisation of Human Right Norms and its impact on the Internally Displaced Kurds'. *Human Rights Quarterly*, 27 (2005): 969-97.
Çelik, E. 'Koruculuk Uygulamalarının Terörle Mücadeledeki yeri: Geçici Köy Koruculuğu sistemi Örneği'. MA diss., Kara Harp Olulu Savunma Birimleri Enstitüsü, Ankara, 2014.
Chandhoke, N., *Democracy and Revolutionary Politics*. London: Bloomsbury Academic, 2015.
Çiçek, C. *Ulus, Din, Sınıf: Türkiye'de Kürt Mutabakatının İnşası*. Istanbul: İletişim Yayınları, 2015.
Çiçek, C. 'Kurdish identity and political Islam under AKP rule'. *Research and Policy on Turkey*, 1:2 (2016): 147-63.
Clark, R. P. *Negotiating with ETA. Obstacles to Peace in the Basque Country, 1975-1988*. Reno: University of Nevada Press, 1990.
Cohen, J. 'Deliberation and Democratic Legitimacy'. In *Deliberative Democracy: Essays on Reason and Politics*, edited by J. Bohman and W. Rehg, 67-92. Boston, MA: MIT Press, 1997.
Cohen, J., Nussbaum, M. and Howard, M. (eds) *Is Multiculturalism Bad for Women?* Princeton: Princeton University Press, 1999.
Cohen, J. and Arato, A. (eds) *Forms of Pluralism and Democratic Constitutionalism*. New York: Columbia University Press, 2018.
Cole, D. and Dempsey, J. *Terrorism and the Constitution: Sacrificing Civil Liberties in the Name of National Security*. Third Edition. New York: The New Press, 2006.
Coller, X., et al., (eds) *Political Power in Spain: The Multiple Divides between MPs and Citizens*. London: Palgrave Macmillan, 2018.
Cumhuriyet Halk Partisi. *CHP 2011 Seçim Bildirgesi*. Place and publisher not stated, 2011.
Cumhuriyet Halk Partisi. *Önce İnsan, Önce Birlik, Önce Türkiye*. Place and publisher not stated, 2015.
Dahl, R. *A Preface to Democratic Theory*. Chicago, IL: Chicago University Press, 1956.
Dahl, R. *Polyarchy: Participation and Opposition*. New Haven, CT: Yale University Press, 1971.
Dalton, R. J., Farrell, D. M. and McAllister, I. *Political Parties and Democratic Linkages: How Parties Organise Democracy*. Oxford: Oxford University Press, 2011.
Darıcı, H. 'Politics of privacy: forced migration and the spatial struggle of the Kurdish youth'. *Journal of Balkan and Near Eastern Studies*, 13:4 (2011): 457-74.
Darıcı, H. '"Adults see politics as a game": Politics of Kurdish Children in Urban Turkey'. *International Journal of Middle East Studies*, 45:4 (2013): 775-90.
Debray, R. *The Revolution in the Revolution? Armed Struggle and Political Struggle in Latin America*. New York: Monthly Review Press, 1967.
Delil, S. and Tanrıkulu, A. *Çermik Termal Turizm Raporu*. Karacadag Kalkınma Ajansı, Diyarbakır, 2012.
Demir, E. *Yasal Kürtler*. Istanbul: Utopya Yayinevi, 2005.
Demir, M. G. *1980'lerden 2000'lere Siyasal Kürt Kadınının İnşası*. Istanbul: Belge Yayınları, 2015.
Demokrasi Partisi (DEP). *Program* (date and place of publication not mentioned).
Demokratik Bölgeler Partisi (DBP). *Demokratik Bölgeler Partisi Demokratik Ekolojik Katılımcı Kadın Özgürlükçü Yerel Yönetim Modeli ve Bir Gasp Aracı Olarak Kayyum Uygulamaları*. Diyarbakır, 2017.
Deniz, H. *Diyarbakır Dış Ticareti 2014 (Export of Diyarbakır 2014)*. Karacadağ Kalkınma Ajansı. Diyarbakır, 2014.
Diken, Ş. and Baysal, N. *Kürdistan'da Sivil Toplum*. Istanbul: İletişim Yayınları, 2015.

Dirik, D. 'The Revolution of Smiling Women: Stateless Democracy and Power in Rojava'. In *Routledge Handbook of Postcolonial Politics*, edited by O. U. Rutazibwa and B. Shilliam, 222–38. London and New York: Routledge, 2018.

Dirik, D. *The Uprising of the Oldest Colony: Patriarchy, State and Capitalist Modernity in Kurdistan*. PhD diss., University of Cambridge, Cambridge, 2018.

Disch, L. 'Toward a Mobilization Conception of Democratic Representation'. *American Political Science Review*, 105:1 (2011): 100–14.

Disch, L. 'The Constructivist Turn in Democratic Representation: A Normative Dead-End?' *Constellations*, 22:4 (2015): 487–99.

Domhoff, G. W. *Who Rules America?* New York: McGraw Hill Education, 7th Edition, 2013.

Donahue, L. 'Terrorism and the counter-terrorist discourse'. In *Global Anti-Terrorism Law and Policy*, edited by V. Ramraj, M. Hor and K. Roach, 13–36. Cambridge: Cambridge University Press, 2005.

Dovi, S. 'Political Representation'. In *The Stanford Encyclopedia of Philosophy*, edited by E. Zalta. Stanford, CA: Stanford University Press, 2007.

Dovi, S. 'Hannah Pitkin: The Concept of Representation'. In *The Oxford Handbook of Classics in Contemporary Political Theory*, edited by J. Levy. Oxford: Oxford University Press, 2015.

Drechselová, L, 'The Kurdish Women's Political Organizing from the Feminist Neo-Institutionalist Perspective'. In *Kurds in Turkey: Ethnographies of Heterogenous Experiences*, edited by A. Çelik and L. Drechselová, 31–58. Lanham: Lexington Books, 2019.

DTK. *Kürt Sorununun Çözümü İçin Demokratik Özerklik*. Diyarbakır: Aram, 2012.

DTP. *Demokratik Toplum Partisi'nin Kürt Sorununa İlişkin Demokratik Çözüm Projesi*. Ankara, 2008.

Eccarius-Kelly, V. *The Militant Kurds. A Dual Strategy for Freedom*. Santa Barbara, CA: Praeger, 2011.

Eisenberg, A. and Spinner-Halev, J. (eds) *Minorities within Minorities: Equality, Rights and Diversity*. Cambridge: Cambridge University Press, 2005.

Ekmekci, F. 'Understanding Kurdish Ethno-nationalism in Turkey: Socio-Economy, Religion, and Politics'. *Ethnic and Racial Studies*, 34:9 (2011): 1608–17.

Emre Cetin, K. B. 'Television and the Making of a Transnational Alevi Identity'. *National Identities*, 20:1 (2018): 91–103.

Entessar, N. *Kurdish Ethnonationalism*. London: Lynne Reinner Publishers, 1992.

Ertur, K. *The Political Integration of the Kurds in Turkey*. PhD diss., Portland State University, Oregon, 1979.

Eşiyok, B. A. 'Kalkınmada Bölgesel Farklılıklar Büyüme Kutupları ve GAP (Tespitler ve Çözüm Önerileri)'. Türkiye Kalkınma Bankası, Ankara, 2012.

Ezrow, N. 'Hybrid Regimes'. In *The SAGE Encyclopedia of Political Behavior*, edited by F. Moghaddam. London: SAGE Publications, 2017.

Fanon, F. *The Wretched of the Earth*. London: Penguin Classics, 2001.

Fekete, L. *Europe's Fault Lines: Racism and the Far Right*. London: Verso, 2017.

Fishkin, J. and Laslett, P. (eds) *Debating Deliberative Democracy*. Hoboken, NJ: Wiley, 2008.

Freeman, J. 'The Tyranny of Structurelessness'. *Berkeley Journal of Sociology*, 17 (1972): 151–65.

Freire, P. *The Pedagogy of the Oppressed*. New York: Continuum, 30th Anniversary Edition, 2000.

Ganser, D. *Nato's Secret Armies. Operation Gladio and Terrorism in Western Europe*. London and New York: Routledge, 2004.

Geary, K., Hildyard, N. and Yildiz, K. 'Holding Investors to Account: The Ilisu Dam Campaign'. In *Listen to the Refugee's Story: How U.K. Foreign Investment Creates Refugees and Asylum Seekers*, edited by E. Schmid. London: Ilisu Dam Refugees Project, The Corner House, and Peace in Kurdistan, 2003.

Geerdink, F. *The Boys are Dead: The Roboski Massacre and the Kurdish Question in Turkey*. London: Gomidas Institute, 2015.

Gerth, H. H. and Wright Mills, C. 'Introduction'. In *From Max Weber: Essays in Sociology*, edited by H. H. Gerth and C. Wright Mills, 3–74. Abingdon, Oxon: Routledge, 1991.

Green, L. 'Internal minorities and their rights'. In *Group Rights*, edited by J. Baker, 257–72. Toronto: University of Toronto Press, 1994.

Grigoriadis, I. N. 'Political Participation of Turkey's Kurds and Alevis: A Challenge for Turkey's Democratic Consolidation'. *Southeast European and Black Sea Studies*, 6:4 (2006): 445–61.

Grigoriadis, I. N. 'Türk or Türkiyeli? The Reform of Turkey's Minority Legislation and the Rediscovery of Ottomanism'. *Middle Eastern Studies*, 43:3 (2007): 423–38.

Göbel, C. 'Semiauthoritarianism'. In *21st Century Political Science: A Reference Handbook*, edited by J. Ishiyame and M. Breuning, 258–67. London: SAGE Publications, 2011.

Gökalp, D. 'A gendered analysis of violence, justice and citizenship: Kurdish women facing war and displacement in Turkey'. *Women Studies International Forum*, 33 (2010): 261–9.

Guevara, E. C. *Guerrilla Warfare: A Method*. Peking: Foreign Language Press, 1964.

Gunes, C. 'Kurdish Politics in Turkey: Ideology, Identity and Transformations'. *Ethnopolitics*, 8:2 (2009): 255–62.

Gunes, C. *The Kurdish National Movement in Turkey: From Protest to Resistance*. London: Routledge, 2012.

Gunes, C. 'Unblocking the Impasse in Turkey's Kurdish Question'. *Peace Review: A Journal of Social Justice*, 24:4 (2012): 462–9.

Gunes, C. 'Accommodating Kurdish Demands in Turkey'. In *The Challenge of Non-Territorial Autonomy: Theory and Case Studies*, edited by E. Nimni, A. Osipov and D. Smith, 71–84. Oxford: Peter Lang International Publishers, 2013.

Gunes, C. 'Explaining the PKK's Mobilization of Kurds in Turkey: Hegemony, Myth and Violence'. *Ethnopolitics*, 12:3 (2013): 247–67.

Gunes, C. 'Political Reconciliation in Turkey'. In *The Kurdish Question in Turkey: New Perspectives on Conflict, Representation and Reconciliation*, edited by C. Gunes and W. Zeydanlıoğlu, 258–81. London and New York: Routledge, 2014.

Gunes, C. 'The ISIS Factor: The Kurds as a Vanguard in the War on the Caliphate'. In *Kurdistan and the Middle East: New Challenges, New Balances?*, edited by S. Torelli, 71–90. Rome: Italian Institute for International Political Studies, 2016.

Gunes, C. 'The Kurdish Political Activism in Turkey: An Overview'. In *Kurdish Issues: Essays in Honor of Robert Olson*, edited by M. Gunter and M. Ahmed, 80–105. Costa Mesa: Mazda Publishers, 2016.

Gunes, C. 'Mobilisation of Kurds in Turkey during the 1980s and 1990s'. In *The Kurdish Question Revisited*, edited by G. Stansfield and M. Shareef, 187–98. London: Hurst and Co., 2017.

Gunes, C. 'Turkey's New Left'. *New Left Review*, 107 (2017): 9–30.

Gunes, C. 'The rise of the pro-Kurdish democratic movement in Turkey'. In *Routledge Handbook on the Kurds*, edited by M. Gunter, 259–69. London and New York: Routledge, 2018.

Gunes, C. *The Kurds in a New Middle East: The Changing Geopolitics of a Regional Conflict*. London: Palgrave MacMillan, 2019.

Gunes, C. 'Unpacking "Democratic Confederalism" and "Democratic Autonomy" Proposals of the Kurdish Movement in Turkey'. In *Autonomy as a Model for Minority Self Government: From Theory to European and Middle Eastern Perspectives*, edited by O. Akbulut and E. Aktoprak, 246–69. Leiden: Brill Publishers, 2019.

Gunes, C. 'Approaches to Kurdish Autonomy in the Middle East'. *Nationalities Papers*, 48(2) (2019): 323–38. doi:10.1017/nps.2019.21.

Gunes, C. 'Political representation of Alevi Kurds in Turkey: Historical trends and main transformations'. *Kurdish Studies* (2020): 71–90.

Gunes, C. and Gürer, Ç. 'Kurdish Movement's Democratic Autonomy Proposals in Turkey'. In *Democratic Representation in Plurinational States: The Kurds in Turkey*, edited by E. Nimni and E. Aktoprak, 159–75. London: Palgrave McMillan, 2018.

Gunes, C. and Lowe, R. *The Impact of the Syrian War on Kurdish Politics Across the Middle East*. London: The Royal Institute of International Affairs, 2015.

Gunes, C. and Zeydanlıoğlu, W. (eds) *The Kurdish Question in Turkey: New Perspectives on Conflict, Representation and Reconciliation*. London and New York: Routledge, 2014.

Gunter, M. *The Kurds and the Future of Turkey*. London: Palgrave, 1997.

Gürbüz, M. *Rival Kurdish Movements in Turkey: Transforming Violent Conflict*. Amsterdam: Amsterdam University Press, 2016.

Gürer, Ç. *Demokratik Özerklik: Bir Yurtdaşlık Heterotopyası*. Istanbul: Notabene Yayınları, 2015.

Gurses, M. 'Is Islam a Cure for Ethnic Conflict? Evidence from Turkey', *Politics and Religion*, 8 (2015): 135–54.

Gurses, M. *Anatomy of a Civil War: Sociopolitical Impacts of the Kurdish Conflict in Turkey*. Ann Arbor: University of Michigan Press, 2018.

Gutmann, A. and Thompson, D. *Why Deliberative Democracy?* Princeton, NJ: Princeton University Press, 2002.

Hacker-Cordón, C. 'Electoral Legitimation, Polyarchy, and Democratic Legitimacy'. *American Political Science Association*. Foundations Section, Washington, DC: 2001.

Hall, S., (ed.) *Representation. Cultural Representation and Signifying Practices*. London: SAGE, 1997.

Happel, K. 'Introduction'. In Abdullah Öcalan, *Prison Writings: The Roots of Civilisation* (translated by Klaus Happel). Pluto Press: London, 2006.

HDP. *Büyük İnsanlık-Bizler Meclise*. Ankara, 2015.

Hobsbawm, E. *Nations and Nationalism since 1780*. Cambridge: Cambridge University Press, 1990.

Houston, C. *Islam, Kurds and the Turkish Nation State*. Oxford and New York: Berg, 2001.

Hroch, M. *The Social Preconditions of National Revival in Europe*. New York: Columbia University Press, 2000.

Ikduygu, A. et al. 'The Ethnic Question in an Environment of Insecurity: The Kurds in Turkey'. *Ethnic and Racial Studies*, 22:6 (1999): 991–1010.

İlyas, A. 'Türkiye'de Aşiret Siyaset İlişkisi: Urfa Örneği (1950-2003)'. MA diss., Selcuk University, Konya, 2009.

International Crisis Group. 'Managing Turkey's PKK Conflict: The Case of Nusaybin' (2017). Brussels, Belgium.

Izady, M. *The Kurds: A Concise Handbook*. London and Washington: Taylor Francis, 1992.

Jarstadt, A. K. and Sisk, T. D. *From War to Democracy: Dilemmas of Peacebuilding*. Cambridge: Cambridge University Press, 2008.

Jenkins, C., Aydın, S. and Cetin, U. (eds) *Alevism as an Ethno-Religious Identity: Contested Boundaries*. London and New York: Routledge, 2018.

Jenkins, G. *Political Islam in Turkey – Running West, Heading East?* London: Palgrave MacMillan, 2008.

Jennings, I. *The Approach to Self-Government*. Cambridge: Cambridge University Press, [1956] 2011.

Jongerden, J. 'Resettlement and reconstruction of identity: the case of Kurds in Turkey'. *Ethnopolitics*, 1:1 (2001): 80–8.

Jongerden, J. and Akkaya, A. H., 'Born From the Left: the Making of the PKK'. In *Nationalims and politics in Turkey: Political Islam, Kemalism and the Kurdish Issue*, edited by M. Casier and J. Jongerden, 123–42. London and New York: Routledge, 2011.

Käser, I., '"Mountain Life is Difficult but Beautiful!": The gendered process of "becoming free" in PKK education'. In *Kurds in Turkey: Ethnographies of Heterogenous Experiences*, edited by A. Çelik and L. Drechselová, 11–30. Lanham: Lexington Books, 2019.

Karadeniz, S. 'Aşiret Sisteminde Dönüşüm: Aşiretlerin Kentte Aldığı Yeni Şekiller – Batman Örneği'. PhD diss., İnönü University, Malatya, 2012.

Karakoç, K. and Sarigil, Z. 'Why Religious People Support Ethnic Insurgency? Kurds, Religion and Support for the PKK', *Politics and Religion*, 13:2 (2020): 245–72.

Kaya, M. S. *The Zaza Kurds of Turkey: A Middle Eastern Minority in a Globalised Society*. London: I.B. Tauris, 2011.

Kendal, N. 'Kurdistan in Turkey'. In *A People Without a Country: The Kurds and Kurdistan*, edited by G. Chaliand, 38–94. Zed Books: London, 1992.

Koefoed, M. 'Martyrdom and Emotional Resistance in the Case of Northern Kurdistan: Hidden and Public Emotional Resistance'. *Journal of Political Power*, 10:2 (2017): 184–99.

KONDA Araştırma ve Danışmanlık, *Siyasal ve Toplumsal Araştırmalar Dizisi*. Istanbul, 2018.

KONDA Araştırma ve Danışmanlık, *7 Haziran Sandık ve Seçmen Analizi*. Istanbul, 2015.

Kukathas, C. 'Are there any cultural rights?'. *Political Theory*, 20:1 (1992): 105–39.

Kurt, M. *Kurdish Hizbullah in Turkey: Islamism, Violence and the State*. London: Pluto Press, 2017.

Kurt, M. '"My Muslim Kurdish brother": colonial rule and Islamist governmentality in the Kurdish region of Turkey'. *Journal of Balkan and Near Eastern Studies*, 21:3 (2019): 350–65.

Kymlicka, W. 'National Cultural Autonomy and International Minority Rights Norms'. *Ethnopolitics*, 6:3 (2007): 379–93.

Laclau, E. and Mouffe, C. *Hegemony and Socialist Strategy*. London: Verso, 1986.

Lapidoth, R. *Autonomy: Flexible Solutions to Ethnic Conflicts*. Washington, DC: United States Institute of Peace, 1996.

Leese, D. *Mao Cult: Rhetoric and Ritual in China's Cultural Revolution*. Cambridge: Cambridge University Press, 2011.

Leezenberg, M. 'Political Islam among the Kurds'. In *The Kurds: Nationalism and Politics*, edited by F. A. Jabar and H. Dawood, 203–30. London: Saqi, 2006.

Leib, E. 'Can Direct Democracy Be Made Deliberative?' *Buffalo Law Review*, 54 (2006): 903–25.

Levitsky, S. and Loxton, J. 'Populism and Competitive Authoritarianism in the Andes'. *Democratization*, 20 (2013): 107–36.

Levitsky, S. and Way, L. *Competitive Authoritarianism: Hybrid Regimes after the Cold War*. Cambridge: Cambridge University Press, 2010.

Lijphart, A. 'Consociational Democracy'. *World Politics*, 25: 2 (1969): 207–25.

Lindblom, C. *Charisma*. Oxford: Oxford University Press, 1993.

Linz, J. 'Early State-Building and Late Peripheral Nationalisms against the State: The Case of Spain'. In *Building States and Nations. Analysis by Region, Vol. II*, edited by N. S. Eisenstadt and S. Rokkan, 32–116. Beverly Hills: Sage Publications, 1973.

Linz, J. 'From Primordialism to Nationalism'. In *New Nationalisms of the Developed West*, edited by Edward A. Tiriyakian and Ronald Rogowski, 203–53. Boston: Allen & Unwin, 1985.

Linz, J. 'State Building and Nation Building'. *European Review*, 1:4 (1993): 355–69.

Linz, J. 'Democracy, Multinationalism, and Federalism'. *Working Paper*, No. 103. Madrid: Centro de Estudios Avanzados en Ciencias Sociales, Instituto Juan March de Estudios e Investigaciones, 1997.

Linz, J. *Totalitarian and Authoritarian Regimes*. Boulder, CO: Lynne Reinner Publishers, 2000.

Linz, J. with Miley, T. 'Cautionary and Unorthodox Thoughts about Democracy Today'. In *Institutions and Democracy: Essays in Honor of Alfred Stepan*, edited by D. Chalmers and S. Mainwaring, 227–52. South Bend, IN: University of Notre Dame Press, 2012.

Linz, J. and Stepan, A. *Problems of Democratic Transition and Consolidation*. Baltimore: The Johns Hopkins University Press, 1996.

Linz, J., Stepan, A. and Yadav, Y. *Crafting State-Nations: India and Other Multi-National Democracies*. Baltimore: The Johns Hopkins University Press, 2011.

Lipovsky, I. P. *The Socialist Movement in Turkey 1960–1980*. Leiden: Brill, 1992.

Loxton, J. 'Competitive Authoritarianism'. In *The SAGE Encyclopedia of Political Behavior*, edited by F. Moghaddam. London: SAGE Publications, 2017.

Lustick, I. *Unsettled States, Disputed Lands: Britain and Ireland, France and Algeria, Israel and the West Bank-Gaza*. Ithaca, NY: Cornell University Press, 1995.

Mainwaring, S. 'Review: From Representative Democracy to Participatory Competitive Authoritarianism: Hugo Chávez and Venezuelan Politics'. *Perspectives on Politics*, 10:4 (2012): 955–67.

Malley, R. and Finer, J. 'The Long Shadow of 9/11. How Counter-terrorism Warps U.S. Foreign Policy'. *Foreign Affairs* (July/August 2018): 58–69.

Manin, B. *The Principles of Representative Government*. Cambridge: Cambridge University Press, 1997.

Mansbridge, J. 'Should Blacks represent Blacks and Women represent Women? A Contingent "Yes"'. *Journal of Politics*, 61:3 (1999): 628–57.

Mansbridge, J. and Parkinson, J. (eds) *Deliberative Systems*. Cambridge: Cambridge University Press, 2012.

Manwaring, M. 'The Environment as a Global Stability-Security Issue'. In *Environmental Security and Global Stability. Problems and Responses*, edited by M. Manwaring. Lanham, MD: Lexington Books, 2002.

Matthews, D. H. and Miley, Thomas J. 'Review of Abdullah Öcalan's *Manifesto for a Democratic Civilization*'. In *Your Freedom and Mine: Abdullah Öcalan and the Kurdish Question in Erdoğan's Turkey*, edited by T. J. Miley and F. Venturini, 337–52. Montreal: Black Rose Books, 2018.

McDowall, D. *A Modern History of the Kurds*. London: I.B. Tauris, 1996.

McGarry, J. and O'Leary, B. 'Consociational Theory and Peace Agreements in Pluri-National Places: Northern Ireland and Other Cases'. In *The Failure of the Middle East Peace Process? A Comparative Analysis of Peace Implementation in Israel/Palestine, Northern Ireland, and South Africa*, edited by G. Ben-Porat, 70–96. London: Palgrave MacMillan, 2008.

Miley, T. J. 'Against the Thesis of the "Civic Nation": The Case of Catalonia in Contemporary Spain'. *Nationalism and Ethnic Politics*, 13 (2007): 1–37.

Miley, T. J. 'Franquism as Authoritarianism: Juan Linz and his Critics'. *Politics, Religion & Ideology*, 12:1 (2011): 27–50.

Miley, T. J. 'Democratic Representation and the National Dimension in Catalan and Basque Politics'. *International Journal of Politics, Culture and Society*, 27 (2014): 291–322.
Miley, T. J. 'State Terror, Human Rights Violations, and Authoritarianism in Turkey. Report of the Third Imrali Peace Delegation Based on its Visit to Turkey, Feb. 13–19, 2017'. In *Your Freedom and Mine: Abdullah Ocalan and the Kurdish Question in Erdoğan's Turkey*, edited by T. J. Miley and F. Venturini, 225–58. Montreal: Black Rose Books, 2018.
Miley, T. J. 'The Nation as Hegemonic Project', *Journal of Political Ideologies*, 23:2 (2018): 183–204.
Miley, T. with Hammy, C. and Yildiz, G. 'The Turkish-Kurdish Conflict in Historical Context'. In *Your Freedom and Mine: Abdullah Öcalan and the Kurdish Question in Erdoğan's Turkey*, edited by T. Miley and F. Venturini, 3–123. Montreal: Black Rose Books, 2018.
Miliband, R. *The State in Capitalist Society*. New York, NY: Basic Books, 1969.
Natali, D. *The Kurds and the State. Evolving National Identity in Iraq, Turkey, and Iran*. Syracuse, NY: Syracuse University Press, 2005.
Nimni, E. 'Introduction: The National Cultural Autonomy Model Revisited'. In *National Cultural Autonomy and Its Contemporary Critics*, edited by E. Nimni, 1–12. London and New York: Routledge, 2005.
Nimni, E. (ed.) *National Cultural Autonomy and its Contemporary Critics*. London and New York: Routledge, 2005.
O'Ballance, E. *The Kurdish Struggle, 1920–1994*. London: Palgrave MacMillan, 1996.
Öcalan, A. *Kürdistan Devriminin Yolu (Manifesto)* (4th Edition). Cologne: Weşanên Serxwebûn, 1992.
Öcalan, A. *Ek Savunma: Kürt Sorununda Çözüm ve Çözümsuzluk İkilemi*. Istanbul: Mem Yayınları, 1999.
Öcalan, A. *Savunma: Kürt Sorununda Demokratik Çözüm Bildirgesi*. Istanbul: Mem Yayınları, 1999.
Öcalan, A. *AİHM Savunmaları (Cilt 1): Sümer Rahip Develtinden Demokratik Cumhuriyete*. Cologne: Mezopotamya Yayınları, 2004.
Öcalan, A. *AİHM Savunmaları (Cilt 2): Sümer Rahip Develtinden Demokratik Cumhuriyete*. Cologne: Mezopotamya Yayınları, 2004.
Öcalan, A. *The Roots of Civilization*. Transmedia Publishing Limited, 2007.
Öcalan, A. *Demokratik Toplum Manifestosu*. Cologne: Mezopotamya Yayınları, 2009.
Öcalan, A. *War and Peace in Kurdistan. Perspectives for a Political Solution to the Kurdish Question*. Cologne: International Initiative, 2009.
Öcalan, A. *Democratic Confederalism*. London and Cologne: Tansmedia Publishing, 2011.
Öcalan, A. *Prison Writings. The PKK and the Kurdish Question in the 21st Century*. Cologne: International Initiative, 2011.
Öcalan, A. *Prison Writings III: The Road Map to Negotiations*. Cologne: International Initiative, 2012.
Öcalan, A. *Prison Writings: The PKK and the Kurdish Question in the Twenty-First Century*. Cologne: International Initiative, 2013.
Öcalan, A. *Liberating Life: Woman's Revolution*. Cologne: International Initiative, 2013.
Öcalan, A. *Manifesto for a Democratic Civilization. Volume One: The Age of Masked Gods and Disguised Kings*. Prosgrunn, Norway: New Compass Press, 2015.
Öcalan, A. *Democratic Nation*. Cologne: International Initiative, 2016.
Öcalan, A. *Manifesto for a Democratic Civilization. Volume Two: The Age of Unmasked Gods and Naked Kings*. Prosgrunn, Norway: New Compass Press, 2017.
Öcalan, A. *The Political Thought of Abdullah Öcalan: Kurdistan, Women's Revolution and Democratic Confederalism*. London: Pluto Press, 2017.

Öcalan, A. 'Seek the Truth'. In *Your Freedom and Mine: Abdullah Öcalan and the Kurdish Question in Erdgoan's Turkey*, edited by T. Miley and F. Venturini, 315–22. Montreal: Black Rose Books, 2018.
O'Donnell, G., Schmitter, P. and Whitehead, L. (eds) *Transitions from Authoritarian Rule: Tentative Conclusions about Uncertain Democracies*. Baltimore: The Johns Hopkins University Press, 1986.
Ölmez, A. O. *Türkiye Siyasetinde DEP Depremi*. Ankara: Doruk Yayınları, 1995.
Oremar, K. *Eyşe Şan: Prensesa Bê Tac û Text*. Diyarbakır: Lis, 2012.
Özar, S., Uçarlar, N. and Aytar, O. *From Past to Present a Paramilitary Organization*. Diyarbakır: Diyarbakır Institute for Political and Social Research (Disa), 2013.
Özcan, A. K. *Turkey's Kurds. A Theoretical Analysis of the PKK and Abdullah Öcalan*. London: Routledge, 2006.
Palermo, F. 'Owned or Shared? Territorial Autonomy in the Minority Discourse'. In *Minority Accommodation through Territorial and Non-Territorial Autonomy*, edited by T. H. Malloy et al., 13–32. Oxford: Oxford University Press, 2015.
Pateman, C. *Participation and Democratic Theory*. Cambridge: Cambridge University Press, 1970.
Phillips, A. *The Politics of Presence*. Oxford: Oxford University Press, 1995.
Pitkin, H. *The Concept of Representation*. Berkeley, CA: University of California Press, 1967.
PKK. *Politik Rapor: Merkez Komitesi Tarafindan PKK 1. Konferansina Sunulmuştur*. Cologne: Weşanên Serxwebûn, 1982.
PKK. *Kürt Sorununda Çözüme Doğru Demokratik Özerklik*. Abdullah Öcalan Sosyal Bilimler Akademisi Yayınları, 2005 (place of publication not stated).
PKK. *Program ve Tüzüğü*. Cologne: Weşanên Serxwebûn, 2005.
PKK. 'Demokratik Özerklik', *Serxwebûn*, 301 (2007): 55–9.
Poulantzas, N. 'The Problem of the Capitalist State'. *New Left Review*, 58 (1969): 67–78.
Poulantzas, N. *Fascism and Dictatorship: The Third International and the Problem of Fascism*. London: NLB, 1970.
Prina, F., Smith, D. J. and Sansum, J. M. 'National Cultural Autonomy in Central and Eastern Europe: Challenges and Possibilities'. In *Democratic Representation in Plurinational States: The Case of Kurds in Turkey*, edited by N. Nimni and E. Aktoprak, 85–111. London: Palgrave Macmillan, 2018.
Przeworski, A. *Democracy and the Limits of Self-Government*. Cambridge: Cambridge, University Press, 2010.
Przeworski, A. and M. Wallerstein. 'The Structural Dependence of the State on Capital'. *The American Political Science Review*, 82:1 (1988): 11–29.
Przeworski, A., et al. (eds) *Democracy, Accountability, and Representation*. Cambridge: Cambridge University Press, 1999.
Redhead, M. *Charles Taylor: Thinking and Living Deep Diversity*. Lanham, MD: Rowman & Littlefield, 2002.
Ricoeur, P. *Freud and Philosophy: An Essay on Interpretation*. New Haven, CT: Yale University Press, 1993.
Robinson, W. *Promoting Polyarchy*. Cambridge: Cambridge University Press, 1996.
Roemer, J. et al. *Racism, Xenophobia, and Distribution: Multi-Issue Politics in Advanced Democracies*. Cambridge: Russell Sage Foundation Books, 2007.
Romano, D. *The Kurdish Nationalist Movement. Opportunity, Mobilization, Identity*. Cambridge: Cambridge University Press, 2006.
Ross, C. *The Leaderless Revolution: How Ordinary People Can Take Power and Change Politics in the 21st Century*. London: Simon and Schuster, 2011.

Saeed, S. *Kurdish Politics in Turkey. From the PKK to the KCK*. London: Routledge, 2017.
Sagnic, C. 'Mountain Turks: State Ideology and the Kurds in Turkey'. *Information, Society and Justice*, 3:2 (2010): 127–34.
Sahin, Z. 'The Political Representation of Kurdish, Kemalist, and Conservative Muslim Women in Turkey (1990–2010)'. PhD diss., The University of Southern California, 2011.
Saraçoğlu, C. *Kurds of Modern Turkey: Migration, Neoliberalism and Exclusion in Turkish Society*. London and New York: I.B. Tauris, 2011.
Sarigil, Z. 'Curbing Kurdish Ethno-nationalism in Turkey: An Empirical Assessment of Pro-Islamic and Socioeconomic Approaches'. *Ethnic and Racial Studies*, 33:3 (2010): 533–53.
Sarigil, Z. *Ethnic Boundaries in Turkish Politics: The Secular Kurdish Movement and Islam*. New York: New York University Press, 2018.
Sarigil, Z. and Fazlioglu, O. 'Religion and ethno-nationalism: Turkey's Kurdish issue'. *Nations and Nationalism*, 19:3 (2013): 551–71.
Saward, M. 'The Representative Claim'. *Contemporary Political Theory*, 5:3 (2006): 297–318.
Saward, M. *The Representative Claim*. Oxford University Press: Oxford, 2010.
Scarrow, S. E. 'Political Parties and Party Systems'. In *Comparing Democracies: Elections and Voting in the 21st Century*, edited by L. LeDuc, R. G. Niemi and P. Norris. London: Sage, 2010.
Schmid, A. 'The Definition of Terrorism'. In *The Routledge Handbook of Terrorism Research*, edited by A. Schmid. Oxford: Routledge, 2011.
Schmid, E. (ed.) *A Permanent State of Terror?* London: Campaign Against Criminalising Communities, CAMPACC, 2003.
Scott, J. *Domination and the Arts of Resistance: Hidden Transcripts*. New Haven, CT: Yale University Press, 1990.
Shaw, S. J. and Shaw, E. K. *History of the Ottoman Empire and Modern Turkey. Volume II: Reform, Revolution and Republic: The Rise of Modern Turkey, 1808–1975*. Cambridge: Cambridge University Press, 1977.
Sirkeci, I. 'Exploring the Kurdish population in the Turkish context', *Genus*, 56:1–2 (2000): 149–75.
Sivanandan, A. *Racism, Liberty and the War on Terror*. London: Institute for Race Relations, 2006.
Smith, R. *Stories of Peoplehood*. Cambridge: Cambridge University Press, 2003.
Smith, D. J. and Cordell, K. 'Introduction: The Theory and Practice of Cultural Autonomy in Central and Eastern Europe'. *Ethnopolitics*, 6:3 (2007): 337–43.
Soleimani, K. *Islam and Competing Nationalisms in the Middle East, 1876–1926*. New York: Palgrave Macmillan, 2016.
Sönmez, M. 'Batı'ya Kürt Göçü ve G.Doğu'yu Kalkındırma Söylemi … '. *Iktisat ve Toplum*, 31–2 (2015): 47–52.
Söyler, M. *The Turkish Deep State: State Consolidation, Civil-Military Relations and Democracy*. London and New York: Routledge, 2015.
Stepan, A. and Miley, T. J. 'Federacy and the Kurds: Might This New Political Form Help Mitigate Hobbesian Conflict in Turkey, Iraq, and Syria'. In *Forms of Pluralism and Democratic Constitutionalism*, edited by J. Cohen and A. Arato. New York: Columbia University Press, 2018.
Sümer, F. 'Yerel Bir Güç Olarak Aşiretin Siyasal Fonksiyonu'. PhD diss., Hacettepe University, Ankara, 2009.
Summers, D. 'Dancing with the Devil'. In *Your Freedom and Mine: Abdullah Öcalan and the Kurdish Question in Erdoğan's Turkey*, edited by T. Miley and F. Venturini, 385–9. Montreal: Black Rose Books, 2018.

Süreç Araştırma Merkezi. *Geçici Köy Koruculuğu Sistemi ve Barış Süreci*. Istanbul, 2015.
Tansey, O. 'Process Tracing and Elite Interviewing: A Case for Non-probability Sampling', *PS: Political Science and Politics*, 40:4 (2007), 765–72.
Tasdemir, S. 'The Feminization of pro-Kurdish Party Politics in Turkey: The Role of Women Activists'. PhD diss., The University of Exeter, Exeter, 2013.
Taylor, C. *Multiculturalism and The Politics of Recognition*. Princeton: Princeton University Press, 1992.
Therborn, G. *What Does the Ruling Class Do When It Rules?* London: NLB, 1978.
Therborn, G. *From Marxism to Post-Marxism?* London: Verso, 2008.
TİHV. *Türkiye İnsan Hakları Raporu 1994*. Ankara: TİHV Yayınları, 1995.
Tong, J. *Comparative Peace Processes*. New Jersey: Wiley, 2014.
Toprak, M. et al. 'Transformations of Turkish Politics: Socio-Political, Economic and Ethnic Particularities'. *bilig*, 50 (2009): 199–232.
Turan, İ. *Turkey's Difficult Journey to Democracy*. Oxford: Oxford University Press, 2015.
Türk, A. *DEP Savunması*. Ankara: Matsa Basımevi,1994.
Turkey Statistical Institute. *Household Labour Force Statistics 2011*. Ankara, 2012.
Türkiye Büyük Millet Meclisi İnsan Hakları İnceleme Komisyonu. *Terör ve Şiddet Olayları Kapsamında Yaşam Hakkı İhlallerini İnceleme Raporu*. Ankara: TBMM, 2013.
Türkiye Cumhuriyeti, Bilim, Sanayi ve Teknoloji Bakanlığı. *81 İl Durum Raporu*. Ankara, 2012.
Türkiye Tekstil İşverenleri Sendikası. 'Tekstil ve Hazır Giyim Sanayiinin Türk Ekonomisindeki Yeri'. Istanbul, 2014.
Uluç, A. V. 'Güneydoğu Anadolu Bölgesinin Toplumsal ve Siyasal Yapısı: Mardin Örnegi'nde Siyasal Katılım'. PhD diss., Istanbul University, Istanbul, 2010.
Uluç, A. V. 'Kürtlerde Sosyal ve Siyasal Örgütlenme: Aşiret'. *Mukaddime*, 2 (2010): 35–52.
Van Bruinessen, M. 'Between Guerrilla War and Political Murder: The Workers' Party of Kurdistan'. *Middle East Report*, 53 (1988).
Van Bruinessen, M. *Agha, Sheikh and State: The Social and Political Structure of Kurdistan*. London: Zed Books, 1992.
Van Bruinessen, M. *Mullahs, Sufis and Heretics: The Role of Religion in Kurdish Society*. Istanbul: The Isis Press, 2000.
Van Bruinessen, M. 'Kurds, states and tribes'. In *Tribes and Power: Nationalism and Ethnicity in the Middle East*, edited by F. A. Jabar and H. Dawod, 165–83. London: Saqi, 2002.
Van Ticaret ve Sanayi Odası (VANSTO). *Mayis Ayi Van İli Ekonomik Istatistikler*. Van, 2016.
Van Ticaret ve Sanayi Odası (VANSTO). *Van Sosyal ve Ekonomik Istatistikleri*. Van, 2016.
Weber, M. 'The Fundamental Concepts of Sociology'. In *The Theory of Social and Economic Organization*, edited by T. Parsons. New York: Free Press, 1964.
Weber, M. 'Politics as a Vocation'. In *From Max Weber: Essays in Sociology*, edited by H. H. Gerth and C. Wright Mills. Abingdon, Oxon: Routledge, 1991.
Weber, M. 'Structures of Power: The Nation'. In *From Max Weber: Essays in Sociology*, edited by H. H. Gerth and C. Wright Mills. Abingdon, Oxon: Routledge, 1991.
Weber, M. 'The Sociology of Charismatic Authority'. In *From Max Weber: Essays in Sociology*, edited by H. H. Gerth and C. Wright Mills. Abingdon, Oxon: Routledge, 1991.
Weismann, I. *The Naqshibandiyya: Orthodoxy and Activism in a Worldwide Sufi Tradition*. London and New York: Routledge, 2007.
White, P. *Primitive Rebels or Revolutionary Modernizers? The Kurdish National Movement in Turkey*. London: Zed Books, 2000.

White, T. (ed.) *Lessons from the Northern Ireland Peace Process*. Madison, WI: The University of Wisconsin Press, 2014.
Wolfenstein, E.V. *Psychoanalytic-Marxism. Groundwork*. Free Association Books, 1993.
Yadirgi, V. *The Political Economy of the Kurds of Turkey: From the Ottoman Empire to the Turkish Republic*. Cambridge: Cambridge University Press, 2017.
Yalçın-Heckmann, L. 'Kurdish Tribal Orbanisation and Local Political Processes'. In *Turkish State, Turkish Society*, edited by Andrew Finkel and Nukhet Sirman, 289–312. London and New York: Routledge, 1990.
Yalçın-Heckmann, L. *Tribe and Kinship among the Kurds*. Frankfurt: Peter Lang Publishers, 1991.
Yanmış, M. 'Diyarbakır Halkının Geleneksel ve Dini Değerlerdeki Değişime Yaklaşımı Üzerine Sosyolojik bir İnceleme'. PhD diss., Uludağ University, Bursa, 2015.
Yanmış, M. and Aktaş, A. 'Diyarbakır Sultan Şeyhmuse Ezzulli Dergahı Örneğinde Tarikatların Sosyal İşlevi'. *International Journal of Kurdish Studies*, 1:1 (2015): 1–26.
Yarkın, G. 'The Ideological Transformation of the PKK Regarding the Political Economy of the Kurdish Regions of Turkey'. *Kurdish Studies*, 3:1 (2015): 26–46.
Yeğen, M. 'Turkish Nationalism and the Kurdish Question'. *Ethnic and Racial Studies*, 30:1 (2007): 119–51.
Yeğen, M. 'The Turkish State Discourse and the exclusion of Kurdish identity'. *Middle Eastern Studies*, 32 (1996): 216–29.
Yeğen, M., Tol, U. U. and Çalışkan, M. A. *Kürtler Ne İstiyor? Kürdistanda Etnik Kimlik, Dindarlık, Sınıf ve Seçimler*. Istanbul: İletişim, 2016.
Yildiz, K. and Breau, S. *The Kurdish Conflict: International Humanitarian Law and Post-Conflict Mechanisms*. London: Routledge, 2010.
Yoruk, E. 'Welfare Provision as Political Containment: The Politics of Social Assistance and the Kurdish Conflict in Turkey'. *Politics & Society*, 40:4 (2012): 517–47.
Yüksel, M. 'A 'Revolutionary' Kurdish Mullah from Turkey: Mehmed Emin Bozarslan and his Intellectual Evolution'. *The Muslim World*, 99 (2009): 356–80.
Zeydanlıoğlu, W. 'Torture and Turkification in the Diyarbakır Military Prison'. In *Rights, Citizenship & Torture: Perspectives on Evil, Law and the State*, edited by J. T. Parry and W. Zeydanlıoğlu, 73–92. Oxford: Inter-Disciplinary Press, 2009.
Zürcher, E. J. *Turkey: A Modern History* (4th edition). London and New York: I.B. Tauris, 2017.

Online sources

Al Jazeera. 'Istanbul police use tear gas to disperse Women's Day marchers' (2019). Available online: https://www.aljazeera.com/news/2019/03/istanbul-police-tear-gas-disperse-women-day-marchers-190308193151561.html (accessed 9 July 2019).
Al Jazeera. 'Kürdsiad İsmine Veto' (2014). Available online: http://www.aljazeera.com.tr/haber/kurdsiad-ismine-veto (accessed 16 October 2015).
Akyol, M. 'Why Erdoğan fired Turkey's top cleric', *Al Monitor* (2017). Available online: http://www.al-monitor.com/pulse/originals/2017/08/turkey-why-erdogan-dismiss-top-cleric.html (accessed 6 August 2017).
Alonso, A. and Verge, T. 'Territorial Dynamics and Gender Equality Policies in Spain', *Fédéralisme Régionalisme* 14 (2014). Available online: http://popups.ulg.ac.be/1374-3864/index.php?id=1365 (accessed 26 July 2010).

Anadolu Ajansı. 'Başbakan Yıldırım: Terör örgütüyle ilişkili bütün öğretmenler açığa alınacak' (2016). Available online: https://www.aa.com.tr/tr/gunun-basliklari/basbakan-yildirim-teror-orgutuyle-iliskili-butun-ogretmenler-aciga-alinacak/640919 (accessed 24 October 2018).

Artı Gerçek. 'AKP'ye Menzilciler desteği' (2018). Available online: https://www.artigercek.com/haberler/akp-ye-menzilciler-destegi (accessed 29 August 2018).

Bagasi, İ. *Kendi Dilinden Hizbullah ve Mücadele Tarihinden Önemli Kesitler* (2004). Available online: www.huseynisevda.biz/Dokumanlar/Kendi_Dilinden_Hizbullah/00.html (accessed 30 July 2018).

BBC. 'IŞİD neden Adıyaman'da örgütlendi?' (2015). Available online: http://www.bbc.com/turkce/haberler/2015/10/151022_isid_adiyaman (accessed 17 November 2015).

BBC. 'Turkey rallies over murder of woman who "resisted rape"' (2015). Available online: http://www.bbc.com/news/world-europe-31476978 (accessed 28 September 2015).

BBC. 'Turkey president Erdoğan: Women are not equal to men' (2014). Available online: http://www.bbc.com/news/world-europe-30183711 (accessed 28 September 215).

BDP. 'Barış ve Demokrasi Partisi Programı' (2008). Available online: https://bdpblog.wordpress.com/parti-programimiz/ (accessed 25 July 2019).

BDP. 'Democratic Özerklik Projesi' (2011). Available online: https://bdpblog.wordpress.com/2011/05/04/demokratik-ozerklik-projesi/ (accessed 25 July 2019).

Bianet. 'Gözaltı Sayısı Beş Günde 1302'yi Buldu' (2015). Available online: https://m.bianet.org/bianet/insan-haklari/166393-gozalti-sayisi-bes-gunde-1302-yi-buldu (accessed 9 July 2019).

Bianet. 'HDP'li Vekillere Tutuklama ve Gözaltıların Kronolojisi' (2017). Available online: http://bianet.org/bianet/siyaset/183856-hdp-li-vekillere-tutuklama-ve-gozaltilarin-kronolojisi (accessed 28 July 2018).

Bianet. 'Issizlik' (2015). Available online: http://bianet.org/bianet/ekonomi/162827-tuik-2014-issizlik-orani-9-9 (accessed 25 September 2015).

Bianet. 'Kadınlar Kongra Jınên Azad'ı Kurdu' (2015). Available online: https://m.bianet.org/bianet/kadin/161974-kadinlar-kongra-jinen-azad-i-kurdu (accessed 30 August 2018)

Bianet. 'KESK'e KCK Operasyonu' (2012). Available online: http://bianet.org/bianet/siyaset/139298-kesk-e-kck-operasyonu (accessed 17 October 2015).

Blaser, N. and Stein, A. 'Islamic State's Network in Turkey' (2015). Available online: https://turkeywonk.wordpress.com/2015/10/30/the-islamic-states-network-in-turkey/ (accessed 12 November 2015).

Boffey, D. 'Turkey should investigate referendum vote "irregularities", says EU commission'. *The Guardian* (2017). Available online: https://www.theguardian.com/world/2017/apr/18/turkey-should-investigate-referendum-vote-irregularities-says-eu-commission (accessed 24 August 2018).

Cumhuriyet. 'Erdoğan, Barzani'yi kabul etti; Kürdistan bayrağı İstanbul'da göndere çekildi' (2017). Available online: http://www.cumhuriyet.com.tr/haber/dunya/685899/Erdogan__Barzani_yi_kabul_etti__Kurdistan_bayragi_istanbul_da_gondere_cekildi.html# (accessed 20 August 2018).

Cumhuriyet. 'Erdoğan: Yozgat milletvekili diye Kürt değil zannetmeyin, Bekir Bey Kürttür, Kürt' (2017). Available online: http://www.cumhuriyet.com.tr/haber/siyaset/796832/Erdogan__Yozgat_milletvekili_diye_Kurt_degil_zannetmeyin__Bekir_Bey_Kurttur__Kurt.html# (accessed 6 August 2017).

Cumhuriyet. 'İşte CHP'nin Kürt sorununa yeni bakışı' (2015). Available online: http://www.cumhuriyet.com.tr/haber/siyaset/262581/iste_CHP_nin_Kurt_sorununa_yeni_bakisi.html# (accessed 31 July 2017).

Demircan, E. 'TRC2 (Diyarbakır-Şanlıurfa) Bolgesi Issizlik Rakamlarinin Degerlendirmesi' (2014). Available online: https://www.karacadag.gov.tr/Dokuman/Dosya/www.karacadag.org.tr_204_KK8K88TO_trc2_diyarbakir_sanliurfa_bolgesi_issizlik_rakamlarinin_degerlendirmesi.pdf (accessed 25 September 2015).

Diken. 'Kürt siyasal hareketinin gençlik yapıları, DEM-GENÇ çatısı altında birleşiyor' (2015). Available online: http://www.diken.com.tr/kurt-siyasal-hareketinin-genclik-yapilari-dem-genc-catisi-altinda-birlesiyor/ (accessed 16 October 2015).

Disiad. 'Üyelerimiz (Members)' (2015). Available online: http://disiad.org.tr/uyelerimiz/ (accessed 15 September 2015).

Disiad. 'Disiad'dan Toplumsal Uzlaşı ve Barış girişimleri' (2015). Available online: http://disiad.org.tr/haber-arsivi/disiaddan-toplumsal-uzlasi-ve-baris-girisimleri/ (accessed 11 October 2015).

DİSK/Genel İş Sendikası. 'Emek Araştırması Raporu 7: Türkiye'de Emeğin Durumu' (2016). Available online: https://www.genel-is.org.tr/turkiyede-emegin-durumu-raporu,2,11091#.XsBkdkBFw2w (accessed 4 October 2016).

Diyarbakır Ticaret ve Sanayi Odası (DSTO). 'Faal Üye Sayısı (Firma Tipine Göre)' (2015). Available online: http://www.dtso.org.tr/2014/index.php/bilgi-bankasi/dtso/istatistik/uye-istatistikleri/faal-uye-firma-tipine-gore (accessed 25 October 2015).

DTK. 'Demokratik Toplum Kongresi Bileşenlerince Hazırlanmış Olan, Demokratik Özerk Kürdistan Modelinin Taslak Sunumu' (2010). Available online: http://bianet.org/files/doc_files/000/000/179/original/demokratiközerklik.htm (accessed 25 July 2019).

Eğitim-Sen. 'Laik, Bilimsel, Anadilinde Eğitim, Demokratik Yaşam ve Eşit Yurttaşlık İçin Mücadelemizi Kararlılıkla Sürdürüyoruz!' (2015). Available online: http://egitimsen.org.tr/laik-bilimsel-anadilinde-egitim-demokratik-yasam-ve-esit-yurttaslik-icin-mucadelemizi-kararlilikla-surduruyoruz/ (accessed 16 October 2015).

Ekinci, B. 'Tekke, Tarikat, Medrese'. *Al-Jazeera Turk Dergi* (2014). Available online: http://dergi.aljazeera.com.tr/2014/10/15/tekke-tarikat-medrese/ (accessed 13 March 2017).

Erdem, T. 'Türkiyeli Kürtler ne kadar?' (2013). Available online: http://www.radikal.com.tr/yazarlar/tarhan-erdem/turkiyeli-kurtler-ne-kadar-1130023/ (accessed 18 October 2015).

Finans Gündem. 'Nihat Özdemir Kürtlere ne söyledi' (2013). Available online: http://www.finansgundem.com/haber/nihat-ozdemir-kurtlere-ne-soyledi/367667 (accessed 2 August 2017).

Financial Times. 'Young Kurds take up arms as clashes increase in south-east Turkey' (2015). Available online: http://www.ft.com/intl/cms/s/0/d11a20a4-4a50-11e5-b558-8a9722977189.html#axzz3quSQYy8d (accessed 18 September 2015).

GAP. 'GAP Eylem Planı' (2010). Available online: http://www.gap.gov.tr/gap-eylem-plani-sayfa-25.html (accessed 10 October 2015).

Güsten, S. 'Mardin elects 25-year old Christian woman as mayor'. *Al Monitor* (2014). Available online: http://www.al-monitor.com/pulse/originals/2014/04/christian-mayor-turkey-rights-bdp-mardin.html#ixzz4WUjzuJYX (accessed 22 January 2017).

Haberdar.com. 'Kılıçdaroğlu: Sol yüzde 35'ten fazla oy alamaz (Röportaj: Amberin Zaman)' (2011). Available online: http://www.haberdar.com.tr/roportaj/kilicdaroglu-sol-yuzde-35ten-fazla-oy-alamaz-h11810.html (accessed 15 September 2015).

Haber Türk. 'Muztazaf-Der'in Kapatılmasına Yargıtay'dan Onay' (2012). Available online: http://www.haberturk.com/gundem/haber/741601-mustazaf-derin-kapatilmasina-yargitaydan-onay (accessed 15 March 2017).

Haber7. 'Kasiyerdi Türkiye'nin en zengini oldu' (2009). Available online: http://ekonomi.haber7.com/ekonomi/haber/421292-kasiyerdi-turkiyenin-en-zengini-oldu (accessed 18 October 2015).

Hacaloğlu, H. 'Erdoğan: Dolmabahçe Mutabakatı Doğru Değil', *VOA* (2015). Available online: https://www.amerikaninsesi.com/a/erdogan-dolmabahce-mutabakini-dogru-bulmuyorum/2690354.html (accessed 15 October 2018).

HAK-PAR. 'Hak ve Özgürlükler Partisi Programı' (2013). Available online: https://www.hakpar.org.tr/root/index.php?option=com_content&view=article&id=60&Itemid=86&lang=tr (accessed 2 August 2018).

HAK-PAR. 'İl Örgütleri' (2018). Available online: https://www.hakpar.org.tr/root/index.php?option=com_content&view=article&id=69&Itemid=66&lang=tr (accessed 2 August 2018).

HDP. *Parti Programı* (2012). Available online: http://www.hdp.org.tr/parti/parti-programi/8 (accessed 8 May 2017).

Hüda-Par. *Parti Programı* (2012). Available online: http://hudapar.org/Detay/Sayfalar/205/parti-programi.aspx (accessed 31 May 2017).

Hürriyet. 'CHP'den AK Parti'yi destekleyen iş adamlarıyla "gizli" görüşme' (2015). Available online: http://www.hurriyet.com.tr/chpden-ak-parti-yi-destekleyen-is-adamlariyla-gizli-gorusme-28559359 (accessed 19 October 2015).

Hürriyet. 'Ege Üniversitesi'nde kavga: Bir öğrenci öldü, biri ağır yaralandı' (2015). Available online: http://www.hurriyet.com.tr/ege-universitesinde-kavga-bir-ogrenci-oldu-biri-agir-yaralandi-28257188 (accessed 16 November 2015).

Hürriyet. 'Hizbullah'ın lideri Hacı İnan gözaltında' (2011). Available online: http://www.hurriyet.com.tr/gundem/hizbullahin-lideri-haci-inan-gozaltinda-16789783 (accessed 23 July 2019);

Hürriyet. 'Hizbullahçıların kaçış planı' (2011). Available online: http://www.hurriyet.com.tr/gundem/hizbullahcilarin-kacis-plani-17547674 (accessed 23 July 2019).

Hürriyet Daily News. 'Turkey set to recruit 5,000 village guards in anti-terror fight' (2015). Available online: http://www.hurriyetdailynews.com/turkey-set-to-recruit-5000-village-guards-in-anti-terror-fight.aspx?pageID=238&nid=88745 (accessed 23 October 2016).

İlke Haber. 'Diyarbakır'da sadece kadınların çalıştığı pazar açıldı' (2013). Available online: http://www.ilkehaberajansi.com.tr/haber/Diyarbakırda-sadece-kadinlarin-calistigi-pazar-acildi.html (accessed 10 November 2015).

İMC TV. 'DÖKH feshedildi, 'Özgür Kadınlar Kongresi' kuruldu' (2015). Available online: http://www.yuksekovahaber.com.tr/video-embed/2361 (accessed 13 October 2015).

Independent. 'Tahir Elci: Kurdish human rights lawyer shot dead during press conference in Turkey' (2015). Available online: http://www.independent.co.uk/news/world/middle-east/tahir-elci-turkish-human-rights-lawyer-shot-dead-during-press-conference-turkey-a6753356.html (accessed 30 November 2015).

İzol Derneği. 'Anasayfa' (2017). Available online: http://izoldernegi.org/#!/Anasayfa (accessed 23 January 2017).

Jones, D. 'Juvenile Detention Guards Sexually Abusing Minority Children in Turkey'. *The Atlantic* (2017). Available online: http://www.theatlantic.com/international/archive/2012/03/juvenile-detention-guards-sexually-abusing-minority-children-in-turkey/255102/ (accessed 18 October 2015).

Joshua Project. 'Country: Turkey' (2017). Available online: https://joshuaproject.net/countries/TU (accessed 22 January 2017).

Kaçar, H. 'Hizbullahçılar artık aramızda', *Hürriyet* (2011). Available online: https://www.sabah.com.tr/gundem/2011/01/05/hizbullahcilar_artik_aramizda (accessed 23 July 2019).

Kahriman, S. '27 Yıllık Deneyimli Yeni Bir Dernek: Hak İnisiyatifi'. *Bianet* (2018). Available online:: https://bianet.org/bianet/insan-haklari/200044-27-yillik-deneyimli-yeni-bir-dernek-hak-inisiyatifi (accessed 3 July 2019).

Kamer, H. 'Diyarbakır Emniyet Müdürü Gaffar Okkan öldürülmesinin 17'nci yılında anıldı'. *BBC Türkçe* (2018). Available online: https://www.bbc.com/turkce/haberler-turkiye-42807355 (accessed 3 August 2018).

Kamer, H. 'HDP milletvekili İdris Baluken'e 16 yıl 8 ay hapis cezası'. *BBC Türkçe* (2018). Available online: http://www.bbc.com/turkce/haberler-turkiye-42565573 (accessed 28 July 2018).

Kayhan, İ. 'Türkiye'de işçi sınıfı Kürtleşti – Erdem Yörük ile söyleşi' (2009). Available online: https://sendika63.org/2009/12/turkiyede-isci-sinifi-kurtlesti-erdem-yoruk-ile-soylesi-ismat-kayhan-anf-38732/ (accessed 4 October 2016).

KCK. 'KCK Sözleşmesi (KCK Contract)' (2005). Available online: https://code.google.com/p/bookstorer/downloads/detail?name=KCK%20S%C3%B6zle%C5%9Fmesi.pdf (accessed 1 June 2017).

Kılınçarslan, C. 'MAZLUMDER'in 16 Şubesi Kapatıldı', *Bianet* (2017). Available online: https://m.bianet.org/bianet/insan-haklari/184643-mazlumder-in-16-subesi-kapatildi (accessed 3 July 2019).

Kurdistan 24, 'HAK-PAR' ın vaadi federasyon' (2018). Available online: https://www.kurdistan24.net/tr/news/80a63019-4097-40da-b999-16c9fa2c514b (accessed 2 August 2018).

Mardin Life. 'Kalenderi Aşiretinin Derneğini AK Partili Akdağ açtı' (2011). Available online: http://www.mardinlife.com/Kalenderi-Asiretinin-Dernegini-AK-Partili-Akdag-acti-haberi-1056 (accessed 23 January 2017).

Mardin Life. 'Mehmet Timurağaoğlu Kimdir?' (2015). Available online: http://www.mardinlife.com/Mehmet-Timuragaoglu-Kimdir-haberi-24508 (accessed 21 January 2017).

Mermer Şirketleri. 'Diyarbakır Mermer Firmalari' (2015). Available online: http://www.dimad.org.tr/index/firmalar/ (accessed 16 September 2015).

Milliyet. '20 yıl aradan sonra ortaya çıkan liste!' (2015). Available online: http://www.milliyet.com.tr/20-yil-aradan-sonra-ortaya-cikan-gundem-2089489/ (accessed 3 November 2015).

Milliyet. 'Avrupalı Kürt İşverenler DTSO'da Yatırım Brifingi Aldı' (2015). Available online: https://www.milliyet.com.tr/yerel-haberler/diyarbakir/avrupali-kurt-isverenler-dtso-dan-yatirim-brifingi-aldi-10768228 (accessed 7 November 2015).

Milliyet, 'Dicle Üniversitesi'nde öğrenci kavgası: 5 yaralı' (2013). Available online: https://www.milliyet.com.tr/gundem/dicle-universitesi-nde-ogrenci-kavgasi-5-yarali-1691072 (accessed 16 October 2015).

Milliyet. 'Gonca Kuriş neden öldürüldü?' (2011). Available online: http://www.milliyet.com.tr/gonca-kuris-neden-olduruldu–gundem-1341564/ (accessed 3 August 2018).

Milliyet. 'HÜDAPAR İstatistikleri' (2014). Available online: http://www.milliyet.com.tr/2014YerelSecim/hudapar/PartiDetay.htm (accessed 30 March 2017).

MyNet. 'Erdoğan ilk kez 'Kürdistan' dedi' (2013). Available online: https://www.mynet.com/erdogan-ilk-kez-kurdistan-dedi-110100862637 (accessed 20 August 2018).

Mynet. 'Hizbullah'ın kilit adamı İsa Altsoy yakalandı' (2007). Available online: http://www.mynet.com/haber/guncel/hizbullahin-kilit-adami-isa-altsoy-yakalandi-277217-1 (accessed 3 August 2018).

OECD. 'Employment Labour Force Participation Rate' (2015). Available online: http://stats.oecd.org/Index.aspx?DataSetCode=GENDER_EMP (accessed 30 March 2016).

Özgür Gündem. 'Nakşibendi Şeyhi: Ak Parti'ye oy vermek Rojava'da Kürt kanının dökülmesine rıza göstermektir' (2013). Available online: https://www.yuksekovahaber.com.tr/haber/s-hayrettin-merci-akpye-oy-vermek-111220.htm (accessed 13 March 2017).

Polat, V. 'Van, Hakkari, Muş ve Bitlis'in geliri Türkiye ortalamasının 4'te 1'i kadar' (2015). Available online: http://t24.com.tr/haber/van-hakkari-mus-ve-bitlisin-geliri-turkiye-ortalamasinin-4te-1i-kadar,292705 (accessed 25 September 2015).

Pulitzer Center. 'Life After Prison: Kurdish Stone-Throwing Kids' (2011). Available online: http://pulitzercenter.org/projects/turkey-kurdish-kids-stone-throwing-jail-terrorists (accessed 16 October 2015).

Radikal. 'Secimin en ilginc rekabeti: bir aile 3 rakip' (2015). Available online: http://www.radikal.com.tr/politika/secimin-en-ilginc-rekabeti-Diyarbakırda-bir-aile-uc-rakip-1312363/ (accessed 17 September 2015).

Resmi Gazete (Official Gazete). *Terörizmin Finansmanının Önlenmesi Hakkında Kanun* (Law No: 6415) (2013). Available online: http://www.resmigazete.gov.tr/eskiler/2013/02/20130216-3.htm (accessed 18 October 2015).

Risale Haber. 'İzzettin Yıldırım cinayetinde sır çözüldü' (2010). Available online: http://www.risalehaber.com/izzettin-yildirim-cinayetinde-sir-cozuldu-72968h.htm (accessed 24 February 2017).

Sarı, Ş. 'Şahımerdan Sarı Hoca Kimdir' (2019). Available online: https://www.mepanews.com/sahimerdan-sari-kimdir-27249h.htm (accessed 23 July 2019).

Sariyuce, I. and Watson, I. 'Turkey detains Kurdish politicians', *CNN* (2016). Available online: https://edition.cnn.com/2016/10/26/middleeast/turkey-detains-kurdish-politicians/index.html (accessed 28 July 2018).

Secim.Haberler.com. '1 Kasım 2015 Genel Seçim Sonuçları' (2015). Available online: https://secim.haberler.com/2015/ (accessed 25 June 2019).

SecimHaberler.com. '2014 BDP Yerel Secim Sonuçları' (2014). Available from: https://secim.haberler.com/2014/bdp-secim-sonucu/ (accessed 26 July 2019).

Secim.Haberler.com. '2018 Milletvekili Seçim Sonuçları' (2018). Available online: https://secim.haberler.com/2018/milletvekilligi-secim-sonuclari/ (accessed 25 July 2019).

Secim.Haberler.com. '31 Mart 2019 Yerel Seçim Sonuçları' (2019). Available online: https://secim.haberler.com/2019/yerel-secimler/ (accessed 2 May 2019).

SecimHaberler.com. 'Diyarbakır 1 Kasım Seçim Sonuçları' (2015). Available online: http://secim.haberler.com/2015/Diyarbakır-secim-sonuclari/ (accessed 30 March 2017).

SeçimHaberler.com. 'Siverek Seçim Sonuçları' (2014). Available online: http://secim.haberler.com/2014/siverek-secim-sonuclari/ (accessed 25 January 2017).

Sendika.org. 'Kadın cinayetleri haritası: 5 yılda en az 1134 kadın öldürüldü' (2015). Available online: https://sendika63.org/2015/11/kadin-cinayetleri-haritasi-5-yilda-en-az-1134-kadin-olduruldu-310904/ (accessed 25 Nobember 2015).

Süddeutsche Zeitung. 'Wir definieren die PKK nicht als eine Terrororganisation' (2016). Available online: https://www.sueddeutsche.de/politik/hdp-politiker-demirta-neue-friedensgespraeche-unter-erdoan-das-ist-nur-ein-leerer-traum-1.3146997-2 (accessed 1 August 2018).

Tajali, M. 'The promise of gender parity: Turkey's People's Democratic Party (HDP)'. *Open Democracy* (2015). Available online: https://www.opendemocracy.net/en/5050/promise-of-gender-parity-turkey-s-people-s-democratic-party-hdp/ (15 November 2015).

The Christian Monitor. 'For Kurdish youth in Turkey, autonomy is no longer enough' (2015). Available online: http://www.csmonitor.com/World/Middle-East/2015/0817/For-Kurdish-youth-in-Turkey-autonomy-is-no-longer-enough (accessed 15 October 2015).

Time Türk. 'Hüda-Par'ın bağımsızları ne kadar oy aldı?' (2015). Available online: https://www.timeturk.com/huda-par-in-bagimsizlari-ne-kadar-oy-aldi/haber-11971 (accessed 19 August 2018).

Turizmde bu Sabah. 'Midyat'tan yurtdışına uzanan bir başarı öyküsü' (2009). Available online: http://www.turizmdebusabah.com/haberler/mithat-yenigun,-250-yillik-evini-otele-donusturdu-48227.html (accessed 18 October 2015).

Türkiye İstatitik Kurumu. *Statistical Bulletin* (2015). Available online: http://www.tuik.gov.tr/PreHaberBultenleri.do?id=18727 (accessed 18 September 2015).

Tremblay, P. 'An immigrant himself, Chobani yogurt founder becomes icon for refugees' (2014). Available online: http://www.al-monitor.com/pulse/originals/2015/10/turkey-usa-kurdish-immigrant-becomes-icon-for-refugees.html (accessed 28 September 2016).

Ufkumuz. 'Dava ve Nübihar Dergileri' (2011). Available online: http://www.ufkumuzhaber.com/dava-ve-nubihar-dergileri-6385htm (accessed 27 February 2017).

Van Haber. 'Van Ekonomisi' (2015). Available online: http://vanhaber.com/van-hakkinda/van-ekonomisi/ (accessed 15 August 2015).

Yayla, A. S. 'Portrait of Turkey's ISIS leader Halis Bayuncuk: Alias Abu Hanzala'. *International Centre for the Study of Violent Extremism* (2016). Available online: http://www.icsve.org/brief-reports/portrait-of-turkeys-isis-leader-halis-bayancuk-alias-abu-hanzala/ (accessed 30 May 2017).

Yesilgazete, 'Hevsel Bahçeleri'ni kurtaran mahkeme kararı: Tarım alanlarında yapılaşmaya iptal' (2015). Available online: https://yesilgazete.org/blog/2015/05/07/hevsel-bahcelerini-kurtaran-mahkeme-karari-tarim-alanlarinda-yapilasmaya-iptal/ (accessed 16 May 2020).

Yüksekova Haber. 'Ahmet Zeydan Vefat etti' (2010). Available online: http://www.yuksekovahaber.com/haber/ahmet-zeydan-vefat-etti-26283.htm (accessed 19 September 2015).

Yüksekova Haber. 'Kadınlar'dan Van'da protesto' (2013). Available online: http://www.yuksekovahaber.com/haber/kadinlardan-vanda-protesto-106215.htm (accessed 17 October 2015).

Index

Adana 6, 46–7, 49, 96, 119
Adıyaman, Tahir 63
Adıyaman 11, 37–8, 40–2, 44, 46, 49–50, 95; religious groups and, 74, 78–9, 121, 190 n13, n17, 194 n26
Agriculture 1, 21, 37, 92–5, 99, 103
Ağrı 11, 20, 24, 38, 40–6, 49, 50, 76
Akman, Yahya 64
AKP (Justice and Development Party): x, 9, 173, 176; representation of Kurds and, 5, 34, 36–43, 52–3, 61–2, 64–5, 67, 73, 77–8, 81, 85–9, 91, 98–103, 116, 121, 136–8, 154, 163, 168–9; repression of Kurdish opposition and, 30, 34, 36, 41, 49, 52, 108, 172; views on Kurdish language, 9, 40; authoritarianism, 13, 172; EU relations 29, 34
Aktay, Yasin 64
Akyol, Februniye 65
Ala Rizgarî 14
Alevis 15, 21, 24, 55, 82–4, 164
Al-Nusra 77
Al-Qaida 74
Altsoy, İsa 27–8, 183 n81, n86
Altun, Rıza 19
ANAP (Motherland Party) 7, 36, 61–2, 76–7, 162
Ankara 11, 14, 45–9, 78, 80, 91, 97–8, 100–1, 113, 117, 121–1, 126–7, 137; University of, 23, 65
Antalya 11, 46, 49, 84
Anti-Terror Law 119
Arabs 46, 64–5, 82
ARGK (Kurdistan People's Liberation Army) 18; see also HPG
Armed struggle xiv, 81, 142–3, 157, 165
Armenian: community 6, 21, 48, 64–6; genocide 64
Arvasi, Sibgatullah 76
Assimilation 6–8, 18, 35, 91, 140, 175
Assyrian 64

Atak, Kamil 63
Atatürk, Mustafa Kemal ix, 161, 199 n12; see also Kemalism
Autonomy 31–32, 59, 119, 136, 147, 153; see also Democratic Autonomy
Avesta, Sozdar 19
Aydar, Zübeyir 19, 166
Aygün, Hüseyin 53
Ayna, Emine 115
Azadi Movement 26, 31–4
Azizoğlu, Yusuf 4, 60

Baluken, İdris 24
Barzani, Massoud xii, 40, 154
Batman 5, 11, 16, 20, 24, 27–8, 30, 38, 41–6, 49–51, 63–4, 69, 76, 78, 80, 85, 93, 95–6, 153, 156, 164
Baydemir, Osman 25, 107
Bayık, Cemil 19
Baykal, Deniz 53
Bayuncuk, Hacı 29
Bayuncuk, Halis (Abu Hanzala) 29
BDP (Peace and Democracy Party) 20–3, 26, 41, 45, 158, 181 n41
Beqaa Valley 14, 152, 164
Beşikçi, İsmail 58
Bingol 11, 15, 37–8, 40–4, 46, 49–51, 80, 96, 190 n13; religious groups 74, 78, 121
Bitlis 4, 11, 20, 23–4, 38, 40–2, 44–6, 49–50, 59, 63–4, 75–8, 80, 86, 95–6, 190 n13
Blessed Birth Week 30, 88
Bookchin, Murray 146, 150, 153, 158
Botan 59
Bozarslan, Mehmet Emin 75
Bozdağ, Bekir 51
Bruki Tribe 4, 59, 61
Bucak tribe 59, 61, 63, 168 n8
Bucak, Ahmet Ersin 68
Bucak, Ali Murat 68

Bucak, Mehmet Celal 61
Bucak, Sedat Edip 61
Bucak, Sertaç 26
Buldan, Pervin 115
Buldan, Savaş 104
Burkay, Kemal 26, 32
Bursa 11, 46
Business enterprises 78, 94, 97–100, 102, 105, 169

Cansız, Sakine 19
Cem Vakfı 83
Cemevi (Alevi temples) 83
Cement 94–5, 98–9
Cevheri, Necmettin 61
Cevheri, Ömer 61
Cevheri, Sabahattin 50, 61
CGP (Republican Reliance Party) 76
Chaldean 64
CHP (Republican People's Party) 9, 26, 36, 48, 53–4, 61–2, 67, 76, 83–4, 91, 102, 161
Cigerxwin (Sheikmous Hasan) 75
Citizenship 6–7, 22
Cizre 63, 120, 171, 185 n25, 194 n16
Cold War 132, 138, 145, 152
Colonialism in Kurdistan 15, 140
Constitutions of Turkey 8, 21–2, 30, 32, 41, 53–5, 156, 162
Constitutional amendments 50, 138
Constitutional Court 8; and closure of parties 8, 20, 45, 202 n29
Construction sector 11, 92, 96–9, 170, 191 n36
Cooperatives 117–8
Counter-insurgency 28, 30, 58, 95, 171
Çermik 53, 94
Çetin, Hikmet 53
Çüngüş 53

Dalar, Ubeydullah 28
DBP (Democratic Regions' Party) x, 21, 24, 31, 53–5, 115, 120, 181 n41, 182 n57, 208 n96
DDKO (Revolutionary Cultural Hearths of the East) 14
DEHAP (Democratic People's Party) 20, 43–4
Delmamikan tribe 62

Demirel, Süleyman 7
Demirtaş, Selahattin 23–5, 48, 50, 107, 136, 157
Democratic autonomy 18, 21–3, 25–6, 129, 158, 165, 172–6, 181 n34, 181 n51, 195 n36, 208 n99
Democratic confederalism 17–8, 32, 151, 153–5, 157–8, 166, 180 n23, 181 n34
DEP (Democracy Party) 8, 19–20
Dersim 82
Descriptive representation of Kurds 3–4, 161
Diaspora 16, 19, 29, 83, 152, 164–5
Dicle, Hatip 8, 115
DİK (Democratic Islam Congress) 74, 80
Disiad (The Industrialists and Business People's Association of Diyarbakır) 97, 103
Diyarbakır 4–5, 11, 14, 15–6, 20, 22–8, 30, 37–46, 49–55, 57, 61–65, 68–9, 75–8, 80, 85, 86, 89, 91, 100, 107, 113, 115–8, 120–3, 126, 156, 164–5, 176, 192 n61, 194 n10, 194 n16; economy 93–9, 102–3; municipality 24, 44
Diyarbakır Military Prison 179 n7
Doğan, Celal 48, 50
Doğan, Mazlum 19
Doğan, Müslüm 48, 84
Doğan, Orhan 8, 115
DOĞUNKAD (Businesswomen's Association of East and South East Anatolia) 114, 117–8
Dora, Erol 65
Doskî tribe 59
DÖDEF (the Federation of Democratic Students Associations) 120
DÖHK (the Democratic Free Women's Movement) 116
DP (Democrat Party) 3–4, 36, 60–1, 67–8, 76–7, 161–2
DTK (Democratic Society Congress) 22, 103, 105, 151
DTP (Democratic Society Party) 8–9, 20–3, 43–5
Durmaz, Hatip 62
Duyan, Mahmut 61–2
DÜÖDER (Dicle University Student Association) 120
DYP (True Path Party) 7, 36, 53, 61–2, 76

Eastern Anatolia Development Agency 103
ECHR (European Court of Human Rights) 17
Eğitim Sen (the Education and Science Workers' Union) 6, 108-9, 117
Eker, Mehmet Mehdi 37, 102-3
Elazığ 11, 15, 23, 36, 41, 51, 86, 96, 190 n13
Elçi, Şerafettin 26
Elçi, Tahir 107, 192 n91
EMEP (Labour Party) 20-1, 43, 45
Ensar Vakfı (The Ensar Foundation) 38
Ensarioğlu, Salim 62
Ensarioğlu, Galip 38, 62, 102
Erbakan, Necmettin 39
Erdoğan, Recep Tayyip 40, 42, 49-52, 91, 138, 158, 162, 172, 176, 196 n3
Erdoğmuş, Nimettullah 23, 37, 54, 86
ERNK (National Liberation Front of Kurdistan) 15; see also PKK
Erol, Abdulbaki 78
Eronat, Oya 116
Ertaş, Ömer 62
Ertuşi tribe 59-60, 63
Erzincan 36, 84
Erzurum 11
ESP (Socialist Party of the Oppressed) 21
Extra-judicial killings 132
Eyyüpoğlu, Seyit 61

Feminism 28, 48, 113, 117, 122-4, 203 n33
Fırat, Abdulmelik 4, 76, 26
Fırat, Mehmet Mir Dengir 23
Food processing 94, 99
Forced displaced 11, 31, 88, 92, 96, 116, 134
FP (Virtue Party) 61

GAP (South-eastern Anatolian Project) 93, 100, 103
Gaydalı, Edip Safter 77
Gaydalı, Mahmut Celadet 23, 77, 86
Gaziantep 11, 15, 46-8, 50, 79, 190 n13
Gender xiv, 116, 118, 124
Gender equality 20, 23, 45, 115-7, 122, 125, 170-1, 175, 208 n96

General election 4, 20, 23-5, 36, 44, 50-1, 61, 63-5, 67-8, 77, 80, 83, 85-6, 113, 137, 162, 167
Genocide 64
Germany 15, 29, 55, 83-4, 143
Geveri, Adem 26, 55
Gezi Park protests 41, 108, 130
Görmez, Mehmet 52
Guerrilla war 15-6, 153, 197 n5, 201 n23
Gülen movement 39, 74, 78-80, 85, 87, 121, 138, 173
Güneştekin, Ahmet 92
Güney, Yılmaz 92
Güngör, Fidan 27-8
Günsiad (Industrialists' and Business Peoples' Association of the South East) 103, 191 n34

HADEP (People's Democracy Party) 8, 20, 43, 80
Hakkari 4, 11, 20, 23-4, 38, 41-6, 49-50, 60-1, 63-4, 80, 96, 185 n25, 190 n13
Hak-Par (Freedom and Rights Party) 5, 26, 31-3, 50
Halkçı Parti (Populist Party) 36
HAS Party (People's Voice Party) 61
Haznevi religious order 77
HDK (Peoples' Democratic Congress) 21
HDP (Peoples' Democratic Party) x, 5, 9, 21, 23-6, 30-5, 41-3, 45-50, 54-5, 61, 63-5, 67, 77, 80, 84-6, 88, 101, 107, 115-6, 120, 122, 126-7, 136, 157-8, 163, 16-8, 171-4, 176, 181 n41, 202 n29, 208 n96
HEP (People's Labour Party) 2, 8-9, 19-20, 62, 113, 166, 202 n29
Hizbullah 27-30, 34-5, 74, 78, 87-8, 121, 168
Honour-killings 118
Hozat, Bese 19
HPG (People's Defence Forces) 19, 115; see also ARGK
Hussein, Feyman (Bahoz Erdal) 19
Hüda-Par (Free Cause Party) 5, 27, 29-34, 39, 50-1, 74, 78, 85, 87-8, 121, 168, 172

Iğdır 20, 38, 41-2, 44, 46, 49-50
İHD (Human Rights Association) 23, 107, 117

İlim group 27; *see also* Hizbullah
İMC TV 173
İmralı prison 134
İnan, Kamran 77
İnan Gaydalı family 4, 23, 76–7
İnan Gaydalı, Selahattin 77
İnan Gaydalı, Abidin 77
Iran xii, xiii, 19, 27, 59, 132, 136, 209 n99
Iraq xii, xiii, 15, 26, 29, 84, 132, 136, 158, 174
Islam 27, 29, 73–5, 78–81, 84, 88, 90, 153–4, 172
Islamic State in Iraq and Syria (ISIS) 29, 42, 48, 74, 96, 114, 119–21, 123, 130
Istanbul 11, 14, 20, 25, 28, 37, 39–40, 42–3, 45–9, 51, 53–5, 65, 74, 78, 83–4, 91–3, 97–8, 100–1, 104, 113, 117, 119, 121–2, 124, 126–7, 137, 175
Izmir 11, 46–8, 84, 92–3, 128
İzol tribe 59, 61, 63, 69
İzol, Zülfikar 68

Jirkî tribe 59, 63

KADEK (Kurdistan Freedom and Democracy Congress) 17
KADEP (Participatory Democracy Party) 26, 31, 33
Kalenderi tribe 69
Kalkan, Duran 19, 197 n5
Karacadağ Development Agency 103
Karakeçili tribe 63
Karasu, Mustafa 19
Karavar, Ahmet 61
Karay, Hacı 104
Karayılan, Murat 19
Karer, Haki 19
Kars 11, 15, 38, 40–2, 44–6, 49–50, 80
Kartal, Kinyas 4, 61
Kartal, Nadir 4, 61
Kartal, Remzi 4, 19, 31, 61, 166
Kaya, Ahmet 91
Kaya, Hüda 48
Kaytan, Ali Haydar 19
KCK (Council of Communities of Kurdistan) 17, 19, 109, 121, 127, 151
KDP (Kurdistan Democrat Party) 26, 34, 172
Kemalism 6, 8, 162; *see also* Atatürk, Mustafa Kemal

KESK (the Confederation of Public Employees Trade Union) 5, 108, 117
Kikan tribe 59, 61
Kılıçdaroğlu, Kemal 53, 84, 91
Kirvar tribe 61
Kışanık, Gültan 24, 115
KJA (Congress of Free Women) 116
KNK (Kurdistan National Congress) 31–3, 164, 166
Kobani 42, 96, 119, 130, 158
Kongra Gel (People's Congress of Kurdistan) 17, 19, 31, 33, 166
KRG (Kurdistan Regional Government) 40
Kurdish emirates 59, 74
Kurdish language 17–9, 22, 26, 30, 35, 40, 76, 78, 83, 128, 140, 166, 170, 172–5; Turkey's policy on 9–10, 47, 52
Kurdish population 1, 10–1, 19, 57, 59, 64, 67, 69, 75, 82, 84, 88, 100, 114, 119, 122, 136, 164–5, 168–9, 178 n36, 200 n17; dispersion of 26, 39, 175
Kurdish Society for Mutual Aid and Progress (Kürt Teavün ve Terraki Cemiyeti) 74
Kurdish students and youth 51, 69, 76, 79, 113–4, 118–21, 126–30, 140, 170–1, 174, 202 n28
Kurdish women ix-x, xiv, 15–6, 21, 23, 52–4, 69, 96, 100, 113–18, 121–6
Kurdishness 81, 139, 143, 154
Kurdism 7
Kurdistan 17, 40, 55, 75, 132, 135, 154, 157, 164; liberation of 15–6, 164
Kurdistan Region of Iraq (KRI) xii–xiii, 32, 34, 40, 59, 79, 82, 95, 100, 154, 158, 171
Kurt, Abdulrahman 37
Küfrevi Sufi lodge 75–6
Küfrevi, Kasım 76
Kürkçü, Ertuğrul 20, 24, 45, 48

Law on the Prevention of Terrorism Financing 104
Lebanon 15, 82
Lök Beyaz, Mine 116

Madrasas 75–6
Mardin 11, 20, 23–4, 26–7, 37–8, 40–6, 49–51, 57, 61–5, 69, 85, 93, 96, 114, 176, 185 n25, 190 n13

Mardin Artuklu University 9
Martyrs 143–4, 150, 152
Marxism-Leninism 75, 132, 146, 150–1, 153, 156
Maşveret group 78
Med-Zehra group 78
Melayê Batê 74
Melayê Cizîrî 74
Menderes, Adnan 36, 162
Menzil bookshop 27–8; *see also* Hizbullah
Menzil group 78
Mersin 11, 20, 23, 43, 45–7, 49, 119
Metinan tribe 59, 62
Metiner, Mehmet 37
MHP (Nationalist Movement Party) 36, 40, 49–50, 172–3
Midyat, Zekiye 114
Military coups 14–5, 77, 79, 113, 162
Milli İrade Platformu (Platform for National Will) 38
Mining 92, 94, 97–9
Ministry of Interior of Turkey 63
Miroğlu, Orhan 37
Mother tongue 8; education in 18, 53, 108, 174
MSP (National Salvation Party) 61
Münir Baba 77
Müsiad (the Independent Industrialists and Businessmen Association) 97, 102–3, 191 n33
Muş 11, 24, 40–1, 45, 51, 64, 80, 95–6, 190 n13, 194 n16
Mutlu, Muhyettin 76
Mutlu, Abdulhaluk 76
Muztazaf-Der (The Association for Solidarity with the Oppressed) 29

Naqshibandiyya 6, 74–8, 86, 188 n6
National Outlook (Milli Görüş) 39
Newroz 16, 30, 130, 152, 165
Nomadism 59
Norşin 76
Nur Movement (Nurculuk or Nur Cemaati) 78
Nursi, Bediüzzaman Said 78
Nûbihar 78

Öcalan, Abdullah 14–17, 19, 22, 25, 35, 47, 63, 115, 127, 134, 140, 144–6, 151–4, 158, 166, 172, 199 n12, 208 n96, 208 n99

Odabaşı, Abdulrahman 61
Okkan, Gaffar 28
Okuyucular (the Readers) 78
Önder, Sırrı Süreyya 20, 45, 48
Orhan, Gülsen 116
Ottoman Empire 6, 59, 74, 157
Özal, Turgut 36, 93, 162, 202 n29
Özcan, Halil 64

PAJK (Freedom Party of Women of Kurdistan) 115
Paylan, Garo 48, 65
Peace Mothers 117
Pinyanişi tribe 4, 23, 59–61, 63–4
Pir Sultan Abdal Cultural Centre 83
Pitkin, Hannah 2–3, 203 n33
PKK (Kurdistan Workers' Party): activities 14–5, 17, 19, 35, 40–1, 47–8, 113–120, 127, 132, 134–5, 141, 143, 151–2, 158, 164–8, 180 n23, 197 n5; counter-insurgency against the 25, 27–8, 35, 48, 52, 58, 63, 69, 71, 88, 92, 94–5, 104, 137, 171–2, 174, 200 n18; political mobilisation by 1, 16, 80–1; women and 16, 19, 113–6, 122–3
Pluralism xiii, 21–2, 29, 31–2, 39, 52–3, 163, 172
Presidency of Religious Affairs (Diyanet) 30, 51–2
Presidential: elections 43, 48, 50–1, 78; system 42, 176
PSK (Kurdistan Socialist Party) 26
PYD (Democratic Union Party) 208 n96

Qadiriyya 73, 75, 77
Qandil Mountains 171
Qur'an 76, 78, 90

Radical democracy 149, 151, 154
Referendum 30, 34, 43, 50–1, 162, 173, 176
Reforms 6, 37, 40–1, 47, 52, 59, 104, 125, 162–3, 169, 176; EU accession/integration 9–10, 29, 35, 79
Religious Leaders' Assistance and Solidarity Association (DİAYDER) 80
Representation: descriptive 2; formal 2; substantive 3; symbolic 3
Roboski massacre 119

Rojava 154, 171, 193 n2, 203 n33, 208 n96
RP (Welfare Party) 36, 61, 73, 80

Sadak, Selim 8, 115
Saladin the Great 74
Şan, Eyşe 114
Sancar, Mithat 65
Saturday Mothers 117
Saward, Michael 3
Sayyids 74
Secularism 6, 37, 39, 73, 81, 83-4, 87, 138, 153-4, 169
Self-determination 26, 31, 150, 155
Self-government 10, 17-8, 22, 31-2, 162, 172-3, 175
Separatism 8, 100, 141, 161, 165, 167
Serhat, Ronahi 19
Serhildan 15-6, 114, 152, 156
Şeyhanlı tribe 59, 61
Seyidoğlu 77
Seyit Hayrettin Merci 77
Seyyid Abdülkadir 74-5
Sheikhs 4, 76, 78, 86
Sheikh Said 4, 74-5
Sheikh Ubeydullah 74
SHP (Social Democratic Populist Party) 9, 19, 36, 43, 48, 61-2, 76, 84
Siirt 11, 16, 20, 24, 38, 41-6, 49-51, 63-4, 76, 93, 96, 190 n13
Şimşek, Mehmet 37, 51
Silvan 4, 52, 61, 194 n16
Siverek 61, 68
Sivil Cuma 80
Şırnak 11, 16, 20, 24, 27, 41, 43-5, 51, 63-4, 80, 93, 96, 120, 171, 190 n13, 194 n16
Society for the Rise of Kurdistan (Kürdistan Teali Cemiyeti) 74
Solmaz, Edip 5
Soviet Union 84, 152
SP (Felicity Party) 39, 50, 61
Substantive representation of Kurds 4, 162
Sufi lodges 75-6
Sufi religious orders xiv, 27, 73, 75-8, 85
Sultan Şeymus Ezzuli 77
Suruç 48, 185 n25
Syriacs 23, 65

Tağiler family 76
Tan, Altan 23, 25, 86
Tanrıkulu, Sezgin 53-4
Tatlıcı, Şeyhmuz 98
Tatlıses, İbrahim 91
TEKEL (Tobacco and Alcohol Beverages Company) 95
Textiles firms 92, 98-9
Timurağaoğlu, Abdulkadir 61
TİP (Workers' Party of Turkey) 14
TKDP (Kurdistan Democrat Party of Turkey) 26, 32, 82
TKSP (Socialist Party of Turkish Kurdistan) 14, 26, 32
TMMOB (the Union of Chambers of Turkish Engineers and Architects) 107
Tourism sector 92, 94, 97-8
Trade unions 5-6, 108-9, 117, 124, 170, 196 n3
Treaty of Lausanne 6, 158
TRT Kurdî 9, 40, 51
TTB (the Turkish Medical Association) 107
Tunceli 11, 20, 24, 36, 38, 41-2, 44-6, 49-50, 82, 84, 91, 96, 185 n25, 190 n13
Turkish nationalism 5-7, 37, 41, 53, 77, 82, 103, 105, 131, 138, 161-2, 168, 172-4, 176
TUSKON (Turkish Confederation of Businessmen and Industrialists) 79
Türk, Ahmet 8, 62

Uca, Feleknas 55, 85
Ulukaya, Hamdi 96
Union of Scholars of Kurdistan (Kürdistan Alimler Birliği) 80
Unity Party (Birlik Partisi) 83
Unity Party of Turkey (Türkiye Birlik Partisi) 83
Urfa/Şanlıurfa 11, 23, 25, 37, 40-2, 46, 50-1, 57, 61, 63-5, 67-8, 80, 85-6, 95-6

Van 4, 11, 20, 24, 26, 38, 41-6, 49-50, 53-5, 57, 61, 63, 65, 68-9, 77-8, 80, 85, 91, 100, 102, 113, 116-7, 120-2, 126, 176, 185 n25, 190 n13, 194 n10; economy 93-7, 99, 103-4, 191 n33, 191 n34; tourism 99; earthquake 94
Velioğlu, Hüseyin 27-8, 168

Village guards 16, 30, 63, 69
Village Institutes 92

Women cooperatives 117–8
Women's rights organisations 114, 117, 123–4, 171, 173

Xan, Meryem 114
Xanî, Ehmadi 74

Yapıcıoğlu, Zekeriya 29, 51
Yazidis 30, 55, 82, 84–5
Yazıcılar (the Writers) 78
YDG-H (Patriotic Revolutionary Youth Movement) 119–20
Yeni Asya group 78
Yıldırım, Adnan 104
Yıldırım, İzzettin 28
Yıldırım, Kadri 86
Yılmaz, Mesut 7
Young Turk Revolution 74
YPS (Civil Protection Units) 119–20

YSP (Green Left Party) 21
YTP (New Turkey Party) 4, 60–1, 76, 162
YÖK (the Council of Higher Education) 128
YÜDER (the Van Yüzüncü Yıl Student Association) 120
Yüksekdağ, Figen 24–5, 32, 54–5, 136
Yüksekova 61, 185 n25
Yurtdaş, Sedat 8

Zana, Mehdi 5
Zana, Leyla 8, 24, 113, 115
Zapsu, Cüneyd 91
Zaza: Kurds 23, 42, 46, 53, 55, 64, 91; language 54, 83
Zehra group 28, 78
Zeydan, Abdullah 23, 25, 61, 64
Zeydan, Ahmet 61
Zeydan, Mustafa 61
Zeydan, Rüstem 61
Zeydan, Teoman 61
Zilan, Abdulkerim 76

www.ingramcontent.com/pod-product-compliance
Lightning Source LLC
Chambersburg PA
CBHW072142290426
44111CB00012B/1952